How to Think about Weird Things

How to Think about Weird Things

Critical Thinking for a New Age

Theodore Schick, Jr.
Muhlenberg College

Lewis Vaughn

Foreword by Martin Gardner

Mayfield Publishing Company
Mountain View, California
London • Toronto

To Erin, Kathy, Katie, Marci, Patrick, and T.J.

LIBRARY OF CONGRESS CATALOGING-IN-PUBLICATION DATA
Schick, Theodore, Jr.
How to think about weird things: critical thinking for a new age
Theodore Schick and Lewis Vaughn.
        p.   cm.
Includes index.
ISBN 1-55934-254-4
1. Critical thinking. 2. Parapsychology. 3. Occultism.
4. Mysticism. 5. Miracles. 6. Curiosities and wonders.
I. Vaughn, Lewis. II. Title.
BC177.S32 1994
001.9'01 — dc20   94-5543
                                                    CIP

Manufactured in the United States of America
10 9 8 7 6 5 4

Mayfield Publishing Company
1280 Villa Street
Mountain View, CA 94041

Sponsoring editor, James Bull; production editor, April Wells-Hayes; manuscript editor, Dale Anderson; text and cover designer, Jeanne M. Schreiber;
art editor, Robin Mouat; art director, Jeanne M. Schreiber; manufacturing
manager, Martha Branch. The text was set in 10.5/13 Weiss by ColorType,
Inc., and printed on 50# Text White Opaque by The Maple-Vail Book
Manufacturing Group.

Cover image: Rene Magritte, *Die Stimme Der Lüfte*. Copyright © Rene Magritte,
Archiv für Kunst und Geschichte, Berlin; by permission.

Photo and illustration credits appear at the back of the book on page 292,
which constitutes an extension of the copyright page.

This book is printed on recycled paper.

Foreword

More than a hundred books are published every year, in English speaking countries alone, that promote the wildest forms of bogus science and the paranormal. The percentage of Americans today who take astrology seriously is larger than the percentage of people who did so in the early Middle Ages, when leading church theologians — Saint Augustine, for example — gave excellent reasons for considering astrology nonsense. We pride ourselves on our advanced scientific technology, yet public education in science has sunk so low that a fourth of Americans and 55 percent of teenagers believe in astrology, not to mention a recent president of the nation and his first lady!

Now and then a courageous publisher, more concerned with enlightening the public than with profits, will issue a book that honestly assesses pseudoscience and the paranormal. Works of this sort now in print can be counted on your fingers. It is always an occasion for rejoicing when such a book appears, and there are several ways in which *How to Think about Weird Things* is superior to most books designed to teach readers how to tell good science from bad.

First of all, this book covers an enormous range of bogus sciences and extraordinary claims that currently enjoy large followings in America. Second, unlike most similar books, the authors heavily stress principles that help you critically evaluate outlandish claims — and tell you *why* these principles are so important. Third, the book's discussions are readable, precise, and straightforward.

I am particularly pleased by the book's clearheaded assessment of scientific realism at a time when it has become fashionable in New Age circles to think of the laws of science as not "out there," but somehow a projection of our minds and cultures. Yes, quantum mechanics has its subjective tinge. There is a sense in which an electron's properties are not definite until it is measured, but this is a technical aspect of quantum theory that has no relevance on the macroscopic level of everyday life. In no way does the mathematical formalism of quantum mechanics imply, as some physicists smitten by Eastern religions claim, that the moon is not there unless someone looks at it. As Einstein liked to ask, will a mouse's observation make the moon real?

The authors give clear, accurate explanations of such much publicized puzzles of quantum mechanics as the notorious EPR paradox named after the initials of Einstein and two colleagues. Quantum theory indeed swarms with mind-boggling experiments that are only dimly understood. None of them justify thinking that $E = mc^2$ is a cultural artifact, or that E might equal mc^3 in Afghanistan or on a distant planet. Extraterrestrials would of course express Einstein's formula with different symbols, but the law itself is as mind independent as Mars.

As the authors say simply: "There is a way the world is." It is the task of science to learn as much as it can about how this universe, not made by us, behaves. The awesome achievements of technology are irrefutable evidence that science keeps getting closer and closer to objective truth.

As the authors tell us, there are two distinct kinds of knowledge: logical and mathematical truth (statements that are certain within a given formal system), and scientific truth, never absolutely certain, but which can be accepted with a degree of probability that in many instances is practically indistinguishable from certainty. It takes a bizarre kind of mind to imagine that two plus two could be anything but four, or that, as the authors put it, cows can jump over the moon or rabbits lay multicolored eggs.

The authors are to be especially cheered for their coverage of unsubstantiated alternative treatments, some of them weird beyond imagining. Preposterous medical claims can cause untold harm to gullible persons who rely on them to the exclusion of treatment by mainstream physicians.

The authors are also to be commended for finding colorful and apt quotations from other writers. Bertrand Russell, for instance, gave three simple rules for curbing one's tendency to accept what he called "intellectual rubbish":

1. When the experts are agreed, the opposite opinion cannot be held to be certain.
2. When they are not agreed, no opinion can be regarded as certain by a non-expert.
3. When they all hold that no sufficient grounds for a positive opinion exist, the ordinary man would do well to suspend judgment.

"These propositions seem mild," Russell added, "yet, if accepted, they would absolutely revolutionize human life."

I am under no illusions about how effective this book will be in persuading readers to adopt Russell's three maxims. I *can* say that to the extent it does, it will have performed a service that our technologically advanced but scientifically retarded nation desperately needs.

— *Martin Gardner*

Preface

Few claims seem to arouse more interest, evoke more emotion, and create more confusion than those dealing with the paranormal, the supernatural, or the mysterious—what in this book we call weird things. Although many such claims are unbelievable, many people believe them, and their belief often has a profound effect on their lives. Billions of dollars are spent each year on people and products claiming supernatural powers. Channelers claim to communicate with aliens from outer space, psychics and astrologers claim to foretell the future, and healers claim to cure everything from AIDS to warts. Who are we to believe? How do we decide which claims are credible? What distinguishes rational from irrational claims? This book is designed to help you answer such questions.

Why do you believe in any given claim? Do you believe for any of the following reasons?

- You had an extraordinary personal experience.
- You embrace the idea that anything is possible—including weird things.
- You have an especially strong feeling that the claim is true or false.
- You have made a leap of faith that compels you to accept the claim.
- You believe in inner, mystical ways of knowing that support the claim.
- You know that no one has ever disproved the claim.
- You have empirical evidence that the claim is true.
- You believe that any claim is true for you if you believe it to be true.

This list of reasons for belief could go on and on. But which reasons are *good* reasons? Clearly, some are better than others; some can help us decide which claims are most likely to be true, and some can't. If we care whether any claim is actually true, whether our beliefs are well-founded (and not merely comfortable or convenient), we must be able to distinguish good reasons from bad. We must understand how and when our beliefs are justified, how and when we can say that we *know* that something is the case.

The central premise of this book is that such an understanding is possible, useful, and empowering. Being able to distinguish good reasons from bad will not only improve your decision-making ability, it will give you a powerful weapon against all forms of hucksterism. This volume shows you step by step how to sort out reasons, how to evaluate evidence, and how to tell when a claim (no matter how strange) is likely to be true. It's a course in critical thinking as applied to claims and phenomena that many people think are immune to critical thinking.

The emphasis, then, is neither on debunking nor advocating specific claims, but on explaining principles of critical thinking that enable you to evaluate any claim for yourself. To illustrate how to apply these principles, we supply analyses of many extraordinary claims, including conclusions regarding their likely truth or falsity. But the focus is on carefully wielding the principles, not on whether a given claim goes unscathed or is cut down.

Often in the realm of the weird, such principles themselves are precisely what's at issue. Arguments about weird things are frequently about *how people know* and *if people know* — the main concerns of the branch of philosophy called *epistemology*. Thinking about weird things, then, brings us face to face with some of the most fundamental issues in human thought. So we concentrate on clearly explaining these issues, showing why the principles in this book themselves are valid, and demonstrating why many alternatives to them are unfounded. We explore alleged sources of knowledge like faith, intuition, mysticism, perception, introspection, memory, reason, and science. We ask: Do any of these give us knowledge? Why or why not?

Since we show how these principles can be used in specific cases, this book is essentially a work of *applied epistemology*. Whether you're a believer or nonbeliever in weird things, and whether or not you're aware of it, you have an epistemology, a theory of knowledge. If you ever hope to discern whether a weird claim (or any other kind of claim) is true, your epistemology had better be a good one.

The principles discussed in this book can help you evaluate any claim — not just those dealing with weird phenomena. We believe that if you can successfully use them to assess the most bizarre, most unexpected claims, you're well prepared to tackle anything run-of-the-mill.

IMPORTANT FEATURES

This volume also includes the following:

- Explanations of thirty-four principles of knowledge, reasoning, and evidence that you can use to enhance your problem-solving skills and sharpen your judgment.
- Discussions of over fifty paranormal, supernatural, or mysterious phenomena, including astrology, ghosts, ESP, psychokine-

sis, UFO abductions, channeling, water witching, near-death experiences, prophetic dreams, demon possession, time travel, parapsychology, and creationism.

• Details of a step-by-step procedure for evaluating any extraordinary claim. We call it the SEARCH formula and give several examples showing how it can be applied to some popular weird claims.

• Numerous boxes offering details on various offbeat beliefs, assessments by both true believers and skeptics of extraordinary claims, and reports of relevant scientific research. We think this material can stimulate discussion or serve as examples that can be assessed using the principles of critical thinking.

• A comprehensive treatment of different views about the nature of truth, including several forms of relativism and subjectivism.

• A detailed discussion of the characteristics, methodology, and limitations of science, illustrated with analyses of the claims of parapsychology and creationism. This includes a complete treatment of science's criteria of adequacy and how those criteria should be used to evaluate extraordinary claims.

• An in-depth treatment of various kinds of evidence appealed to in health issues, including personal experience, testimonials, case studies, test-tube and animal studies, human non-intervention studies, and clinical trials. It covers several principles that will help you assess any health claim, including popular ones in alternative medicine and holistic health.

• An appendix that explores various informal logical fallacies. These fallacies are also explained in the text.

MYSTERIES IN PERSPECTIVE

This book is about solving mysteries. Some people wish we would leave well enough alone. They don't want to solve mysteries, but preserve them. They want to put mysteries on the endangered species list. To them, a mystery is precious, a thing of beauty, a source of enchantment, part of what makes life interesting and meaningful. We recall the radio commentator who decried the attempts of scientists to solve the mystery of the crop circles in Britain. To her, the cause and meaning of the crops that had been flattened in strange patterns was a near perfect mystery, a pure delight in itself, a relief from the world of dull facts, something to enjoy as one would a fine painting.

We must agree with the commentator, to a point. We know—as lovers, artists, storytellers, and scientists know—that the allure of the mysterious can be profound. After all, it was in part infatuation with mysteries that led us to write this book. But unlike the commentator, we don't view mysteries as an end, but as a beginning — the beginning of inquiry and on to even greater mysteries. This is essentially the view of scientists. To always preserve mysteries for mystery's sake would mean the cessation of inquiry and the end of the pursuit of knowledge — a high price for the worship of the unknown.

We also know that mysteries are nowhere near the edge of extinction. Mysteries dot the universe like stars, as every scientist knows. Often the deepest, most awe-inspiring mysteries are absolutely real, as sections of this book will attest. Quantum physics, black holes, the human brain — these alone harbor mysteries more evocative than most figments of the imagination because they're actual. No one had to protect these mysteries; they were discovered by those who make it their business to solve them. Indeed, if other mysteries hadn't been explored — and solved — first, these mysteries would never have been revealed.

Then too, there are consequences for holding fast to mystery against all reason. As we make clear in the discussion of the hundredth-monkey story and other phenomena, belief in alleged mysteries affects people's lives, sometimes dramatically and not always for the good. It's imperative then that our beliefs regarding a mystery be as well founded as possible.

So we prefer to help make the world safe for critical thinking, knowing that there are plenty of mysteries waiting for it.

We can add that, contrary to what many may believe, critical thinking is not the enemy of art, poetry, laughter, or love. We say this for benefit of those who fear that the practice of critical thinking means becoming a walking logic machine with a heart as cold as a computer chip. Without taking the time now to argue the point, we can say that nothing in this book is antithetical to the abovementioned sides of human existence. If anything, critical thinking informs these other sides of us, just as they can inform critical thinking. To paraphrase the philosopher Bertrand Russell, the good life is one guided by reason and inspired by love.

ACKNOWLEDGMENTS

The authors shared equally in the work of writing this book and thus share equally in responsibility for any of its shortcomings. But we are not alone in the project. We're grateful to Muhlenberg College for the research funds and library resources made available to us, to the Muhlenberg Scholars who participated in the course based on this book, and to the many people who helped us by reviewing the manuscript for accuracy, giving expert advice and offering insightful commentary. These include Brad Art, Westfield State College; Stephen Barrett, consumer health advocate; Linda Bomstad, California State Polytechnic University, San Luis Obispo; Andrew Chrucky, Albright College; Jack DeBellis, Lehigh University; Frank Fair, Sam Houston State University; Stephen Gehlbach, University of Massachusetts; Nori Geary, New York Hospital–Cornell Medical Center; Paul Jacques, Tufts USDA Human Nutrition Research Center; Alison King, California State University, San Marcos; Manfred Kroger, Pennsylvania State University; Brooke Noel Moore, California State University at Chico; Andrew Neher, Cabrillo College; David Reed, Muhlenberg College; John Renner, Consumer Health Information Research Institute; Lud Schlecht, Muhlenberg College; Tom Theis, Thomas J. Watson Research Center; Thomas Vogt, Kaiser Permanente Center for Health Research; Graham Ward, Boston University School of Medicine; Perry Weddle, California State University, Sacramento; Robert Wind, Muhlenberg College; and Merrit Yorgey, Passer Books.

Contents

ONE

Introduction:
Close Encounters
with the Strange

THIS BOOK IS FOR you who have stared into the night sky or the dark recesses of a room, hairs raised on the back of your neck, eyes wide, faced with an experience you can't explain but about which you have never stopped wondering, "Was it real?" It's for you who have read and heard about UFOs, psychic phenomena, time travel, out-of-body experiences, ghosts, monsters, astrology, reincarnation, mysticism, acupuncture, iridology, incredible experiments in quantum physics, and a thousand other extraordinary things and asked, "Is it true?" Most of all, it's for you who believe, as Einstein did, that the most beautiful experience we can have is the mysterious and yet, like him, have the courage to ask tough questions until the mystery yields answers.

Wonder is the feeling of a philosopher, and philosophy begins in wonder.
—PLATO

But this is not primarily a book of such answers, though several will be offered. This book is about *how to find the answers for yourself* — how to test the truth or reality of some of the most influential, mysterious, provocative, bewildering puzzles we can ever experience. It's about how to think clearly and critically about what we authors have dubbed *weird things* — all the unusual, awesome, wonderful, bizarre, and antic happenings, real or alleged, that bubble up out of science, pseudoscience, the occult, the paranormal, the mystic, and the miraculous.

THE IMPORTANCE OF WHY

Skeptical habits of thought are essential for nothing less than our survival — because baloney, bamboozles, bunk, careless thinking, flimflam and wishes disguised as facts are not restricted to parlor magic and ambiguous advice on matters of the heart.
—CARL SAGAN

Pick up almost any book or magazine on such subjects. It will tell you that some extraordinary phenomenon is real or illusory, that some strange claim is true or false, probable or improbable. Plenty of people around you will gladly offer you their beliefs (often unshakable) about the most amazing things. In this blizzard of assertions, you hear a lot of *whats*, but seldom any good *whys*. That is, you hear the beliefs, but seldom any solid reasons behind them — nothing substantial enough to justify your sharing the beliefs; nothing reliable enough to indicate that these assertions are likely to be *true*. You may hear naiveté, passionate advocacy, fierce denunciation, one-sided sifting of evidence, defense of the party line, leaps of faith, jumps to false conclusions, plunges into wishful thinking, and courageous stands on the shaky ground of subjective certainty. But the good reasons are missing. Even if you do hear good reasons, you may end up forming a firm opinion on one extraordinary claim but fail to learn any principle that would help you with a similar case. Or you hear good reasons but no one bothers to explain why they're so good, why they're most likely to lead to the truth. Or no one may dare to answer the ultimate why — why good reasons are necessary to begin with.

Without good whys, humans have no hope of understanding all that we fondly call *weird* — or anything else, for that matter. Without good whys, our beliefs are simply arbitrary, with no more claim to knowledge than the random choice of a playing card. Without good whys to guide us, our beliefs lose their value in a world where beliefs are already a dime a dozen.

We especially need good whys when faced with weirdness. For statements about weird things are almost always cloaked in swirling mists of confusion, misconception, misperception, and our own yearning to disbelieve or believe. Our task of judging the reality of these weird things isn't made any easier by one fact that humbles and inspires every scientist: Sometimes the weirdest phenomena are absolutely real; sometimes the strangest claims turn out to be true.

The best scientists and thinkers can never forget that sometimes wondrous discoveries are made out there on the fringe of experience, where anomalies prowl.

Space aliens are abducting your neighbors. You were a medieval stable boy in a former life. Nostradamus predicted JFK's assassination. Herbs can cure AIDS. Levitation is possible. Reading tarot cards reveals character. Science proves the wisdom of Eastern mysticism. Some people can imprint their thoughts on photographic film. We are all God. Near-death experiences prove there's life after death. Crystals heal. Bigfoot stalks. Elvis lives.

Do you believe any of these claims? Do you believe that some or all of them deserve a good horselaugh, that they're the kind of hooey that only a moron could take seriously? The big question then is *why?* Why do you believe or disbelieve? Belief alone—without good whys—can't help us get one inch closer to the truth. A hasty rejection or acceptance of a claim can't help us tell the difference between what's actually likely to be true (or false) and what we merely want to be true (or false). Beliefs that do not stand on our best reasons and evidence simply dangle in thin air, signifying nothing except our transient feelings or personal preference.

What we authors offer here is a compendium of good whys. As clearly as we can, we explain and illustrate principles of rational inquiry for assessing all manner of weirdness. We give you the essential guides for weighing evidence and drawing well-founded conclusions. Most of these principles are simply commonplace, wielded by philosophers, scientists, and anyone else interested in discovering the facts. Many are fundamental to scientific explorations of all kinds. We show why these principles are so powerful, how anyone can put them to use, and *why they're good whys to begin with*—why they're more reliable guides for discovering what's true and real than any alternatives.

We think this latter kind of explanation is sorely needed. You may hear that there's no reliable scientific evidence to prove the reality of psychokinesis (moving physical objects with mind power alone). But you may never hear a careful explanation of why scientific evidence is necessary in the first place. Most scientists would say that the common experience of thinking of a friend and then suddenly getting a phone call from that person doesn't prove telepathy (communication between minds without use of the five senses). But why not? Only a few scientists and a handful of others bother to explain why. Say a hundred people have independently tried eating a certain herb and now swear that it has cured them of cancer. Scientists would say that these one hundred stories constitute anecdotal evidence that doesn't

Call him wise whose actions, words, and steps are all a clear "because" to a clear "why."

—JOHANN KASPAR LAVATER

prove the effectiveness of the herb at all. But why not? There is indeed a good answer, but it's tough to come by.

The answer is to be found in the principles that distinguish good reasons from bad ones. You needn't take these principles (or any other statements) on faith. Through your own careful use of reason, you can verify their validity for yourself.

Nor should you assume that these guides are infallible and unchangeable. They're simply the best we have until someone presents sound, rational reasons for discarding them.

These guides shouldn't be a surprise to anyone. Yet to many, the principles will seem like a bolt from the blue, handing them a detailed map to a country they thought was uncharted. Even those of us who are unsurprised by these principles must admit that we probably violate at least one of them daily — and so run off into a ditch of wrong conclusions.

BEYOND WEIRD TO THE ABSURD

To these pages, we cordially invite all those who sincerely believe that this book is a gigantic waste of time — who think that it's impossible or pointless to use rational principles to assess the objective truth of weird claims. To this increasingly prevalent attitude, in all its forms, we offer a direct challenge. We do the impossible, or at least what some regard as impossible. We show that there are good reasons for believing that the following claims are, in fact, false:

- There's no such thing as objective truth. We make our own truth.
- There's no such thing as objective reality. We make our own reality.
- There are spiritual, mystical, or inner ways of knowing that are superior to our ordinary ways of knowing.
- If an experience seems real, it is real.
- If an idea feels right to you, it is right.
- We are incapable of acquiring knowledge of the true nature of reality.
- Science itself is irrational or mystical. It's just another faith or belief system or myth, with no more justification than any other.
- It doesn't matter whether beliefs are true or not, as long as they're meaningful to you.

We discuss these ideas because they're unavoidable. If you want to evaluate weird things, sooner or later you'll bump into notions that challenge your most fundamental assumptions. Weirdness by definition is out of the norm, so it often calls into question our normal ways

A man is a small thing, and the night is very large and full of wonders.
—LORD DUNSANY

I really think we are all creating our own reality. I think I'm creating you right here. Therefore I created the medium, therefore I created the entity, because I'm creating everything.
—SHIRLEY MACLAINE

of knowing. It invites many to believe that in the arena of extraordinary things, extraordinary ways of knowing must prevail. It leads many to conclude that reason just doesn't apply, that rationality has shown up at the wrong party.

You can learn a lot by seriously examining such challenges to basic assumptions about what we know (or think we know) and how we know it. In fact, in this volume you learn three important lessons about the above ideas:

1. If some of these ideas *are* true, knowing anything about anything (including weird stuff) is *impossible*.
2. If you honestly believe any of these ideas, you cut your chances of ever discovering what's real or true.
3. Rejecting these notions is liberating and empowering.

The first lesson, for example, comes through clearly when we examine the idea that there's no such thing as objective truth. This notion means that reality is literally whatever each of us believes it to be. Reality doesn't exist apart from a person's beliefs about it. So truth isn't objective, it's subjective. The idea is embodied in the popular line "It may not be true for you, but it's true for me." The problem is, if there's no objective truth, then *no* statement is objectively true, including the statement "There's no such thing as objective truth." The statement refutes itself. If true, it means that the statement and *all* statements — ours, yours, or anybody else's — aren't worthy of belief or commitment. Every viewpoint becomes arbitrary, with nothing to recommend it except the fact that someone likes it. There could be no such thing as knowledge, for if nothing is true, there can be nothing to know. The distinction between asserting and denying something would be meaningless. There could be no difference between sense and nonsense, reasonable belief and illusion. For several reasons, which we'll discuss later, people would be faced with some intolerable absurdities. For one thing, it would be impossible to agree or disagree with someone. In fact, it would be impossible to communicate, to learn a language, to compare each other's ideas, even to think.

The point of the third lesson is that if such outrageous notions shackle us, rejecting them sets us free. To reject them is to say that we *can* know things about the world — and that our ability to reason and weigh evidence is what helps us gain that knowledge. In part, the purpose of much that follows is to demonstrate just how potent this ability is. Human reason empowers us, like nothing else, to distinguish between fact and fiction, understand significant issues, penetrate deep mysteries, and answer large questions.

Light — more light.
—JOHANN WOLFGANG VON GOETHE

A WEIRDNESS SAMPLER

How many people actually care about weird things? Plenty. Book sales, coverage in magazines and on television, and opinion polls suggest that there's widespread interest in things psychic, paranormal, occult, ghostly, and otherworldly. A Gallup Poll conducted in June 1990, for example, shows that:

- 49 percent of Americans believe in ESP (extrasensory perception).
- 25 percent feel that they've experienced telepathy.
- 21 percent believe in reincarnation.
- 17 percent feel that they've been in touch with someone who had died.
- 25 percent believe in ghosts.
- 14 percent feel that they've been in a haunted house.
- 55 percent believe in the Devil — and 10 percent believe they've either talked to or been talked to by the Devil.
- 14 percent have consulted a fortuneteller or psychic.
- 25 percent believe in astrology.
- 46 percent believe in psychic or spiritual healing; 25 percent feel they've healed their body using mental power alone.
- 27 percent believe that extraterrestrial beings have visited Earth in the past.

There are many, many more extraordinary things that thousands of people experience, believe in, and change their lives because of. Several will be discussed in this book. Here's a sampling:

• Hundreds of people who were near death but did not die have told of blissful experiences in the beyond. Their reports vary, but certain details keep recurring: While they were at death's door, a feeling of peace overcame them. They watched as they floated above their own bodies. They traveled through a long, dark tunnel. They entered a bright, golden light and glimpsed another world of unspeakable beauty. They saw long-dead relatives and a being of light that comforted them. Then they returned to their own bodies, awoke, and were transformed by their incredible experience. In each case, the experience seemed nothing like a dream or a fantasy; it seemed vividly *real*. Such episodes are known as near-death experiences (NDEs). Many who have had such an experience say that their NDE gives undeniable proof of life after death.

• Some people report the often chilling experience known as a precognitive dream, a dream that seems to foretell the future. Here's an example: "I dreamed I was walking along a steep ridge with my father.

Pseudoteachers

Two social scientists—sociologist Ray Eve and anthropologist Dana Dunn of the University of Texas at Arlington—tried to find out where pseudoscientific beliefs might come from. They theorized that teachers might be passing such ideas on in school.

To test their theory, they surveyed a national sample of 190 high-school biology and life-science teachers. Their findings: forty-three percent thought that the story of the flood and Noah's ark was definitely or probably true; 20 percent believed in communication with the dead; 19 percent felt that dinosaurs and humans lived at the same time; 20 percent believed in black magic; and 16 percent believed in Atlantis. What's more, 30 percent wanted to teach creation science; 26 percent felt that some races were more intelligent than others; and 22 percent believed in ghosts.

Although 30 to 40 percent of the teachers were doing a good job, says Eve, "it boils down to the observation that a large number of the teachers are either football coaches or home-economics teachers who have been asked to cover biology."

Is there hope for change? "Much like the Department of Defense," says Eve, "the education bureaucracy has become so intractable that even when you know something is wrong, the chances of fixing it are not great."[1]

He was stepping too close to the edge, making the dirt cascade to the rocks far below. I turned to grab his arm, but the ridge fell away under his feet, leaving him to dangle from my hands. I pulled as hard as I could, but he grew larger and heavier. He fell, in slow motion, crying out to me but making no sound. Then I woke up screaming. Three weeks later my father fell to his death from a second-story window while he was painting the window sill. I was in the room with him at the time but wasn't able to reach him fast enough to prevent his fall. I rarely remember any dreams, and I had never before dreamed about someone falling." Such dreams can have a profound emotional impact on the dreamer and may spark a firm belief in the paranormal.

• There are probably hundreds of people claiming that they once lived very different lives in very different places — long before they were born. Tales of these past lives surface when people are "regressed" during hypnosis back to their alleged long-hidden selves. It all started in 1952 when Virginia Tighe, an American housewife, was apparently hypnotically regressed back to a previous life in nineteenth-century Ireland. Speaking in an uncharacteristic Irish brogue, she related an astounding account of her former life. Many others during hypnosis have related impressively detailed past lives in early Rome, medieval France, sixteenth-century Spain, ancient Greece or Egypt, Atlantis, and more, all the while speaking in what often sounds like authentic language or accents. A lot of famous people claim that they too have been hypnotically regressed to discover earlier existences. Shirley MacLaine, for example, has said that she's been a pirate with a wooden leg, a Buddhist monk, a court jester for Louis XV, a Mongolian nomad, and assorted prostitutes. Many believe that such cases are proof of the doctrine of reincarnation.

• Some U.S. military officers have expressed strong interest in an astonishing psychic phenomenon called *remote viewing*. It's the alleged ability to accurately perceive information about distant geographical locations without using any known sense. The officers claimed that the former Soviet Union was way ahead of the United States in developing such powers. Remote viewing is said to be available to anyone, as it needs no special training or talents. Experiments have been conducted on the phenomenon, and some people have said that these tests prove that remote viewing is real. If it is real, science would be turned on its head. Textbooks would have to be rewritten, research redirected, and our understanding of psychology, physiology, and physics would be transformed.

• A lot of people look to psychics, astrologers, and tarot card readers to obtain a precious commodity: predictions about the future. You can get this commodity through newspapers, magazines, books, TV talk shows, 900 numbers, and private sessions with a seer. Predictions may concern the fate of movie stars, momentous events on the world stage, or the ups and downs of your personal life. Everywhere, there's word that some startling, unlikely prediction has come true. Here's an example (now notorious, for reasons to be explained later): On April 2, 1981, four days after the assassination attempt on President Reagan, the world was told that a Los Angeles psychic *had predicted the whole thing weeks earlier.* On that April morning, NBC's "Today" show, ABC's "Good Morning America," and Cable News Network aired a tape showing the psychic, Tamara Rand, offering a detailed prediction of the assassination attempt. The tape was said to have been made on January 6, 1981. She foresaw that Reagan would be shot by a sandy-haired young man with the initials "J.H," that Reagan would be wounded in the chest, that there would be a "hail of bullets," and that the fateful day would occur in the last week of March or first week of April.

• Something strange is going on in physics, something so strange, in fact, that some people who've bothered to think about the strangeness now declare that physics is looking more and more like Eastern mysticism. This weirdness is taking place in the branch of physics known as quantum mechanics, which studies subatomic particles, the tiny bits that make up everything in the universe. The notorious weirdness is this: In the quantum realm, particles don't acquire some of their characteristics *until they're observed by someone.* They seem not to exist in a definite form until scientists measure them. This spooky fact didn't sit well with Einstein, but it has been confirmed repeatedly in rigorous tests. It has caused some people to speculate that reality is subjective, that we as observers create the universe ourselves — that the universe is a product of our imagination. This quantum freakiness has prompted some people, even a physicist or two, to seriously ask: "Is a tree really there when no one's looking?"

• In 1894 the Society for Psychical Research published the first survey of personal encounters with ghostly phenomena. There were hundreds of first-hand accounts by people who claimed to have seen real apparitions. A recent scholarly history of apparitions documents an unsurprising fact: People have been reporting such encounters for centuries. Today things haven't changed much. You're likely to hear at least one first-hand account yourself from somebody you know — somebody who says it's not a ghost *story* at all, but fact. Research suggests that the experiences can happen to perfectly sane persons, appear vividly real, and have a powerful emotional impact. There are also reports of people feeling a "sense of presence," as though another person, invisible, is close by. There's no end to the stories of more famous apparitions, told and retold, with eerie details that raise bumps on the skin. And you don't have to read a tabloid newspaper (more reputable newspapers will do) to discover that when someone wonders "who ya gonna call?" there are real ghostbusters ready to handle a haunting.

Fat Woman's Bra Snaps — 13 Injured!
—WEEKLY WORLD NEWS

• *The Exorcist* dramatized it. *The Amityville Horror* reinforced awareness of it. The Catholic Church endorses it. The news media eagerly report it. It is the idea of demon possession — that people and places can be haunted, harmed, and controlled by supernatural entities of immense evil. A typical case: On August 18, 1986, the Associated Press reported that demons were said to be haunting a house in West Pittston, Pennsylvania. Jack and Janet Smurl lived there with their four children and claimed that the demons were terrorizing them. According to the report: "The Smurls said they have smelled the stench of smoke and rotten meat, heard pig grunts, hoofbeats, and blood-curdling screams and moans. Doors have opened and shut, lights have gone on and off, formless ghostly glows have traveled before them, and the television set has shot across the room. Even the

Oh God, how did I get into this room with all these weird people?
—STEWART BRAND

family dog, a 75-pound German shepherd, has been slammed against the wall while [Jack] Smurl said he stood nearby."[2] Later, Jack Smurl was quoted in the *New York Daily News* as saying that "at least a dozen times [a female demon, or Succubus] has had intercourse with me in bed. I was awake, but I was immobile." The Smurls invited demonologist Ed Warren, who had been involved in the Amityville case, to investigate. Warren declared that several demons did indeed inhabit the house.

• Long ago the Earth was visited by extraterrestrial beings who imparted advanced technology and learning to primitive humans. So say many people, who ask: How else do you explain the stunning engineering of the pyramids in Egypt and the New World? The ancient designs cut into the Nazca plain in Peru that look like airfield markings meant for approaching spacecraft? The highly accurate Piri Reis map of 1513 that must have been created by some kind of aerial photography? The facts possessed by the primitive Dogon tribe of Africa about a star that no one can see with the naked eye and wasn't even discovered by astronomers until the nineteenth century? In myths and legends, they say, our ancestors told of the visitation of these "gods." This theme is sounded by many, most notably Erich von Däniken in his books *Chariots of the Gods, Gods from Outer Space,* and *Von Däniken's Proof.* Sparks still fly when somebody asserts that somebody else's ancestors were too primitive to have managed certain engineering feats without alien help.

• Many have turned to a method of disease treatment shunned by mainstream medicine and at odds with modern science: homeopathy. Around since the 1700s, it now has several hundred practitioners in the United States and is built on two main doctrines. One is that "like cures like"—symptoms of a sick person can be cured by substances that actually produce the same symptoms in healthy people. The other doctrine is that the smaller the dose of this substance, the mightier the healing effect. Homeopathic drugs are diluted for maximum power—and are often so watered down that not one molecule of the original substance remains. That such dilutions could possibly heal anything flies in the face of the laws of chemistry. Yet in recent years there's been an increase in homeopathic remedies offered in drugstores and health-food stores. And growing numbers of people who believe in it (including members of the British Royal Family).

• The story of a strange, miraculous event has been circulating for fifteen or so years. It was first told by author Lyall Watson in his 1979 book *Lifetide,* who said he gleaned it from scientists, and it's been repeated by countless other writers. Watson reported that in the 1950s some wild Japanese monkeys on the island of Koshima were given raw sweet potatoes for the first time. One of the monkeys, Imo, learned to wash the potatoes in a stream to remove the sand and grit. Over the years, Imo taught this skill to other monkeys in the colony. Then one day, when a certain number of monkeys, say 100, had learned the washing trick, the impossible happened. Suddenly almost all the other monkeys knew how to do it, too. "Not only that," says Watson, "but the habit seems to have jumped natural barriers and to have appeared spontaneously, like glycerin crystals in sealed laboratory jars, in colonies on other islands."[3] With the hundredth monkey, a kind of "critical mass" had been reached, he says, forcing a kind of group mind. This, then, is the hundredth monkey phenomenon. Some believe that the story is fact and that the phenomenon is at work in all of humanity. If so, we're faced with an astounding implication: When enough people believe something is true, it becomes true for everyone. Others say that it's pointless to ask whether the story is factual — it's a metaphor or myth and, as such, is as true as science. Still, we stubbornly ask: Did the incident actually happen? And does it really matter after all?

What we need is not the will to believe, but the will to find out.

—BERTRAND RUSSELL

NOTES

1. Paul McCarthy, "Pseudoteachers," *Omni*, July 1989, p. 74.
2. Associated Press, August 18, 1986.
3. Lyall Watson, *Lifetide* (New York: Bantam Books, 1979), p. 148.

TWO

The Possibility of the Impossible

THE TROUBLE WITH paranormal phenomena is that they're just not normal. It's not simply that they're rare and unusual (which they are); it's that they seem to violate the natural order of things. (That's why we sometimes call them *supernatural*.) Their very existence seems to contradict certain fundamental laws that govern the universe. Since these laws define reality for us, anything that violates them appears impossible. Consider, for example, the phenomena collectively known as ESP, or extra-sensory perception, namely, telepathy (reading another's mind), clairvoyance (viewing a distant object without using your eyes), and pre-cognition (seeing the future). What makes these phenomena seem so weird is that they appear to be physically impossible. Physicist Milton Rothman explains:

12

Transmission of information through space requires transfer of energy from one place to another. Telepathy requires transmission of an energy-carrying signal directly from one mind to another. All descriptions of ESP imply violations of conservation of energy [the principle that mass-energy can be neither created nor destroyed] in one way or another, as well as violations of all the principles of information theory and even of the principle of causality [the principle that an effect cannot precede its cause]. Strict application of physical principles requires us to say that ESP is impossible.[1]

According to Rothman, anything that violates physical principles is impossible; ESP violates these principles; therefore ESP is impossible.

PARADIGMS AND THE PARANORMAL

But according to the true believers (those who accept the reality of the paranormal), nothing is impossible. As Erich von Däniken, author of *Chariots of the Gods*, puts it, *"nothing* is incredible any longer. The word 'impossible' should have become literally impossible for the modern scientist. Anyone who does not accept this today will be crushed by the reality tomorrow."[2] What von Däniken is referring to here is the fact that many things that scientists once considered impossible are now considered real. The most notorious example is meteorites. For many years, the scientific community dismissed meteorites as impossible. The great chemist Lavoisier, for example, argued that stones couldn't fall from the sky because there were none up there. No less a free thinker than Thomas Jefferson, after reading a report by two Harvard professors claiming to have observed meteorites, remarked, "I could more easily believe that two Yankee professors would lie than that stones would fall down from heaven."[3] The true believers hold that Lavoisier and Jefferson were blinded by science. There was no place in their world view for stones that fell from the sky, so they refused to accept the reality of meteorites. Many of today's scientists, say the true believers, suffer from a similar myopia. They're unable to see beyond the narrow confines of their pet theories.

This defect is a potentially serious one, for it can block scientific development. The historian Thomas Kuhn in his seminal work, *The Structure of Scientific Revolutions*, has shown that science advances only by recognizing and dealing with *anomalies* (phenomena that don't seem to obey known laws). According to Kuhn, all scientific investigation takes place within a *paradigm*, or theoretical framework, that determines what questions are worth asking and what methods should be used to answer them. From time to time, however, certain phenomena are discovered that don't fit into the established paradigm; that is,

How many things, too, are looked upon as quite impossible until they have been actually effected?
—PLINY THE ELDER

they can't be explained by the current theory. At first, as in the case of meteorites, the scientific community tries to dismiss or explain away these phenomena. But if no satisfactory account of them is forthcoming, the scientific community is forced to abandon the old paradigm and adopt a new one. In such a case, the science is said to have undergone a *paradigm shift*.

There have been many paradigm shifts in the past. Galileo's discovery of the moons of Jupiter and the phases of Venus helped lead to a shift from a geocentric (earth-centered) view of the solar system to a heliocentric (sun-centered) one. Darwin's discovery of the strange creatures of the Galapagos islands helped support the shift from creationism to evolution. The failure to detect the "luminiferous ether" (the medium in which light waves were supposed to travel) contributed to a shift from Newtonian physics to Einsteinian physics. Similarly, say the true believers, paranormal phenomena may lead to another paradigm shift. The resulting world view may be as different from ours as ours is from the aborigines'. We may have to give up many of our most cherished beliefs about the nature of reality. But it's happened before, and, they claim, there's no reason to think it won't happen again. As Shakespeare so eloquently put it: "There are more things in heaven and earth, Horatio, than are dreamt of in your philosophy."

So whom are we to believe? Should we follow the scientist who dismisses paranormal phenomena on the grounds that they contradict fundamental physical principles or the true believer who sees paranormal phenomena as a harbinger of a new age? To evaluate the relative merits of these positions, we'll have to take a closer look at the notions of possibility, plausibility, and reality.

LOGICAL POSSIBILITY VERSUS PHYSICAL IMPOSSIBILITY

One can't believe impossible things.

—ALICE, IN *THROUGH THE LOOKING GLASS*

Although it's fashionable to claim that anything is possible, such a claim is mistaken, for there are some things that can't possibly be false, and others that can't possibly be true. The former—such as "2 + 2 = 4," "All bachelors are unmarried," and "Red is a color"—are called *necessary truths* while the latter—such as "2 + 2 = 5," "All bachelors are married," and "Red is not a color" are called *necessary falsehoods*.[4] The Greek philosopher Aristotle (Plato's pupil) was the first to systematize our knowledge of necessary truths. The most fundamental of them—the ones upon which all other truths rest—are often called the *laws of thought*. They are:

> *The law of non-contradiction:* Nothing can both have a property and lack it at the same time.

The law of identity: Everything is identical to itself.

The law of excluded middle: For any particular property, everything either has it or lacks it.

These principles are called the laws of thought because without them thought — as well as communication — would be impossible. In order to think or communicate, our thoughts and sentences must have a specific content; they must be about one thing rather than another. If the law of non-contradiction didn't hold, this wouldn't be the case, for there would be no fact of the matter as to what we are thinking or saying. Without the law of non-contradiction, it would be impossible to distinguish one thought or sentence from another, for whatever would be true of one would be true of the other. No claim could be considered to be more correct than any other, for all would be equally true (and false). Thus those who deny the law of non-contradiction can't claim that their position is superior to those who accept that law.

One of the most effective techniques of refuting a position is known as *reductio ad absurdum*: reduction to absurdity. If you can show that a position has absurd consequences, you've provided a powerful reason for rejecting it. The consequences of denying the law of non-contradiction are about as absurd as they get. Any position that makes thought and communication theoretically impossible is, to say the least, suspect. Aristotle, in Book IV of the *Metaphysics*, put the point this way:

> If all are alike both wrong and right, one who is in this condition will not be able either to speak or to say anything intelligible; for he says at the same time both "yes" and "no." And if he makes no judgment but "thinks" and "does not think," indifferently, what difference will there be between him and a vegetable?[5]

What difference indeed. Without the law of non-contradiction, we can't believe things to be one way rather than another. But if we can't believe things to be one way rather than another, we can't think at all.

Logic is the study of correct thinking. As a result, the laws of thought are often referred to as the laws of logic. Anything that violates these laws is said to be *logically impossible*, and whatever is logically impossible can't exist. We know, for example, that there are no round squares, no married bachelors, and no largest number because such things violate the law of non-contradiction — they attribute both a property and its negation to a thing and are thus *self-contradictory*. The laws of thought, then, not only determine the bounds of the rational; they also determine the bounds of the real. Whatever is real must obey the law of non-contradiction. That is why the great German

Why, sometimes before breakfast I've believed as many as six impossible things.
— THE WHITE QUEEN, IN *THROUGH THE LOOKING GLASS*

Aristotle on Demonstrating the Laws of Thought

Since the laws of thought are the basis for all logical proofs, they can't be proven by means of a logical demonstration. But, says Aristotle, they can nevertheless be demonstrated negatively:

> There are some who, as we said, both themselves assert that it is possible for the same thing to be and not to be, and say that people can judge this to be the case. And among others many writers about nature use this language. But we have now posited that it is impossible for anything at the same time to be and not to be, and by this means have shown that this is the most indisputable of all principles. Some indeed demand that even this shall be demonstrated, but this they do through want of education, for not to know of what things one should demand demonstration, and of what one should not, argues want of education. For it is impossible that there should be demonstration of absolutely everything (there would be an infinite regress, so that there would still be no demonstration); but if there are things of which one should not demand demonstration, these persons could not say what principle they maintain to be more self-evident than the present one.

> We can, however, demonstrate negatively even that this view is impossible. . . . The starting point for all such proofs is that our opponent shall say something which is *significant* both for himself and for another; for this is necessary, if he really is to say anything. For, if he means nothing, such a man will not be capable of reasoning, either with himself or with another. But if any one says something that is significant, demonstration will be possible; for we shall already have something definite. The person responsible for the proof, however, is not he who demonstrates but he who listens; for while disowning reason he listens to reason. And again he who admits this has admitted that something is true apart from demonstration."[6]

In other words, the law of non-contradiction can't be demonstrated to someone who won't say something definite, for demonstration requires that our words mean one thing rather than another. On the other hand, the law of non-contradiction need not be demonstrated to someone who will say something definite, for in saying something definite he or she has already assumed its truth.

logician, Gottlob Frege, called logic "the study of the laws of the laws of science."

Thus, von Däniken is mistaken in thinking that anything is possible. That which is logically impossible is simply not possible. There are limits to what can exist, and those limits are most broadly defined by the laws of logic.

Rothman claims that ESP is impossible. Now if he means that ESP is logically impossible, then, provided he's right, we can dismiss it out of hand, for in that case, it couldn't possibly be real. But ESP isn't logically impossible. The notions of reading another's mind, viewing distant objects, and even knowing the future are not self-contradictory in the way that married bachelors or round squares are. Neither are such paranormal phenomena as psychokinesis, spontaneous dematerialization, spontaneous combustion, UFOs, reincarnation, plant communication, dowsing, or out-of-body experiences. What, if anything, these phenomena violate are not the laws of logic, but the laws of physics, or more generally, the laws of science. If they violate those laws, they're *physically impossible*.

Many things that are logically possible are physically impossible. For example, it's logically possible for a cow to jump over the moon because that feat doesn't violate a law of logic. But it's not physically possible. The laws governing bovine physiology and gravitation forbid such feats. Similarly, it's logically possible for bunnies to lay multicolored eggs. Unfortunately, mammalian physiology can't produce such treasures. Even if we take von Däniken to be claiming that nothing is physically impossible, he's still mistaken. Our universe is governed by physical laws, and whatever violates them cannot occur.

What *is* von Däniken claiming then? His point seems to be not that paranormal phenomena don't violate physical laws, but that our understanding of physical laws may change. In other words, he seems to be saying that it is logically possible that our notion of physical possibility will change; that we may someday adopt a paradigm that permits such phenomena. And indeed we may. But this possibility doesn't give us any reason for believing that paranormal phenomena are real — for reasonable belief must be based on current evidence. The fact that we may someday come to believe that something is real gives us no reason for believing that it is. The principle that should guide our thinking in these matters is this:

> Just because something is logically possible doesn't mean that it's real.

If it did, all sorts of fantastic things would have to be considered real, like moon-jumping cows and egg-laying rabbits.

THE APPEAL TO IGNORANCE

There are those, however, who measure the credibility of a claim not in terms of the evidence in its favor, but in terms of the lack of evidence against it. They argue that since there is no evidence refuting their position, it must be true. Although such arguments have great

> *We have to live today by what truth we can get today, and be ready tomorrow to call it falsehood.*
> —WILLIAM JAMES

psychological appeal, they are logically fallacious. Their conclusions don't follow from their premises because a lack of evidence is no evidence at all. Arguments of this type are said to commit the *fallacy of appeal to ignorance*. Here are some examples:

> "No one has shown that Jones was lying. Therefore he must be telling the truth."

> "No one has shown that there are no ghosts. Therefore they must exist."

> "No one has shown that ESP is impossible. Therefore it must be possible."

All a lack of evidence shows is our own ignorance; it doesn't provide a reason for believing anything.

If a lack of evidence against a claim actually constituted evidence for it, all sorts of weird claims would be well-founded. For example, the existence of mermaids, unicorns, and centaurs — not to mention Bigfoot, the Loch Ness monster, and the abominable snowman — would be beyond question. Unfortunately, substantiating a claim is not that easy. The principle here is:

> Just because a claim hasn't been conclusively refuted doesn't mean that it's true.

A claim's truth is established by the amount of evidence in its *favor*, not by the lack of evidence against it.

In addition, the strategy of placing the burden of proof on the nonbeliever is unfair because doing so asks him or her to do the impossible, namely, to prove a universal negative. (A universal negative is a claim to the effect that nothing of a certain sort exists.) Suppose someone claims that there are no white ravens, supporting this claim by pointing out that no one has ever reported seeing a white raven. From this it doesn't follow that there are no white ravens, for no one may have looked in the right place or someone may have seen one but not reported it. To prove a universal negative, you would have to be able to exhaustively investigate all of time and space. Since none of us can do that, demanding such an investigation of anyone is unreasonable. Whenever someone proposes something — a policy, a fact, or a theory — the burden of proof is on that person to provide reasons for accepting the proposition.

It's not only true believers who commit the fallacy of appeal to ignorance, however. Skeptics often take this approach: No one has proven that ESP exists, therefore it doesn't. This, too, is fallacious reasoning; it's an attempt to get something for nothing. The operative principle here is the converse of the one cited earlier:

> Just because a claim hasn't been
> conclusively proven doesn't mean
> that it's false.

Even if no one has yet found a proof of ESP, we can't conclude that none ever will be found. Someone could find one tomorrow. So even if there is no good evidence for ESP, we can't claim that it doesn't exist. We *can* claim that there is no compelling reason for thinking that it does exist.

THE POSSIBILITY OF ESP

What about Rothman's claim that ESP is physically impossible? Is it? If so, is investigating it really worth our while? Let's tackle the second question first. Even if our best scientific theories seem to indicate that ESP is physically impossible, investigating it still has some value, for our best scientific theories may be wrong. The only way we can tell whether or not they're wrong is to test them, and investigating ESP constitutes one such test. Failure to come up with any credible examples of ESP (or other paranormal phenomena) serves to confirm our current theories. But if we were to find good evidence for ESP—if, for example, someone were to consistently score well above the score predicted by chance on ESP tests for a number of years under conditions that ruled out any possibility of fraud—we would have to rethink our current scientific theories.

But we still wouldn't necessarily have to reject them. For what at first appears to be a contradiction may, upon further examination, turn out not to be. Meteorites provide a case in point. As we've seen, the scientific establishment of the seventeenth and eighteenth centuries refused to admit the existence of meteorites because they seemed to conflict with the accepted model of reality. But once their existence was verified and scientists took seriously the task of explaining them, it was found that they violated no physical laws. None of Newton's laws had to be rejected in order to accommodate them. In fact, as scientists came to understand the physics of planetary development, they found that Newton's laws actually *predicted* the existence of meteorites. This teaches us another principle:

> Just because something seems
> physically impossible doesn't mean
> that it is.

Certainly nothing is unnatural that is not physically impossible.
—RICHARD BRINSLEY SHERIDAN

This principle is particularly applicable to the study of miracles. A miracle is commonly considered to be a violation of natural (physical) law. Since only something supernatural can violate natural law, miracles are often taken as evidence for the existence of God. But in light of the preceding principle, it's difficult to see how we could ever be justified in believing that a miracle occurred. For an event's seeming impossibility may simply be due to our ignorance of the operative forces or principles. As the Roman Catholic theologian St. Augustine noted, "A miracle is not contrary to nature but contrary to our knowledge of nature."[7] The scientific ignorance of the ancient Jews and early Christians may explain why they reported so many miraculous occurrences. In any event, it's important to realize that just because you can't explain something doesn't mean it's supernatural.

As our knowledge of the physical world has increased, our conception of the limits of physical possibility has expanded. Many things that were formerly considered physically impossible are now considered within the bounds of physical possibility. Take, for example, the miracle of Joshua bringing down the walls of Jericho by blowing his horn. How can a horn bring down a wall? In the same way that a tone generator can shatter a champagne glass — by vibrating the object at its resonant frequency. It's possible, if improbable, that Joshua and his fellow trumpeters simply blew a note whose pitch matched the resonant frequency of the wall. Given that our knowledge of the natural world isn't perfect, the most reasonable response to a recalcitrant fact is not to invoke the supernatural but to look for a natural explanation.

Paranormal phenomena are like miracles in that they seem to violate physical law though — again like miracles — their seeming impossibility may simply be due to our ignorance of the operative forces or principles. In the absence of any good evidence, it's not reasonable to believe in the existence of paranormal phenomena. But when faced with good evidence that a paranormal event took place, the most reasonable thing to do is to start looking for a natural explanation.

THEORIES AND THINGS

Skeptics who wish to maintain that paranormal phenomena are physically impossible often write as if the phenomena themselves contradict physical law, but a phenomenon can't contradict a law anymore than a tree can get married. Since marriage is a relation between people, only people can get married. Similarly, since contradiction is a relation between propositions, only propositions can contradict one another. It isn't the phenomena themselves that contradict physical law,

Bad Vibes

The power of vibration is considerable. A suspension bridge was destroyed when wind vibrated the bridge at its resonant frequency. Armies never march in step across bridges because they do not want to set up such destructive vibrations. Lyall Watson claims that just as vibrations can destroy bridges, so they can destroy human beings. He writes:

> Professor Gavraud is an engineer who almost gave up his post at an institute in Marseille because he always felt ill at work. He decided against leaving when he discovered that the recurrent attacks of nausea only worried him when he was in his office at the top of the building. Thinking that there must be something in the room that disturbed him, he tried to track it down with a Geiger counter, but he found nothing until one day, nonplused, he leaned back against the wall. The whole room was vibrating at a very low frequency. The source of this energy turned out to be an air-conditioning plant on the roof of a building across the way, and his office was the right shape and the right distance from the machine to resonate in sympathy with it. It was this rhythm, at seven cycles per second, that made him sick.

> Fascinated by the phenomena, Gavraud decided to build machines to produce infrasound so that he could investigate it further. In casting around for likely designs, he discovered that the whistle with a pea in it issued to all French gendarmes produced a whole range of low-frequency sounds. So he built a police whistle six feet long and powered it with compressed air. The technician who gave the giant whistle its first trial blast fell down dead on the spot. A postmortem revealed that all his internal organs had been mashed into an amorphous jelly by the vibrations.[8]

Believe it or not.

but rather our theories about them. Since these theories may be mistaken, we must approach claims of physical impossibility with extreme caution.

The philosopher C. J. Ducasse notes that 200 years ago, making one's voice heard all the way across the Atlantic would have seemed physically impossible.[9] People of that time would have assumed that the only way to do so would be to use air as a means of transmission, and air can't carry a message that far. But if you use a telephone wire or radio waves, you can make yourself heard across the Atlantic fairly easily. The seeming impossibility of the feat, then, was based on a particular theory of what was involved. By changing the theory, the impossibility disappears. Similarly, the seeming impossibility of ESP is based on a particular theory of what is involved. If that theory is mistaken, so may be the claim that ESP is physically impossible.

Rothman's claim that ESP is impossible is based on the theory that ESP is a transmission of information from one object to another and that the information transfer has features (like the failure to degrade over distance) that violate physical law. If his theory is correct, his claim is justified. If not, it's unfounded.

Adrian Dobbs, a parapsychologist, argues that there's no good reason for believing that ESP signals actually do violate physical law. In the first place, according to Dobbs, there's no evidence that ESP signals don't degrade over distance. "We have," he tells us, "no systematically compiled data to test whether it has happened as frequently over long distances as over short distances, taking into account the number of occasions when it has been tried experimentally."[10] Secondly, even electromagnetic signals don't always get weaker the farther they travel. "Every experienced operator of radio transmitters," he explains, "knows that 'breakthrough' conditions occur sporadically when signals are picked up 'loud and clear' over distances far in excess of those their transmitters are designed to reach under normal working conditions."[11] Perhaps the purported cases of long-distance ESP are caused by some such special conditions. Thirdly, even if a signal is picked up over a great distance, it doesn't mean that it has not attenuated, "for modern radio technology has shown that it is practicable for a receiver to detect exceedingly weak electromagnetic signals; and by using systems of Automatic Gain Control, to amplify incoming signals . . . in such a way that both strong and weak signals appear at the output stage of the loudspeaker with subjectively equal audible strengths."[12] Perhaps there's some sort of "automatic gain control" at work in ESP so that both weak and strong signals are output at the same level. In any case, contrary to what Rothman would have us believe, the evidence available concerning ESP doesn't rule out a physical explanation.

Many physical explanations of ESP have, in fact, been offered. None are fully satisfactory, however. Often they postulate entities or processes that are unobservable. Recent research in quantum mechanics, though, has revealed physical processes that some believe bear a striking resemblance to purported cases of ESP. Consequently, they conclude that a physical explanation of ESP may soon be forthcoming.[13]

According to one interpretation of quantum mechanics, any two particles that have interacted in the past remain inseparably linked so that whatever happens to one can instantaneously affect the other, no matter how far apart they have become. As the physicist John Gribbin notes, "particles that were once together in an interaction remain in some sense parts of a single system which responds together to further interactions."[14] Since our best theory of the origin of the universe, the Big Bang Theory, holds that all matter came from a point in space smaller than the diameter of a proton, every particle in the universe may be "connected" in this mysterious way to every other. Einstein recognized early on that quantum mechanics implied this sort of spooky action at a distance. Because he considered such interactions physically impossible, he could never accept the truth of quantum mechanics. He considered them physically impossible because they seemed to violate either the principle that nothing travels faster than the speed of light (which is the cornerstone of his theory of relativity) or the principle that objects have properties independently of our observing them (which is the cornerstone of our common-sense theory of reality).[15] And Einstein was unwilling to give up either relativity or common sense.

To avoid making such a choice, Einstein tried to prove that quantum mechanics is incomplete, that it leaves something out of the account. He and his colleagues Nathan Rosen and Boris Podolsky described an experiment designed to show that we can know a property of a particle—like its position or momentum—without measuring it. Since quantum mechanics says that such properties can be known only through measurement, Einstein, Podolsky, and Rosen concluded that quantum mechanics doesn't provide a complete description of physical reality.[16] There must be a "deeper" theory, which avoids the bizarre implications of quantum mechanics.

At the time the paper was written (1935), the experiment described by Einstein and his colleagues was technically impossible. But in 1964, the Scottish physicist John Bell, then of the European Laboratory for Particle Physics (CERN), formulated a version of the experiment that could be performed using existing technology.[17] Since that time, a number of Bell-type experiments have been performed, and these experiments have shown that Einstein's, Podolsky's, and Rosen's interpretation of the situation was mistaken.[18] They assumed that the distinction between the system being measured and the apparatus doing the measuring was absolute. Not so, said physicist and Nobel laureate Niels Bohr. In a reply to their paper, Bohr argued that the distinction was, at best, relative. Just as Einstein's theory of relativity shows that space and time are indissolubly linked, so quantum mechanics shows that the measuring apparatus and the thing being measured are part of one system.[19]

The upshot is that things seem to be connected to each other in rather remarkable ways. Physicists David Bohm and B. J. Hiley describe "the quantum interconnectedness of distant systems" this way:

> A quantum many-body system cannot properly be analyzed into independently existent parts, with fixed and determinate dynamical relation-

There is nothing impossible in the existence of the supernatural.
—GEORGE SANTAYANA

ships between each of the parts. Rather, the "parts" are seen to be in an immediate connection, in which their dynamical relationships depend, in an irreducible way, on the state of the whole system (and indeed on that of broader systems in which they are contained, extending ultimately and in principle to the entire universe). Thus one is led to a new notion of *unbroken wholeness* which denies the classical idea of analyzability of the world into separately and independently existent parts.[20]

Such a view seems to echo the mystics' claim that everything is one. If there really are no separate entities, instantaneous interaction between seemingly distant objects becomes easier to accept. And if subatomic particles can instantaneously interact with one another over great distances, why not people?

A likely impossibility is always preferable to an unconvincing possibility.
—ARISTOTLE

Even if subatomic particles do engage in spooky action at a distance, though, it doesn't follow that larger objects do. What is true of the parts is not necessarily true of the whole. To believe otherwise is to commit the *fallacy of composition*. Further, even if larger objects, like human beings, could instantaneously affect one another, it doesn't follow that any meaningful information could be transmitted between them. In fact, because of the uncertainty involved in quantum mechanical events, it appears that quantum connections can't be used to carry meaningful signals.[21] Nevertheless, quantum mechanics has shown us that things are related to one another in ways that were undreamed of several decades ago. It is possible that a fuller understanding of quantum mechanics will yield a physical explanation of ESP. But until we know more, a fully adequate physical theory of ESP remains nothing more than a tantalizing (logical) possibility.

But suppose we had a theory demonstrating the physical possibility of ESP. Would that mean ESP is real? No, for the following reason:

> Just because something is physically possible doesn't mean that it's real.

The possibility of a phenomenon doesn't imply its actuality. To establish the reality of a phenomenon, we need reliable evidence showing that it exists.

ON KNOWING THE FUTURE

No chapter on possibility would be complete without a discussion of precognition, for precognition is widely believed to be logically impossible. To precognize an event is to know what will happen before it actually does. Precognition, then, is a form of fortunetelling—it's seeing into the future. Such an ability certainly appears physically impossible, for it seems to be at odds with the principle of causality, which states that an effect cannot precede its cause. But more importantly, it also appears logically impossible, for it seems to suggest that the future exists now, and that's a contradiction in terms. We can perceive only that which currently exists. If we perceive the future, the future must currently exist, but the future, by definition, doesn't currently exist. It will exist, when the time comes, but does not exist now. So precognition seems to commit us to an existing nonexistent, which is a logical impossibility.

The problem with this view is that there are models of physical reality, consistent with all known physical laws, in which the future does exist now. Such models draw their inspiration from Hermann Minkowski's interpretation of Einstein's special theory of relativity.

It is easy to see, hard to foresee.
—BENJAMIN FRANKLIN

In his special theory of relativity, published in 1905, Einstein showed that space and time are much more intimately related than anyone had previously thought. He showed, for example, that the faster you travel, the slower you age. At the speed of light, you don't age at all; time stands still, so to speak. If you were to go faster than the speed of light, you would go backwards in time.[22] But if you went backwards in time, you could get into all sorts of trouble. You could, for example, kill your father before he met your mother. What, then, would happen to you? In Einstein's theory, we don't have to worry about such things, for nothing can travel faster than the speed of light.

One reason that nothing can travel faster than the speed of light is that the faster something travels, the more massive it becomes until, at the speed of light, it becomes infinitely massive. Since mass is a measure of an object's resistance to force, this means that even if you could apply an infinite amount of force to an object travelling at the speed of light, you couldn't make it travel any faster. (Photons, which do travel at the speed of light, aren't infinitely massive because they don't have any mass to begin with. In the language of physics, they have zero rest mass.)

Although Einstein's theory prohibits time travel into the past, it does permit a sort of time travel into the future. To see this, consider the infamous "twin paradox." Twins Mike and Spike have pursued different careers. Spike is an astronaut while Mike is a miner. Now suppose that Spike travels to Alpha Centauri in a rocketship capable of travelling at almost the speed of light while Mike toils away inside the bowels of the earth. Alpha Centauri is 4.4 light-years away from Earth, so at the speed of light it would take 4.4 years to get there. Taking into account the time needed for acceleration, deceleration, and exploration, let's suppose that the round trip actually takes 10 years. During that time, Mike, who stays on Earth, would age 10 years. But

Tachyons and Precognition

According to relativity theory, anything that travels faster than the speed of light must go backward in time. Furthermore, no ordinary object (having a rest mass greater than zero) can go faster than the speed of light for, at that speed, it would have infinite mass. By plugging different numbers into the variables for mass in Einstein's equations, however, physicist Gerald Feinberg found that if something had imaginary mass (mass represented by an imaginary number), it would be physically possible for it to travel faster than the speed of light. Such particles he dubbed "tachyons."[23]

If tachyons exist, they must travel backwards in time because they travel faster than light. Consequently, some have thought that tachyons might be able to explain precognition. Prescient individuals may simply have especially sensitive tachyon receptors. According to electrical engineer Laurence Beynam,

> The fact that precognition involves information transfer in the reverse time direction necessitates, due to the theory of relativity, the adoption of faster-than-light (superluminal or supraluminal) processes as a possible explanatory cause allowed for by the laws of physics. . . . Physicist Gerald Feinberg and Mathematician Adrian Dobbs . . . have theorized superluminal particles of (mathematically) imaginary mass. . . . Tachyons can be viewed either as carrying negative energy backwards in time or positive energy forwards in time. This interchangeability allows us to view a tachyon as a bidirectional discontinuous field line, microminiature "warp," "wormhole," or short-circuit that carries information across space-time regardless of direction, somewhat as light photons carry information within ordinary space-time.[24]

Although tachyons are physically possible, to date no one has detected one. In fact, G. A. Benford, D. L. Book, and W. A. Newcomb argue in "The Tachyonic Antitelephone" that no one ever will, because tachyonic communication involves a logical contradiction.[25] Martin Gardner explains:

> Suppose physicist Jones on the earth is in communication by tachyonic antitelephones with physicist Alpha in another galaxy. They make the following agreement. When Alpha receives a message from Jones, he will reply immediately. Jones promises to send a message to Alpha at three o'clock earth time, if and only if he has not received a message from Alpha by one o'clock. Do you see the difficulty? Both messages go back in time. If Jones sends his message at three, Alpha's reply could reach him before one. "Then," as [Benford, Book, and Newcomb] put it, "the exchange of messages will take place if and only if it does not take place . . . a genuine . . . causal contradiction."[26]

Spike, who travels nearly the speed of light during the trip, would age hardly at all. He would return to an Earth 10 years older while he himself would have aged only a few months. In effect, he would have time-travelled into the Earth's future.

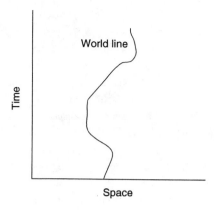

World line

Time

Space

A Minkowskian space-time diagram. The complete history of an object is represented by its "world line."

But time-dilation isn't the only bizarre effect of high-speed travel that Einstein discovered. He also discovered space-contraction: the faster you go, the more you shrink in the direction of travel. At 90 percent of the speed of light, you would have shrunk to 14 percent of your normal (stationary) length.[27]

In 1908, Minkowski developed a mathematically elegant and conceptually appealing way of representing time-dilation and space-contraction: regard space and time not as separate entities but as aspects of a single entity, namely, *space-time*. "Henceforth," he proclaimed, "space by itself and time by itself, are doomed to fade away into mere shadows, and only a kind of union of the two will preserve an independent reality."[28] According to Minkowski, time should be viewed as a fourth dimension, and physical objects should be viewed as four-dimensional entities existing immutably in space-time. You can begin to get a feel for what this means by imagining a Cartesian coordinate system in which the three dimensions of space are represented by the x (horizontal) axis, and time is represented by the y (vertical) axis. Your entire life history could be represented on this graph by a single somewhat squiggly line. The line as a whole would indicate every place you occupy at every moment of your life. The times at which you're at rest would be indicated by straight vertical line segments, and the times at which you're moving would be indicated by curved line segments. Such a line is called by some a *world line* and by others a *space-time worm*. The advantage of this conception is that it graphically depicts the perceived effects of time-dilation and space-contraction.[29]

For our purposes, however, what's interesting about Minkowski's conception of space-time is that the past and the future are just as real

People like us, who believe in physics, know that the distinction between past, present and future is only a stubborn, persistent illusion.

—ALBERT EINSTEIN

Precognition, Free Will, and the Many-Worlds Interpretation

You may be wondering how there can be free will if what Minkowski says is true and the future already exists. If our entire history is already laid out in the unchanging realm of space-time, it's difficult to see how what we do can be up to us. Perhaps free will is an illusion. The Dutch philosopher Baruch Spinoza thought so, noting that if a falling rock had consciousness, it, too, would think it had free will. Many scientists concur. Psychologist B. F. Skinner, for example, claimed that our false belief in the existence of free will has kept us from developing the technology necessary to cure our social ills. According to Skinner, our belief in free will is a prescientific one that has no more to commend it than does a belief in evil spirits. But interestingly enough, there does appear to be a model of the universe that is consistent with both precognition and free will, namely, the many-worlds interpretation of quantum mechanics.

Quantum mechanics allows us to compute the probability that a subatomic event will occur by treating each possible outcome as a wave that propagates according to a formula known as the Schrödinger wave equation (named after its discoverer, Erwin Schrödinger). These waves of probability interfere with one another like waves on the surface of a pond, sometimes cancelling one another, sometimes reinforcing one another. According to the standard interpretation of quantum mechanics, known as the Copenhagen interpretation (named after the birthplace of its champion, Niels Bohr), no actual event occurs until a measurement is made. The act of measurement is said to collapse the wave function and bring one of the possibilities into actuality. In other words, according to this interpretation of quantum mechanics, we create the world in the act of measuring it. One begins to see why Einstein railed against quantum mechanics.

The notion that things are not real until they are measured is a hard one to swallow. In as the present. In his view, past, present, and future all coexist in the unvarying realm of space-time. So in a Minkowskian universe, it's not a logical contradiction to say that you perceive the future, for the future does exist now.

Space-time is static. It never changes. But the world around us is constantly changing. What, then, accounts for our perception of the passing of time? In one view, the world line of each of us is like a movie film unrolled and laid out flat. Each point on a world line is like a frame in a movie; it's a snapshot of us at one particular place and time. Our consciousness functions as a movie viewer that moves along our world line. In this model, the "change" we observe in reality is like the "change" we observe in the movie theater. The film itself doesn't change, but viewing the frames sequentially creates the illusion of change.

order to avoid this consequence, Hugh Everett showed that the waves described by quantum mechanics need not be taken to represent different possibilities. Instead, they can be taken to represent different real worlds—alternate parallel universes, if you will. When an observation is made, the universe "splits" and we find ourselves in one of its "branches." In other words, according to Everett, everything that can possibly happen actually does happen. But each possibility is realized in a different world. According to this theory, if it is physically possible for you to be President of the United States, then there is a real world in which you are the president of the United States. Since these other worlds are inaccessible to us, however, they will probably not give presidential contenders much solace.

If we wed Everett's many-worlds interpretation of quantum mechanics with Minkowski's view of space-time, however, we arrive at a model of reality that some say can account for free will. Mathematician Rudolf v. B. Rucker, for example, asks, "Is there some way to set up the universe so that the different possible futures are real possibilities instead of theoretical possibilities?" And he answers, "Yes there is. The idea is that we can work with a branching universe."[30] For Rucker, our will somehow determines which path through the many worlds our consciousness takes.[31] In this model, precognition could be viewed as catching a glimpse of one of Everett's many worlds. It wouldn't be seeing into *the* future, however, for there isn't just one future. Rather, it would be seeing into one possible future, a future that might not occur if we make decisions that lead to other futures. (Perhaps this explains why so many supposed precognitions turn out wrong.) In any event, it's interesting to note that it *may* be physically possible for both precognition and free will to coexist.

Such a model, crude as it is, provides a way of understanding precognition. In normal perception, our consciousness travels up adjacent world lines in a smooth, continuous fashion. In the case of precognition, however, our consciousness jumps ahead to a spot farther up our world lines. In that case, we would actually be seeing the future.[32]

This model can also account for memory. When we remember, we experience the past, so to speak. Perhaps when we remember, our consciousness travels down our world line to the place where the event is recorded. Indeed, some cases of recollection are so vivid that it does seem that we have actually returned to the time at which they occurred. In "A New Refutation of Time," the Argentinean writer, Jorge Luis Borges, argues for just such a view of memory.[33]

Although imagining our consciousness moving up and down world lines provides one way of accounting for precognition and

Time is the moving image of eternity.
—PLATO

memory, this approach is problematic because it assumes that consciousness exists in another time separate from space-time.[34] That may be the case, but such an assumption isn't necessary. As the physicist David Park has shown, if we simply accept as a given that points on a world line containing memories are "later" or farther up the world line than the events remembered, there is no need to suppose that our consciousness "moves" in its own separate time.[35] In this view, we are conscious at each point along our world line. What creates the illusion of the passing of time is just the structure of the universe itself.

These considerations suggest that even precognition may be physically possible. But remember that this possibility does not establish that precognition is real. The fact that the world may be constructed so as to permit such things gives us no reason to believe that it actually is so constructed. A theory, by itself, doesn't provide a good reason for believing in ESP. Only a well-confirmed theory can do that.

SUGGESTED READINGS

Bradley, Raymond, and Norman Swartz. *Possible Worlds*. Indianapolis: Hackett, 1979.

Davies, Paul. *Other Worlds*. New York: Simon and Schuster, 1980.

Gamow, George. *One, Two, Three . . . Infinity*. New York: Bantam, 1947.

Gardner, Martin. *Time Travel and Other Mathematical Bewilderments*. New York: W. H. Freeman, 1988.

Kuhn, Thomas. *The Structure of Scientific Revolutions*. Chicago: University of Chicago Press, 1970.

Moore, Brooke Noel, and Richard Parker. *Critical Thinking*. Palo Alto, Calif.: Mayfield, 1991.

NOTES

1. Milton A. Rothman, *A Physicist's Guide to Skepticism* (Buffalo: Prometheus Books, 1988), p. 193.

2. Erich von Däniken, *Chariots of the Gods* (New York: Bantam, 1970), p. 30.

3. Saul-Paul Sirag, "The Skeptics," in *Future Science*, ed. John White and Stanley Krippner (Garden City, N.J.: Doubleday, 1977), p. 535.

4. For a more in-depth examination of necessity, see Raymond Bradley and Norman Swartz, *Possible Worlds* (Indianapolis: Hackett, 1979).

5. Aristotle, *Metaphysics*, Book IV, 1008b, trans. Richard McKeon (New York: Random House, 1941), p. 742.

6. Ibid., Book IV, 1006a, p. 737.

7. St. Augustine, *The City of God*, XXI, 8.

8. Lyall Watson, *Supernature: A Natural History of the Supernatural* (New York: Bantam, 1973), pp. 82–83.

9. C. J. Ducasse, "Some Questions Concerning Psychical Phenomena," *The Journal of the American Society for Psychical Research*, 48 (1954): 5.

10. Adrian Dobbs, "The Feasibility of a Physical Theory of ESP," in *Science and ESP*, ed. J. R. Smythies (London: Routledge and Kegan Paul, 1967), p. 230.

11. Ibid., pp. 230–31.

12. Ibid., p. 234.

13. R. Targ and H. Puthoff, *Mind Reach* (New York: Delta, 1972), p. 170.

14. John Gribbin, *In Search of Schrödinger's Cat* (New York: Bantam, 1984), p. 229.

15. *Science*, 217 (1982): 435.

16. A. Einstein, B. Podolsky, and N. Rosen, "Can Quantum Mechanical Description of Physical Reality be Considered Complete?" *Physical Review*, 47 (1935): 777–80.

17. J. S. Bell, "On the Einstein-Podolsky-Rosen Paradox," *Physics*, 1 (1964): 195–200.

18. See, for example, Bernard d'Espagnat, "Quantum Theory and Reality," *Scientific American*, 241 (1979): 158–81; and A. Aspect, P. Granger, and G. Roger, "Experimental Realization of Einstein-Podolsky-Rosen-Bohm *Gedankenexperiment*: A New Violation of Bell's Inequalities," *Physical Review Letters*, 49 (1982): 91–94.

19. N. Bohr, "Can Quantum Mechanical Description of Physical Reality Be Considered Complete?" *Physical Review*, 48 (1935): 696–702.

20. D. J. Bohm and B. J. Hiley, "On the Intuitive Understanding of Nonlocality as Implied by Quantum Theory," *Foundations of Physics*, 5 (1975): 95–96.

21. Victor J. Stenger, "The Spooks of Quantum Mechanics," *Skeptical Inquirer*, 15 (1990): 51–61.

22. George Gamow, *One, Two, Three . . . Infinity* (New York: Bantam, 1979), p. 104.

23. Gerald Feinberg, "Particles That Go Faster Than Light," *Scientific American*, February 1970, pp. 69–77.

24. Laurence M. Beynam, "Quantum Physics and Paranormal Events," in *Future Science*, White and Krippner, pp. 317–18.

25. G. A. Benford, D. L. Book, and W. A. Newcomb, "The Tachyonic Antitelephone," *Physical Review D*, 3d ser., 2 (1970): 63–65.

26. Martin Gardner, "Time Travel," in *Time Travel and Other Mathematical Bewilderments* (New York: W. H. Freeman, 1988), p. 4.

27. Gamow, *One, Two, Three. . .Infinity*, p. 100.

28. H. Minkowski, "Space and Time," in H. A. Lorentz, A. Einstein, H. Minkowski, and H. Weyl, *The Principle of Relativity* (New York: Dover, 1952), p. 75.

29. Gamow, *One, Two, Three,* p. 66ff.

30. Rudolf v. B. Rucker, *Geometry, Relativity, and the Fourth Dimension* (New York: Dover, 1977), pp. 63–64.

31. Ibid.

32. Lee F. Werth, "Normalizing the Paranormal," *American Philosophical Quarterly,* 15 (1978): 47–56.

33. Jorge Luis Borges, *A Personal Anthology* (New York: Grove Press, 1967), pp. 44–64.

34. Paul Davies, *Other Worlds* (New York: Simon and Schuster, 1984), pp. 45–46.

35. David Park, "The Myth of the Passage of Time," in *The Study of Time,* ed. J. T. Fraser, F. C. Haber, and G. H. Muller (Berlin: Springer-Verlag, 1972), pp. 110–21.

THREE
Looking for Truth in Personal Experience

"I SAW IT WITH MY own eyes."

"I *know* what I heard and felt."

"I could no longer doubt my own senses—what seemed utterly impossible was . . . *real.*"

Such words have come from many of us who've experienced, up close and personal, the extraordinary, the bizarre, the *weird*. They're often spoken with conviction, with an air of certainty. After all, we trust our own sensory experiences and the interpretations we put on them. We trust them because relying on our senses works, at least for most purposes. Doing so proves accurate enough, often enough, for us to make our way in the world. So in the aftermath of an extraordinary personal experience, it's no wonder if someone asks "Can we reasonably deny the evidence of our own senses?"— and concludes: "No!"

If you believe everything, you are not a believer in anything at all.
—SUFI SAYING

SEEMING AND BEING

Everard Feilding, an amateur magician and researcher of psychic phenomena, was such a someone. In the first decade of this century, he investigated Eusapia Palladino, the world-famous medium (a person said to contact spirits). He was a skeptic concerning such matters and had helped to expose trickery among many who claimed paranormal powers. But he changed his tune after the unforgettable experience of sitting in on several seances with Palladino. Here's what he said about those encounters:

> All my own experiments in physical mediumship had resulted in the discovery of the most childish frauds. Failure had followed upon failure. . . . The first seance with Eusapia, accordingly, provoked chiefly a feeling of surprise; the second, of irritation — irritation at finding oneself confronted with a foolish but apparently insoluble problem. . . . After the sixth, for the first time, I find that my mind, from which the stream of events has hitherto run off like rain from a macintosh, is at last beginning to be capable of absorbing them. For the first time I have the absolute conviction that our observation is not mistaken. I realize, as an appreciable fact in life, that, from an empty cabinet I have seen hands and heads come forth, that from behind the curtain of that empty cabinet I have been seized by living fingers, the existence and position of the very nails of which could be felt. I have seen this extraordinary woman sitting visible outside the curtain, held hand and foot by my colleagues, immobile except for the occasional straining of a limb, while some entity within the curtain has over and over again pressed my hand in a position clearly beyond her reach. I refuse to entertain the possibility of a doubt that we were the victims of hallucination.[1]

Such compelling stories of personal experience leading to belief in the paranormal are numerous in past and present. Maybe you even have one of your own. In several surveys, people who believe in the paranormal have cited personal experience as the most important reason for their belief. In one study, believers were asked their main reason for their belief in ESP. Personal experience got more votes than media reports, experiences of friends or relatives, and laboratory evidence. Even many of the skeptics in this study put a high premium on personal experience. They said that they disbelieved because they hadn't yet experienced ESP.[2] So Feilding's emphasis on personal experience seems typical.

But there's a problem here. Despite Feilding's experience being direct and firsthand, despite how impressive his experience seems, despite his certainty in concluding that the paranormal phenomena in question were real, there are good reasons to believe that his conclusion was in fact *wrong*. (We'll discuss his case in more detail later.)

These reasons do not involve questioning Feilding's integrity, intelligence, or sanity. Neither do they involve the unjustified assertion that paranormal events are impossible. More important, what we've said about Feilding's conclusion could be said about many similar conclusions based on other equally impressive extraordinary experiences.

The fact is, though our experiences (and our judgments about those experiences) are reliable enough for most practical purposes, they often mislead us in the strangest, most unexpected ways — especially when the experiences are exceptional or mysterious. This is because our perceptual capacities, our memories, our states of consciousness, our information-processing abilities have perfectly natural but amazing powers and limits. Apparently, most people are unaware of these powers and limits. But these odd characteristics of our minds are very influential. Because of them, as several psychologists have pointed out, we should *expect* to have many natural experiences that seem for all the world like supernatural or paranormal events. So even if the supernatural or paranormal didn't exist, *weird things would still happen to us.*

The point is not that every strange experience must indicate a natural phenomenon — nor is it that every weird happening must be supernatural. The main point is that some ways of thinking about personal experience help increase our chances of getting to the truth of the matter. If our minds have peculiar characteristics that influence our experience and how we judge that experience, we need to know about those characteristics and understand how to think our way through them — all the way through, to conclusions that make sense. This feat involves critical thinking. But it also requires *creative* thinking — a grand leap powered by an open mind past the obvious answer, beyond the will to believe or disbelieve, toward new perspectives, to the best solution among several possibilities. This chapter shows you how to take the first step. The chapters that follow tell you how to finish the job.

That first step is to understand and apply a simple but potent principle:

> Just because something seems
> (feels, appears) real doesn't mean
> that it is.

We can't know for sure that an event or phenomenon has objective reality — that it's not imagination, not "all in our heads" — just because it appears to us to have objective reality. This is simply a logical fact. We can't infer what is from what seems. To draw such a

The Will to Believe or Disbelieve

Part of the task of critically evaluating an unusual claim is to control our tendency to believe or disbelieve without good reason. For some people, the need to believe in paranormal phenomena is very strong—so strong that in some cases people have refused to accept the confessions of others, who admit (and sometimes demonstrate) that their paranormal feats are fraudulent. Gustav Jahoda provides this example:

> I found myself in the company of six other people after dinner, and the conversation veered toward the supernatural. An impromptu seance was proposed, and all of us settled around a large circular table. The idea was that questions would be asked, and the spirits would answer by rapping once for "yes" and twice for "no." The first question was asked, but nothing happened. We sat for several minutes in the semi-darkness, with tension rising. Getting rather stiff, I shifted in my chair, accidentally knocking the table, and was staggered to find that this was taken as the expected answer. After a brief struggle with my conscience, the desire to experiment gained the upper hand; I told myself that after a while I would reveal the deception and pass it off as a joke. For another half-hour or so I knocked the table quite blatantly with the tip of my shoes, without arousing the slightest suspicion. I was just about to summon my courage to come clean, when one of the persons present asked the spirit to materialize. Another long tense silence followed, then one person whispered, "He's there, in the corner—a little grey man." It was said with such conviction that I almost expected to see something when I looked. There was in fact nothing except a faint shadow cast by a curtain moving in a slight breeze. Two others claimed to see the homunculus quite clearly. . . . About a year after the seance I met one of the participants. Recalling the evening, he said that he had previously been sceptical about the occult, but this experience had convinced him. On hearing this my guilt feelings were thoroughly aroused, and I decided to make a clean breast of it. Once more I had badly miscalculated—he just would not believe me.[3]

conclusion is to commit an elementary fallacy of reasoning: It's clearly fallacious to say, "This event or phenomenon seems real; therefore, it *is* real." What's more, the peculiar nature of our minds guarantees that what seems will frequently *not* correspond to what is.

Now, in our daily routines, we usually do assume that what we see is reality—that seeming is being. And we're generally not disappointed. But we're at much greater risk for being dead wrong with such assumptions when (1) our experience is uncorroborated (no one else has shared our experience), (2) our conclusions are at odds with all known previous experience, or (3) any of the peculiarities of our minds could be at work.

Here's how some of these peculiarities operate and how powerful they can be.

PERCEIVING: TRUE OR FALSE?

The idea that our normal perceptions have a direct, one-to-one correspondence to external reality — that they are like photographs of the outer world — is wrong. Much research now suggests that perception is *constructive*, that it's in part something that our minds manufacture. Thus what we perceive is determined not only by what our eyes and ears and other senses detect, but also by what we know, what we expect, what we believe, and what our physiological state is. This constructive tendency has survival value — it helps us make sense of and deal successfully with the world. But it also means that seeing is often *not* believing — rather, the reverse is true.

·Believing is seeing.
—JOHN SLADER

Perceptual Constancies

Consider what psychologists call perceptual constancies — our tendency to have certain perceptual experiences even in the absence of relevant input from our senses. Research has demonstrated these constancies again and again; they're stock items in basic psychology texts. Psychologist Terence Hines believes that they're some of the best illustrations of our constructive perception at work, and he cites three examples.[4]

One is color constancy. People often perceive an object as a certain color because they know that the object is supposed to be that color — even if the object is not that color at all. In one early experiment, people were shown cutouts of trees and donkeys, which they perceived as green and gray, as they should be — even though all the cutouts were made from the same green material and lit by a red light to make them appear gray.[5] Such findings help to explain how we sometimes can be quite wrong when remembering colors.

Another example, also involving color constancy, shows that we can perceive color even when it's physically impossible for our eyes to see any color at all. The vision cells that let us see color are located in the middle of the retina. This means that we should be able to see colors only in the center of our visual field — objects in our peripheral vision should be in black and white. But we perceive color throughout our *whole* visual field. How can this be? When we *know* what color something in our peripheral vision should be, our minds supply that color. If we don't know, we perceive the object in black and white until it's closer to the center of our field of vision. Hines illustrates the phenomenon like this:

> As I sit here writing this, there is an orange red door off to my left. I can just see the door out of the corner of my eye and I clearly see it as colored, in spite of the fact that the light being reflected off the door to my retina is falling on a part of the retina where there are no color receptors. Since I know what color the door is — it is very familiar to me — my brain constructs a perception of the color. How the brain manages this is not known . . . but the phenomenon demonstrates the great importance of knowledge in even the simplest types of perception.[7]

Then there's the example of size constancy. If you watch a truck rumble past you and speed into the distance, do you perceive the truck to become smaller? Of course not. You perceive the size of familiar objects as roughly constant no matter how far away they are. The image on your retinas shrinks as an object gets farther away, but you perceive the size of the object as unchanging. The reason is that you *know* that distance has no effect on the actual size of physical objects. With this knowledge your brain gives you perceptions of size constancy, despite shrinking retinal images.

Amazingly enough, our knowledge of size constancy is learned. We're not born with it. And there have been reports of people in the world who haven't learned it. Anthropologist Colin Turnbull told of the Ba Mbuti people who didn't get a chance to learn about size constancy because they lived in thick jungle where the only objects that could be seen were always just a few yards away. When Turnbull took one of these people out on an open plain, they saw several buffalo grazing a few miles away. The Ba Mbuti asked what kind of insects they were! Turnbull told him that they were buffalo twice the size of the ones his people were used to. Turnbull's companion refused to believe him. So they drove to where the buffalo were. As they got closer to the animals, and the buffalo appeared to get larger and larger, the Ba Mbuti became frightened and said that it was witchcraft. Turnbull writes, "Finally, when he realized that they were real buffalo he was no longer afraid, but what puzzled him still was why they had been so small, and whether they *really* had been small and had so suddenly grown larger, or whether it had been some kind of trickery."[7]

The Role of Expectation

We're usually completely unaware of our many perceptual constancies — just as we're often oblivious to all the other ways that our brains get into the construction business. One of these other ways is

Collective Hallucinations

Can the same hallucination be experienced by two or more persons? Yes, say psychologists Leonard Zusne and Warren H. Jones, and here's how it happens:

It is expectation that plays the coordinating role in collective hallucination. Although the subject matter of individual hallucinations has virtually no limits, the topics of collective hallucinations are limited to certain categories. These categories are determined, first, by the kinds of ideas that a group of people may be excited about as a group, for emotional excitement is a prerequisite of collective hallucinations. The most common causes of emotional excitement in groups are religious, and, indeed, phenomena related to religion are most often the subject of collective hallucinations. Second, the categories are limited by the fact that all participants in the hallucination must be informed beforehand, at least concerning the broad outlines of the phenomenon that will constitute the collective hallucination. This may take the form of a publicly announced prophecy, for example, or someone suddenly looking up and saying, "Lo, in the sky!" or words to that effect. Things in the sky, or at least overhead, are the most commonly seen collective hallucinations: radiant crosses, saints, religious symbols, flying objects, sometimes all these in combination. Once the general type of hallucination is established, it is easy to harmonize individual differences in the accounts. This may take place during the hallucination or in subsequent conversations.

Even in cases of emotional contagion that so often takes place in crowds moved by strong emotions, there will be always some who will not see the hallucination. It is uncommon for them to speak out and deny it. They usually keep quiet, doubtful perhaps of their worthiness to have been granted the vision for which so many of their fellows all around them are fervently giving thanks. Later on, influenced by the accounts of others, they may even begin to believe that they saw it too. The "reliable eyewitness," who, as it turns out upon closer examination did not see anything unusual at all, is an all-too-frequent experience of the investigator of phenomena seen by many.[8]

based on the power of expectancy: We sometimes perceive exactly what we *expect* to perceive, regardless of what's real.

Research has shown that when people expect to perceive a certain stimulus (for example, see a light or hear a tone), they often do perceive it — even when no stimulus is present. In one experiment, subjects were told to walk along a corridor until they saw a light flash. Sure enough, some of them stopped, saying they had seen a flash — but the light hadn't flashed at all. In other studies, subjects expected to experience an electric shock, or feel warmth, or smell certain odors, and many did experience what they expected even though none of the appropriate stimuli had been given. All that was really given was the suggestion that a stimulus might occur. The subjects had hallucinated (perceived, or apparently perceived, objects or events that have no objective existence). So if we're normal, expectancy or suggestion can cause us to perceive what simply isn't there. Studies show that this is especially true when the stimulus is vague or ambiguous or when clear observation is difficult.

We've all had such hallucinations. Psychologist Andrew Neher cites the common experience of looking at a clock and "seeing" the second hand move — then realizing that the clock isn't running.[9] Have you ever seen someone standing in the shadows on a dark night as you walk home alone and then discovered that the person was a shrub? Have you ever been in the shower and heard the phone ring, only to realize that the ringing was all in your mind?

Looking for Clarity in Vagueness

Another kind of perceptual construction happens every time we're confronted with a vague, formless stimulus but nevertheless perceive something very distinct in it. Take the moon, for instance. In this country, we see the figure of a man in it. But East Indians see a rabbit, Samoans a woman weaving, and Chinese a monkey pounding rice. We often look at clouds, wallpaper, smoke, fire, fuzzy photos, murky paintings, water stains on walls and see elephants, castles, faces, demons, nude figures — you name it. This trick is technically a type of illusion, or misperception, called *pareidolia.* We simply see a vague stimulus as something it's not. We etch meaning into the meaningless. Psychologists point out that once we see a particular image in the clouds or smoke, we often find it difficult to see anything else, even if we want to. This tendency takes on more importance when we consider some of the conclusions people have reached when they failed to take it into account.

Things are not always what they seem.
—PHAEDRUS

Consider: On the surface of the planet Mars, there's a stone monument of a human face, one mile wide — and this amazing artifact is clearly revealed in a NASA photograph. This startling claim has been made by several people in books, magazines, and on television. They have suggested that the face is the work of an alien civilization.

The NASA photo is real enough. It was taken by the Viking spacecraft in 1976, along with many others. But it's an ambiguous mixture of light and shadow, suggestive of a face but subject to various interpretations. Planetary scientists have emphasized that the photo shows a natural formation. Indeed, Mars experts who've seen the photo don't consider it to show anything unusual at all. A key space scientist who was involved in the Viking mission said, "The object does not even look very much like a face, but the correlating sense of

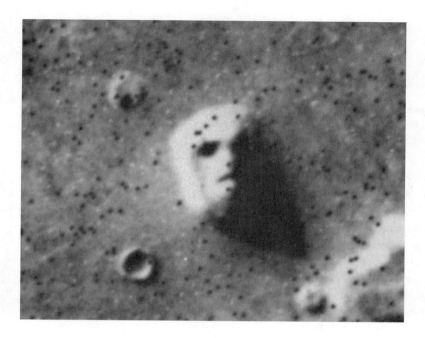

The famous stone "face" on Mars, photographed by the Viking 1 orbiter in 1976, is one mile across and has a nose and mouth formed by shadows. Planetary geologists say that the feature is due to natural processes.

the human brain fills in the missing details to make one think of a face."[10] Science writer Martin Gardner wryly points out that if you're really looking for it, you can see something else in the photo when you look at it from a different angle: "the nude torso of a woman, complete with dark pubic hair, small breasts, and an enlarged belly button slightly off center."[11]

Now it is possible that an alien civilization sculpted a massive human face on Mars. But given our tendency to overlay our own patterns onto vague stimuli, it's a mistake to look at something as ambiguous as the Mars photo and conclude that it is, in fact, a sculpted human face. To do so is to ignore at least one other very good possibility: our own constructive perception.

Overlooking or rejecting this possibility plays a part in countless bizarre cases of pareidolia—like the New Mexico housewife who in 1978 noticed the odd shape of skillet burns on one of her tortillas. She thought that the tortilla looked like the face of Jesus Christ with a crown of thorns—and took it as a sign of Christ's second coming. Pilgrims by the thousands came to see the tortilla, encased in glass. Another example of pareidolia is backward masking, the belief that satanic messages are embedded in rock music. Many people have claimed that such messages can influence us subconsciously and can be heard clearly when the music is played backwards. But researchers say that what you get when you play rock music backwards is mostly

PK Parties and Self-Delusion

In 1988 the National Academy of Sciences issued a scientific evaluation of extraordinary techniques alleged to improve human performance. The report had this to say about certain instances in which personal experience had been used as evidence to support the existence of psychokinesis (PK):

> Another example of beliefs generated in circumstances that are known to create cognitive illusions is macro-PK, which is practiced at spoon bending, or PK, parties. The 15 or more participants in a PK party, who usually pay a fee to attend and bring their own silverware, are guided through various rituals and encouraged to believe that, by cooperating with the leader, they can achieve a mental state in which their spoons and forks will apparently soften and bend through the agency of their minds.
>
> Since 1981, although thousands of participants have apparently bent metal objects successfully, not one scientifically documented case of paranormal metal bending has been presented to the scientific community. Yet participants in the PK parties are convinced that they have both witnessed and personally produced paranormal metal bending. Over and over again we have been told by participants that they know that metal became paranormally deformed in their presence. This situation gives the distinct impression that the proponents of macro-PK, having consistently failed to produce scientific evidence, have forsaken the scientific method and undertaken a campaign to convince themselves and others on the basis of clearly nonscientific data based on personal experience and testimony obtained under emotionally charged conditions.

Consider the conditions that leaders and participants agree facilitate spoon bending.

garbled music — garbled enough to allow people who hear it to construct messages for themselves. Often what people hear in the muddled sounds is exactly what someone suggests they should hear.

The Blondlot Case

Perceptual construction, in all its forms, explains some of the strangest episodes in the history of science. It explains why scientists in Nazi Germany thought they could see nonexistent physical differences between the blood particles of Jews and those of the Aryan man. It explains why over 100 years ago the Italian astronomer Giovanni Schiaparelli (and later the American astronomer Percival Lowell) claimed to see canals on Mars. (Lowell even published a detailed map of the canals.) Photos taken by Mariner 9 show nothing on Mars that corresponds to what Schiaparelli and Lowell said they saw.[13] And perceptual construction explains the infamous case of Professor René Blondlot.

Efforts are made to exclude critics because, it is asserted, skepticism and attempts to make objective observations can hinder or prevent the phenomena from appearing. As [J.] Houck, the originator of the PK party, describes it, the objective is to create in the participants a peak emotional experience. To this end, various exercises involving relaxation, guided imagery, concentration, and chanting are performed. The participants are encouraged to shout at the silverware and to "disconnect" by deliberately avoiding looking at what their hands are doing. They are encouraged to shout Bend! throughout the party. "To help with the release of the initial concentration, people are encouraged to jump up or scream that theirs is bending, so that others can observe." Houck makes it clear that the objective is to create a state of emotional chaos. "Shouting at the silverware has also been added as a means of helping to enhance the emotional level in a group. This procedure adds to the intensity of the command to bend and helps create pandemonium throughout the party."

A PK party obviously is not the ideal situation for obtaining reliable observations. The conditions are just those which psychologists and others have described as creating states of heightened suggestibility and implanting compelling beliefs that may be unrelated to reality. It is beliefs acquired in this fashion that seem to motivate persons who urge us to take macro-PK seriously. Complete absence of any scientific evidence does not discourage the proponents; they have acquired their beliefs under circumstances that instill zeal and subjective certainty. Unfortunately it is just these circumstances that foster false beliefs.[12]

Blondlot (1849–1930) was a member of the French Academy of Sciences and a highly respected physicist at the University of Nancy in France. In 1903, not long after scientists discovered x-rays and other forms of radiation, Blondlot announced the discovery of yet another type of radiation. He called it N-rays, after his university. His research indicated that the presence of N-rays could be detected by the human eye and that they were emitted by certain metals (but not wood). They increased the brightness of a spark. When they were directed at objects coated with luminous paint, the objects became brighter. And when N-rays were present, they helped the eye see better in dim light. Soon dozens of research studies confirmed Blondlot's discovery. Many scientists reported other amazing properties of N-rays.[14]

But all was not well. Scientists outside France weren't able to duplicate Blondlot's results. Many physicists doubted the existence of N-rays because all the tests were based on subjective judgments.

The Experience Behind the Ouija Experience

Have you ever used a Ouija board and wondered what its secret was? Were you really getting messages from the spirit world—or just talking to yourself? Psychologists say the latter is a distinct possibility. Here, psychologist Andrew Neher explains why:

> A Ouija board is a smooth-surfaced board printed with numbers, letters, and words such as yes and no. Ouija players rest their hands on a pointer, which glides easily on felt-covered legs, and concentrate on a question they want answered. Studies have shown that thinking about a certain pattern is sufficient to produce small subconscious movements in the hand in the appropriate directions. Exaggerated, this movement directs the pointer to an answer, which seems to have been arrived at mysteriously since the Ouija player ordinarily has no conscious awareness of having moved the pointer and is often genuinely surprised at the answer. From my own informal experience, it seems possible to elicit memories, as well as subliminal impressions, using a Ouija board, which are otherwise lost to consciousness. . . .
>
> Although the Ouija board, or the planchette, seems to be a handy device for tapping subconscious impressions, there do not seem to be any studies to indicate that Ouija is, in any way, paranormal in its operation.[15]

Instead of using instruments to gather objective data, people's observations determined the results. For example, people were used to judge whether there was an increase in brightness of an object (a standard test for the presence of N-rays). Most scientists knew then, as they know now, that such subjective judgments can be affected by belief or expectancy.

One of those skeptical scientists was American physicist Robert W. Wood. In 1904 he paid a visit to Blondlot's laboratory. There, without Blondlot's knowledge, he tested Blondlot and others to see if N-rays were real or just wishful thinking. In one N-ray experiment, Wood was to assist Blondlot by placing a sheet of lead between a source of N-rays and a card coated with luminous paint. N-rays were supposed to make the paint brighter, except when the lead sheet was placed in their path. (Blondlot had found that lead completely blocked N-rays.) Blondlot was to observe the changes in the paint's brightness as the lead sheet was inserted or removed. But without Blondlot's knowledge, Wood tried something that revealed the truth about N-rays. Wood repeatedly told Blondlot that the lead sheet was in place when in fact it wasn't or that the sheet had been removed when it was really still there. Blondlot's observations then followed an amazing pattern. If he believed that the lead sheet wasn't in place, and

"I can't believe that," said Alice. "Can't you?" the Queen said in a pitying tone. "Try again: draw a long breath and shut your eyes."

—Lewis Carroll

thus not blocking N-rays, he reported that the paint was brighter. If he believed that the lead sheet was there, blocking N-rays, he reported that the paint was dimmer. His observations depended on his belief and had *nothing to do with whether or not the lead sheet was actually in place.*

Wood secretly manipulated other experiments in Blondlot's laboratory with similar results. If Blondlot or some other observer believed N-rays were present, he could see that they were — even in situations where Wood had secretly changed the experiments so that N-rays should have been impossible to detect.

In 1904 Wood published his findings in the British scientific journal *Nature.* It became clear that Blondlot and other French scientists had been victims of perceptual construction. They weren't lying about their observations, and they didn't imagine their experience. Their strong belief in N-rays simply changed the way they perceived. Being scientists didn't protect them from a kind of perceptual distortion that affects us all.

"Constructing" UFOs

This uncomfortable fact — that a phenomenon can be radically misperceived by people who are sane, sober, honest, educated, and intelligent — is seen even more clearly in UFO reports. Case in point: On March 3, 1968, a UFO was sighted by multiple witnesses in several states. In Tennessee, three intelligent, educated people (including the mayor of a large city) saw a light in the night sky moving rapidly toward them. They reported that they saw it pass overhead at about 1,000 feet up; what they saw was a huge, metallic craft moving in silence. They observed orange-colored flames shooting out from behind it, with many square-shaped windows lit from inside the object. In a report to the U.S. Air Force, one of the witnesses said that the craft was shaped "like a fat cigar . . . the size of one of our largest airplane fuselages, or larger."

At about the same time, six people in Indiana spotted the same UFO. Their report to the Air Force said that it was cigar-shaped, moving at treetop level, shooting rocketlike exhaust from its tail, and having many brightly lit windows. Around the same time, two people in Ohio saw it too. But they said that they saw three luminous objects, not one. One of these witnesses used her binoculars to get a good look at the UFO. She submitted a detailed report to the Air Force that said the objects were shaped like "inverted saucers," flying low and in formation, silently cruising by.[16]

Fortunately, we know exactly what these witnesses (and many others) saw in the sky that night. Records from the North American

Air Defense Command (NORAD) and other evidence show that at the time of the UFO sighting, the rocket used to launch the Soviet Zond 4 spacecraft reentered the atmosphere, breaking into luminous fragments as it sped across the sky. It zoomed in the same southwest-to-northeast trajectory noted by the witnesses, crossing several states. The witnesses simply saw the light show produced by the breakup of a rocket.[17]

So where did those interesting details come from — the giant craft, the inverted saucers, the square-shaped windows, the metallic cigar-shape? They were constructed. As Hines says,

> These additions and embellishments were purely the creation of the witnesses' minds: not because they were crazy, drunk, or stupid, but because that is the way the human brain works. It can be said that these witnesses did perceive what they said they did. This doesn't mean, however, that what they perceived was the same as what was really there. Note, too, how inaccurate was the estimate of the object's altitude. . . . [Witnesses] estimated about 1,000 feet while, in fact, the reentering rocket was miles high and scores of miles away. This type of gross inaccuracy frequently occurs when one sees a light in the sky with no background, as is the case at night. Under these circumstances, the many cues the brain uses to judge distance are not present, so no accurate basis for judgment exists.[18]

Even pilots, who are presumed to be experts at accurately observing objects in the sky, can be fooled by UFO construction of the perceptual kind. For example, on June 5, 1969, near St. Louis, the pilots of two airliners and an Air National Guard fighter plane had a close encounter with what they said was a whole squadron of UFOs. It was late afternoon when the copilot of one of the airliners first spotted the UFOs. A Federal Aviation Administration traffic controller who happened to be riding in the cockpit as an observer later reported that it seemed that the squadron would collide with the airliner. He said they seemed to come frighteningly close — within several hundred feet of the airliner! They were the color of "burnished aluminum" and shaped like a "hydroplane." Moments later, the crew of the other airliner (eight miles west of the first) radioed the tower reporting that the UFOs had just zoomed past them. Later the fighter pilot, flying behind the second airliner at 41,000 feet, radioed a near-collision with the UFOs. "Damn, they almost got me," he said. At the last moment the UFOs seemed to suddenly change course and climb out of his way, suggesting that they were "under intelligent control."

What was going on up there? UFO investigator Philip Klass has shown that:

> The identity of this "squadron of UFO's" not only is now known beyond all doubt, but they were photographed by an alert newspaper photogra-

A UFO with a Message

UFO investigator Philip Klass reports the following strange "close encounter"—a peculiar type of UFO experience that's more common than people realize:

A professional musician from Bridgeport, Connecticut, who is a member of Mensa (an organization whose membership is limited to persons of very high I.Q.), after having seen a strange-looking lighted craft in the night skies with a friend, decided to carry his home movie camera, loaded with high-speed color film, in his car in the hope of again seeing, and photographing, the curious object. Some months later, he and his young son spotted the same object with its blinking lights in the night sky. He jumped out of the car and managed to take a few feet of film before the camera jammed. The next evening, at about the same time, the musician spotted the UFO again and managed to obtain about twenty seconds of movies before the object disappeared. "I could hardly contain my emotions," the musician later wrote me.

Later that evening, when he called the friend who had been with him during the initial sighting to report his good fortune, she told him that she too had seen the UFO and had decided to chase after it in her car. When she managed to get underneath the UFO and got out of the car to look up at it, she saw: "ANTHONY'S AUTO BODY—FREE ESTIMATES." The UFO was an advertising plane, a small aircraft equipped with strings of electric lights that spell out advertising messages. When such advertising aircraft are viewed at an oblique angle, they frequently generate UFO reports. The operators of such aircraft are not unhappy at the UFO reports they generate, because it prompts many more people to search the skies on subsequent nights, providing a larger potential audience for their message.[19]

pher in Peoria, Illinois, named Alan Harkrader, Jr. His photo shows a meteor fireball, with a long, luminous tail of electrified air, followed by a smaller flaming fragment, also with a long tail, flying in trail behind. Harkrader told me that he saw another fragment break off but was unable to get a photo of it.[20]

The Harkrader photo and many eyewitness reports from the ground in Illinois and Iowa show that the fireball and its fragments were *not* just a few hundred feet from the planes. The actual distance was at least *125 miles*.

UFO sightings are also complicated by another kind of perceptual construction called the autokinetic effect. This effect refers to how, for most people, a small stationary light in the dark will be perceived as moving. This happens even if the person's head remains perfectly still. Psychologists theorize that the cause of this apparent movement is small, involuntary movements of the eyeball. So a star or

Ghosts in the Bedroom

You awake, startled, to find an eerie image of your dead grandmother floating at the foot of your bed. Is this a ghost? A forlorn spirit from beyond the grave? Maybe. Psychologists, however, have an alternative explanation for experiences like this. Psychologist Graham Reed:

> The drowsiness experienced as one falls asleep, and again as one wakes up, is often accompanied by pronounced imagery. . . . The intermediate state between wakefulness and sleep is referred to as hypnagogic; that which precedes full wakefulness after sleep is termed hypnopompic. . . .
>
> Both hypnagogic and hypnopompic images are notably autonomous, in the sense that they occur suddenly and are not under voluntary control. Very often they are vivid and realistic, although their content may be bizarre.
>
> The most common type of hypnagogic visual imagery is probably the "faces in the dark" which often terrify children as they are falling asleep, and which are also reported by some adults. The "faces" are often distorted in size and shape, and may be in bright but unnatural colours. . . .
>
> It has been noted how hypnagogic images may be invested with fear-providing qualities. They may also be attributed to supernatural causes or to telepathy. Subjects who are interested in spiritualism, ghosts or witchcraft may interpret their images as representing the attempts of spirit contacts to "come through." Those who are interested in ESP (extra-sensory perception) may credit themselves as being "percipients"; their images are then interpreted as telepathic communications. Ironically enough, experiments in telepathy have often required subjects to maintain "watch" late at night, preferably at bedtime, on the grounds that they are more likely to "receive" communications when they are relaxed and unlikely to be distracted. Furthermore the "messages" in such experiments often take the form of coloured geometric shapes such as yellow diamonds or blue squares. Approximations to geometric shapes or patterns are amongst the most common types of hypnagogic images, and as we have seen these are usually coloured. Again, as noted earlier, hypnopompic images often have reference to the subject's anticipations about his forthcoming day. So it is not surprising that they are often interpreted as examples of precognition by those who are interested in ESP, or as premonitions by the superstitious. Hypnagogic imagery may also be interpreted as a pathological phenomenon by adolescents and by persons who are worried about their mental health.[21]

bright planet can appear to move, creating the illusion of a UFO. Research has shown that the autokinetic effect can be influenced by the opinion of others. If someone says a light in the dark is moving in a certain way, others will be more likely to report similar observations.[22] Klass says that no single object has been mistaken as a flying saucer more often than the planet Venus, a very bright object in the morning sky, and the autokinetic effect helps explain why.[23]

Perceptual construction in UFO sightings has been documented many times, enough to demonstrate that no one is immune to it — not pilots, not astronomers, not reliable witnesses of all kinds, not pillars of the community. This fact, of course, doesn't explain every UFO sighting. (To explain many more sightings, other facts would need to be — and have been — brought to bear.) But it does help to show that personal observations alone aren't proof that UFOs — that is, spacecraft of extraterrestrial origin — are real. In fact, when clear observation is difficult (which is usually the case, as in the examples above), personal experience by itself can never tell us whether or not a UFO is real. What *seems* real may not *be* real.

REMEMBERING: DO WE REVISE THE PAST?

Your memory is like a mental tape recorder — it whirrs day and night, picking up your experience, making a literal record of what happens, and letting you play back the parts you want to review. Does this sound about right? It's wrong.

A lot of research now indicates that our memories *aren't* literal records or copies. Like our perceptual powers, our memories are constructive or, rather, creative. When we remember an experience, our brains reach for representation of it; then, piece by piece, they *reconstruct* a memory based on this fragment. This reconstructive process is inherently inexact. It's also vulnerable to all kinds of influences that guarantee that our memories will frequently be inaccurate.

For an example of your memory's reconstructive powers try this: Remember an instance when you were sitting today. Recall your surroundings, how you were dressed, how you positioned your legs and arms. Chances are, you see the scene from the perspective of someone looking at it, as though you were watching yourself on television. But this memory can't be completely accurate because during the experience you never perceived yourself from this perspective. You now remember certain pieces of the experience, and your brain constructed everything else, television perspective and all.

For well over a half century, research has been showing that the memory of witnesses can be unreliable, and the constructive nature of memory helps explain why. Studies demonstrate that the recall of eyewitnesses is sometimes wrong because they reconstruct events from memory fragments and then draw conclusions from the reconstruction. Those fragments can be a far cry from what actually transpired. Further, if eyewitnesses are under stress at the time of their observations, they may not be able to remember crucial details, or their recall may be distorted. Stress can even distort the memories of expert witnesses, which is one of several reasons why reports of UFOs, seances, and ghosts must be examined carefully: The experiences are stressful. Because memory is constructive and liable to warping, people can sincerely believe that their recall is perfectly accurate—and be perfectly wrong. They may report their memory as honestly as they can, but, alas, it's been worked over.

Like perception, memory can be dramatically affected by expectancy and belief. Several studies show this, but a classic experiment illustrates the point best. Researchers asked students to describe what they had seen in a picture. It portrayed a white man and a black man talking to each other on the subway. In the white man's hand was an open straight razor. When the students recalled the picture, one-half of them reported that the razor was *in the hand of the black man*. Memory reconstruction was tampered with by expectancy or belief.[24]

The same kind of thing can happen in our successful "predictions." After some event has occurred, we may say," I knew that would happen; I predicted it." And we may truly believe that we foretold the future. But research suggests that our desire to believe that we accurately predicted the future can sometimes alter our memories of the prediction. We may remember our prediction even though we actually made no such prediction. Apparently this can occur despite our knowing that our memories can be checked against records of the actual predictions.[25]

Research also shows that our memory of an event can be drastically changed if we later encounter new information about the event—even if the information is brief, subtle, and dead wrong. Here's a classic example: In one experiment people were asked to watch a film depicting a car accident. Afterwards, they were asked to recall what they had seen. Some of the subjects were asked: "About how fast were the cars going when they smashed into each other?" The others were asked the same question with a subtle difference. The word "smashed" was replaced by "hit." Strangely enough, those who were asked the "smashed" question estimated higher speeds than those asked the "hit" question. Then a week later, all the subjects were asked to recall whether they had seen broken glass in the film. Compared to the subjects who got the "hit" question, more than twice as many of those exposed to the "smashed" question said they had seen broken glass. But the film showed *no broken glass at all*.[26] In a similar study, subjects recalled that they had seen a stop sign in another film of a car accident even though no stop sign had appeared in the film. The

Our beliefs are not automatically updated by the best evidence available. They often have an active life of their own and fight tenaciously for their own survival.

—D. Marks and
   R. Kammann

Past Life Remembered or Cryptomnesia?

If, under hypnosis, you recall living 200 years ago and can vividly remember doing and seeing things that you've never experienced in your present life, isn't this proof that you lived a "past life"? Isn't this evidence of reincarnation? Some people would think so. There is, however, another possibility, explained by Ted Schultz:

> Beatle George Harrison got sued for rewriting the Chiffons' "He's So Fine" into "My Sweet Lord." He was the innocent victim of the psychological phenomenon of cryptomnesia. So was Helen Keller, the famous blind and deaf woman, when she wrote a story called "The Frost King." After it was published in 1892, she was accused of plagiarizing Margaret Canby's "The Frost Fairies," though Helen had no conscious memory of ever reading it. But, sure enough, inquiries revealed that Canby's story had been read to her (by touch) in 1888. She was devastated....
>
> Cryptomnesia, or "hidden memory," refers to thoughts and ideas that seem new and original, but which are actually memories of things that you've forgotten you knew. The cryptomnesic ideas may be variations on the original memories, with details switched around and changed, but still recognizable.
>
> Cryptomnesia is a professional problem for artists; it also plays an important role in past-life regression. In the midst of the hoopla surrounding the Bridey Murphy [reincarnation] case the Denver Post decided to send newsman William J. Barker to Ireland to try to find evidence of Bridey's actual existence. [Bridey was the alleged past-life personality of Virginia Tighe.] Unfortunately for reincarnation enthusiasts,

careful checking failed to turn up anything conclusive. Barker couldn't locate the street Bridey said she lived on, he couldn't find any essays by Bridey's husband in the Belfast News-Letter between 1843 and 1864 (during which time Bridey said he was a contributor), and he couldn't find anyone who had heard of the "Morning Jig" that Bridey danced.

> Research by reporters from the Chicago American and later by writer Melvin Harris finally uncovered the surprising source of housewife Virginia Tighe's past-life memories. As a teenager in Chicago, Virginia had lived across the street from an Irish woman named Mrs. Anthony Corkell, who had regaled her with tales about the old country. Mrs. Corkell's maiden name was Bridie Murphy! Furthermore, Virginia had been active in high school dramatics, at one point memorizing several Irish monologues which she learned to deliver with a heavy Irish brogue. Finally, the 1893 World's Columbian Exposition, staged in Chicago, had featured a life-size Irish Village, with fifteen cottages, a castle tower, and a population of genuine Irish women who danced jigs, spun cloth, and made butter. No doubt Virginia had heard stories of this exhibition from many of her neighbors and friends while growing up in Chicago in the '20s.

> Almost every other case of "past-life memory" that has been objectively investigated has followed the same pattern: the memories, often seemingly quite alien to the life experiences of the regressed subject, simply cannot be verified by historical research; on the other hand, they frequently prove to be the result of cryptomnesia.[27]

subjects had simply been asked a question that presupposed a stop sign and thus created the memory of one in their minds.[28]

These studies put in doubt any long-term memory that's subjected to leading questions or is evoked after exposure to a lot of new, seemingly pertinent information. Psychologist James Alcock cites the example of reports of near-death experiences collected by Raymond Moody in his books *Life After Life* (1975) and *Reflections on Life After Life* (1977). These are stories of people who had been close to death (for example, clinically dead but later resuscitated) and later reported that while in that state they felt the sensation of floating above their body, traveling through a dark tunnel, seeing dead loved ones, or having other extraordinary experiences. Researchers generally agree that people do experience such things; whether their experiences show that they literally leave their bodies and enter another world is another question. Moody's cases were based on the memories of people who came to him with their stories, sometimes years after the experience, frequently after they had heard Moody lecture or read newspaper stories about his work. Alcock explains:

> Since there was such great similarity in the reports, Moody argued that these reports must reflect reality. (There are physiological reasons for expecting such similarities. . . .) Considering how memory can be shaped after the event, it is not unlikely that one's memory of near-death experience will conform to the pattern described in the lecture or reading one has just experienced. Moreover, Moody's questions to his subjects certainly would not have been without influence.[29]

But our memories are more than just constructive — they're also selective. We selectively remember certain things and ignore others, setting up a memory bias that can give the impression that something mysterious, even paranormal, is going on. Our selective memories may even lead us to believe that we have ESP. As Hines says:

> A classic example is to be thinking of someone and, minutes later, having them call. Is this sort of instance amazing proof of direct mind-to-mind communication? No — it's just a coincidence. It seems amazing because we normally don't think about the millions of telephone calls made each day and we don't remember the thousands of times we have thought of someone when they *haven't* called.[30]

Selective memory is also at work in many cases of seemingly prophetic dreams. Research has shown that we all dream during sleep. In fact, if we're normal, we'll have at least 250 dreams a night! But we won't remember most of them. But, as Hines points out, we're likely to remember the ones that "come true":

If a dream doesn't "come true" there is very little chance that it will be remembered. We have all had the experience of awakening and not remembering any dreams. Then, sometime later during the day, something happens to us, or we see or hear something, that retrieves from our long-term memory a dream we had had, but which, until we were exposed to what is called a *retrieval cue*, we were unable to recall voluntarily. Of course, if we had not been exposed to the retrieval cue, we would never have been aware that the dream had occurred. Thus, the nature of memory for dreams introduces a strong bias that makes dreams appear to be much more reliably prophetic than they are—we selectively remember those dreams that "come true."[31]

JUDGING: THE HABIT OF UNWARRANTED ASSUMPTIONS

Human judgment is fallible. We've all seen enough foul-ups in our lifetimes to be convinced of this. In fact, it could be the understatement of the millennium. But many people don't realize that our judgment is fallible in special ways. It's often biased in such strange fashion that it can lead us to conclude that something is paranormal or supernatural when that's not the case at all.

Man prefers to believe what he prefers to be true.
—FRANCIS BACON

Against All Odds

Consider: A woman finds herself thinking about an old friend she hasn't thought about for ages or seen in twenty years. Then she picks up the newspaper and is stunned to see her friend's obituary. Or a man reads his daily horoscope, which predicts that he'll meet someone who'll change his life. The next day he's introduced to the woman he eventually marries. Or a woman dreams in great detail that the house next door catches fire and burns to the ground. She wakes up in a cold sweat and writes down the dream. Three days later her neighbor's house is struck by lightning and is damaged by fire. Are these stories simply cases of coincidence? Could the eerie conjunction of events have happened by chance?

Many would say absolutely not—the odds against mere coincidence are too great, astronomical. But research shows that people—even trained scientists—are prone to misjudge probabilities. When we declare that an event couldn't have occurred by chance, we're frequently way off in our estimates of the odds. Test yourself: Let's say you're at a party, and there are twenty-three people present including yourself. What are the chances that two of those twenty-three people have the same birthday? Is it (a) 1 chance in 365, or 1/365; (b) 1/1000; (c) 1/2; (d) 1/40; or (e) 1/2020? Contrary to most people's intuitive sense of the probabilities, the answer is c—1 chance in 2, or 50−50.[32]

Here's another one: You toss an unbiased coin five times in a row. The chances of it landing heads on the first toss is, of course, 1 in 2. Let's say it does land heads on the first toss—and, amazingly enough, on each of the other four tosses. That's five heads in a row. What are the chances of it landing heads on the sixth toss? The answer is 50–50, the same as on the first toss. The probability of heads (or tails) on any toss is always 50–50. What happened in previous tosses has no effect on the next toss; coins have no memory. The idea that previous events can affect the probabilities in a current random event is called the *gambler's fallacy*. And most people act as though this idea were valid.

One problem is that most of us don't realize that because of ordinary statistical laws, *incredible coincidences are common and must occur.* An event that seems highly improbable can actually be highly probable—even virtually certain—given enough opportunities for it to occur. Drawing a royal flush in poker, getting heads five times in a row, winning the lottery—all these may seem incredibly unlikely in any instance. But they're virtually certain to happen sometime to *someone.* With enough chances for something to happen, it will happen.

Consider prophetic dreams, mentioned earlier. If a normal person has about 250 dreams per night and over 250 million people live in the United States, there must be billions of dreams dreamed every night and trillions in a year. With so many dreams and so many life events that can be matched up to the dreams, it would be astounding if some dreams didn't seem prophetic. The really astonishing thing may not be that there are prophetic dreams but that there are so few of them.

Suppose you're reading a novel. Just as you get to the part that mentions the peculiar beauty of the monarch butterfly, you look up and see one on your window. Suppose you're sitting in an airport, musing over the last name of an old classmate. Just then the person sitting next to you says that very name aloud in a conversation with someone else. These are indeed uncanny pairings of events, strange couplings that provoke wonder—or the idea that psychic forces are at work. But just how likely are such pairings? The answer is *very.* A demonstration of this fact by psychologists David Marks and Richard Kammann goes something like this: Let's say that in an ordinary day a person can recall 100 distinct events. The total number of pairings of these events for a single person in a single day is thus 4,950 (99 + 98 + 97 . . . + 3 + 2 + 1).[33] Over a period of 10 years (or about 3,650 days), 1,000 people are thus expected to generate over 18 billion pairs (4,950 × 3,650 × 1,000 = 18,067,500,000). Out of so many pairs of events, it's *likely* that some of those 1,000 people will experience some weird, incredible pairings.[34] Thus, the seemingly impossible becomes commonplace.

It is likely that unlikely things should happen.
—ARISTOTLE

What Are the Odds? You Wouldn't Believe It

When we try to judge the probabilities involved in events, we're often wrong. Sometimes we're *really* wrong because the true probabilities are completely counter to our intuitive "feel" for the odds. Mathematician John Allen Paulos offers this surprising example of a counterintuitive probability:

> First, take a deep breath. Assume Shakespeare's account is accurate and Julius Caesar gasped "You too, Brutus" before breathing his last. What are the chances you just inhaled a molecule which Caesar exhaled in his dying breath? The surprising answer is that, with probability better than 99 percent, you did just inhale such a molecule.
>
> For those who don't believe me: I'm assuming that after more than two thousand years the exhaled molecules are uniformly spread about the world and the vast majority are still free in the atmosphere. Given these reasonably valid assumptions, the problem of determining the relevant probability is straightforward. If there are N molecules of air in the world and Caesar exhaled A of them, then the probability that any given molecule you inhale is from Caesar is A/N. The probability that any given molecule you inhale is not from Caesar is thus $1-A/N$. By the multiplication principle, if you inhale three molecules, the probability that none of these three is from Caesar is $[1-A/N]^3$. Similarly, if you inhale B molecules, the probability that none of them is from Caesar is approximately $[1-A/N]^B$. Hence, the probability of the complementary event, of your inhaling at least one of his exhaled molecules, is $1-[1-A/N]^B$. A, B (each about 1/30th of a liter, or 2.2×10^{22}), and N(about 10^{44} molecules) are such that this probability is more than .99. It's intriguing that we're all, at least in this minimal sense, eventually part of one another.[35]

How easy it would be to gather some eerie pairings into a book and offer them as proof that something psychic or cosmic had transpired.

How likely is it that someone will recall a person he knew (or knew of) in the last thirty years and, within exactly five minutes, learn of that person's death? More likely than you might think. In fact, it's possible to calculate the approximate probability of this strange occurrence. One such calculation assumes that a person would recognize the names of 3,000 people from the past thirty years and that the person would learn of the death of each of those 3,000 people in the thirty years. With these assumptions and some statistical math, it can be determined that the chances of the strange occurrence happening are 0.00003. This is, as you would expect, a low probability. But in a population of 100,000 people, even this low probability means that about ten of these experiences should occur every day.[36]

The mathematical probabilities of rare events, in particular, often run counter to intuition, but it is the mathematics, not our intuition, that is correct.

—BARRY SINGER

Rationalizing *Homo Sapiens*

People not only jump to conclusions, they frequently rationalize or defend whatever conclusion they jump to. Psychologist Barry Singer summarizes research findings that show just how good our rationalizing skills are:

Numerous psychological experiments on problem solving and concept formation have shown that when people are given the task of selecting the right answer by being told whether particular guesses are right or wrong, they will tend to do the following:

1. They will immediately form a hypothesis and look only for examples to confirm it. They will not seek evidence to disprove their hypothesis, although this strategy would be just as effective, but will in fact try to ignore any evidence against it.

2. If the answer is secretly changed in the middle of the guessing process, they will be very slow to change the hypothesis that was once correct but has suddenly become wrong.

3. If one hypothesis fits the data fairly well, they will stick with it and not look for other hypotheses that might fit the data better.

4. If the information provided is too complex, people will cope by adopting overly simple hypotheses or strategies for solution, and by ignoring any evidence against them.

5. If there is no solution, if the problem is a trick and people are told "right" and "wrong" about their choices at random, people will nevertheless form all sorts of hypotheses about causal relationships they believe are inherent in the data, will believe their hypotheses through thick and thin, and will eventually convince themselves that their theories are absolutely correct. Causality will invariably be perceived even when it is not present.

It is not surprising that rats, pigeons, and small children are often better at solving these sorts of problems than are human adults. Pigeons and small children don't care so much whether they are always right, and they do not have such a developed capacity for convincing themselves they are right, no matter what the evidence is.[37]

Now none of this shows that truly prophetic dreams or psychic connections among events can't happen. But it does demonstrate that our personal experience of improbabilities doesn't prove that they're miraculous or paranormal. Our personal experience alone simply can't reveal to us the true probability of a single impressive event. This is so despite the strong feelings that an odd conjunction of events may cause in us. When events that people view as too much of a coincidence happen, we may be awestruck, mystified, or frightened. We may get a sense of strangeness that invites us to believe that something unusual is happening. But these feelings aren't evidence that something significant is occurring, any more than the feeling of dizziness means that the world is swaying from side to side.

Selective Attention

Confounding our troubles with probabilities is something else that we're often unaware of: selective attention. We notice certain things and ignore others. It's as if we have a kind of radar that locks on specific events to the exclusion of everything else. After we buy a new car, we seem to see more of that same model on the road. We see that every time we plan a picnic, it rains. We think that every time we wear a certain pair of socks, we encounter the same person. As we've seen, incredible runs of odd events do happen, but often their real cause is that our radar is working overtime.

People often support their beliefs through selective attention or by otherwise misconstruing the pertinent evidence. They ignore facts that contradict their beliefs and look for those that confirm them — or mentally tinker with facts so they no longer contradict. This process is sometimes called *subjective validation*. Science has documented it, and the whole human race practices it regularly. It shows up when our most beloved beliefs are at stake — including those involving the paranormal. For example, in one study, researchers showed subjects either a "successful" demonstration of ESP or an "unsuccessful" one. Some subjects already believed in ESP, and some were skeptics. Afterwards the researchers checked the subjects' recall of the demonstrations. The results showed that the skeptics accurately recalled both demonstrations. Believers who saw the successful demonstration remembered it correctly, but those who watched the unsuccessful demonstration actually recalled it as successful![38]

The Lunar Effect   There's a popular theory that the moon has a powerful impact on human behavior. It's called the lunar effect. Crimes, hospital admissions, and assorted craziness are supposed to be on the upswing during a full moon. A multitude of studies, however, haven't detected any moon influence at all on human behavior, but an experiment did suggest something interesting about subjective validation. Nurses were asked to report on any unusual behavior they observed in patients during a full moon. Sure enough, the nurses who believed in the lunar effect noted more unusual behavior than the nurses who didn't believe.[39]

The Forer Effect   The following is a personality profile, one that could very well describe *you*. Read it carefully:

> Some of your aspirations tend to be pretty unrealistic. At times you are extroverted, affable, sociable, while at other times you are introverted, wary and reserved. You have found it unwise to be too frank in revealing

Spooky Presidential Coincidences

In the spirit of fun and skeptical inquiry, some clever fellows have derived the ultimate answer to those lists of weird coincidences in the lives of American Presidents:

This offering is an idea that springs from a bull session among us computer programmers at the University of Texas Data Processing Department. Ann Landers had just reprinted, for the zillionth time, a list of chilling parallels between the assassinations of Abraham Lincoln and John F. Kennedy. In the same spirit of skepticism that led Crash Davis, in the film Bull Durham, to wonder why every believer in reincarnation was always someone famous in a past life, we wondered aloud why no one ever talks about the chilling similarities between William McKinley and James Garfield. Sure enough, those of us who know American history were able to find a dozen similarities between McKinley and Garfield.

Well, the joke took on a life of its own. Before long, we thought of common themes in the lives of Zachary Taylor and William Henry Harrison. In fact, Thomas Jefferson and Richard Nixon seemed to have as much in common as Lincoln had with Kennedy. . . .

Coincidence? You Decide . . .

1. William McKinley and James Garfield were both Republicans.
2. McKinley and Garfield were both born and raised in Ohio.
3. McKinley and Garfield were both Civil War veterans.
4. McKinley and Garfield both served in the House of Representatives.
5. McKinley and Garfield both supported the gold standard and tariffs for protection of American industry.
6. "McKinley" and "Garfield" both have eight letters.
7. McKinley and Garfield were both replaced by vice-presidents from New York City (Theodore Roosevelt and Chester Alan Arthur).
8. Both of their vice-presidents wore mustaches.
9. McKinley and Garfield were both shot in September, in the first year of their current terms.
10. "Chester Alan Arthur" and "Theodore Roosevelt" have seventeen letters each.
11. Both of their assassins, Charles Guiteau and Leon Czolgosz, had foreign-sounding names.
12. Garfield had a cat named McKinley; McKinley had a cat named Garfield. (Okay, okay, so I made this one up.)

. . . You get the idea. Finding Spooky Parallels is easy. So why should I have all the fun? I figure that with minimal effort, anyone should be able to think of five or six eerie similarities between any two presidents.[40]

yourself to others. You pride yourself on being an independent thinker and do not accept others' opinions without satisfactory proof. You prefer a certain amount of change and variety, and become dissatisfied when hemmed in by restrictions and limitations. At times you have serious doubts as to whether you have made the right decision or done the right thing. Disciplined and controlled on the outside, you tend to be worrisome and insecure on the inside.

Your sexual adjustment has presented some problems for you. While you have some personality weaknesses, you are generally able to compensate for them. You have a great deal of unused capacity which you have not turned to your advantage. You have a tendency to be critical of yourself. You have a strong need for other people to like you and for them to admire you.[41]

Now answer this honestly: How well does this profile match your personality? Most people, if told that the profile is created specifically for them, think that it describes them fairly well — maybe even perfectly. Even though the profile could apply to almost anyone, *people believe that it describes them specifically and accurately.* This phenomenon of believing that a general personality description is unique to oneself, which has been thoroughly confirmed by research, is known as the *Forer effect* (named after the man who first studied it). For the Forer effect to work, people have to be told that the catchall description really pinpoints them specifically. If people suspect what's really going on, they're less likely to fall for the phenomenon.

But why *do* we fall for it? Marks and Kammann explain it this way:

> From our point of view, Forer's result is a special case of subjective validation in which we find ways to match ourselves up with the description given. Our personalities are not fixed and constant as we usually imagine. Everybody is shy in one situation, bold in another, clever at one task, bumbling at another, generous one day, selfish the next, independent in one group of people but conforming in another group. Thus, we can usually find aspects of ourselves that will match up with a vague statement, although the specific examples of self will be different from one person to the next.[42]

Astrology, biorhythms, graphology (determining personality characteristics from handwriting), fortunetelling, palmistry (palm reading), tarot card reading, psychic readings — all these generally involve the Forer effect. So if the Forer effect is likely to be at work in any of these systems in any instance, we can't conclude that the system has any special power to see into our character. Our sincere feeling that the readings are true does not — and cannot — validate the system.

Vague Prophecies Probably no prophet has a bigger reputation than Michel Nostradamus (1503–1566), who composed a thousand verses that some people believe foretell many historical events. He's been credited with predicting both World Wars, the atomic bomb, the rise

The Will to Believe—in Fairies?

The following case, detailed by psychologist Terence Hines, wins first place in the category of Most Intriguing True Tale of Weird Stuff. We'll let you decide for yourself what the moral of the story is. Hines has some ideas of his own:

The story starts in Cottingley, England, in 1917. Two girls—Elsie Wright, thirteen, and a cousin, Frances Griffiths, ten—claimed to have taken two photographs of fairies who played with them. Three more photos were apparently taken in the summer of 1920. It was [Sir Arthur Conan Doyle, the creator of the fictional detective Sherlock Holmes] who brought the photos to the public's awareness, and he later wrote a book arguing for the real existence of fairies, based largely on these photos. The photographs . . . have always looked fake. But neither this nor the inherent absurdity of the claim has stopped many people, in addition to Doyle, from taking the existence of fairies seriously. . . . UFOlogists have been interested in fairy sightings, believing they may be related to the UFO phenomenon and extraterrestrials.

Various reports of fairies, leprechauns, and the like are all brought together to argue that maybe there really is some substance to the reports. And, again, the skeptic is challenged to explain away each and every report. Just as in the case of [purported evidence for Santa Claus], however, it's impossible to explain every case. For example, we can never expect each child who has reported seeing fairies to admit lying. But the Cottingley photos can be explained. They were—and this should come as no great surprise to the reader—a hoax. The "fairies" were cutouts from a children's book of the time, and many years later Frances and Elsie admitted the hoax. Finally, [investigator R. Sheaffer] has subjected the photographs to computer enhancement and found evidence of a string that was used to hang the cutouts from shrubs while the photos were taken. So, what began as a hoax and concerned a clearly absurd hypothesis—that fairies really exist—turned into pseudoscientific belief that required sixty years and much effort to put to rest.[43]

and fall of Hitler, and more. Now, clearly, if a prophet consistently offers unequivocal, precise predictions of events that can't reasonably be expected, we must take serious notice of that seer. How about Nostradamus?

In fact, his predictions are neither unequivocal nor precise, and this fact has allowed subjective validation to convince some that his prophecies have come true. Nostradamus himself said that he deliberately made his verses puzzling and cloudy. As a result, they are open to multiple interpretations. For example:

Quatrain 22

That which shall live shall leave no direction,
Its destruction and death will come by stratagem,

This is one of the notorious Cottingley photos, which Sir Arthur Conan Doyle took to be good evidence for the existence of fairies. The pictures were later shown to be part of a hoax; the "fairies" were cutouts from a children's book.

Autun, Chalons, Langres, and from both sides,
The war and ice shall do great harm.[44]

Quatrain 27

Underneath the cord, Guien struck from the sky,
Near where is hid a great treasure,
Which has been many years a gathering,
Being found, he shall die, the eye put out by a spring.[45]

What do you think these verses from Nostradamus mean? Andrew Neher asks that people compare their own interpretations of the verses with those of Henry Roberts, one of several authors of books on Nostradamus's prophecies. According to Roberts, Quatrain 22 is "a forecast of the use of supersonic weapons, traveling in the near absolute zero temperature above the stratosphere." And Roberts says that Quatrain 27 means "paratroopers alight near the Nazi's plunder hoard and, captured, they are executed."[46] Did you come to a different conclusion? Do you see how easy it is to come up with alternative interpretations that seem to fit?

Neher also suggests a telling comparison between the interpretations offered by two Nostradamus experts commenting on the same verses. One is Roberts; the other is Erika Cheetham, also a Nostradamus author:

> ### Quatrain 9
>
> Roberts: "A remarkably prophetic description of the role of Emperor Haile Selassie, in World War II."[47]
>
> Cheetham: "Lines 1–2 . . . refer . . . to Henry IV. The man who troubles him from the East is the Duke of Parma. . . . Lines 3–4 most probably refer to the siege of Malta in 1565."[48]
>
> ### Quatrain 26
>
> Roberts: "The taking over of Czechoslovakia by Hitler, the resignation of President Benes, the dissensions over the matter between France and England and the dire warning of the consequences of this betrayal, are all remarkably outlined in this prophecy."[49]
>
> Cheetham: "The first three lines here may apply to the assassinations of the two Kennedy brothers."[50]

As Neher points out, "In comparing the conflicting interpretations of the quatrains, it is apparent that Roberts and Cheetham are projecting into them meanings that exist in their own minds, which leads them to think that Nostradamus had great precognitive ability."[51]

This is subjective validation at work. And once an interpretation is overlaid on a vague prophecy, it may be difficult to see any other possibility.

THE LIMITS OF PERSONAL EXPERIENCE

Now you know some of the mind's peculiarities that affect our personal experience. Now we can say more clearly how much our personal experience can tell us about what's real and what isn't.

It's in part because of all the limitations of our personal experience — perceptual construction, memory construction, the effects of stress, the impact of expectancy and belief, selective attention, misjudgments of probabilities, subjective validation, altered states of consciousness, and much more — that we must add this corollary to our earlier principle:

> It's reasonable to accept personal
> experience as reliable evidence
> only if there's no reason to doubt
> its reliability.

Reasons for doubting include any of the limitations just mentioned. Other reasons include poor observational conditions (like limited visibility, bad lighting, faint stimuli, unusual circumstances, and so on), anything that renders the observer physically impaired (like alcohol, drugs, fatigue, bad eyesight, poor hearing, and so on), and conflicts with other propositions we have good reason to believe.

When there's reason to think that any of these limitations or conditions may be present, our personal experience can't prove that something is the case. In fact, when we're in situations where our subjective limitations could be operating, the experiences that are affected by those limitations not only can't give us proof that something is real or true, they can't even provide us with low-grade evidence. The reason is that at those moments, we can't tell where our experience begins and our limitations end. Is that an alien spacecraft in the night sky or Venus, embellished for us by our own high level of expectancy? Is that strange conjunction of events a case of cosmic synchronicity or just our inability to appreciate the true probabilities? If subjective limitations might be distorting our experience, our personal evidence is tainted and can't tell us much at all. An honest assessment of the situation would be "I don't know."

Our beliefs may predispose us to misinterpret the facts, when ideally the facts should serve as the evidence upon which we base beliefs.
—ALAN M. MACROBERT AND TED SCHULTZ

Science is a systematic attempt to get around such limitations. Thus, scientific work is largely the business of not taking any one person's word for it. Most scientists know that the limitations of our own unaided experience work overtime, and prestige and authority and good intentions are no protection. So science tries to remove the element of unsystematic personal experience from the scientific process. It attempts to use objective measurements, not subjective judgments, wherever possible. It insists on the corroboration of findings by other scientists. It demands public evidence open to public scrutiny, not private data subject to personal confirmation. Its facts must rest not on the say-so of some authority, but on objective evidence. When scientists err (as did Professor Blondlot), it's often because the limitations of the subjective creep in. When science progresses, it's in large measure because these limitations are overcome.

By now you probably have guessed why Everard Feilding's personal experience in Palladino's seances wasn't a good enough reason for him to conclude that he had witnessed genuine paranormal phenomena. As an eyewitness, in a darkened room, in unusual circumstances, feeling the stress of the situation, he was open to possible distortions of perception and judgment. The testimony of any eyewitness—or several eyewitnesses—in similar circumstances would be suspect. (Chapter 5 discusses an even more important

The Tamara Rand Hoax

In Chapter 1 we mentioned the purported prediction of the assassination attempt on Ronald Reagan. Now here's the rest of the story, told by Kendrick Frazier and James Randi:

On the morning of April 2, 1981, you will remember — four days after the assassination attempt on President Reagan in Washington — the NBC-TV "Today" show and ABC-TV's "Good Morning America" joined the Cable News Network in broadcasting a tape that was claimed to have been made on January 6, 1981, by Tamara Rand, a noted Los Angeles "psychic" who makes a handsome living by advising movie stars whether or not to sign contracts. On that videotape, viewers saw and heard Rand predict that Reagan would be shot in the chest area by a sandy-haired young man from a wealthy family. The assailant, said Rand, would have the initials, "J.H.," first name possibly Jack, last name something like "Humley." She foresaw a "hail of bullets"

as well. All this was to take place during the last week of March or the first week of April.

It was an impressive apparent prediction, the kind of thing that can turn a local "psychic" into a world-class celebrity, with the fame and fees that go with that exalted status. Yet to veteran psychic watchers the prediction was too precise. . . .

The wire services had already helped broadcast Rand's miracle prediction worldwide, but Paul Simon, an Associated Press reporter in Los Angeles, contacted CSICOP [Committee for the Scientific Investigation of Claims of the Paranormal] chairman Paul Kurtz in Buffalo. Simon was skeptical about Rand's claims. Kurtz asked whether it was certain the videotape had been prepared before the assassination attempt as claimed and urged that Simon check the time sequence. Simon called Kurtz back several times that day to report on his investigation. He said he had contacted station

reason not to jump to conclusions when confronted with extraordinary experiences like Feilding's.)

In Palladino's case, there are additional grounds for doubting that she had extraordinary powers. She cheated. Like countless other mediums of her day, she used trickery to deceive her sitters. Some say she used trickery only occasionally; others say all the time. In any case, she was caught red-handed several times. In one instance, she was caught using her foot to skillfully reach behind her into the spirit cabinet from which objects often appeared.

So if we have an unforgettable personal experience of the extraordinary, we can enjoy it, learn from it, be inspired by it, use it as a starting point for further investigation. But unless we rule out the prevalent and persistent reasons for doubt, we can't use the experience as a foundation for some towering truth.

personnel at WTBS in Atlanta, Georgia, which Rand claimed had broadcast the tape Saturday night, March 28, two days before the predicted event. They denied that such a tape had been aired. He then called KTNV in Las Vegas, where the tape was said to have been prepared, and technicians there told him that they had taped it on Tuesday night, March 31, more than 24 hours after the shooting of Reagan.

Simon said that Arthur Lord, bureau chief in Los Angeles for NBC, admitted that he had accepted the word of the producer of the TV tape and of Tamara Rand and that he had been bamboozled. Unfortunately, at the same time, NBC-TV officials in Los Angeles were telling the press that they "stood by every word" of the broadcast. That evening Kurtz sent telegrams on behalf of CSICOP to the "Today" show (NBC) and to "Good Morning America" (ABC) requesting that they retract the "pre-diction" story since all the evidence pointed toward a hoax.

Fortunately, most of the network programs did eventually acknowledge that the affair had been a hoax and they had fallen for it.

The coup de grace arrived when Dick Maurice, host of the faked TV show, who had maintained the prediction was genuine, finally admitted that it was an outright hoax. In a front-page column in the Los Angeles Sun on April 5, Maurice proclaimed:

"I am sorry.

"I have committed a terrible wrong. I have committed the cardinal sin of a columnist. I have perpetrated a hoax on the public and feel very much ashamed.

"My interview with Tamara Rand in which she predicted the assassination attempt on President Ronald Reagan is a lie. Ed Quinn's (vice president and general manager of KTNV-TV) statement about the actual taping taking place on March 31 is the truth."[52]

SUGGESTED READINGS

Gilovich, Thomas. *How We Know What Isn't So*. New York: Free Press, 1991.

Hines, Terrence. *Pseudoscience and the Paranormal*. Buffalo: Prometheus Books, 1988.

Neher, Andrew. *The Psychology of Transcendence*. New York: Dover, 1990.

Reed, Graham. *The Psychology of Anomalous Experience*. Buffalo: Prometheus Books, 1988.

Zusne, Leonard, and Warren H. Jones. *Anomalistic Psychology*. Hillsdale, N.J.: Lawrence Erlbaum Associates, 1982.

NOTES

1. E. Feilding, W. W. Baggally, and H. Carrington, *Proceedings of the SPR*, 23 (1909): 461–62, reprinted in E. Feilding, *Sittings with Eusapia Palladino and Other Studies* (New Hyde Park, NY: University Books, 1963).

2. James Alcock, *Parapsychology: Science or Magic?* (Oxford: Pergamon Press, 1981), pp. 35–37, 64.

3. Gustav Jahoda, *The Psychology of Superstition* (Baltimore: Penguin,1969), pp. 50–51.

4. The following discussion is drawn from Terence Hines, *Pseudoscience and the Paranormal* (Buffalo: Prometheus Books, 1988), pp. 168–70.

5. K. Duncker,"The Influence of Past Experience upon Perceptual Properties,"*American Journal of Psychology,* 52 (1939): 255–65.

6. Hines, *Pseudoscience and the Paranormal,* pp. 169–70.

7. C. M. Turnbull, "Some Observations Regarding the Experiences and Behavior of the Ba Mbuti Pygmies," *American Journal of Psychology,* 74 (1961): 304–8.

8. Leonard Zusne and Warren H. Jones, *Anomalistic Psychology* (Hillsdale, N.J.: Lawrence Erlbaum Associates, 1982), p. 135.

9. Andrew Neher, *The Psychology of Transcendence* (Englewood Cliffs, N.J.: Prentice-Hall, 1980), p. 64.

10. Conway W. Snyder, correspondence reproduced in *Skeptical Inquirer,* Summer 1988, pp. 340–43.

11. Martin Gardner, *The New Age: Notes of a Fringe Watcher* (Buffalo: Prometheus Books, 1988), p. 76.

12. From Committee on Techniques for the Enhancement of Human Performance, Commission on Behavioral and Social Sciences and Education, National Research Council, *Enhancing Human Performance: Issues, Theories, and Techniques* (Washington, D.C.: National Academy Press, 1988), pp. 204–5.

13. Carl Sagan and P. Fox, "The Canals of Mars: An Assessment after Mariner 9," *Icarus,* 25, 602–12.

14. The following account draws on I. Klotz, "The N-Ray Affair," *Scientific American,* 242, no. 5, 168–75.

15. Neher, *Psychology of Transcendence,* pp. 182–83.

16. Philip J. Klass, *UFO's Explained* (New York: Random House, 1974), pp. 9–14.

17. Philip J. Klass, "UFOs," in *Science and the Paranormal* (New York: Scribner's, 1981), pp. 313–15.

18. Hines, *Pseudoscience and the Paranormal,* p. 175.

19. Klass, "UFOs," pp. 316–17.

20. Ibid., pp. 315–16.

21. Graham Reed, *The Psychology of Anomalous Experience* (Buffalo: Prometheus Books, 1988), pp. 37–40.

22. Zusne and Jones, *Anomalistic Psychology,* p. 336.

23. Philip Klass, *UFO's Explained,* p. 77.

24. G. W. Allport and L. J. Postman, "The Basic Psychology of Rumor," *Transactions of the New York Academy of Science,* 2d ser., 8 (1945): 61–81.

25. B. Fischhoff and R. Beyth, "'I Knew It Would Happen': Remembered Probabilities of Once-Future Things," *Organizational Behavior and Human Performance,* 120 (1972): 159–72.

26. E. F. Loftus and J. C. Palmer, "Reconstruction of Automobile Destruction: An Example of the Interaction Between Language and Memory," *Journal of Verbal Learning and Verbal Behavior,* 13, no. 5 (1974): 585–89.

27. Ted Schultz, "Voices from Beyond: The Age-Old Mystery of Channeling," in *The Fringes of Reason: A Whole Earth Catalog,* ed. Ted Schultz (New York: Harmony Books, 1989), pp. 60, 62.

28. E. Loftus, D. Miller, and H. Burns, "Semantic Integration of Verbal Information into a Visual Memory," *Journal of Experimental Psychology: Human Learning and Memory,* 4 (1978): 19–31.

29. Alcock, *Parapsychology,* p. 76.

30. Hines, *Pseudoscience and the Paranormal,* p. 52.

31. Ibid., p. 51.

32. John Allen Paulos, *Innumeracy* (New York: Hill and Wang, 1988), p. 27.

33. You can understand better why this formula works by considering a smaller number of events, say five (A, B, C, D, E). Event A can be paired with C, D, and E producing four possible pairs. Event B can be paired with C, D, and E (not A to avoid repeating a pair), producing three pairs. Event C can be paired with D and E (not A and B to avoid repeats), and so on. So the total possible pairs (without duplicates) of five events is given by the formula 4 + 3 + 2 + 1, or 10.

34. David Marks and Richard Kammann, *The Psychology of the Psychic* (Buffalo: Prometheus Books, 1980), p. 166.

35. Paulos, *Innumeracy,* p. 24.

36. L. W. Alvarez, letter to the editors, *Science,* June 18, 1965, p. 1541.

37. Barry Singer, "To Believe or Not to Believe," in *Science and the Paranormal* (New York: Scribner's 1981), p. 18.

38. W. H. Jones, D. Russell, and T. W. Nickel, "Personality and Behavioral Correlates of Superstitious Beliefs" (Paper delivered at the Midwestern Psychological Association conference, Chicago, 1976).

39. M. Angus, "The Rejection of Two Explanations of Belief" (unpublished master's thesis, Simon Frazer University, British Columbia, 1973).

40. John Leavy, "Our Spooky Presidential Coincidences Contest," *Skeptical Inquirer,* Spring 1992, pp. 316–20.

41. C. Snyder and R. Shenkel, "The P. T. Barnum Effect," *Psychology Today,* March 1975, pp. 52–54.

42. Marks and Kammann, *Psychology of the Psychic,* p. 189.

43. Hines, *Pseudoscience and the Paranormal*, pp. 4–5.

44. Henry Roberts, *The Complete Prophecies of Nostradamus* (Great Neck, NY: Nostradamus, 1969), p. 16., as cited in Neher, *Psychology of Transcendence*, p. 188.

45. Roberts, p. 18, as cited in Ibid.

46. Roberts, pp. 16, 18, as cited in Ibid.

47. Roberts, p. 12, as cited in Ibid.

48. Erika Cheetham, *The Prophecies of Nostradamus* (New York: Putnam's/ Capricorn Books, 1974), p. 25, as cited in Ibid.

49. Roberts, *Complete Prophecies*, p.17, as cited in Ibid.

50. Cheetham, *Prophecies*, p. 33, as cited in Ibid.

51. Neher, *Psychology of Transcendence.*, p. 159.

52. Kendrick Frazier and James Randi, "Predictions After the Fact: Lessons of the Tamara Rand Hoax," *Skeptical Inquirer*, Fall 1981, pp. 4–7.

FOUR
Relativism, Truth, and Reality

W E GIVE YOU A parable:

Seven men came upon a duck—or what seemed a duck.

"It quacks like a duck. It waddles like a duck. It's a duck," said

the first man.

"To you it's a duck, but to me it's not a duck, for my belief is

true for me, and your belief is true for you," said the second man.

"In your society it may be a duck, but in mine it's not; truth is

relative to societies," said the third man.

"Your conceptual scheme may classify it as a duck, but mine

doesn't; truth is relative to conceptual schemes," said the fourth man.

"It's a duck if I believe it's a duck, for we each create our own

reality," said the fifth man.

"If enough of us believe that it's not a duck but a raccoon, it will

become a raccoon," said the sixth man.

There is nothing so powerful as truth, and often nothing so strange.
—DANIEL WEBSTER

"It doesn't matter whether it's an actual duck or not; the idea of 'duck' is a metaphor with a deeper, larger truth," said the seventh man.

This is a strange discussion if there ever was one. But like many parables, this one cuts deep. It may be surreal or amusing, but it's really about the nature of truth. The first four men imply or express notions about *what truth is*. Their notions aren't about what is true (what the specific truths are), but *what it means for statements or beliefs to be true*.

These views are far from being merely academic. Each one is taken seriously or assumed without question by many people today. Every one of us, if we make any judgments at all, adopts a notion about the nature of truth—and that notion is probably one of these four or a variation thereof. And what you assume about the idea of truth influences every decision you make.

While the statements of the last three men are not about the nature of truth, they reflect ideas that often come up when the concept of truth is at issue. These too have been influential. If you really believe them, they must radically affect the way you view the world.

The concept of truth implied by the first man's statement is the one assumed by most people without question. It says that truth is objective—that there's a way things *are* independently of what we think about them and that statements are true if they say how things are. Discovering what's true may be difficult (maybe even impossible), and people attempting to discover what's true are sometimes wrong. But, most people would say, there can be no doubt that truth depends on what is objectively the case. The second, third, and fourth men in our parable deny this, and many people agree with them. They assume that there is no way the world is independent of what we think about it. For them, objective truth is a worn-out myth. In a sense, because the idea of objective truth is so fundamental, its rejection is the weirdest of all weird claims.

So what is the truth about truth? In the following pages we'll provide an answer to this question—a question that some people believe is either not worth asking or impossible to answer. Let's proceed by looking closer at the notions about truth in our parable.

"TRUTH IS RELATIVE TO INDIVIDUALS"

This is the claim of our second man, who says that truth depends on what each person believes it to be. If you believe that a proposition is true, then it is true. In this view, truth is subjective, not objective. Those who accept the subjectivist view must admit that statements like the following are *not* objectively true (or false):

The earth moves around the sun.

2 + 2 = 4.

Bachelors have no wives.

Dogs aren't cats.

World War II actually happened.

The view that truth is subjective runs deep in the New Age movement, where disagreements have been stopped dead in their tracks by statements like "Well, this is *my* truth, and that's *your* truth." People with New Age beliefs, some critics say, often make such pronouncements when they're losing an argument or when they're faced with evidence that contradicts their claims. There's nothing new, though, about the subjectivist notion of truth. The ancient philosopher Protagoras (c. 490–c. 421 B.C.) is thought to have put forth the first classic statement of the view, declaring that "man is the measure of all things."

Despite its appeal to many, however, the proposition that truth is subjective has many bizarre consequences. For one thing, if we could make a statement true by simply believing it to be true, we would be infallible. We could never hold an erroneous belief because any belief we held, simply because we held it, would be true. Furthermore, if everyone made their own truth, disagreement would be pointless. Disagreements arise when there is reason to believe that another is mistaken. If subjectivism were true, however, there would be no reason to believe that anyone is mistaken. It would be useless to try to convince anyone that they're wrong, for they couldn't be.

That a subjective view of truth renders disagreement futile often goes unnoticed. As biologist Ted Schultz observes:

> Paradoxically, many New Agers, having demonstrated to their satisfaction that objective truth is the unattainable bugaboo of thick-headed rationalists, often become extremely dogmatic about the minutiae of their own favorite belief systems. After all, if what is "true for you" isn't necessarily "true for me," should I really worry about the exact dates and locations of the upcoming geological upheavals predicted by Ramtha or the coming of the "space brothers" in 2012 predicted by José Arguellas?[1]

You shouldn't, for if subjectivism were true, you couldn't help but be right. But then again, neither could your rivals.

There's the rub. If everyone is always right, then even those who reject subjectivism would be right. The belief that subjectivism is false would be just as true as the belief it is true. The Greek philosopher Plato (c. 427–347 B.C.) was perhaps the first to recognize this

Whoever tells the truth is chased out of nine villages.
— TURKISH PROVERB

You may not be coming from where I'm coming from, but I know that relativism isn't true for me.
— ALAN GARFINKEL

strange consequence of subjectivism. "Protagoras," he tells us, "for his part, admitting as he does that everybody's opinion is true, must acknowledge the truth of his opponents' belief about his own belief, where they think he is wrong."[2] If subjectivism were true, the subjectivists couldn't claim that their theory is any more correct than that of the objectivists. The sense of intellectual superiority felt by Schultz's New Agers, then, is misplaced. They can't claim the intellectual high ground because, in their own view, there is no high ground; everybody's view is as good as everybody else's.

It would be nice if we were always right, but as we all know all too well, we aren't. Much as we must hate to admit it, we all make mistakes. Even the most fervently relativistic New Ager must confess that he or she dials a wrong number, bets on a losing football team, or forgets a friend's birthday. These admissions reveal that reality is not constituted by our beliefs. We all recognize the truth of this principle:

> Just because you believe that something is true doesn't mean that it is.

We can't make something true simply by believing it to be true. If we could, the world would contain a lot fewer unfulfilled desires, unrealized ambitions, and unsuccessful projects than it does.

"TRUTH IS RELATIVE TO SOCIETIES"

Most men live like raisins in a cake of custom.

— Brand Blanshard

To avoid the absurd consequences of subjectivism, some people, like our third man, adopt the view that truth is relative to societies. This theory, known as social relativism, holds that society — not the individual — determines what is true. If your society believes that a proposition is true, then it is. Something can be true for the French, but false for the Chinese; true for the ancient Greeks, but false for us. Since individuals can be mistaken about what their society believes, individuals are not infallible. But society is. As philosopher Roger Trigg points out, in social relativism:

> [the] possibility of false beliefs is ruled out, so that a whole community could not be judged mistaken. What its members believe is true for them, just as what we believe is true for us. Facts are then dependent on the way people think, and no room is left for the idea that things can be the case whether anyone thinks they are or not. In other words, the possibility of something being objectively the case is ruled out. Truth must always be considered *relative* to a society, whether it consists of

the believers in a particular religion, the holders of a certain scientific theory, the members of one tribe, or any other identifiable grouping.[3]

The social relativist, then, trades individual infallibility for social infallibility.

But is this a wise trade? Have we any more reason for believing that society is infallible than that individuals are? It wouldn't seem so. Society used to believe that the Earth was flat, that the sun orbited the Earth, and that storms were caused by angry gods. In each case, society was wrong. We must conclude, then, that:

> Just because a group of people believe that something is true doesn't mean that it is.

Groups are just as prone to error as individuals are — perhaps more so. We can't justify our beliefs by claiming that everyone shares them, for everyone may be mistaken. To attempt to do so is to commit the *fallacy of appeal to the masses*.

Moreover, if society is infallible, it would be impossible to disagree with society and be right. Since truth is whatever society says it is, any claim that society is wrong would have to be false. Thus social reformers could never justifiably claim that truth is on their side.

According to social relativism, then, our founding fathers were deluded in believing that there were truths that applied universally to all people regardless of what society they belonged to — truths like: everyone is created equal, everyone has the right to life, liberty, and the pursuit of happiness, and everyone has the right to alter or abolish any government that becomes destructive of these rights. If truth is relative to society, no such universal truths exist. Whatever society says goes. Here's tyranny of the majority with a vengeance.

The exact contrary of what is generally believed is often the truth.

— Jean de la Bruyere

But suppose (as may well be the case) that our society agrees with our founding fathers that not all truth is socially constructed. Does this mean that social relativism is false? According to the relativist doctrine, it does. You see, social relativism faces the same problem that subjectivism does: if every society's belief is as true as every other's, then a society's belief that the opposite is true is also true. Just as a subjectivist must recognize the truth of another individual's opposing view, so a social relativist must recognize the truth of another society's opposing view.

This means that no one can legitimately criticize another society. As long as a society is doing what it thinks is right, no one can defensibly claim that what they're doing is wrong. Suppose, for example, that during World War II the German people agreed with the Nazis that the Jews should be exterminated. If so, then, according to social relativism, the Holocaust was justified. Since the Nazis were just doing what society said they should, they were doing the right thing. What they did might not have been right for us, but according to social relativism, it was right for them. Like Protagoras, we have to recognize that their point of view is just as valid as our own.

If you disagree — if you believe that what the Nazis did was wrong even if they had the support of the German people — then you can't be a social relativist, for you have admitted that society can be mistaken. Given the history of civilization, such a conclusion seems unavoidable. Society has been wrong about many things: that kings have a divine right to rule, that letting blood cures disease, or that women shouldn't have the right to vote, just to name a few. So the doctrine of social relativism has little to recommend it.

Since social relativism holds that what makes a proposition true is that society believes it to be true, it follows that whenever individuals disagree about the truth of a proposition, what they must really be disagreeing about is whether society believes it or not. But are all of our disputes really about what society believes? Suppose we disagree about whether the universe contains black holes. Can we really resolve this dispute by simply polling the members of our society? Of course not. Even disagreements about morality can't be settled by opinion surveys. Whether abortion is moral, for example, can't be determined by simply canvassing the populace. So truth must be more than just social consensus.

If it isn't — if consensus created truth — then there can be no truth without consensus. In other words, if no view claims a clear majority, no view is true. Usually, when there is no consensus, people try to create one by persuading others of the truth of their position. But if social relativism is true, to do so is to attempt the impossible because without consensus, no one can legitimately claim to have the truth. In other words, according to social relativism, there can be no rational persuasion in the absence of consensus. The only form of persuasion available in such circumstances is brute force. For the social relativists, then, might makes right — not a comforting thought for those of us in the minority.

Even if truth is manufactured by society, it wouldn't be any easier to find, for there is no single society to which each of us clearly belongs. Suppose, for example, that you were a black Jewish communist living in Bavaria in the 1960s. What would be your real society? The blacks? The Jews? The communists? Bavarians? Unfortunately, there is no way to answer this question because we all belong to a

Universal Human Rights

To embrace social relativism is to reject the notion of universal human rights. As you might expect, the most vocal proponents of social relativism are the most flagrant violators of human rights. Columnist Ellen Goodman had this to say about the U.N. conference on human rights held in 1993 in Vienna, Austria:

> The first conference on human rights in 25 years was called in the heady months after the fall of the Berlin Wall. A world that had been divided into East and West, locked into a Cold War and superpower politics, was turned inside out. There was real hope that the human rights impulse which had been released in Eastern Europe would catch on across the world. . . . But in recent years a backlash of sorts has emerged, especially from some Third World governments in Asia and Africa. Waving the banner of multiculturalism, they have come here to insist that their country cannot be judged by some universal standard but only by its own "particularities," its own cultural and economic context. They resist the notion that democratic or human rights strings should be tied to financial aid from the West or North.

There are serious questions that emerge out of any clash of countries or cultures, but many of the governments claiming special exemptions to universal rights are abusers of those rights: Burma, China, Yemen, Syria and others that a jaded U.N. spokesperson called "the usual suspects." In stark contrast, activists in these countries disagree with their own government's view of "cultural differences." They insist there is no culture that favors discrimination, torture, "disappearings."

In a strong speech on opening day in which he proposed an international tribunal, Secretary of State Warren Christopher put the issue bluntly: "We cannot let cultural relativism become the last refuge of repression."

At the heart of the human rights movement in this fractionalized world is the notion that these rights are the same everywhere for everyone. As [UN Secretary-General Boutros] Boutros-Ghali said, these values are the way "we affirm together that we are a single human community . . . [a] world community that accepts anything less is just flags flying in the wind."[4]

number of different societies, none of which can claim to be our *real* society. So not only is social relativism not a very reasonable theory, it's not a very useful one either.

"TRUTH IS RELATIVE TO CONCEPTUAL SCHEMES"

Common sense tells us that neither individuals nor societies are infallible. Both can believe things that are false, and something can be true even if no individual or society has ever believed it. To preserve these insights, some relativists, like our fourth man, have claimed that truth is relative not to individuals or societies but to conceptual schemes. A *conceptual scheme* is a set of concepts for classifying objects. These concepts provide categories into which the items of our experience can be placed. Just as the post office uses pigeonholes to sort mail into deliverable piles, so we use our conceptual schemes to sort things into meaningful groups. Different people may sort things differently, however. One person may believe that an item falls under one concept while someone else may believe that it falls under another. So even though two people share the same concepts, they may apply them differently.[5]

To account for individual and social fallibility, the conceptual relativist must maintain that simply believing something to fall under a certain concept isn't enough to make it so. There must be a fact of the matter as to how it should be classified, and that fact can't be determined solely by belief. What is it determined by then? According to the conceptual relativist, it is determined, at least in part, by the world. So the conceptual relativist must admit that the world plays a role in determining what's true.[6]

Although the world constrains the truth, conceptual relativists do not believe that the world uniquely determines the truth, for in their view there is no *one* way the world is. Rather, different conceptual schemes create different worlds.

For the conceptual relativist, the relationship between conceptual schemes and the world is analogous to that of a cookie cutter to dough. Just as dough takes on whatever shape is imparted to it by a cookie cutter, so the world takes on whatever properties are imparted to it by a conceptual scheme. The world has some properties that are not affected by the conceptual scheme, just as the dough has some properties that are not affected by the cookie cutter. This is what allows the conceptual relativist to account for mistaken classifications. Nevertheless, in an important sense, the world is a product of a conceptual scheme. As philosopher Nelson Goodman puts it, conceptual schemes are ways of making worlds.[7] So people with different conceptual schemes live in different worlds.

Conceptual relativists contend that it is possible for one and the same proposition to be true in one conceptual scheme and false in another. But is this really possible? No, because one and the same proposition can't be both true and false. To suppose otherwise is to violate the principle of non-contradiction discussed earlier. As philosopher W. Newton-Smith puts it, "propositions are individuated in terms of their truth conditions. It is just incoherent to suppose that the same proposition could be true in ϕ and false in ψ [where ϕ and ψ stand for different conceptual schemes]."[8] Propositions with different truth values can't be identical, any more than lines with different lengths can be identical. Since one and the same proposition can't be true in one conceptual scheme and false in another, conceptual relativism can't be correct.

Here's another way to look at it. According to the conceptual relativist, the world as we know it is constituted by our conceptual scheme, and our language refers to the world as we know it. But if the language of each conceptual scheme refers to a different world, then it's impossible for these languages to share any common meanings. As philosopher Chris Swoyer explains:

> Put simply, the problem is that to get a strong version of relativism we need some one thing that could be true in F and false in F' [where F and F' are different conceptual schemes, or frameworks]. And whatever its exact nature, it will surely involve meanings. We need not demand anything so strong as strict synonymy, but unless two sentences have roughly the same meaning, there will be no justification for speaking of something that is true in one framework and false in another. Yet if F and F' involve "different worlds," as a natural interpretation of the strong relativistic conception of truth requires, how can a sentence of F mean, even roughly, the same thing as one of F'? The problem is that the sentences of F and F' are *about* different things, and any move from F to F' seems simply to involve a change of subject.[9]

The situation, then, is this: Conceptual relativism makes sense only if two different conceptual schemes can share the same meanings. But if meaning is constituted by conceptual schemes, two different conceptual schemes *can't* share the same meanings. So conceptual relativism doesn't make sense.

If the world really was constituted by conceptual schemes, it would be difficult to account for the fact that people with different conceptual schemes can understand and communicate with one another because access to a shared world is a necessary condition of translation. Philosopher Roger Trigg explains:

> The result of granting that "the world" or "reality" cannot be conceived as independent of all conceptual schemes is that there is no reason to suppose that what the peoples of very different communities see as the world is similar in any way. Unfortunately, however, this supposition is absolutely necessary before any translation or comparison between languages of different societies can take place. Without it, the situation would be like one where the inhabitants of two planets which differed fundamentally in their nature met each other and tried to communicate. So few things (if any) would be matters of common experience that their respective languages would hardly ever run parallel.[10]

A harmful truth is better than a useful lie.
—THOMAS MANN

Since translation is possible among all the different conceptual schemes we know of, the world must not be constituted by conceptual schemes.

Translation requires a common point of reference. Consequently some argue that the very notion of an alternate conceptual scheme makes no sense. Donald Davidson, for example, claims that if we can translate an alien's utterances into our own, our conceptual schemes must be essentially the same. And if we can't translate the alien's utterances, we have no reason to suppose that the alien species even has a conceptual scheme.[11]

As long as we don't take truth to be relative to conceptual schemes, however, we need not reject the notion of alternate conceptual schemes. An analogy may be helpful here. Instead of viewing conceptual schemes as cookie cutters, we can view them as maps. The countryside can be mapped in many different ways. For example, there are road maps, topographical maps, relief maps, and so on. Different maps will use different symbols, and the features that are represented on one map may not be represented on another. But this doesn't mean that those who use different maps are traveling on different terrain. The terrain is what it is. Whatever is true in one map is true in another. So changing the nature of the representation doesn't change the nature of what's represented. Different conceptual schemes represent the world differently; they don't create different worlds.

Since different maps are used for different purposes, it makes no sense to say that any map is absolutely better than any other. Some maps are good for some things, and some are good for others. The goodness of a map will be determined by how well it helps us accomplish our purposes. So we may agree with the conceptual relativist that there is no one "best" way of conceptualizing the world. But this doesn't mean that there is no one way the world is.

THE RELATIVIST'S PETARD

The foregoing considerations weigh heavily against relativism. But the most serious flaw of relativism in all its forms is a purely logical one: it's self-defeating because its truth implies its falsity. That is, it refutes itself.

All generalizations are dangerous, even this one.

— ALEXANDRE DUMAS FILS

According to the relativist, the statement "All truth is relative" is true. But in what sense is that statement true? Is it objectively true or relatively true? Either way, the relativist is in trouble.

To refute a universal generalization, all you have to do is find one counterexample to it. For example, if someone says that all ravens are black, all you have to do to refute him is to find one nonblack raven. If someone says that all truth is relative, all you have to do to refute him is to find one objective truth. If the proposition "All truth is relative" is an objective truth, it refutes itself because it serves as its own counterexample. So if the statement "All truth is relative" is objectively true, it's objectively false.

To avoid such self-contradiction, the relativist may claim that the statement "All truth is relative" is only *relatively* true. But this won't help, because to say that is just to say that the relativist (or his society or his conceptual scheme) takes relativism to be true. Such a claim should not give the non-relativist pause, for the fact that relativists take relativism to be true is not in question. The question is whether a non-relativist should take relativism to be true. He should do so only if the relativist can provide some objective evidence for believing that relativism is true. But this is precisely the kind of evidence that the relativist can't provide for, in his view, there is no objective evidence.

So the relativist faces a dilemma: if he interprets his theory objectively, he defeats himself by providing evidence against it. If he interprets his theory relativistically, he defeats himself by failing to provide any evidence for it. Either way, he defeats himself.

Philosopher Harvey Siegel describes the dilemma this way:

> First the framework relativist must, in order to join the issue with the non-relativist, defend framework relativism non-relativistically. To "defend" framework relativism relativistically (i.e. "according to my framework, framework relativism is true (correct, warranted, etc.)") is to fail to defend it, since the non-relativist is appropriately unimpressed with such framework-bound claims. But to defend framework relativism non-relativistically is to give it up, since to defend it in this way is to acknowledge the legitimacy of framework-neutral criteria of assessment of claims, which is precisely what the framework relativist must deny. Thus to defend framework relativism relativistically is to fail to defend it; to defend it non-relativistically is to give it up. Thus framework relativism is self-defeating.[12]

And anything that is self-defeating cannot be true.

The problem with the relativist is that he wants to eat his cake and have it too. On the one hand, he wants to say that he or his society or his conceptual scheme is the supreme authority on matters of truth. But on the other hand, he wants to say that other individuals, societies, or conceptual schemes are equally authoritative. He can't have it both ways. As philosopher W. V. O. Quine explains:

> Truth, says the cultural relativist, is culture-bound. But if it were, then he, within his own culture, ought to see his own culture-bound truth as

absolute. He cannot proclaim cultural relativism without rising above it, and he cannot rise above it without giving it up.[13]

If individual, social, or conceptual relativism were true, there would be no standpoint outside of yourself, your society, or your conceptual scheme from which to make valid judgments. With no such standpoint, however, you would have no grounds for thinking that relativism is true. In proclaiming that truth is relative, then, the relativist hoists himself on his own petard; he blows himself up, so to speak.

FACING REALITY

The foregoing considerations indicate that truth isn't relative to individuals, societies, or conceptual schemes. Belief is often relative to these things because different individuals, societies, and conceptual schemes often have different beliefs. But that doesn't mean that truth is relative to them, for as we've seen, you can't make something true by simply believing it to be true. The upshot, then, is that:

> There is such a thing as objective truth.

In other words, there is a way the world is. We can represent the world to ourselves in many different ways, but that which is being represented is the same for all of us.

So the concept of objective truth is not optional, something we can take or leave. Each time we assert that something is the case or we think that something is a certain way, we assume that there is objective reality. Each time a relativist denies it, he entangles himself in self-refutation and contradictions. In the very argument over the existence of objective truth, both those who accept it and those who deny it must assume it or the argument would never get off the ground.

"But wait," you say. "Still, there must be some things that are 'true for me' and not 'true for you.' If I say that I hate opera, isn't that statement true for me? If I love Bart Simpson, have a pain in my left leg, or am bored silly by discussions of politics, aren't these assertions true for me?"

The truth may not be helpful, but the concealment of it cannot be.
— MELVIN KONNER

Clearly there are things about ourselves that are relative—that are a certain way to us and a different way to others. Personal characteristics—peculiarities of psychology and physiology—are relative to persons (Jane likes pizza, but Jack doesn't; Jane has a mole on her nose, and Jack doesn't). The effects that anything might have on a person are also relative to that person (Jane is intrigued by quantum mechanics, but Jack isn't; loud music gives Jane a headache, but not Jack). Certain states-of-affairs, then, may be relative to individuals.

But the truth about those states-of-affairs isn't relative. Let's say that Jane loves white wine and Jack doesn't. On their first dinner date, Jane says, "I love white wine." Is Jane's statement true for her but not true for Jack? No. Her statement reports a fact about herself, and because she does love white wine, her statement is true. It's not true for her and false for Jack; it's just true. If Jack says, "I don't love white wine," his statement refers to a fact about himself and is also true for both of them. In each statement, the "I" refers to a different person, and so the statements correctly report on different states-of-affairs.

Now we come to the fallacy that seems to give many people their most compelling pretext for rejecting the concept of objective truth. It's the claim that belief in objective truth leads to — or is synonymous with — intolerance and arrogance. It says that objectivists tend to think they have a monopoly on truth and eventually are tempted to repress those who disagree with them. Weren't all persecutions in history perpetuated by those who believed in objective truth and knew beyond doubt that they alone possessed it? Relativism, on the other hand, is supposed to foster tolerance, implying that different views are entitled to equal respect because they're all equally true.

We've probably all known people who thought they were in possession of the truth and couldn't abide anyone who disagreed with them. But this fact doesn't have any bearing on the real question here: does belief in objective truth *necessarily* entail intolerance and arrogance?

The answer is no. The objectivist believes that when there's disagreement, it's theoretically possible to determine the truth through rational argument. After all, if there is a way things are, then the only way to resolve disputes is by appeal to that way. But as Trigg points out,

> there is no reason why someone who believes that basic disagreement *can* admit of solution firstly should arrogantly assume that he himself has a monopoly of truth, and secondly should then make others accept his views by force. The mere fact that a disagreement is capable of solution does not of itself suggest which side is right. When two sides contradict each other, whether in the fields of morality, religion or any other area, each will recognize (if they are objectivists) that at least one side must be mistaken. There need be no contradiction between strongly believing that one is right and yet realizing that one could be wrong. Arrogance is not entailed by any objectivist theory.[14]

True, an objectivist might indeed be tempted to force his views upon others — but so might a relativist. A relativist might use force to get others to agree with him because he has no other recourse. After

Truth is a great flirt.
—Franz Liszt

all, he can't persuade anyone by appealing to objective standards or using rational argument since he doesn't believe that's possible. If he wants to persuade others, what is left besides force and manipulation?

Certainly, dogmatism isn't ruled out by relativism. It crops up among relativists just as it does among some objectivists. It's apparent, for example, among some who have espoused New Age subjectivism. So relativism doesn't entail tolerance, any more than objectivism entails intolerance.

Also, if the relativist does embrace the virtue of tolerance, she once again gets herself stuck in contradictions. If she says that tolerance of other views is a good thing, does she mean that this is objectively true or not? If she means that it's objectively true, she denies her relativism because she regards something as objectively true. If she means that it's only relatively true that tolerance is a good thing, then she must admit that the opposite view could be equally justified. Consequently she can't consistently claim that everyone should be tolerant.

Truth does not do so much good in the world as the appearance of it does evil.

— La Rochefoucauld

The relativist may say that some things are true for her and some things are true for others, and we should respect the right of people to be different. But she can't consistently uphold this right — she can't say that others should respect this right. (After all, someone could believe just the opposite and, since all positions are equally true, there is no reason not to act intolerantly.) She can't even condemn those who would trample this right. She can say only that she supports it.

On the other hand, there's no contradiction at all for the objectivist who says all of the following: statements are objectively true or false; it's often difficult to tell whether statements are true or false; we may be mistaken about their truth or falsity; and, because of our fallibility, we must be tolerant of those who have opposing views and uphold their right to disagree.

Understand this as well: just because there is an objective reality (and thus objective truth) doesn't mean that people can't view this objective reality differently. In fact, some people are tempted by relativism precisely because they are aware that there are different perspectives on reality — and plenty of disagreements about it. But it doesn't follow from the existence of disagreements and differing perspectives that there is no objective reality or objective truth.

"WE CREATE OUR OWN REALITY"

Our fifth man is not alone in claiming that people create their own reality. Many people, past and present, have embraced this idea and thought it both liberating and profound. Shirley MacLaine, for example, declared in the introduction to her book *Out on a Limb*:

If my search for inner truth helps give you, the reader, the gift of insight, then I am rewarded. But my first reward has been the journey through myself, the only journey worth taking. Through it all I have learned one deep and meaningful lesson: LIFE, LIVES, and REALITY are only what we each perceive them to be. Life doesn't happen to us. We make it happen. Reality isn't separate from us. We are creating our reality every moment of the day. For me that truth is the ultimate freedom and the ultimate responsibility.[15]

Later, to the amazement of her friends, she followed this claim to its logical conclusion — to solipsism, the idea that I alone exist and create all of reality. In *It's All in the Playing*, she tells how she scandalized guests at a New Year's Eve party when she expressed solipsistic sentiments:

> I began by saying that since I realized I created my own reality in every way, I must therefore admit that, in essence, *I was the only person alive in my universe.* I could feel the instant shock waves undulate around the table. I went on to express my feeling of total responsibility *and power* for all events that occur in the world because the world is happening only in my reality. *And* human beings feeling pain, terror, depression, panic, and so forth, were really only aspects of pain, terror, depression, panic and so on, in *me!* . . . I knew *I* had created the reality of the evening news at night. It was my reality. But whether anyone else was experiencing the news *separately* from me was unclear, because *they* existed in my reality too. And if they reacted to world events, then I was creating them to react so I would have someone to interact with, thereby enabling myself to know me better.[16]

In 1970, long before MacLaine spoke of creating reality, a book called *The Seth Material* was published. It was to be one of many bestsellers based on the words of a putative entity named Seth (a personality "no longer focused in physical reality") and "channeled" by novelist Jane Roberts. A major theme of the book is that physical reality is our own creation:

> Seth says that we form the physical universe as unselfconsciously as we breathe. We aren't to think of it as a prison from which we will one day escape, or as an execution chamber from which all escape is impossible. Instead *we form matter* in order to operate in three-dimensional reality, develop our abilities and help others. . . . Without realizing it we project our ideas outward to form physical reality. Our bodies are the materialization of what we think we are. We are all creators, then, and this world is our creation.[17]

So *do* we make our own reality? First, let's be clear about the meaning of this claim. If it's just another way of saying "truth is subjective," we now know that this view has a big problem. It means that

The mind does not create what it perceives, any more than the eye creates the rose.
— RALPH WALDO EMERSON

The Crime of Gabriel Gale

A number of writers have wrestled with the problem of solipsism. According to Martin Gardner, none have expressed this struggle quite as eloquently as G. K. Chesterton:

> Although there has never been a sane solipsist, the doctrine often haunts young minds. G. K. Chesterton is a case in point. In his autobiography he writes about a period in his youth during which the notion that maybe nothing existed except himself and his own phaneron [sense experiences] had caused him considerable anguish. He later became a realist, and there are many places in his writings where he warns against the psychic dangers of solipsistic speculation. . . . But nowhere did GK defend his realism with more passionate intensity than in a story called "The Crime of Gabriel Gale." It can be found in *The Poet and the Lunatic,* my favorite among GK's many collections of mystery stories about detectives other than Father Brown.
>
> Since this book may be hard to come by, here is a brief summary of the story's plot. Gabriel Gale, poet, artist, and detective, is accused of a terrible crime. It seems that on a wild and stormy night Gale had thrown a rope around the neck of a young man who was preparing for the Anglican ministry. After dragging the poor fellow into a wood, Gale pinned him for the night against a tree by forcing the two prongs of a large pitchfork into the trunk on either side of the man's neck. After Gale is arrested for attempted murder, he suggests to the police that they obtain the opinion of his victim.
>
> The surprising reply comes by telegraph: "Can never be sufficiently grateful to Gale for his great kindness which more than saved my life."
>
> It turns out that the young man had been going through the same insane phase that had tormented GK in his youth. He was on the verge of believing that his phaneron did not depend on anything that was not entirely inside his head. Gabriel Gale, always sensitive to the psychoses of others (having felt most of them himself), had realized that the man's mind was near the snapping point. Gale's remedy was radical. By pinning the man to the tree he had convinced him, not by logic (no one is ever convinced by logic of anything important) but by an overpowering experience. He found himself firmly bound to something that his mind could in no way modify.
>
> "We are all tied to trees and pinned with pitchforks," Gale tells the half-comprehending police. "And as long as these are solid we know the stars will stand and the hills will not melt at our word. Can't you imagine the huge tide of healthy relief and thanks, like a hymn of praise from all nature, that went up from that captive nailed to the tree, when he had wrestled till the dawn and received at last the great and glorious news; the news that he was only a man?"
>
> The story ends when the man, now a curate, remarks casually to an atheist, "God wants you to play the game."
>
> "How do you know what God wants?" asks the atheist. "You never were God were you?"
>
> "Yes," says the clergyman in a queer voice. "I was God once for about fourteen hours. But I gave it up. I found it was too much of a strain."[18]

there's no objective reality, which, of course, is to say that there's no objective truth. As we've already shown, this claim is unreasonable.

What MacLaine and Roberts mean by "we create our own reality," however, is a more limited claim than that there's no objective reality. They want to say that we each create *physical* reality. We each create the Milky Way galaxy, the trees in the park, the cat next door, the office building on Main Street, and the electrons whirring in our hands and the heavens. The solipsist would go one step further and say "It's not that we each create our own universe. I alone create it—and the appearance of other minds as well."

Notice also that even if your mind somehow creates everything in the universe, there would still be an objective reality and an objective truth. There would be the objective facts about your mind—it would be a certain way and not some other. There would then be the objective truth that you were omnipotent.

So even if you were a god making worlds by the very act of believing that those worlds existed, a statement would still be true only if it says what is the case in objective reality—regardless of whether you had a hand in bringing about some of that reality. Even as a god, you couldn't escape the three principles discussed earlier.

So do we each make physical reality? At one time, Ted Schultz was attracted to this idea, but he soon came to have doubts about it.

> I began to wonder about the logical extensions of "consensus reality," "personal reality," and the power of belief. Supposing a schizophrenic was totally convinced that he could fly. Could he? If so, why weren't there frequent reports from mental institutions of miracles performed by the inmates? What about large groups of people like the Jehovah's Witnesses, who devoutly believed that Jesus would return on a particular day? Hadn't he failed to appear twice in that religion's history (in 1914 and 1975), forcing the faithful to reset the dates? What if the inhabitants of some other solar system believed astronomical physics to work differently than we believe they do on earth? Could both be true at the same time? If not, which would the universe align itself with? Does the large number of Catholics on earth make the Catholic God and saints a reality? Should I worry about the consequences of denying the Catholic faith? Before Columbus, was the earth really flat because everyone believed it to be? Did it only "become" round after the consensus opinion changed?[19]

What could be more appealing than the notion that if we just believe in something, it will come true? Just the same, as Schultz indicates, there are serious problems with the idea that belief alone can transfigure reality. For one thing, it involves a logical contradiction. If it's true that our beliefs can alter reality, then what happens when different people have opposing beliefs? Let's say that one person, A, believes *p* (a statement about reality), and *p* therefore becomes true. Another person, B, however, believes not-*p*, and it becomes true. We would then have the same state-of-affairs both existing and not existing simultaneously—a logical impossibility. What if A believes that all known terrorists are dead, and B believes that they're not dead? What if A believes that the Earth is round, and B believes it's flat? Since the supposition that our beliefs create reality leads to a logical contradiction, we must conclude that reality is independent of our beliefs.

Solipsists can avoid this problem because, in their view, there is only one person in the world and hence only one person doing the believing. But is it reasonable to believe that there is only one person in the world and that that person creates everything there is by merely thinking about it? Consider your own experience.

You have a leaking faucet. You position a bucket to catch the drops. You leave the room. When you return, the bucket is full of water, the sink is overflowing, and the carpet is soaked. Simple events like this—and billions of other experiences—lead us to believe that causal sequences continue whether we're experiencing them or not, as though they were independent of our minds.

You open a closet door, and—surprise!—books fall on your head. The last thing on your mind was falling books. It's as though such events are causally connected to something *outside* your mind.

You fall asleep on your bed. When you awaken the next day, everything in the room is just as it was before you drifted off. It's as though your room continued to exist whether you were thinking about it or not.

You hold a rose in your hand. You see it, feel it, smell it. Your senses converge to give you a unified picture of this flower—as though it existed independently. If it's solely a product of your mind, this convergence is more difficult to account for.

Every day of your life, you're aware of a distinction between experiences that you yourself create (like daydreams, thoughts, imaginings) and those that seem forced upon you by an external reality (like unpleasant smells, loud noises, cold wind). If there is an independent world, this distinction makes sense. If there isn't and you create your own reality, the distinction is mysterious.

The point is that the existence of an independent world explains our experiences better than any known alternative. We have good reason to believe that the world—which seems independent of our minds—really is. We have little if any reason to believe that the world is our mind's own creation. Science writer Martin Gardner, in an essay on solipsism, puts the point like this:

> We, who of course are not solipsists, all believe that other people exist. Is it not an astonishing set of coincidences — astonishing, that is, to anyone who doubts an external world — that everybody sees essentially the same phaneron? We walk the same streets of the same cities. We find the same buildings at the same locations. Two people can see the same spiral galaxy through a telescope. Not only that, they see the same spiral structure. The hypothesis that there is an external world, not dependent on human minds, made of *something*, is so obviously useful and so strongly confirmed by experience down through the ages that we can say without exaggerating that it is better confirmed than any other empirical hypothesis. So useful is the posit that it is almost impossible for anyone except a madman or a professional metaphysician to comprehend a reason for doubting it.[20]

If there is indeed a world out there independent of our minds — a world not fashioned by our very thoughts — then the principle stated earlier takes on added meaning: *Just because you believe something to be true doesn't mean that it is true.*

"WE CREATE REALITY BY CONSENSUS"

The basic idea behind the sixth man's claim is that if enough people believe that something is true, it literally becomes true for everyone. We don't each create our own separate realities, we all live in one reality — but we can radically alter this reality for everybody if a sufficient number of us believe. If within our group we can reach a kind of consensus, a critical mass of belief, then we can change the world.

Probably the most influential articulation of this idea was a book called *The Crack in the Cosmic Egg* by Joseph Chilton Pearce.[21] In it, Pearce asserted that people have a hand in shaping physical reality — even the laws of physics. We can transform the physical world, or parts of it, if enough of us believe in a new reality. If we attain a group consensus, we can change the world any way we want — for everyone.

Facts do not cease to exist because they are ignored.
— ALDOUS HUXLEY

In recent years, this extraordinary thesis — that if enough people believe in something, it suddenly becomes true for everyone — has been enormously influential. It got its single biggest boost from the hundredth monkey phenomenon mentioned in Chapter 1, a story told by Lyall Watson in his book *Lifetide.* This tale has been told and retold in a bestselling book by Ken Keyes called *The Hundredth Monkey,* in a film with the same name, and in several articles.

Here's the story: Watson tells of reports coming from scientists in the 1950s about wild Japanese monkeys on the island of Koshima.

After the monkeys were given raw sweet potatoes for the first time, one of them, named Imo, learned to wash the sand and grit off the potatoes by dunking them in a stream. In the next few years, Imo taught this skill to other monkeys in the colony. "Then something extraordinary took place," says Watson.

> The details up to this point in the study are clear, but one has to gather the rest of the story from personal anecdotes and bits of folklore among primate researchers, because most of them are still not quite sure what happened. And those who do suspect the truth are reluctant to publish it for fear of ridicule. So I am forced to improvise the details, but as near as I can tell, this is what seems to have happened.
>
> In the autumn of that year [1958] an unspecified number of monkeys on Koshima were washing sweet potatoes in the sea, because Imo had made the further discovery that salt water not only cleaned the food but gave it an interesting new flavor. Let us say, for argument's sake, that the number was ninety-nine and that at eleven o'clock on a Tuesday morning, one further convert was added to the fold in the usual way. But the addition of the hundredth monkey apparently carried the number across some sort of threshold, pushing it through a kind of critical mass, because by that evening almost everyone in the colony was doing it. Not only that, but the habit seems to have jumped natural barriers and to have appeared spontaneously, like glycerin crystals in sealed laboratory jars, in colonies on other islands and on the mainland in a troop at Takasakiyama.[22]

Watson uses the story to support the consensus-truth thesis. But you might ask at this point, "Is the story true? Did these events really happen?" (Many people who retold the story in books and articles never bothered to ask this question.)

If it did happen, it would be of enormous scientific interest. But it still wouldn't constitute proof of the thesis that a critical mass of humans can make something true for everyone else. For one thing, the evidence could easily support alternative hypotheses. Perhaps the potato-washing habit wasn't really spread, but resulted from independent experimentation and learning by different monkeys (in other words, other monkeys learned it the way Imo did).

On the other hand, if the story didn't happen, this wouldn't prove that the consensus-truth thesis was false, either. It would simply mean that one potential piece of empirical evidence that would justify our believing in the thesis was not valid.

As it turns out, *the story didn't happen,* at least not as told by Watson and others. (See the accompanying boxes for a critical evaluation of the Watson story and for Watson's reply to the critique and his admission that the story wasn't literally true.)

A Closer Look at the Hundredth Monkey Phenomenon

Lyall Watson, a writer specializing in paranormal topics, was the first to tell the hundredth monkey story, which seemed to many to support the idea of paranormal group consciousness. The story focuses on a troop of macaques living on islands in Japan and is documented by references to research reports by Japanese primatologists. The story says that the monkeys suddenly and miraculously learned the habit of potato-washing. Surprisingly, few people questioned whether Watson's story ever actually happened. Ron Amundson, a professor of philosophy, did question it. He checked to see if Watson's story accurately reflected what was contained in the research reports. He concluded that it did not. Here are excerpts from his analysis:

> Almost all of the information about the Koshima [island] troop appears in a journal article by Masao Kawai in 1965; the other articles are secondary on this topic. Kawai's article is remarkably detailed in its description of the Koshima events. The troop numbered 20 in 1952 and grew to 59 by 1962. (At least in the numerical sense, there was never a "hundredth monkey" on Koshima.) Watson states that "an unspecified number" of monkeys on Koshima had acquired the potato-washing habit by 1958. Actually this number was far from unspecified. Kawai's data allows the reader to determine the dates of acquisition of potato washing (and two other food behaviors), as well as the dates of birth and genealogical relationships, of every monkey in the Koshima troop from 1949 to 1962. In March 1958, exactly 2 of 11 monkeys over seven years old had learned potato washing, while exactly 15 of 19 monkeys between two and seven had the habit. This amounts to 17 of 30 non-infant monkeys. There is no mention in this paper (or in any other) of a sudden learning event in the fall of 1958. However, it is noted that by 1962, 36 of the 49 monkeys had acquired the habit. So both the population and the number of potato washers had increased by 19 during this four-year period. Perhaps this is what suggested to Watson that a sudden event occurred in the fall of 1958. And perhaps (since one can only surmise) this idea was reinforced in Watson's mind by the following statement by Kawai: "The acquisition of [potato washing] behavior can be divided into two periods: before and after 1958."

> So Kawai does not give a time of year, a day of the week, or even the season for any sudden event in 1958. But he does at least identify the year. And is Kawai mystified about the difference between pre- and post-1958 acquisition? Is he "not quite sure what happened"? Is he reluctant to publish details

(continued)

(continued)

"for fear of ridicule"? No, he publishes the whole story, in Gothic detail. The post-1958 learning period was remarkable only for its normalcy. . . .

So there was nothing left unsaid in Kawai's description. There was nothing mysterious, or even sudden, in the events of 1958. Nineteen fifty-eight and 1959 were the years of maturation of a group of innovative youngsters. The human hippies of the 1960s now know that feeling. In fact 1958 was a singularly poor year for habit acquisition on Koshima. Only two monkeys learned to wash potatoes during that year, young females named Zabon and Nogi. An average of three a year had learned potato washing during the previous five years. There is no evidence that Zabon and Nogi were psychic or in any other way unusual.

Let us try to take Watson seriously for a moment longer. Since only two monkeys learned potato washing during 1958 (according to Watson's own citation), one of them must have been the "Hundredth Monkey." Watson leaves "unspecified" which monkey it was, so I am "forced to improvise" and "say, for argument's sake" that it was Zabon. This means that poor little Nogi carries the grim metaphysical burden of being the "almost everyone in the colony" who, according to Watson, sud-denly and miraculously began to wash her potatoes on that autumn afternoon.

Watson claims that the potato-washing habit "spontaneously" leaped natural barriers. Is there evidence of this? Well, Japanese primatologists Masao Kawai and Atsuo Tsumori report that the behavior was observed off Koshima, in at least five different colonies. Their reports specifically state that the behavior was observed only among a few individual monkeys and that it had not spread throughout a colony. There is no report of when these behaviors occurred. They must have been observed sometime between 1953 and 1967. But there is nothing to indicate that they followed closely upon some supposed miraculous event on Koshima during the autumn of 1958, or that they were in any other way remarkable. In fact there is absolutely no reason to believe in the 1958 miracle on Koshima. There is every reason to deny it. Watson's description of the event is refuted in great detail by the very sources he cites to validate it. In contrast to Watson's claims of a sudden and inexplicable event, "Such behavior patterns seem to be smoothly transmitted among individuals in the troop and handed down to the next generation," according to Tsumori."[23]

"A Metaphor of My Own Making"

Lyall Watson, the creator of the hundredth monkey story, responded to philosopher Ron Amundson's critique of the tale by saying that the story wasn't literally true after all. Here's an excerpt from his response:

> I find the cavils of self-appointed committees for the suppression of curiosity very tedious.
>
> And I am deeply suspicious of those who feel the need to set themselves up as defenders of the scientific faith.
>
> But I have to say that I admire Ron Amundson. His analysis of the Hundredth Monkey Phenomenon is lucid, amusing and refreshingly free of the emotional dismissals that characterize much of the usual output of the Committee for the Scientific Investigation of Claims of the Paranormal.
>
> I accept Amundson's analysis of the origin and evolution of the Hundredth Monkey without reservation. It is a metaphor of my own making, based—as he rightly suggests—on very slim evidence and a great deal of hearsay. I have never pretended otherwise.
>
> I take issue, however, with his conclusion that, therefore, the Hundredth Monkey Phenomenon cannot exist.
>
> It might have come to be called the Hundredth Cockroach or Hairy Nosed Wombat Phenomenon if my travels had taken me in a different direction. As it happened, I was already interested in the non-linear manner in which ideas and fashions travel through our culture, and the notion of quantum leaps in consciousness (a sort of punctuated equilibrium of the mind) was taking shape in my own mind when I arrived in Japan. It was off-the-record conversations with those familiar with the potato-washing work that led me to choose a monkey as the vehicle for my metaphor. And I still contend that there is more to those studies than meets the eye or reaches Hawaii in scientific journals.[24]

Like the seventh man in our parable, some people may declare that it doesn't even matter whether Watson's tale is literally true because it's a myth or metaphor. Myths and metaphors, they say, have their own kind of truth. Well, this latter point is true enough — myths and metaphors can, indirectly, say things about reality, just as literal statements can. There's a problem, though, if the point is supposed to imply that in myth or metaphor, concerns about truth or falsity don't apply. A claim about reality, whether embodied in mythic or metaphoric language or not, is still a claim about reality. As such, it's either true or false, and discovering which is still a job for critical thinking.

Regardless of the literal truth of Watson's story, though, we can still scrutinize his thesis. In *Lifetide* he says, "It may be that when enough of us hold something to be true, it becomes true for everyone."[25] If by this he means that consensus belief by groups of people can literally alter physical reality (Pearce's notion), he's mistaken, because this notion would entail a logical contradiction, as we've seen.

But he may have something else in mind. He may mean that people's consensus beliefs don't really alter reality (that is, what's true); they just change other people's beliefs (what people think is true). If enough of us fervently hold certain beliefs, then somehow everyone else will suddenly come to hold those beliefs too. Once the magic number of believers is attained, nonbelievers everywhere become believers.

This view conjures up the chilling specter of instant, mass brainwashing (see the box "On Good Myth and Bad Myth"). But the possible unpleasant consequences of these views are no grounds to judge them false. As an empirical claim, a hypothesis, about how people acquire their personal beliefs, we can judge its validity only by considering it alongside alternative hypotheses and asking which is the best of the bunch—which is superior or most likely to be true. As we'll see in later chapters, often the choice comes down to which hypothesis has the most supporting evidence.

There are, in fact, commonplace alternative hypotheses explaining how people come to hold a certain belief: they want to believe what their friends believe; they've been manipulated by messages from television, radio, print media, movies and more; their belief is psychologically comforting; they fear adverse consequences for not believing; their belief makes sense (is justified or is supported by evidence). The list could go on. Each of these explanations has been confirmed by an enormous amount of empirical evidence, in both science and our daily experience. On the other hand, the notion that beliefs get inserted into everyone's minds by a critical mass of believers has, so far, no clear empirical support. Just as there's no reason to believe that we can make something true by simply believing it to be true, so there's no reason to believe that we can make others believe that something is true by simply believing it to be true.

On Good Myth and Bad Myth

Psychologist Maureen O'Hara was the first to publish a skeptical analysis of Lyall Watson's hundredth monkey story of a paranormal critical mass of consciousness. She's aware that many have embraced the tale as a significant myth. She acknowledges the importance of myth in our lives but contends that as a myth, the Watson story is "profoundly non-humanistic" and a "betrayal of the whole idea of human empowerment":

> There are major contradictions in the present idealization of critical mass — seen not only in the Hundredth Monkey story, but in the ideologies of such organizations as est, Bhagwan Rajneesh, and the "Aquarian conspirators." In promoting the idea that, although our ideas are shared by only an enlightened few (for the time being), if we really believe them, in some magical way what we hold to be true becomes true for everyone, proponents of the critical mass ideal ignore the principles of both humanism and democratic open society. The basis for openness in our kind of society is the belief that, for good or ill, each of us holds his or her own beliefs as a responsible participant in a pluralistic culture. Are we really willing to give up on this ideal and promote instead a monolithic ideology in which what is true for a "critical mass" of people becomes true for everyone? The idea gives me the willies. . . .
>
> My objection to the Hundredth Monkey Phenomenon, then, is not that it is a myth, but that it is bad myth, and that it draws its force not from the collective imagination, but by masquerading as science. It leads us (as I have tried to show) in the direction of propaganda, manipulation, totalitarianism, and a worldview dominated by the powerful and persuasive — in other words, business as usual. . . .
>
> . . . I most emphatically cannot agree that the "Hundredth Monkey myth empowers." In fact, I believe it to be a betrayal of the whole idea of human empowerment. In this myth the individual as a responsible agent disappears; what empowers is no longer the moral force of one's beliefs, not their empirical status, rather, it is the number of people who share them. Once the magic number is reached curiosity, science, art, criticism, doubt and all other such activities subversive of the common consensus become unnecessary or even worse. Individuals no longer have any obligation to develop their own worldview within such a collective — it will come to them from those around. Nor are we called on to develop our arguments and articulate them for, by magic, those around us will catch them anyway. This is not a transformation myth impelling us toward the fullest development of our capacities, but one that reduces us instead to quite literally nothing more than a mindless herd at the mercy of the "Great Communicators." The myth of the Hundredth Monkey Phenomenon is more chillingly Orwellian than Aquarian."[26]

SUGGESTED READINGS

Gardner, Martin. *The Whys of a Philosophical Scrivener*. New York: Quill, 1983.

Krausz, Michael. *Relativism: Interpretation and Confrontation*. South Bend, Ind.: University of Notre Dame Press, 1989.

Scheffler, Israel. *Science and Subjectivity*. Indianapolis: Bobbs-Merrill, 1967.

Siegel, Harvey. *Relativism Refuted*. Dordrecht, Netherlands: D. Reidel, 1987.

Trigg, Roger. *Reason and Commitment*. London: Cambridge University Press, 1973.

NOTES

1. Ted Schultz, "A Personal Odyssey Through the New Age," in *Not Necessarily the New Age* (Buffalo: Prometheus Books, 1988), p. 342.

2. Plato, "Theaetetus," 171a, trans. by F. M. Conford, ed. Edith Hamilton and Huntington Cairns, *The Collected Works of Plato* (Princeton: Princeton University Press, 1961), p. 876.

3. Roger Trigg, *Reason and Commitment* (London: Cambridge University Press, 1973), p. 2.

4. Ellen Goodman, column in *The Morning Call*, June 15, 1993, p. A11.

5. Israel Scheffler, *Science and Subjectivity* (Indianapolis: Bobbs-Merrill, 1967), pp. 36ff.

6. Chris Swoyer, "True For," in *Relativism: Cognitive and Moral*, ed. Jack W. Meiland and Michael Krausz (South Bend, Ind.: University of Notre Dame Press, 1982), p. 97.

7. Nelson Goodman, *Ways of World Making* (Indianapolis: Hackett, 1978).

8. W. Newton-Smith, "Relativism and the Possibility of Interpretation," in *Rationality and Relativism*, ed. Martin Hollis and Steven Lukes (Cambridge: MIT Press, 1982), pp. 107–8.

9. Swoyer, "True For," p. 101.

10. Trigg, *Reason and Commitment*, pp. 15–16.

11. "Presidential Address" (Speech made to the Seventieth Annual Eastern Meeting of the American Philosophical Association in Atlanta, December 28, 1973).

12. Harvey Siegel, *Relativism Refuted* (Dordrecht, Netherlands: D. Reidel, 1987), pp. 43–44.

13. W. V. Quine, "On Empirically Equivalent Systems of the World," *Erkenntnis*, 9 (1975), pp. 327–28.

14. Trigg, *Reason and Commitment*, pp. 135–36.

15. Shirley MacLaine, *Out on a Limb* (New York: Bantam Books, 1983).

16. Shirley MacLaine, *It's All in the Playing* (New York: Bantam Books, 1987), pp. 171–72.

17. Jane Roberts, *The Seth Material* (New York: Bantam Books, 1970), p. 124.

18. Martin Gardner, *The Whys of a Philosophical Scrivener* (New York: Quill, 1983), pp. 30–31.

19. Schultz, "Personal Odyssey," p. 345.

20. Gardner, *Philosophical Scrivener*, p. 15.

21. Joseph Chilton Pearce, *The Crack in the Cosmic Egg* (New York: Julian Press, 1971).

22. Lyall Watson, *Lifetide* (New York: Bantam Books, 1979), pp. 147–48.

23. Ron Amundson, "The Hundredth Monkey Debunked," in *The Fringes of Reason: A Whole Earth Catalog*, ed. Ted Schultz (New York: Harmony Books, 1989), pp. 175–80.

24. Lyall Watson, "Lyall Watson Responds," in *Fringes of Reason*, Schultz, pp. 180–81.

25. Watson, *Lifetide*, pp. 148–49.

26. Maureen O'Hara, "Of Myths and Monkeys: A Critical Look at Critical Mass," in *Fringes of Reason*, Schultz, pp. 182–86.

FIVE
Knowledge, Belief, and Evidence

IT IS WRITTEN in the scriptures, proclaimed by Francis Bacon, and enshrined in common sense: knowledge is power.[1] Those in the know are more likely to get their way than those who aren't because their views are based on reality—not on fantasy, illusion, or wishful thinking. Their projects have a greater chance of success because their knowledge gives them the ability to foresee obstacles and devise ways of overcoming those obstacles. Prediction and control are keys to survival, and knowledge makes prediction and control possible.

But knowledge is not only valuable for what we can do with it; it is also valuable for its own sake. We all would like to know why things are as they are. Our desire for this knowledge, however, is not motivated by purely practical considerations. We often seek such understanding simply for the sake of understanding — because understanding, like virtue, is its own reward. Solving a mystery, discovering the truth, and acquiring insight are among the most exhilarating experiences we can have.

Since knowledge is needed to help us attain our goals and to make sense of the world, we must be clear about what knowledge is and how to acquire it.

BABYLONIAN KNOWLEDGE-ACQUISITION TECHNIQUES

Our thirst for knowledge, especially of the future, has inspired many strange techniques for acquiring it. Among the earliest and most elaborate are those of the Babylonians, the inventors of astrology. But astrology was not the Babylonians' first or preferred method of prophecy. Those distinctions belong to hepatoscopy — divination through inspection of the liver.[2] Having realized that blood is essential to life, the Babylonians apparently concluded that the organ richest in blood — the liver — is where the life force is located. By offering this valuable organ (usually taken from sheep) in sacrifice, they presumably believed that the gods would reward their generosity by revealing the future. Why they thought the gods would choose this particular means of showing their gratitude is unclear. Nevertheless, the Babylonians were convinced that every feature of a sacrificed liver — its shape, its blood vessels, its lobes, and so on — disclosed something about the future. All manner of problems, from agricultural to military, were settled by consulting this organ.

In Mesopotamia, hepatoscopy was considered to be such an effective knowledge-acquisition technique that only kings and nobles were allowed to use it. The inspection of a sheep's liver by a seer was considered a solemn act of state.[3] The seer's interpretation of a liver, however, was not a purely subjective matter. Particular features of the liver were thought to correspond to particular kinds of events. The Babylonians systematized this knowledge in the form of stenciled clay models of sheep's livers, which were used to teach aspiring hepatoscopists their trade. But while over 700 tablets containing hepatoscopic prophecies have come down to us, none explain how the correspondences between liver features and human affairs were established.[4]

While hepatoscopy is no longer big business, that other form of divination pioneered by the Babylonians — astrology — still is. There are over 10,000 professional astrologers in the United States alone. What does astrology have that hepatoscopy doesn't? Well for one thing, it's less messy. For another, dates and places of birth are easier

Prediction is very difficult, especially about the future.
— NIELS BOHR

to come by than sheep's livers. Astrology differs from hepatoscopy in another way, too. Astrology claims a causal relationship between the prophetic sign (the stars and planets) and the events to which they correspond that hepatoscopy doesn't. In hepatoscopy, the liver isn't the *cause* of the events it foretells; it is merely a record of them. In astrology, on the other hand, the stars and planets supposedly help to bring about the events they portend.

The Babylonians' view of how heavenly bodies acted upon humans, however, is not one many would accept today. According to the Babylonians, each of the seven "planets" that influence our lives—the sun, the moon, Mercury, Venus, Mars, Saturn, and Jupiter—is the seat of a different god, and each of these gods has a different effect on us.[5] Nowadays, astrologers are wont to explain the effects of heavenly bodies in more scientific terms, by appeal to such forces as gravity or electromagnetism. But neither the ancient nor the modern astrologers explain how the purported cause and effect relationships between heavenly bodies and human affairs were established. Are we to suppose that the Babylonians did a statistical survey correlating personal characteristics with star positions? If not—if it is not based on any reliable evidence—why take it seriously? If it is just the fantasy of some Babylonian priest (as hepatoscopy arguably is), can it really be considered a source of knowledge? To answer these questions, we'll first have to examine what knowledge involves.

PROPOSITIONAL KNOWLEDGE

We know many different types of things. We know, for example, who raised us, which pair of shoes is our favorite, what pain feels like, how to read, and that ducks quack. In each case, the object of our knowledge (what our knowledge is about) is different. In the first case, our knowledge is about a person; in the second, a physical object; in the third, an experience; in the fourth, an activity; and in the fifth, a fact. Our concern will be with the fifth, for we are interested in how we come to know the facts.

A fact, in the sense we are using it here, is a true proposition. Thus, factual knowledge is often referred to as *propositional knowledge.* One of the first and foremost attempts to characterize propositional knowledge can be found in the works of Plato. In his dialogue *Meno,* Socrates remarks, "it is not, I am sure, a mere guess to say that right opinion and knowledge are different. There are few things that I should claim to know, but that at least is among them, whatever else is."[6] The point that Plato is trying to make here is that while having right opinions (true beliefs) may be a necessary condition for knowledge, it is not sufficient—there must be something more to having knowledge than just having true beliefs.

True belief is necessary for knowledge because we can't know something that's false, and if we know something, we can't believe that it's false. For example, we can't know that 2 + 2 equals 5 because 2 + 2 does not equal 5. In other words, we can't know what isn't so. Similarly, if we know that 2 + 2 equals 4, we can't believe that it doesn't. To know that something is true is to believe that it's true.[7]

True belief is not sufficient for knowledge because we can have true belief and yet not have knowledge. To see this, consider the following situation. Suppose you believe that it's raining in Hong Kong right now, and suppose that it is. Does this mean that you *know* that it's raining in Hong Kong right now? Not if you have no good reason for believing so, for in that case, your belief is nothing more than a lucky guess. Having knowledge, then, would seem to require having good reasons for what you believe. Plato agrees. "True opinions," Socrates tells Meno, "are a fine thing and do all sorts of good so long as they stay in their place, but they will not stay long. They run away from a man's mind; so they are not worth much until you tether them by working out the reason. . . . Once they are tied down, they become knowledge."[8] For Plato, then, knowledge is true belief that is grounded in reality. What grounds our beliefs in reality are the reasons we have for them.

Not all reasons provide equally good grounds for belief, however. Circumstantial evidence, for example, is not as good as eyewitness testimony. So how good must our reasons be to adequately ground our beliefs? To answer this question we'll have to examine the evidential role of reasons.

REASONS AND EVIDENCE

Reasons confer probability on propositions. The better the reasons, the more likely it is that the proposition they support is true. But having reasons that make a proposition only somewhat more likely than its denial is not enough to justify our claim to know it. Suppose a geologist discovered a rock formation indicating that it was somewhat more likely than not that there was gold in the nearby hills. Could he legitimately claim to know that there is gold in the hills? No, for even if there is gold there, his claim would be little more than a guess—an educated guess, perhaps, but a guess nonetheless. And guesses, whether lucky or educated, don't constitute knowledge.

Does knowledge require certainty then? To know a proposition, must we have reasons that establish it beyond a shadow of a doubt?

The word "knowledge," strictly employed, implies three things: truth, proof, and conviction.
—RICHARD WHATELY

To doubt everything or to believe everything are two equally convenient solutions; both dispense with the necessity of reflection.
—JULES HENRI POINCARÉ

Some people think so. Suppose for example, that you and a million other people each purchased one lottery ticket. In such a case, your chance of winning is one in a million, or .000001 percent. As a result, you have a very good reason for believing that you will lose. But do you *know* that you will lose? It wouldn't seem so.

If knowledge requires certainty, however, there is little that we know, for there are precious few propositions that are absolutely indubitable. You might object that there are many things you know for certain, such as that you are reading a book right now. But do you? Isn't it possible that you are dreaming at this moment? Haven't you, during dreams, been just as convinced as you are right now that what you're perceiving is real? If so, there's not much you can be certain of (except, as Descartes pointed out, that you're thinking).

There are many possibilities that, because they can't be ruled out, undermine our certainty. It's possible, for example, that this is the twenty-ninth century and that you are watching a superadvanced television set that controls all of your sensory input. If so, you aren't really reading a book right now; you're watching a television program about reading a book. To demand that a proposition be certain in order to be known, then, would severely restrict the extent of our knowledge, perhaps to the vanishing point.

Those who believe that we can't know what isn't certain are *philosophical skeptics*. According to these thinkers, most of us are deluded about the actual extent of our knowledge. In defense of their position, philosophical skeptics often cite examples like the lottery case, which seem to suggest that nothing less than conclusive proof can give us knowledge. But for each such example, there are many that suggest otherwise. That the earth is inhabited, that cows produce milk, that water freezes at 32 degrees Fahrenheit, and so on, are all propositions we would ordinarily claim to know, yet none of them is absolutely certain. In light of these counterexamples, can philosophical skeptics legitimately claim to *know* that knowledge requires certainty? No, for unless they are certain that knowledge requires certainty, they can't know that it does. (Philosophical skeptics, remember, claim that we can only know what is certain.) And they can't be certain that knowledge requires certainty because the counterexamples cited above provide good reason for doubting that it does.

So if knowledge doesn't require certainty, how much evidence does it require? It does not need enough to put the claim beyond *any* possibility of doubt, but rather enough to put the issue beyond any *reasonable* doubt. There comes a point beyond which doubt, although possible, is no longer reasonable. It's possible, for example, that our minds are being controlled by aliens from outer space, but to reject the evidence of our senses on that basis would not be reasonable. To have knowledge, then, we must have adequate evidence, and our evidence is adequate when it puts the proposition in question beyond a reasonable doubt. So:

> We are justified in believing a
> proposition when we have no good
> reason to doubt it.

A proposition is beyond a reasonable doubt when it provides the best explanation of something. Chapter 8 spells out the notion of best explanation in some detail. For now, it's important to realize that a claim doesn't have to possess any particular degree of probability in order to be beyond a reasonable doubt. All that is required is that it fully account for the phenomena better than any of its competitors.

Epistemologist Alan Goldman provides the following example: Suppose that an expectant mother who has just had her fetus genetically tested is told that it is male. Suppose further that the chances of the test being mistaken are greater than the chances of her winning a lottery. In such a situation, even though she can't legitimately claim to know that she will lose the lottery, she *can* legitimately claim to know that her fetus is male. Why? Because the proposition that her fetus is male provides the best explanation of the results of the genetic test. As the most reasonable explanation, there's no good reason to doubt it. The proposition that she will lose the lottery, however, doesn't provide the best explanation of the results of the lottery.[9] Since her losing the lottery is a consequence of her ticket not being chosen, it cannot explain *why* her ticket will not be chosen. So the philosophical skeptics are right in claiming that no one can legitimately claim to know that they will lose a lottery, no matter how large it is, but they are wrong in claiming that this shows that knowledge requires certainty. In our view, it merely shows that the claim that someone will lose a lottery is never beyond a reasonable doubt because it doesn't provide the best explanation of anything.

Just as we are justified in convicting someone if we have established his or her guilt beyond a reasonable doubt, so we are justified in believing a proposition if we have established its truth beyond a reasonable doubt. But being justified in believing a proposition no more guarantees its truth than being justified in convicting someone guarantees his or her guilt. For it is always possible that we have overlooked something that undermines our justification. Since we are not omniscient, we can never be sure that we have considered all of the relevant evidence. Nevertheless, if we are justified in believing a proposition, we are justified in *claiming* that it is true; indeed, we are justified in *claiming* that we know it. Such a claim could be mistaken, but it would not be improper, for our justification gives us the right to make such a claim.

If our belief in a proposition is not justified—if we have good reason to doubt it—then we have no right to claim that we know it. We have reasonable grounds for doubt when we have credible evidence to the contrary. Suppose, for example, that we are looking at a surface that appears to be pink and are told either that there is no pink surface in the room or that there is a red light shining on the surface. In such a case, as epistemologist Ernest Sosa explains:

> Anyone who still believes in a pink surface before him after accepting either testimony would lack justification—this because we consider rational coherence the best overall guide. Even if the testimony is in each case false, given only adequate reason to accept it, one still loses one's justification to believe in the pink surface.[10]

In other words, if we have good reason for believing a proposition to be false, we are not justified in believing it to be true, even if all of our sensory evidence indicates that it is. When two propositions conflict with one another, we know that at least one of them must be false. Until we determine which one it is, we cannot claim to know either. Thus:

> There is good reason to doubt a proposition if it conflicts with other propositions we have good reason to believe.

The conflict of credible propositions provides reasonable grounds for doubt. And where there are reasonable grounds for doubt, there cannot be knowledge.

The search for knowledge, then, involves eliminating inconsistencies among our beliefs. When the conflict is between different reports of current observations, as in the case of the surface that appears to be pink, it's easy enough to find out which one is mistaken: look more closely. When the conflict involves propositions that can't be directly verified, finding the mistaken belief can be more difficult.

Sometimes we observe or are informed about things that seem to conflict with our background information—that vast system of well-supported beliefs we use to guide our thought and action, much of which falls under the heading "common sense." When this happens, we have to decide whether the new piece of information is credible

Doubt grows with knowledge.
—GOETHE

Is All Justified True Belief Knowledge?

We have seen that if we have knowledge, then we have justified true belief, but does it work the other way around? If we have justified true belief, then do we have knowledge? Recent scholarship suggests not. Consider the following case. Suppose that on a perfectly clear day you come upon a field in which a sheep appears to be grazing. As a result, you form the belief that there is a sheep in the field. Now suppose that what appears to you to be a sheep is actually a sheep dog although hidden behind a rock is a real sheep. In such a situation your belief that there is a sheep in the field is true and since you have no reason to doubt your perception, your belief is justified. But do you *know* that there is a sheep in the field? It would seem not, for although you have a true belief based on adequate evidence, your evidence is not appropriately related to that which makes your belief true. So not all justified true belief is knowledge. Some have suggested that a justified true belief is knowledge as long as it has been caused (in the appropriate way) by that which makes it true. Others have suggested that a justified true belief is knowledge as long as it is *undefeated*, and it is undefeated as long as there is no evidence that would undermine its justification. Neither of these suggestions (nor any other) has received universal acceptance.[11] Whatever the correct analysis of knowledge turns out to be, however, Plato's basic insight still stands: knowledge is properly grounded true belief. If you have this, then you have knowledge.

enough to make us give up some of our old beliefs. When we cannot directly verify a questionable claim, one way to assess its credibility is to determine how much is at stake in accepting it. When all other things are equal:

> The more background information a proposition conflicts with, the more reason there is to doubt it.

The structure of our belief system can be compared to that of a tree. Just as certain branches support other branches, so certain beliefs support other beliefs. And just as bigger branches support more branches than little ones, so fundamental beliefs support more beliefs than ancillary ones. Accepting some dubious claims is equivalent to cutting off a twig, for it requires giving up only peripheral beliefs. Accepting others, however, is equivalent to cutting off a limb or even part of the trunk, for it requires giving up some of our most central beliefs.

For example, suppose that after listening to the nightly weather report you come to believe that it will be sunny tomorrow. Suppose further that when you get to work the next morning, a trusted friend informs you that it is going to rain that afternoon. Your friend's report. conflicts with what you heard on the news last night, but given the variability of the weather and the possibility that your friend might have heard a more recent weather report, the claim is not altogether implausible. You may even decide to change your belief about the day's weather on its basis. Such a change would have little effect on your overall belief system, for not much hangs on your beliefs about the weather.

Now suppose that somebody claimed to be able to walk through walls without disturbing them or becoming harmed. On the credibility scale, such a claim would be close to zero because it conflicts with so much of what we believe about the physical world. Unlike the case of the weather report, you would be right in dismissing such a claim out of hand, for if it were true, large portions of your belief system would be false.

But suppose your claimant offers to provide you with supporting evidence. Suppose he proposes to demonstrate his ability by walking through as many different walls in as many different buildings as you choose. If he could perform this feat regularly and repeatedly, you would have little choice but to start pruning your belief system. But if he could perform the feat only under special circumstances controlled by him, there would be less reason to alter your beliefs, for in that case, you couldn't be sure that the feat wasn't just a conjuring trick.

Most of the dubious claims we encounter fall somewhere between the extremes of the weather report and wall-walker cases. They are not so outrageous that we can simply dismiss them, but the evidence in their favor is not compelling enough to justify their acceptance. What should be our attitude toward such propositions? We should believe as the evidence warrants. In other words:

> When there is good reason to doubt a proposition, we should proportion our belief to the evidence.

The more evidence we have for a proposition, the more credence we should give it.

The probability of a proposition may range from close to 0 (e.g., "Humans can walk through walls") to 1 (e.g., "Either it's raining or it

The Ethics of Belief

"Everybody's entitled to their own opinion" goes the platitude, meaning that everybody has the right to believe whatever they want. But is that really true? Are there no limits on what is permissible to believe? Or, as in the case of actions, are some beliefs immoral? Surprisingly, perhaps, many have argued that just as we have a moral duty not to perform certain sorts of actions, so we have a moral duty not to have certain sorts of beliefs. No one has expressed this point of view more forcefully than the distinguished mathematician W. K. Clifford: "It is wrong always, everywhere, and for anyone to believe anything on insufficient evidence."[12] Others of similar stature have echoed this sentiment. Biologist Thomas Henry Huxley, for example, declared, "It is wrong for a man to say that he is certain of the objective truth of any proposition unless he can produce evidence which logically justifies that certainty."[13] And Brand Blanshard has proclaimed "that where great human goods and ills are involved, the distortion of belief from any sort of avoidable cause is immoral, and the more immoral the greater the stakes."[14] These men think it wrong for belief to outstrip the evidence because our actions are guided by our beliefs, and if our beliefs are mistaken,

our actions may be misguided. As Blanshard indicates, the more important the decision, the greater our duty to align our beliefs with the evidence, and the greater the crime if we don't.

Where not much hangs on the belief, it might be thought that what one believes has little importance. But Clifford claims that even in trivial matters we have a duty to proportion our belief to the evidence:

> Every time we let ourselves believe for unworthy reasons, we weaken our powers of self-control, of doubting, of judicially and fairly weighing evidence. We all suffer severely enough from the maintenance and support of false beliefs and the fatally wrong actions which they lead to. . . . But a greater and wider evil arises when the credulous character is maintained and supported, when a habit of believing for unworthy reasons is fostered and made permanent.[15]

According to Clifford, responsible believing is a skill that can be maintained only through constant practice. And since responsible believing is a prerequisite for responsible acting, we have a duty to foster that skill.

isn't"). Similarly, our belief in a proposition may range from total incredulity to complete acceptance. Ideally, our belief in a proposition should correspond to its probability. If there's a good chance that the proposition is true, we should believe it strongly. If not, we shouldn't. This match with probability is needed because if the strength of our convictions doesn't match the strength of our evidence, we dramatically increase our chances of error. As any good gambler will tell you, the more you miscalculate the odds, the more you stand to lose. Unfortunately, many of us are not good gamblers, especially when it comes to estimating the chances of a proposition's truth. As a result, we end up believing all sorts of outlandish things for no good reason.

EXPERT OPINION

Bertrand Russell was acutely aware of the difficulty many of us have in getting our beliefs to correspond to the evidence. To remedy this situation, he suggested that we adopt the following principle: "it is undesirable to believe a proposition when there is no ground whatever for supposing it true."[16] Russell felt that "If such an opinion became common, it would completely transform our social life and our political system" because it would not only require rejecting many of our most cherished beliefs, but also "tend to diminish the incomes of clairvoyants, bookmakers, bishops, and others who live on the irrational hopes of those who have done nothing to deserve good fortune here or hereafter."[17] More to the point, adopting such a proposal would help alleviate a good deal of unnecessary suffering.

To adopt his proposal, Russell claimed, we need only accept the following propositions:

(1) that when the experts are agreed, the opposite opinion cannot be held to be certain; (2) that when they are not agreed, no opinion can be regarded as certain by a non-expert; and (3) that when they all hold that no sufficient grounds for a positive opinion exist, the ordinary man would do well to suspend his judgment.[18]

If our beliefs were guided by these principles, he insisted, the world would be completely transformed:

These propositions may seem mild, yet, if accepted, they would absolutely revolutionize human life.

The opinions for which people are willing to fight and persecute all belong to one of the three classes which this skepticism condemns. When there are rational grounds for an opinion, people are content to set them forth and wait for them to operate. In such cases, people do not hold their opinions with passion; they hold them calmly, and set forth their reasons quietly. The opinions that are held with passion are always those for which no good ground exists; indeed the passion is the measure of the holder's lack of rational conviction.[19]

Unfortunately, Russell seems to be right. There often appears to be an inverse correlation between degree of conviction and evidence — the less evidence there is for a proposition, the more fervently it is believed. Such a situation, as Russell realized, is not conducive to harmonious human relations.

To avoid holding unjustified beliefs, then, it's important to develop a healthy *common sense skepticism*. Unlike philosophical skepticism, common sense skepticism does not consider everything that lacks certainty suspect. Rather, it considers everything that lacks adequate evidence suspect. Common sense skeptics won't believe something unless they have a good reason for believing it, and their belief will be proportionate to the evidence.

Russell argues that one way to foster such common sense skepticism is to give experts their due. We should not defer to the experts because they are always right—they aren't. But they are more likely to be right than we are. One reason for this is that they are usually privy to more information than we are. Another is that they are usually better judges of that information than we are. They know, for example, what kinds of observations are accurate, what kinds of tests are valid, and what kinds of studies are reliable. Since they are more knowledgeable than we are, their judgments are usually more trustworthy than ours. Consequently:

> There is good reason to doubt a proposition if it conflicts with expert opinion.

But the opinion of experts is superior to our own *only* in their field of expertise. Outside of their specialty, what they say carries no more weight than what anyone else says. Unfortunately, people have a tendency to treat the opinions of experts as authoritative even when they're speaking out of their depth.

For example, Clive Backster was one of the FBI's foremost lie detector experts. One day while sitting in his office, he decided to see what would happen if he put a lie detector on his philodendron. After the machine was attached, he decided to see what would happen if he burned one of its leaves. To his surprise, just as he formulated this idea, the lie detector jumped off the scale. Backster concluded that his philodendron was responding to his thoughts! After conducting a number of other experiments, he published his results in an article entitled "Evidence of a Primary Perception in Plant Life."[20] Backster's experiments and others like them were chronicled in a 1975 book by Peter Tompkins and Christopher Bird called *The Secret Life of Plants*, which became an international best seller. As a result of the claims made in this book, people all over the world began playing music and talking to their plants. When scientists tried to replicate Backster's results, however, they failed.[21] It turned out that his experiments had not been conducted with adequate controls. Backster may have been an

Men will cease to commit atrocities only when they cease to believe absurdities.
— VOLTAIRE

expert in the use of the lie detector, but that did not make him an expert in scientific method or plant physiology. What this shows is that:

> Just because someone is an expert
> in one field doesn't mean that he
> or she is an expert in another.

Just as disturbing as our tendency to treat experts in one area as experts in another is our tendency to treat nonexperts as experts, especially when they're famous. You may have heard the television commercial for a medicine that began, "I'm not a doctor, but I play one on TV, and I recommend . . ." Playing a doctor on television hardly qualifies someone as a medical expert. Consequently any medical advice he offers should be taken with a grain of salt.

To cite a nonexpert as an expert is to make a *fallacious appeal to authority*. It's fallacious because it doesn't provide the type of evidence it purports to. Instead, it attempts to deceive us about the quality of the evidence presented. To avoid being taken in by this kind of subterfuge, we need to know what makes someone an expert.

An expert is someone who knows some of the worst mistakes that can be made in his subject, and how to avoid them.
— WERNER HEISENBERG

Contrary to what the Wizard of Oz says, being an expert requires more than having a certain piece of paper. Where the paper comes from is also important. The opinions of people with degrees from institutions that advertise on the inside of matchbook covers are not as credible as those of people with degrees from Ivy League institutions. But even having a degree from a reputable institution does not necessarily qualify you as an expert, especially if you have never practiced in the field in which you offer expert opinion. The designation "expert" is something you earn by showing that your judgments are reliable. To be considered an expert, you must have demonstrated an ability to correctly interpret data and arrive at conclusions that are justified by the evidence. In other words, you must have shown yourself capable of distinguishing truth from falsehood in a particular field. If you have a good education but make faulty judgments, you can't be considered an expert. A good indication of the quality of someone's judgment is to be found in the recognition he or she has received from his or her peers. The views of those who have achieved positions of authority or won prestigious awards are to be trusted more than those who have not, for such distinctions are usually a mark of intellectual virtue.

Expert testimony, like any testimony, is credible only to the extent that it is unbiased. If there is reason to believe that an expert is motivated by something other than the search for truth, there is good reason to doubt his or her testimony. If, for example, the expert has

The Botanical Witness

Here's one of Backster's more intriguing experiments, as described in *The Secret Life of Plants*:

To see if a plant could display memory, a scheme was devised whereby Backster was to try to identify the secret killer of one of two plants. Six of Backster's polygraph students volunteered for the experiment, some of them veteran policemen. Blindfolded, the students drew from a hat folded slips of paper, on one of which were instructions to root up, stamp on, and thoroughly destroy one of two plants in a room. The criminal was to commit the crime in secret; neither Backster nor any of the other students was to know his identity; only the second plant would be a witness. By attaching the surviving plant to a polygraph and parading the students one by one before it, Backster was able to establish the culprit. Sure enough, the plant gave no reaction to five of the students, but caused the meter to go wild whenever the actual culprit approached. Backster was careful to point out that the plant could have picked up and reflected the guilt feelings of the culprit; but as the villain had acted in the interests of science, and was not particularly guilty, it left the possibility that a plant could remember and recognize the source of severe harm to its fellow."[22]

Do our lawns recognize us? How about the weeds in our gardens?

something to gain or lose by espousing one position rather than another, that expert's testimony cannot be trusted. Where there is a conflict of interest, there are reasonable grounds for doubt. When considering the opinions of others, then, we must always look for the presence of bias.

According to Russell, any proposition that flies in the face of expert opinion cannot be certain. More importantly, since credible opinion to the contrary provides reasonable grounds for doubt, any proposition that flies in the face of expert opinion cannot be known (unless, of course, we can show beyond a reasonable doubt that the experts are mistaken). These considerations have important implications for our beliefs about weird things. Such beliefs often conflict with expert opinion. When they do, we cannot claim to know them. We can believe them, but without adequate evidence showing that the experts are mistaken, we cannot know them. If we do claim to know them, it is *we* who are weird.

When you know a thing, hold that you know it; when you know not a thing, allow that you know it not; this is knowledge.
— CONFUCIUS

COHERENCE AND JUSTIFICATION

Ordinarily, if a proposition fails to cohere with the rest of our beliefs, we are not justified in believing it. So coherence is a necessary condition for justification. But is it also sufficient? If a proposition coheres with the rest of our beliefs, are we justified in believing it? Remarkably enough, the answer to this question is no. Just because a proposition coheres with our beliefs, it is not necessarily likely to be true.

To see this, consider the case of David Koresh, the former leader of the Branch Davidians, who died when the cult's headquarters near Waco, Texas, burned down in 1993. Koresh believed that he was Jesus Christ. He maintained that this belief was based on a coherent interpretation of the scriptures. Suppose it was. And suppose that everything else that he believed cohered with that belief. Does that mean that he was justified in believing that he was God? Of course not. Just because someone consistently believes something doesn't mean that it's likely to be true.

But suppose that it wasn't only Koresh that believed he was God; suppose (as is likely) that all of his followers did, too. Does that justify his belief that he is God? Does the number of people who believe a proposition increase its likelihood? Again, the answer is no. When it comes to knowledge, there is no safety in numbers. Even if a large number of people consistently believe something, its credibility may be negligible.

If cohering with a certain group's beliefs justified a proposition, then both a proposition and its negation could be equally justified because both could be consistently believed by different groups. Do we want to say that Koresh's position is or could be just as justified as the denial of his position (as long as *that* is part of a coherent belief system)? If we do, we must give up the notion that justification is a reliable indication of truth because whatever justification a proposition had, its denial could have as well. The price for taking coherence to be a sufficient condition for justification, then, is rather high.

Coherence alone is not enough for justification because a coherent set of propositions may not be grounded in reality. A fairy tale may be coherent, but that doesn't justify our believing it. Since justification is supposed to be a reliable guide to the truth, and since truth is grounded in reality, there must be more to justification than mere coherence.

SOURCES OF KNOWLEDGE

Perception has traditionally been considered our most reliable guide to the truth. That perception is considered a source of knowledge should not surprise us, for most of our information about the world comes to us through our senses. If our senses weren't reliable, we could not have survived as long as we have. But even though senses are reliable, they're not infallible. The existence of illusions and hallucinations demonstrates that our senses can't always be trusted.

Illusions and hallucinations occur only under certain circumstances, however. Only when we, our tools, or our environment are in a state that impedes the accurate flow of information do our senses lead us astray. For example, if we are injured, anxious, or drugged; if our glasses are cracked, our hearing aid broken, or our measuring devices malfunctioning; or if it is dark, noisy, or foggy, then our observations may be mistaken. But if we have good reason to believe that no such impediments to accurate perception are present, then we have good reason to believe what we perceive.

Just as perception is considered a source of knowledge about the external world, introspection is considered a source of knowledge about the internal world, that is, about our mental states. Some have considered this source of knowledge to be infallible. We may be mistaken about many things, they argue, but we cannot be mistaken about the contents of our own minds. We may be mistaken, for example, about whether we see a tree, but we cannot be mistaken about whether we *seem* to see a tree. But we must be careful here. While we may infallibly *know what* our experience is like, we may not infallibly *know that* it is of a certain sort. In other words, we may miscategorize or misdescribe what we experience. Infatuation, for example, may be mistaken for love, jealousy for envy, rage for anger. So the beliefs we form through introspection about our current experience are not infallible.

Similarly, the beliefs we form through introspection about our dispositional mental states are not infallible. There are certain mental states (like believing, wanting, hoping, fearing, and so on) that we may be in even though we are not currently feeling or doing anything in particular. Such states are called *dispositional* because to be in them is to have a tendency to feel or do certain things under certain conditions. For example, if you are afraid of snakes, you will normally have a tendency to feel fear and run away when you see one. Unfortunately, we can deceive ourselves about our dispositional mental states. We may believe, for example, that we are in love when we really aren't. Or we may believe that we don't have a certain desire when we really do. Since introspection is not error free, it is not an infallible source of knowledge about our mental states.

Though introspection is fallible, it can still be trusted. Our beliefs about our mental states are about as certain as they come. We rarely misdescribe our current mental states, and when we do, the fault often

All our knowledge has its origins in our perceptions.
—LEONARDO DA VINCI

lies not with our faculty of introspection, but with our carelessness or inattentiveness.[23] While mistakes regarding our dispositional mental states are more common, they, too, can often be traced to our being in an abnormal state. Normally, then, beliefs arrived at through introspection are justified. As long as we have no reason to doubt what our introspection tells us, we are justified in believing it.

Although much of what we know originates in introspection and perception, we have to rely on our memory to preserve and retrieve that information. So memory is also a source of knowledge, not in the sense of generating it, but in the sense of transmitting it. Normally memory performs its functions without error. But, as we saw in Chapter 3, situations can arise where the information entrusted to it is mishandled. We may forget certain details of events we've experienced or we may embellish them with imaginative flourishes. We may even seem to remember events that never happened. Psychologist Jean Piaget had a vivid memory of his nurse fighting off a kidnapper on the Champs-Elysées when he was only two. Years later, his nurse confessed in a letter to his parents that she made up the whole story about that event. Even though our memory is fallible, it's not totally unreliable. If we seem to clearly remember something, then, as long as we have no good reason to doubt it, we are justified in believing it.

Reason has also been considered a source of knowledge, for it too can reveal how things are. Consider the proposition, "Whatever has a shape has a size." We know that it's true, but we don't have to perform any experiments or gather any data to see that it is. Through the use of reason alone we can see that these concepts necessarily go together. Reason is the ability we have to discern the logical relationships between concepts and propositions. Reason shows us, for example, that if A is bigger than B, and B is bigger than C, then A is bigger than C.

As with introspection, some think that reason is an infallible guide to the truth. History has taught us otherwise, however. Many propositions once thought to be self-evident are now known to be false. That every event has a cause, that every property determines a class, that every true mathematical theorem has a proof were all thought, at one time, to be self-evident. We now know that they're not. Even the clear light of reason does not shine only on the truth.

But most of the time, reason is not wrong. What seems to be self-evident usually is. Self-evident propositions are ones whose denial is unthinkable, like "Whatever has a shape has a size." To understand a self-evident proposition is to believe that it's true. If someone denies a self-evident proposition, the burden of proof is on them to provide a counterexample. If they can't, their denial is groundless. So in the ab-

Everyone complains of his memory, and no one complains of his judgment.
—La Rochefoucauld

Reason in man is rather like God in the world.
—St. Thomas Aquinas

sence of any evidence to the contrary, we are justified in believing what reason reveals.

The traditional sources of knowledge—perception, introspection, memory, and reason—are not infallible guides to the truth, for our interpretation of them can be negatively affected by all sorts of conditions, many beyond our control. But if we have no reason to believe that such conditions are present, then we have no reason to doubt what these sources of knowledge tell us. The principle that emerges from these considerations is this:

> If we have no reason to doubt what's disclosed to us through perception, introspection, memory, or reason, then we're justified in believing it.

In other words, the traditional sources of knowledge are innocent until proven guilty. Only if we have good reason for believing that they are not functioning properly should we doubt them.

THE APPEAL TO FAITH

"Faith," as it is ordinarily understood, is "belief that does not rest on logical proof or material evidence."[24] To believe something on faith is to believe it in spite of, or even because of, the fact that we have insufficient evidence for it. No one has expressed this cavalier attitude toward evidence better than Tertullian: "It is to be believed," he said, "because it is absurd."[25] St. Thomas Aquinas considered faith to be superior to opinion because it is free from doubt, but inferior to knowledge because it lacks rational justification. In the case of faith, the gap between belief and evidence is filled by an act of will—we choose to believe something even though that belief isn't warranted by the evidence. Can such a belief be a source of knowledge? No, for we cannot make something true by believing it to be true. The fact that we believe something doesn't justify our believing it. Faith, in the sense we are considering, is unquestioning, unjustified belief, and unjustified belief cannot constitute knowledge.

The problem with the appeal to faith is that it is unenlightening; it may tell us something about the person making the appeal, but it tells us nothing about the proposition in question. Suppose someone presses you about why you believe something and you say, "My belief is based on faith." Does this help us evaluate the truth of your belief? No. To say that you believe something on faith is not to offer any justification for it; in fact, you are admitting that you have no justification. Since believing something on faith doesn't help us determine the plausibility of a proposition, faith can't be a source of knowledge.

Faith is used not only to denote a kind of belief in propositions but also a kind of trust in people. When we say, "I have faith in you," we mean that we have trust or confidence in you. Often this trust is justified. If you've acted responsibly in the past, then we have good reason to believe that you will do so in the future. Sometimes, however, we have to trust people who haven't earned it. If trusting such a one is the only way to get out of a predicament, we may have no choice but to do so, hoping that the trust will be vindicated. Unfortunately, there is no guarantee that it will.

Some claim, however, that even when we have no evidence of a person's character or attitudes, faith in that person can still be rational because that faith may bring the desired character trait or attitude into existence. Philosopher and psychologist William James provides the following example of what is called *precursive faith*:

> *Do you like me or not?*—for example. Whether you do or not depends, in countless instances, on whether I meet you half-way, am willing to assume that you must like me, and show you trust and expectation. The previous faith on my part in your liking's existence is in such cases what makes your liking come. But if I stand aloof, and refuse to budge an inch until I have objective evidence . . . ten to one your liking never comes.[26]

Although I have no evidence that you like me, if I believe that you do, you may come to do so. This shows, says James, that belief without evidence can be rational. Since unfounded beliefs can bring about desirable consequences, James believes that only a fool would not have unfounded beliefs.

But are these beliefs really unfounded? No, for they are based on well-known facts about human behavior. We know, for example, that if we treat people with kindness and respect, they will usually return the favor. This knowledge was gained through experience and serves as the evidence upon which our precursive faith rests. Far from being groundless, then, precursive faith is actually well-rooted in our knowledge of human nature. James is right in claiming that the decision to show kindness to strangers can be rational. He is wrong, however, in claiming that no evidence supports such a decision.

Moreover, James's claim that our faith can transform others is misleading. It is not our faith that brings about the change; it is our behavior. By *acting* as if we like someone, we may get them to like us. For such a strategy to work, however, it is not necessary that we actually like them. All that is required is that we get them to believe that we

Mind Viruses

Biologist Richard Dawkins, author of *The Selfish Gene* and *The Blind Watchmaker*, argues that certain thoughts can function in the mind like computer viruses in a computer, subverting its normal functioning. The thought that faith is a source of knowledge, he argues, is one such:

> Like computer viruses, successful mind viruses will tend to be hard for their victims to detect. If you are the victim of one, the chances are that you won't know it, and may even vigorously deny it. Accepting that a virus might be difficult to detect in your own mind, what telltale signs might you look out for? I shall answer by imagining how a medical textbook might describe the typical symptoms of a sufferer (arbitrarily assumed to be male).
>
> 1. The patient typically finds himself impelled by some deep, inner conviction that something is true, or right, or virtuous: a conviction that doesn't seem to owe anything to evidence or reason, but which, nevertheless, he feels as totally compelling and convincing. We doctors refer to such a belief as "faith.". . .
>
> 2. Patients typically make a positive virtue of faith's being strong and unshakable, in spite of not being based upon evidence. Indeed, they may feel that the less evidence there is, the more virtuous the belief. . . .
>
> 3. A related symptom, which a faith-sufferer may also present, is the conviction that "mystery," *per se,* is a good thing. It is not a virtue to solve mysteries. Rather we should enjoy them, even revel in their insolubility . . . .
>
> 4. The sufferer may find himself behaving intolerantly toward vectors of rival faiths, in extreme cases even killing them or advocating their deaths. He may be similarly violent in his disposition toward apostates (people who once held the faith but have renounced it); or toward heretics (people who espouse a different—often, perhaps significantly, only very slightly different—version of the faith). He may also feel hostile toward other modes of thought that are potentially inimical to his faith, such as the method of scientific reason that may function rather like a piece of antiviral software.[27]

like them. It's our actions rather than our beliefs that produces the desired results.

James is trying to drive a wedge between rationality and evidence by purporting to show that there are situations where belief without evidence is rational. But the examples he gives do not show this. Moreover, his project seems doomed from the start, for just as you cannot coherently present a logical argument showing that logic is ineffectual, so you cannot coherently provide evidence for a position claiming that evidence is unnecessary. If a belief is rational, there is some reason to hold it, and if there is some reason to hold it, there is some evidence in its favor. Since belief without evidence is not rational,

They who imagine truth in untruth and see untruth in truth, never arrive at truth, but follow vain desires.

—THE DHAMMAPADA

faith is not rational. But as we've learned, only rational belief can yield knowledge. So faith *cannot* be a source of knowledge.

THE APPEAL TO INTUITION

Intuition is sometimes claimed to be a source of knowledge. "How did you know that they would get married?" we might ask. "I knew by intuition," might be the reply. But what sort of thing is this intuition? Is it a sixth sense? Are those who claim to know by intuition claiming to have extrasensory perception? Perhaps they are, but to take such a claim seriously, we would need evidence showing that there is such a thing as ESP and that it is a reliable guide to the truth. Without such evidence, intuition in this sense can't be considered a source of knowledge.

But the claim to know by intuition need not be construed as a claim to possess ESP. It can instead be construed as a claim to possess what might be called HSP — hypersensory perception. Some people, like the fictional Sherlock Holmes, are much more perceptive than others. They notice things that others don't and consequently make inferences that others may think are unwarranted but really aren't — they are simply based on data that most people aren't aware of. To know by intuition that a couple will get married, for example, you need not have read their minds. You need only to have noticed them exhibiting some of those subtle behaviors that indicate true love.

One of the most remarkable examples of HSP comes from the animal kingdom. In 1904, a retired Berlin school teacher, Wilhelm von Osten, claimed that his horse — who came to be known as "Clever Hans" — possessed an intelligence equivalent to humans. He seemed to be able to correctly answer arithmetic problems, tell time, and correctly recognize photographs of people he had met, among other things. Clever Hans would answer the questions put to him by tapping his hoof. He had learned the alphabet, and when he was asked a word-problem, he would spell out the answer in German by tapping once for "A," twice for "B," and so on. A panel of thirteen of the best scientists in Germany rigorously tested Clever Hans to determine whether his master was somehow communicating the answers to him. Since he performed almost as well without his master as with him, they concluded in their report that Clever Hans was a genuine phenomenon worthy of the most serious scientific consideration.

One of those assisting in this investigation, however, remained skeptical. Oskar Pfungst couldn't believe that a horse possessed such extraordinary intellectual powers. What made him skeptical was the fact that Clever Hans would not get the right answer when the answer was unknown to any of those present or when he was unable to see those who did know the right answer. Pfungst concluded that the horse needed some sort of visual aid. The remarkable thing was, the aid did not have to be given intentionally.[28]

It turns out that Hans would get the right answer by attending to very subtle changes in people's posture — some of those changes were by less than one fifth of a millimeter. Those who knew the answer, for example, would unconsciously tense their muscles until Hans produced it. Hans perceived this tension and used it as a cue. Pfungst learned to consciously make the same body movements that were unconsciously made by Hans's examiners and was thus able to elicit from Hans all of his various reactions without asking him any questions or giving him any commands.[29] This showed beyond a reasonable doubt that Clever Hans's cleverness lay not in his intellectual prowess but in his perceptual acuity.

Our ability to perceive subtle behavioral cues is no less remarkable than Clever Hans's. Psychologist Robert Rosenthal has studied this ability in depth. In an attempt to determine the extent to which psychological experimenters can nonverbally influence their subjects, he devised the following experiment. Student subjects were asked to look at photographs of ten people and rate them in terms of their success or failure. The scale ranged from +10 (extreme success) to −10 (extreme failure). The photographs used had been independently determined to elicit a success rating of close to 0 from most people. The experimenters were told that their task was to replicate the results achieved in previous experiments. They were paid one dollar an hour for conducting the experiment, but were promised two dollars an hour if they achieved the desired results. One group of experimenters was told that the people in the photographs had received an average rating of +5 in previous experiments while the other group was told that they had received an average rating of −5. The experimenters were not allowed to talk to their subjects; they could read the experimental instructions to them but could say nothing else. Without telling their subjects how to evaluate the people in the photographs, the experimenters who expected high scores nevertheless received higher scores than any of those who expected low ones.[30] This result has been repeated in other similar experiments.[31] How did the subjects know what ratings the experimenters wanted? By attending to subtle behavioral cues. Call it intuition if you will, but it is really nothing more than acute sensory perception.

It is these sorts of experimenter effects that those investigating ESP must be particularly wary of. Any experiment that does not eliminate them cannot provide evidence for ESP, for the results obtained could be due to experimenter signaling. Early telepathy experiments

The Strange Case of Ilga K.

Clever Hans is not alone in his ability to correctly interpret minute muscular movements in humans. Ilga Kirks could correctly interpret the lip and throat movements made by people thinking to themselves. Until this peculiar form of hypersensory awareness was discovered, she was thought to be telepathic. Here is psychologists Leonard Zusne and Warner Jones's description of the strange case of Ilga K.:

> In 1935, the Director of the Forensic Institute of the Latvian State University in Riga, Dr. F. von Neureiter, published a monograph describing his experimental observations of a 9-year-old mentally retarded (I.Q. of 48) Latvian girl, Ilga Kirks, who supposedly was able to read the thoughts of her teacher and mother as well as other individuals. Even though she had great difficulty

reading Latvian from a book, she could read Latvian as well as foreign languages rather fluently if these were read silently by another person. Von Neureiter thought that the girl had genuine telepathic ability, and the case of Ilga K., as she is referred to in the literature, became well known both in Latvia and abroad. In 1936 and 1937, a specially formed Commission, made up of 13 professionals representing psychology, physics, medicine, and speech and hearing disorders, conducted an extensive series of tests of Ilga K. Some of these were conducted in a soundproof room and in a Faraday cage (an insulated cubicle that keeps out electromagnetic waves). In their report, the Commission concluded that no paranormality was involved in Ilga's ability.

did not take these effects into account, and consequently their results are unconvincing. Simon Newcomb, first president of the American Society for Psychical Research and a distinguished astronomer, describes one of these early experiments: "When the agent drew cards from a pack one by one, and at each drawing the percipient named a card at random, it was found that the proportion of correct guesses was much greater than it should have been as the result of chance, which would, of course, be 1 out of 52."[33] If the percipient could see the agent, however, the success of the experiment could be due to hypersensory perception rather than extrasensory perception. These experimental results thus do not provide evidence for ESP. An experiment can provide evidence for extraordinary abilities only if its results can't be accounted for in terms of ordinary abilities.

ASTROLOGY REVISITED

Now that we have a better idea of what's involved in making claims about knowledge, what are we to make of astrology? Is it reasonable

When the agent was Ilga's mother, the word that the mother was thinking of was "sent" to her daughter by breaking it down into separate phonemes and tacking these onto the ends of the words of encouragement uttered by the mother. Ilga would pick them out and put them together into a whole word. When the mother was made to keep quiet or was isolated in a soundproof room, Ilga failed to receive, or else was only partly successful by using the highly expressive gestures and lip movements of the mother. Ilga was most successful with individuals who strongly moved their lips, tongue,and larynx while thinking or reading, which was the case with her teacher who had first brought Ilga's ability to the attention of the scientists. She could learn nothing from her mathematics teacher, whose subvocal speech was very weak, but a special teacher assigned by the Latvian Commission to tutor Ilga at home learned the communication method that Ilga and her mother were using and was able to replicate and even better the mother's performance. Ilga's ability was apparently one that she had developed on her own to compensate for her rather severe intellectual deficit. In spite of the fact that the Latvian Commission's work leaves not the slightest doubt as to the true nature of Ilga K.'s phenomenon, and the additional fact that von Neureiter was one of the Commission's members, some parapsychologists still present her case as a genuine case of telepathy ignoring the Commission's report altogether.[32]

to believe that the position of the stars and planets at the time and place of your birth controls your destiny? Let's examine the evidence.

Astrology, as noted above, was invented by the Babylonians as a means of foretelling the future. Their belief was (and the belief of present-day astrologers is) that each person's physical and emotional makeup is caused, not by their heredity and environment, but by the particular arrangement of stars and planets at their birth. Given what the Babylonians knew about the universe at that time, such a view was not unreasonable. Anyone can see that the position of heavenly bodies is correlated with the seasons. The belief that heavenly bodies cause the seasons is therefore quite a natural one. And if heavenly bodies control the Earth's destiny, maybe they control ours as well. Although such a view makes sense from a Babylonian perspective, the question is whether it makes sense from ours.

There is no evidence that the Babylonian astrologers established the alleged correlations between personal characteristics and star positions by conducting statistical surveys. They do not appear to have sent out questionnaires asking people to describe themselves and to

I shall always consider the best guesser the best prophet.

—Marcus Tullius Cicero

give the time and place of their birth. Rather, it appears that they assumed that those born under the influence of a particular planet or constellation would acquire the characteristics of the person, god, or animal for which the planet or constellation was named.[34] Thus people born under the sign of Aries, for example, are said to be ramlike — courageous, impetuous, and energetic — while those born under the sign of Taurus are said to be oxlike — patient, persistent, and obstinate.[35]

St. Augustine, one of the patriarchs of the Roman Catholic Church, realized long ago that if the stars really determined our fate, then astral twins (people who are born at the same time and place) should lead the same sort of lives. When he learned of a pair of astral twins — a slave and an aristocrat — who were as different as night and day, he gave up his belief in astrology and became an outspoken critic of it. The twins, for him, were conclusive proof that our destiny is not written in the stars.

In our century, many attempts have been made to statistically verify the predictions of astrology, but none has succeeded. Psychologists Zusne and Jones describe some of these studies:

> In 1937, Farnsworth failed to find any correspondence between artistic talent and either the ascendant sign or the sun in the sign of Libra for the birth dates of 2000 famous painters and musicians. Bok and Mayall (1941) found no predominance of any one sign of the zodiac among scientists listed in a directory of scientists, the *American Men of Science.* Barth and Bennett (1973) did a statistical study on whether more men who had chosen a military career had been born under the influence of the planet Mars than men who had chosen non-military careers. They found no such relationship. Very large numbers of birth dates were used by McGervey (1977), who tabulated the number of scientists and politicians (a total of 16,634 scientists and 6,475 politicians) born on each day of the year, and found no astrological sign favoring either one of the callings. . . . In another recent study, Bastedo (1978) tested statistically whether persons with such characteristics as leadership ability, liberalism/conservatism, intelligence, and 30 other variables, many of them attributed to astral influence, would cluster on certain birth dates — that is, according to the astrological sign that governs the appropriate characteristics. The results for a 1000-person, cross sectional, stratified cluster sample taken from the San Francisco Bay area were entirely negative.[36]

More recent research confirms these findings. R. B. Culver and P. A. Ianna surveyed hundreds of people to determine if there is any truth to the astrologists' claim that there is a correlation between sun sign (the zone of the zodiac that the sun was in when you were born) and physical features. They studied such attributes as neck size, skin

Julius Caesar — A Confirming Instance?

A Caesarean section is a method for delivering a baby that involves cutting through the mother's abdominal and uterine walls. The procedure is so named because Julius Caesar was supposedly born this way. But legend has it that the procedure was performed not for medical reasons, but for astrological ones. It seems that Caesar's mother had consulted an astrologer to determine the most propitious time to have a baby. After a thorough study of the heavens, the astrologer identified a time and place of birth that would result in a child that was destined for fame and fortune. When the time came, the story goes, Caesar's mother ordered a doctor to surgically remove the infant Caesar. And as we all know, the prophecy came true. Does this story improve the credibility of astrology?

complexion, body build, height, and weight. Contrary to what the astrologers would have us believe, no set of physical features occurred more in one sign than another.[37]

Professional astrologers might find these studies unconvincing because they focus on the sun sign rather than the astrological chart. To get an accurate prediction, they might argue, the positions of the planets at the time of birth must also be taken into account. When this is done, however, the results are still negative. For his doctoral dissertation at North Texas State University, Jonus Noblitt tried to determine if the angular relations among planets could predict an individual's personality traits. He gave 155 volunteers the 16PF personality questionnaire and compared the results with their horoscopes. None of the predictions of astrology were born out by the data.[38] David Fourie, Charles Coetzee, and Darby Costello gave two prominent South African astrologers the sex, birth place, and times of birth of sixteen men and thirty-four women. Their task was to construct a personality profile for each of these people on the basis of their horoscope. The profiles arrived at by the two astrologers not only did not agree with each other, they also did not agree with the results of a 16PF personality test given to each subject.[39]

Geoffrey Dean and Arthur Mather, after reviewing over 700 astrology books and 300 scientific works on astrology, concluded:

> Astrology today is based on concepts of unknown origin but effectively deified as "tradition." Their application involves numerous systems, most of them disagreeing on fundamental issues, and all of them supported by anecdotal evidence of the most unreliable kind. In effect, astrology

You can make a better living in the world as a soothsayer than as a truthsayer.

— GEORGE LICHTENBERG

presents a dazzling and technically sound superstructure supported by unproven beliefs; it starts with fantasy and then proceeds entirely logically. Speculation is rife, as are a profusion of new factors (each more dramatically "valid" than the last) to be conveniently considered where they reinforce the case and ignored otherwise.[40]

There is simply no reliable data establishing any of astrology's claims.

Not only is there no trustworthy evidence supporting astrology, but the very notion that stars and planets determine our physical and psychological makeup conflicts with a good deal of what we know about human physiology and psychology. Research has shown that our physical characteristics are determined by the information encoded in our genes. All of the tissues in our body are manufactured according to this information, and all of our genes are present in the fertilized egg from which we developed. So our basic physical constitution is determined by our genes at the moment of conception—not by the heavens at the moment of birth, as astrologers would have us believe.

Our genes also play a role in determining our personality, but they are not the only factor involved: upbringing and early childhood experiences are important as well. The position of the stars or planets at the time of birth, however, seems to have little effect on our psyches. Only one study seems to suggest otherwise. Michel Gauquelin, a French scientist who spent years investigating astrology only to conclude that it's bogus, nevertheless claims to have found a correlation between planetary positions at birth and certain careers. His data suggest, for example, that more sports champions are born when Mars is rising or culminating than would be expected by chance alone. Similarly, Jupiter is correlated with the birth of actors and politicians while Saturn is correlated with the birth of scientists and physicians.[41]

Some astrologers believe that Gauquelin's research vindicates astrology. John West and Jan Toonder, for example, claim that "Gauquelin's work proves once and for all, and incontestably, that there is *something* to astrology."[42] Gauquelin himself is very clear that his results do nothing of the sort:

> Every attempt, whether of astrologers or scientists, to produce evidence of astrological laws, has been in vain. It is now quite certain that the signs in the sky which presided over our births have no power whatever to decide our fates, to affect our heredity, characteristics, or to play any part however humble in the totality of effects, random and otherwise, which form the fabric of our lives and mold our impulses to action.[43]

Gauquelin's findings don't vindicate astrology because the correlations he found were not those predicted by astrology. So even if the correlations exist, they don't support astrology.

More important, the existence of these correlations doesn't prove that the planets affect our personalities because correlation doesn't prove causation. Rises in the stock market are correlated with rises in women's hemlines, but few would want to claim that one causes the other. To establish a cause-and-effect relationship, you must establish a theory that accounts for the correlation better than its rivals, and that Gauquelin has not done.

He has proposed a theory, however.[44] Gauquelin speculates that children inherit from their parents a tendency to be born when a certain planet is rising or culminating in the same way that they inherit artistic or athletic ability. The fetus senses the position of the planet by sensing subtle changes in the earth's magnetic field. The changes in the earth's magnetic field are caused by changes in solar activity, which are caused by the position of the planets. So Gauquelin's theory involves four separate claims: (a) the position of the planets affects solar activity, (b) solar activity affects the earth's magnetic field, (c) the earth's magnetic field affects when a fetus is born, and (d) people with similar electromagnetic sensitivities will pursue similar careers.

Gauquelin believes that fetuses with different genetic structures respond differently to electromagnetic radiation, just as people with different skin colors respond differently to solar radiation. When the right sort of electromagnetic field is present, fetuses with the right sort of genetic structure change in ways that induce labor. Since other abilities are also determined (at least in part) by genetics, there will be a correlation between planetary positions and careers. Gauquelin's claim, then, is that *if* planetary position affects solar activity in the right way, *if* solar activity affects the earth's electromagnetic field in the right way, *if* the earth's electromagnetic field affects fetuses in the right way, and *if* genetic structure affects career choice in the right way, then there will be a correlation between planetary positions and careers. That's a lot of ifs. None of them has been established, but at least they provide a direction for future research.

You can only predict things after they've happened.
—Eugene Ionesco

It is the difficulty of explaining how stars and planets could possibly influence our personalities and careers that makes the claims of astrology so hard to swallow. To the best of our knowledge, the universe contains only four forces — gravity, electromagnetism, the strong nuclear force, and the weak nuclear force. Everything that happens in the world results from the action of one or more of these forces. The range of the strong and weak nuclear forces, however, is very limited — they can only affect things in and around atoms. So if stars and planets affect us, it cannot be by their means.

That leaves gravity and electromagnetism. Their range is potentially unlimited. But the strength of these forces diminishes the farther they get from their source. The gravitational and electromagnetic forces reaching us from the stars and planets are extremely weak. The book you are now reading, for example, exerts a gravitational force about a billion times greater at the point you're holding it than does Mars when it is closest to the Earth. Similarly the electromagnetic radiation from the radio and television transmitters all around us is hundreds of millions of times greater than that from the planets.[45] Thus there is no known way that stars or planets could significantly affect us. That's not to say that they don't; it's just to say that no one has given us a plausible theory of how they do.

In 1975, 186 scientists published a letter alerting the public to the fact that there is no evidence for the claims of astrology. They proclaimed:

> We, the undersigned—astronomers, astrophysicists, and scientists in other fields—wish to caution the public against the unquestioning acceptance of the predictions and advice given privately and publicly by astrologers. Those who wish to believe in astrology should realize that there is no scientific foundation for its tenets. . . . It is simply a mistake to imagine that the forces exerted by stars and planets at the moment of birth can in any way shape our futures. Neither is it true that the position of distant heavenly bodies make certain days or periods more favorable to particular kinds of action, or that the sign under which one was born determines one's compatibility or incompatibility with other people.[46]

Unfortunately, the letter seems to have had little effect. A 1984 Gallup Poll found that 55 percent of American teenagers believe that astrology works. Even more ominous, during the 1980s, then President Ronald Reagan was making decisions regarding affairs of state on the basis of astrological predictions.[47]

Why, with so little evidence to support it, do people continue to believe in astrology? For one thing, most people are probably unaware of the many studies that have found no substantiation for astrology. These studies have not received much media coverage, and newspapers running astrology columns don't usually preface them with caveats such as "for entertainment purposes only." For another, astrologers like to give the impression that it all makes perfectly good scientific sense. Linda Goodman, for example, writes, "Science recognizes the Moon's power to move great bodies of water. Since man himself consists of seventy percent water, why should he be immune to such forceful planetary pulls?"[48] He isn't. But as we have seen, the effect must be negligible given the miniscule level of the force, and there is no reason to believe that extraterrestrial gravity significantly affects our physical or psychological development.

Why, then, does belief in astrology persist? Some, like the scientists objecting to its widespread acceptance, claim that its appeal derives from the diminished sense of personal responsibility it provides:

> In these uncertain times many long for the comfort of having guidance in making decisions. They would like to believe in a destiny predetermined by astral forces beyond their control. However, we must all face the world, and we must realize that our futures lie in ourselves, and not in the stars.[49]

Others believe that its appeal derives from an increased sense of unity it provides. Historian Theodore Roszak writes: "The modern fascination with astrology — even in its crudest forms — stems from a growing nostalgia for that older, more unified sense of nature in which the sun, moon and stars were experienced as a vast network of living consciousness."[50] There is probably an element of truth in both of these assessments.

Many people probably find astrology appealing because it seems to describe them accurately. It seems to do so because the descriptions offered are so general that they apply to practically everybody (see the discussion of the Forer effect in Chapter 3). One of the most dramatic examples of the Forer effect comes from Michel Gauquelin. Gauquelin placed an advertisement in a French newspaper offering a personalized horoscope to anyone who would send him their name, address, birthday, and birthplace. About 150 people responded to the ad, and Gauquelin sent them a ten-page horoscope, a questionnaire, and a return envelope. The horoscope read, in part, as follows:

> As he is a Virgo-Jovian, instinctive warmth of power is allied with the resources of the intellect, lucidity, wit. . . . He may appear as someone who submits himself to social norms, fond of property, and endowed with a moral sense which is comforting — that of a worthy, right-thinking, middle-class citizen. . . . The subject tends to belong wholeheartedly to the Venusian side. His emotional life is in the forefront — his affection towards others, his family ties, his home, his intimate circle . . . sentiments . . . which usually find their expression in total devotion to others, redeeming love, or altruistic sacrifices . . . a tendency to be more pleasant in one's own home, to love one's house, to enjoy having a charming home.[51]

Ninety-four percent of those who returned the questionnaire said that the horoscope described them accurately, and 90 percent said that their friends and relatives agreed with that assessment. The horoscope, however, was that of notorious mass murderer, Dr. Marcel Petoit, who lured unsuspecting Nazi escapees into his home with promises of aid only to rob them, murder them, and dissolve their bodies in quicklime. He was accused of twenty-seven murders but boasted of sixty-three. Funny that so many fine upstanding citizens of France would claim the horoscope of a mass murderer as their own.

How, then, should we think about astrology? The first thing to note is that no one can legitimately claim to know that astrology is true. Such a claim conflicts with expert opinion, and, as we have seen, claims that conflict with expert opinion cannot be known (unless it can be shown beyond a reasonable doubt that the experts are mistaken). Astrology also conflicts with a lot of our background beliefs. Accepting astrology would mean rejecting large tracts of physics, astronomy, biology, and psychology. When faced with such conflicts, the thing to do is to proportion our belief to the evidence. In the case of astrology, however, there is no evidence to proportion it to, for none of its claims has been verified. So the degree of belief it warrants is negligible.

SUGGESTED READINGS

Audi, Robert. *Belief, Justification, and Knowledge.* Belmont, Calif.: Wadsworth, 1988.

Blanshard, Brand. *Reason and Belief.* New Haven: Yale University Press, 1975.

Chisholm, Roderick. *Theory of Knowledge.* Englewood Cliffs, N.J.: Prentice-Hall, 1988.

Goldman, Alan. *Empirical Knowledge.* Berkeley: University of California Press, 1988.

Russell, Bertrand. *Let the People Think.* London: William Clowes, 1941.

Culver, R. B., and P. A. Ianna. *The Gemini Syndrome: A Scientific Evaluation of Astrology.* Buffalo: Prometheus Books, 1984.

NOTES

1. Proverbs 4:7–9; Francis Bacon, "De Haeiresibus," *Meditationes Sacrae.*
2. Richard Lewinsolhn, *Science, Prophecy, and Prediction* (New York: Harper Brothers, 1961), p. 53.
3. Ibid., p. 54.
4. Ibid., p. 54.
5. Ibid., p. 59.
6. Plato, "Meno," 98b, trans. by W. K. C. Guthrie, ed. Edith Hamilton and Huntington Cairns, *The Collected Works of Plato* (Princeton: Princeton University Press, 1961), p. 382.
7. We sometimes say things which seem to suggest that knowledge doesn't require belief. For example, after winning a prize we might remark, "I know that I won, but I still don't believe it." What we mean, though, is

not that we doubt that we've won the prize, but that we haven't gotten used to the fact that we did. Intellectually we've accepted the situation, but emotionally we haven't.

8. Plato, "Meno," 98a, p. 381.

9. Alan H. Goldman, *Empirical Knowledge* (Berkeley: University of California Press, 1988), p. 52.

10. Ernest Sosa, "Knowledge and Intellectual Virtue," *Monist,* March 1985.

11. For an account of recent attempts to analyze the concept of knowledge, see Robert K. Shope, *The Analysis of Knowing: A Decade of Research* (Princeton: Princeton University Press, 1983).

12. W. K. Clifford, "The Ethics of Belief," in J. Burr and M. Goldinger, *Philosophy and Contemporary Issues* (New York: Macmillan, 1984), p. 142.

13. T. H. Huxley, *Science and Christian Tradition* (London: Macmillan, 1894), p. 310.

14. Brand Blanshard, *Reason and Belief* (New Haven: Yale University Press, 1975), p. 410.

15. Clifford, "Ethics of Belief," p. 142.

16. Bertrand Russell, *Let the People Think* (London: William Clowes, 1941), p. 1.

17. Ibid.

18. Ibid., p. 2.

19. Ibid.

20. Clive Backster, "Evidence of a Primary Perception in Plant Life," *International Journal of Parapsychology,* 10 (1968): 329–48.

21. K. A. Horowitz, D. C. Lewis, and E. L. Gasteiger, "Plant 'Primary Perception': Electrophysical Unresponsiveness to Brine Shrimp Killing," *Science,* 189 (1975): 478–80.

22. Peter Tompkins and Christopher Bird, *The Secret Life of Plants* (New York: Avon Books, 1974). pp. 24–25.

23. Sosa, "Knowledge and Intellectual Virtue," pp. 230ff.

24. *The American Heritage Dictionary of the English Language* (Boston: Houghton Mifflin, 1970), p. 471.

25. Tertullian, "On the Flesh of Christ," *Apology.*

26. William James, "The Will to Believe," in *Philosophy and Contemporary Issues,* ed. by J. Burr and M. Goldinger (New York: Macmillan, 1984), pp. 146–47.

27. Richard Dawkins, "Viruses of the Mind," *Free Inquiry,* 13, no. 3 (Summer 1993): 37–39.

28. Oskar Pfungst, *Clever Hans: The Horse of Mr. von Osten,* ed. Robert Rosenthal (New York: Rinehart and Winston, 1965), p. 261.

29. Ibid., pp. 262–63.

30. Robert Rosenthal, *Experimenter Effects in Behavioral Research* (New York: Irvington Publishers, 1976), pp. 143–46.

31. Ibid., pp. 146–49.

32. Leonard Zusne and Warren H. Jones, *Anomalistic Psychology* (Hillsdale, N.J.: Lawrence Erlbaum Associates, 1982), p. 320.

33. Simon Newcomb, "Modern Occultism," *A Skeptic's Handbook of Parapsychology*, ed. Paul Kurtz (Buffalo: Prometheus Books, 1985), p. 151.

34. George O. Abell, "Astrology," in *Science and the Paranormal* (New York: Scribner's, 1981), pp. 83–84.

35. Ellic Howe, "Astrology," *Man, Myth and Magic*, ed. Richard Cavendish (New York: Marshall Cavendish, 1970), p. 155.

36. Zusne and Jones, *Anomalistic Psychology*, p. 219.

37. R. B. Culver and P. A. Ianna, *The Gemini Syndrome: A Scientific Evaluation of Astrology* (Buffalo: Prometheus Books, 1984).

38. Cited in I. W. Kelly, "Astrology, Cosmobiology, and Humanistic Astrology," in *Philosophy of Science and the Occult*, ed. Patrick Grim (Albany: State University of New York Press, 1982), p. 52.

39. David Fourie, Cas. Coetzee, and Darby Costello, "Astrology and Personality: Sun-sign or Chart?" *South African Journal of Psychology*, 314, no. 10 (1980): 104–6.

40. Geoffrey Dean and Arthur Mather, *Recent Advances in Natal Astrology: A Critical Review 1990–1976* (Rockport: Para Research, 1977), p. 1.

41. Michel Gauquelin, *Cosmic Influences on Human Behavior* (London: Garnstone Press, 1974).

42. John Anthony West and Jan Gerhard Toonder, *The Case for Astrology* (Baltimore: Penguin Press, 1973), p. 172.

43. Michel Gauquelin, *The Scientific Basis of Astrology: Myth or Reality?* (New York: Stein and Day, 1969), p. 145.

44. See Michel Gauquelin, *Cosmic Influences.*

45. George O. Abell, "Astrology," p. 87.

46. "Objections to Astrology," *The Humanist*, 35, no. 5 (September/October 1975): 4–6.

47. Donald T. Regan, *For the Record: From Wall Street to Washington* (San Diego: Harcourt Brace Jovanovich, 1988).

48. Linda Goodman, *Linda Goodman's Sun Signs* (New York: Bantam Books, 1972), p. 477.

49. "Objections to Astrology."

50. Theodore Roszak, *Why Astrology Endures* (San Francisco: Robert Briggs Associates, 1980), p. 3.

51. Quoted in Michel Gauquelin, *Astrology and Science* (London: Peter Davies, 1969), p. 149.

SIX
Mystical Knowing

BEYOND THE SENSES, beyond the intellect, beyond these mundane means we use to acquire knowledge lies a more direct path to truth: mystical experience. So say many who claim that mystical experience bypasses our normal modes of cognition and yields a deeper insight into the nature of reality. According to physicist Fritjof Capra, author of the best selling *The Tao of Physics*, "What the Eastern mystics are concerned with is a direct experience of reality which transcends not only intellectual thinking but also sensory perception."[1] Attaining such an experience, however, often requires years of preparation and involves practices that are both mentally and physically taxing. Because such practices are known to induce altered states of consciousness, many dismiss mystical experience as nothing more than delusion or hallucination.

If the doors of perception were cleansed, every thing would appear to man as it is, infinite.
—WILLIAM BLAKE

As Bertrand Russell put it: "From a scientific point of view we can make no distinction between the man who eats little and sees heaven and the man who drinks much and sees snakes. Each is an abnormal physical condition, and therefore has abnormal perception."[2]

But Capra argues that the mystics' claim to knowledge can't be so easily dismissed — because their vision of reality agrees with that of modern physics. "The principal theories and models of modern physics," he says, "lead to a view of the world which is internally consistent and in perfect harmony with the views of Eastern Mysticism."[3] Mystics, like scientists, are seekers after truth. But whereas scientists use their senses to explore nature's mysteries, mystics use only their intuition. What is remarkable, contends Capra, is that the reality revealed by these two types of experience appears to be the same. Psychologist Lawrence LeShan agrees:

> The physicist and the mystic follow different paths: they have different technical goals in view; they use different tools and methods; their attitudes are not the same. However, in the world-picture they are led to by these different roads they perceive the same basic structure, the same reality.[4]

Mysticism is just tomorrow's science dreamed today.
— MARSHALL
  McLUHAN

According to Capra and LeShan, although the mystic and the scientist have traveled different paths, they have arrived at the same destination. Consequently, they claim, mystical experience must be considered a privileged source of knowledge.[5]

But is there really such a royal road to the truth? Has modern physics vindicated the visions of the mystics? To find out, we'll have to take a closer look at what the mystics tell us about the nature of reality.

TRUE MYSTIC MOMENTS

Mystical experiences are ecstatic, awesome, extraordinary experiences in which you seem to enter into a mysterious union with the source and ground of being. During this encounter, it seems as if the deepest secrets of the universe are revealed to you. What you formerly took to be real seems nothing more than an illusion. You become convinced that now, as never before, you understand the true nature of reality. The Christian mystic, St. John of the Cross, describes the experience this way:

> The end I have in view is the divine Embracing, the union of the soul with the divine Substance. In this loving, obscure knowledge God unites Himself with the soul eminently and divinely. . . . This knowledge consists in a certain contact of the soul with the Divinity, and it is God Him-

self Who is then felt and tasted, though not manifestly and distinctly, as it will be in glory. But this touch of knowledge and of sweetness is so deep and so profound that it penetrates into the inmost substance of the soul. This knowledge savors in some measure of the divine Essence and of everlasting life.[6]

For some, the union appears to be an almost sexual one. St. Theresa, another Christian mystic, writes:

I saw an angel close by me, on my left side, in bodily form. . . . I saw in his hand a long spear of gold, and at the iron's point there seemed to be a little fire. He appeared to me to be thrusting it at times into my heart, and to pierce my very entrails; when he drew it out, he seemed to draw them out also and to leave me all on fire with a great love of God. The pain was so great that it made me moan; and yet so surpassing was the sweetness of this excessive pain that I could not wish to be rid of it. The soul is satisfied now with nothing less than God.[7]

The God of which St. John and St. Theresa speak is the God of the Bible: a personal being with thoughts, feelings, and desires. For them, mystical experiences are the result of entering into a peculiarly intimate relationship with Him. But in their view, even though you unite with God, you don't become God. You may be deeply moved — even transformed—by the experience, but you're not annihilated by it. Through it all, you retain your personal identity.

Not all mystics describe their experience this way, however. Hindus of the Advaita Vedanta school, for example, do not believe that mystical union is a relationship between two persons for, in their view, the world does not contain two persons. According to them, there is only one thing in the universe — Brahman — and mystical experience reveals that we are identical to it. As the founder of this school, Shankara (686–718 A.D.), relates: "Through his transcendental vision he [the mystic] has realized that there is no difference between man and Brahman, or between Brahman and the universe — for he sees that Brahman is all."[8] In the mystical state, according to Shankara, all individuality, all distinctions, all boundaries disappear. Reality is experienced as a seamless, indivisible whole. No line can be drawn between the self and the nonself, for the self is all. You are god.

Christians would consider this view blasphemous. No mere human being can be god. Yet that's what Shankara says we are. The central teaching of the Hindu scriptures, the *Vedas* and the *Upanishads*, is: "That art Thou." The word *that* refers to Brahman, the Supreme Hindu Deity — god in his impersonal, absolute aspect — and the word *thou* refers to Atman, your individual soul.[9] The true meaning of this teaching, according to Shankara, is that we and god are one. "The

Not I, but the whole world says it: everything is one.
—HERACLITUS

scriptures establish the absolute identity of Atman and Brahman," he informs us, "by declaring repeatedly: 'That art Thou.'"[10] Obviously Shankara does not share St. John's or St. Theresa's view of the mystical experience.

Nor does he share their view of god. The Christian God is a person—an immensely powerful, intelligent, and good person perhaps—but a person nonetheless. Brahman, however, is not a person. It is reality itself.[11] Shankara describes Brahman this way:

> From the standpoint of the illumined soul, Brahman fills everything—beginningless, endless, immeasurable, unchanging, one without a second. In Brahman there is no diversity whatsoever.
>
> Brahman is pure existence, pure consciousness, eternal bliss, beyond action, one without a second. In Brahman there is no diversity whatsoever.[12]

Even though Brahman is not a person, it can be seen as a person just as a rope lying in the grass can be seen as a snake even though it isn't one. (The three primary "person-aspects" of Brahman are Brahma, the Creator; Vishnu, the Preserver; and Shiva, the Destroyer. Together they comprise the Hindu trinity.) But Brahman is no more a person than the rope is a snake. Rather, it is pure being, pure consciousness, pure bliss.

Since all is Brahman, and Brahman is pure, blissful consciousness, it follows that the world contains no matter as we think of it in the West. It seems to contain matter, but that is just an illusion. "The apparent world is caused by our imagination, in its ignorance," Shankara tells us. "It is not real. It is like seeing the snake in the rope. It is like a passing dream."[13] According to Shankara, all there is is consciousness. The objects that we ordinarily take to be real—rocks, trees, houses, and so on—are merely figments of our imagination. Consciousness alone is the true reality.

In the West, we're used to thinking of matter as the fundamental reality. "All there is is matter in motion" says one version of this idea. In this view, everything is composed of minute particles of matter. Consciousness exists, but it is derivative; it emerges when matter reaches a sufficient degree of complexity, as in our brains. For Shankara, however, it's the other way around: consciousness is primary; matter is derivative. Matter is a manifestation of consciousness, not vice versa.

Shankara holds that Brahman, the one and only true reality, is unchanging and eternal. The Buddha (563–483 B.C.), another Eastern mystic and teacher, maintains that reality is constantly changing and ephemeral. As he remarked to one of his followers, "The world is in

When one sees that everything exists as an illusion, one can live in a higher sphere than ordinary man.

—THE BUDDHA

continuous flux and is impermanent."[14] The Buddha, then, denies the existence of Shankara's Brahman.

The Buddha's vision of the world as a ceaseless flux came to him during a mystical experience he had while sitting underneath a tree on the banks of the river Neranjara near Gaya, India. In sermons to his disciples, he drew out the implications of his insight. If everything is constantly changing, then the self is constantly changing, and if the self is constantly changing, then there are no eternal souls. Rather, each of us is being created anew every instant. The Buddhist theologian, Walpola Rahula, describes the Buddha's revelation this way:

> One thing disappears, conditioning the appearance of the next in a series of cause and effect. There is no unchanging substance in them. There is nothing behind them that can be called a permanent Self (Atman), individuality, or anything that can in reality be called "I."[15]

The Buddha, then, also denies the existence of Shankara's Atman. (This is not surprising, however, for, as we have seen, Shankara identifies Atman with Brahman. If you deny one, you deny the other.)

Change alone is unchanging.
—HERACLITUS

According to the Buddha, the false belief in a continuing self is responsible for all the pain and suffering in the world, for it gives rise to desire, and desire is what causes pain and suffering. Rahula explains:

> Buddhism stands unique in the history of human thought in denying the existence of such a Soul, Self, or Atman. According to the teaching of the Buddha, the idea of self is an imaginary, false belief which has no corresponding reality, and it produces harmful thoughts of "me" and "mine," selfish desire, craving, attachment, hatred, ill-will, conceit, pride, egoism, and other defilements, impurities and problems. It is the source of all the troubles in the world from personal conflicts to wars between nations. In short, to this false view can be traced all the evil in the world.[16]

Since belief in a continuing self causes all of the world's misery, the only way to put an end to that misery is to give up the belief in a continuing self. If you do, you attain Nirvana—a state of perfect bliss, free of any desire, craving, or thirst. Giving up the belief in a continuing self, however, is no easy task. It requires following the noble Eightfold Path: you must practice Right Understanding, Right Thought, Right Speech, Right Action, Right Livelihood, Right Effort, Right Mindfulness, and Right Concentration. By practicing these virtues you will avoid the extremes of self-indulgence and self-mortification and, perhaps eventually give up the idea of the "self" altogether.

The no-mind not-thinks no-thoughts about no-things.
—THE BUDDHA

Despite their differences, Shankara and the Buddha share a common vision of human purpose. Both agree that our ultimate goal is to attain Enlightenment; that to attain Enlightenment, we must understand the true nature of reality; and that to understand the true nature of reality, we must understand the true nature of the self. But they disagree about the nature of reality and the nature of the self. For Shankara, reality (Brahman) is a single, unchanging substance. For the Buddha, reality is an ever-changing process. For Shankara, your self (Atman) is identical to Brahman and thus is eternal. For the Buddha, there are no unchanging substances and thus there are no eternal selves. Both traditions claim to derive their insight from mystical experience. Hindu mystics report that the self is everything while Buddhist mystics report that the self is nothing. But both agree that in the mystical state — which is the only state in which we can perceive the true nature of reality — no distinction can be made between the self and the nonself. Indeed, no distinction can be made between any two things. The Hindus believe that this is due to the fact that there is only one thing in the world — Brahman. The Buddhists believe that it is due to the fact that there are no things (continuing substances) in the world. So on both accounts, although for different reasons, everything is one.

It's this sense of unity experienced by Eastern mystics that forms the basis of Capra's claim that mystics and physicists share a common vision of reality. He writes:

> The basic oneness of the universe is not only the central characteristic of the mystical experience, but is also one of the most important revelations of modern physics. [Modern physics has discovered] that the constituents of matter and the basic phenomena involving them are all interconnected, interrelated and interdependent; that they cannot be understood as isolated entities, but only as integrated parts of the whole. [17]

But notice: If everything is one — in either the Hindu or the Buddhist sense — then there can be no interconnections, interrelations, or interdependence, for such associations require the existence of at least two things, and both the Hindus and the Buddhists tell us that the world doesn't contain even two things. In other words, if there are connections, relations, or dependents, there must be more than one thing in the world. But if there is more than one thing in the world, it cannot be the case that everything is one. So if Capra is right that modern physics has discovered that everything is interconnected, interrelated, and interdependent, he must be wrong that modern physics vindicates the views of either the Hindu or Buddhist mystics.

The true value of a human being is determined primarily by the measure and sense in which he has attained liberation from the self.
— ALBERT EINSTEIN

The One and the Many

It's important to realize that the belief that everything is one is not a recent revelation of modern science. In fact, it is the oldest scientific theory known. Science began when Thales — one of the seven wise men of ancient Greece — tried to discover the one substance out of which everything was made. Ever since, scientists have been searching for the one behind the many; the unity behind the diversity. Einstein spent the last years of his life looking for a "unified field theory" that would explain the workings of both gravity and electromagnetism (the only forces known to exist during his lifetime). Nowadays scientists believe they are close to developing a "theory of everything" that would explain all four of the known forces (and thus everything else in the universe) in terms of one underlying substance: superstrings.[18] If everything turns out to be composed of superstrings, Thales' vision will have been vindicated, and we will have good reason for believing that everything is one.

Furthermore, Capra can't claim that modern physics vindicates the world view of Eastern mystics in general, for as we've seen, the Eastern mystics don't share a common world view. The Hindus and the Buddhists have radically different conceptions of the nature of reality. In fact, mystical world views seem to be at least as various as mystical traditions themselves. According to theologian John Hick, "As we listen to the world-wide company of those who have spoken about the divine reality out of direct personal experience, we find that they have conceptualized their experiences in many different and often incompatible ways, each in accordance with his own environing tradition and culture."[19] Mystics, even Eastern ones, do not speak with a single voice. Consequently it can't coherently be maintained that modern physics confirms their view of things.

Even the more limited claim that modern physics vindicates the world view of one particular group of mystics is problematic. For if one group of mystics is right, the others must be wrong. How, then, would we account for the fact that Christian mystics were mistaken? Is the answer that their experiences weren't really mystical? But how would we distinguish real mystical experiences from false ones? Is the answer that the Christians didn't interpret their experiences correctly? But how would we distinguish correct interpretations from incorrect ones? Once we admit that only certain mystical experiences are revelatory, we have abandoned the claim that all mystical experience yields knowledge.

The Holographic Paradigm

As we saw in Chapter 2, subatomic particles that have interacted with one another somehow remain inseparably linked, so that what happens to one almost instantaneously affects the other, no matter how far apart they have become. Physicists have been hard-pressed to come up with a plausible model for this phenomenon, especially since faster-than-light travel is prohibited by relativity theory. Some believe, however, that the hologram provides such a model.

A hologram is a three-dimensional picture created by means of a laser. What makes it a plausible model for long-distance particle interactions is that each part of a hologram contains the whole. For example, if you broke the hologram of a rose into smaller pieces, each piece of it would contain an image of the entire rose. (The image produced by the smaller pieces would be fuzzier than that of the original, but it would nevertheless be complete.) In other words, every part of a hologram "knows"

about every other. Similarly, according to current physics every particle seems to "know" about every other. Physicist Enos Witmer, for example, claims, "Thus we seem to be led step by step to the idea that a particle in quantum physics is a kind of entity that maintains a very efficient intelligence agency that keeps it informed at all times of what is happening throughout the universe."[20] Viewing the universe as a hologram, it has been claimed, could help account for the strange behavior of subatomic particles.

It has also been claimed that the holographic model can illuminate certain mysterious psychological phenomena as well. Experiments conducted by Karl Lashley over a period of thirty years demonstrated that memory was not located in any specific part of the brain. By training animals to perform a task and then removing various parts of their brains, he found that although their performance diminished, their memory of it was never completely de-

SPEAKING ABOUT THE UNSPEAKABLE

The way that can be told is not the eternal way.
—Lao Tzu

To preserve the view that all mystical experience yields knowledge, it has been claimed that although there are many different descriptions of mystical experience, the experience itself is the same for everyone. The different descriptions arise from the fact that mystical experience transcends our ordinary linguistic categories. It's so unlike any other experience we've had that we lack the words to describe it. Thus mystical experience is said to be *ineffable*.[22]

According to philosopher Walter Stace, to say that something is ineffable is to say that nothing can truthfully be predicated of it. Thus, for example, to say that God is ineffable is to say that "any statement of the form 'God is x' [where x is a predicate] is false."[23] If

stroyed. Many researchers, including Karl Pribram at Stanford University, hypothesized that information in the brain is stored like information in a hologram. That's why memory survives destruction of various parts of the brain—it is distributed throughout the brain. According to Pribram, both the brain and the universe are holograms which interact with one another. Such a model, he claims, could easily account for mystical experience. Here's Marilyn Ferguson's description of Pribram's theory:

> Recently a Stanford neuroscientist, Karl Pribram, proposed an all-encompassing paradigm that marries brain research to theoretical physics; it accounts for normal perception and simultaneously takes the "paranormal" and transcendental experiences out of the supernatural by demonstrating that they are part of nature.
>
> The paradoxical sayings of mystics suddenly make sense in the radical reorienta-tion of this "holographic theory." . . .

> In a nutshell, the holographic super-theory says that our brains mathematically construct "hard" reality by interpreting frequencies from a dimension transcending time and space. The brain is a hologram, interpreting a holographic universe.

> Mystical experience, Pribram says, is no stranger than many other phenomena in nature, such as the selective derepression of DNA to form first one organ, then another. "If we get ESP or paranormal phenomena— or nuclear phenomena in physics—it simply means that we are reading out of some other dimension at that time. In our ordinary way, we can't understand that.". . .

> Pribram engagingly admits at times, "I hope you realize that I don't understand any of this." The admission generally provokes a sigh of relief in even the most scientific audiences.[21]

mystical experience is ineffable in this sense, however, nothing can truthfully be said about it.[24] In particular, it can't truthfully be said that mystical experience is a source of knowledge because to say that is to predicate something of it, and any such predication is false. Someone convinced of the ineffability of mystical experience, then, would do well to follow the advice of philosopher Ludwig Wittgenstein: "Whereof one cannot speak, thereof one must be silent."[25] Furthermore, if no description of mystical experience is true, there are no grounds for believing that it's the same for everyone. Our only access to others' experience is through their descriptions of it. If these descriptions can't be trusted, we have no way of knowing whether their experiences are similar, for totally indescribable experiences can't be compared.

Most likely, what mystics mean by calling their experience ineffable isn't that it can't be described, but that the descriptions offered can't, by themselves, provide knowledge of what it's like to have the experience. In this respect mystical experiences are no different from any other experiences. Certainly it would be very difficult to describe, for example, an orgasm to someone who had never had one. And simply reading a description of an orgasm won't normally produce one. To know what it is to have either an orgasm or a mystical experience, you simply have to have one.

Given that descriptions of mystical experience are no substitute for the real thing, what can we learn from them? Do they support the view that mystical experience is the same for everyone? It wouldn't seem so, for mystics in different traditions describe their experience in radically different ways. Christians, for example, describe their experience as an intimate relationship with a personal god whereas Buddhists describe their experience as an awareness of emptiness. According to theologian Steven Katz, "There is no intelligible way that anyone can legitimately argue that a 'no self' experience of empty calm is the same experience as the experience of intense, loving, intimate relationship between two substantial selves, one of whom is conceived of as the personal God of Western religion and all that this entails."[26] The writings of the mystics, then, rather than establishing the similarity of their experiences, attest to their diversity.

The diversity of their experiences should come as no surprise, however, because mystics in different traditions are exposed to different beliefs and, as we've seen, beliefs condition experience. What we expect to experience affects what we do experience. For example, consider the case of the Jewish mystics:

> The entire life of the Jewish mystic is permeated from childhood up by images, concepts, symbols, ideological values and ritual behavior which there is no reason to believe he leaves behind in his experience. Rather, these images, beliefs, symbolism, and rituals define, *in advance*, what the experience he *wants to have* and which he then does have, will be like.[27]

Mystics in different traditions have different experiences because they have different expectations about what the experience will be like.

The most compelling evidence for the importance of expectancy effects in mystical experience is to be found in the writings of the mystics themselves. Mystics in one tradition rarely describe their experiences in terms used by another. As Katz notes, "The absence of the kinds of experience of unity one often, but mistakenly, associates with mysticism, even as 'the essence of mysticism,' in the Jewish mystical context is very strong evidence that pre-experiential condition-ing affects the nature of the experience one actually has."[28] If we take the writings of the mystics seriously (which is how we have to take them if we are to derive any information from them), we must con-clude that the mystical experience is not the same for everyone.

But even if all mystics did have the same experience, that wouldn't prove that their experiences are a source of knowledge. For we've all shared with others what seems to be the same perceptual experience, then discovered that the experience wasn't real. Lots of people, for ex-ample, have reported identical perceptual illusions, like mirages in the desert. But this agreement among the experiences doesn't prove that the oasis in the distance is real. Experiences can be common, but false. We must remember the relevant principle:

> Just because a group of people believe that something is true doesn't mean that it is.

A lot of people used to believe that the Earth was flat. We now know that they were mistaken. To find out what's real, we always need fur-ther tests—more than the fact that everybody is in agreement.

Some believe that mystical experience is a privileged source of knowledge because it involves a direct experience of reality, unmedi-ated by any intellectual constructs.[29] The idea is that our ordinary concepts function like a veil, hiding from us the true nature of reality. By removing the veil, we can come to know reality as it is in itself, undistorted by our conceptual filters.[30]

Many Eastern mystical traditions teach that we can free ourselves from our intellectual blinders by "silencing our minds."[31] Only by emptying our minds of all thoughts, can we open the door to true per-ception. In the words of mystic Sri Aurobindo, "The cup [has to be] left clean and empty for the divine liquor to be poured into it."[32] In a mystical state of consciousness, then, the mind is not directed upon anything. With no objects to limit awareness, it may seem as if con-sciousness has expanded to infinity; as if all there is is consciousness; as if everything is one. But if that is what is going on in mystical ex-perience—if mystical experience is simply consciousness without an object—then it can't give us knowledge of reality because in that case, mystical experience would not put us in contact with reality. As philosopher Robert Nozick notes, "It would be a mistake to think there is an unusual reality being encountered, when that merely is what it feels like when the experience-mechanism is turned on yet nothing is present to be experienced."[33] An empty mind may not be the best tool for acquiring knowledge.

Refusal to believe until proof is given is a rational position; denial of all outside of our own limited experience is absurd.
—ANNIE BESANT

If mystical experience is a source of knowledge, what it reveals must be true. (Truth, remember, is a necessary condition of knowledge.) If it's true, however, it should be consistent with other things we know to be true. That's why Capra and LeShan are at such pains to establish a link between the claims of the mystics and the physicists. If there were substantial agreement between them, there would be grounds for considering mystical experience to be a source of knowledge. But at present, as we have seen, whatever agreement exists is suggestive, but not substantial.

THE CAUSES OF THE MYSTICAL

While orgasms are relatively easy to induce, mystical experiences are relatively difficult to bring about. Those who've had mystical experiences have usually led lives of extreme self-denial and self-discipline. Often they've renounced worldly goods, repressed physical desires (especially sexual ones), and rejected normal human companionship. In an effort to see god or realize the true nature of reality, they've filled their lives with prayers, devotions, and rituals. One effect of such behaviors is sensory deprivation, which is known to produce altered states of consciousness.

Research has demonstrated that when the nervous system is deprived of its normal level of sensory input, it will generate its own in the form of hallucinations.[34] Psychologist Charles Brownfield has shown that the sort of isolation experienced by religious ascetics is sufficient to produce sensory deprivation effects.[35] An interesting example of the effects of isolation was reported by Joshua Slocum, the first person to sail alone around the world. Several times during his journey he claims to have been visited by a sailor who appeared on the deck of his ship and kept him company.[36]

Research indicates that the self-denial and self-discipline practiced by the mystics can have the same effect on the brain as hallucinogenic drugs.[37] As we all know from our dreams, the brain is capable of producing vivid hallucinations. The practices of the mystics can apparently induce the brain to manufacture the chemicals needed to produce hallucinations during the waking state.

When a stimulus remains unvarying for a period of time, the nervous system ceases to respond to it. In such a case, the nervous system is said to have become habituated to it. The unchanging posture and repetitive thought patterns practiced by mystics during their prayers

The Miracle of Marsh Chapel

Timothy Leary was not the only person experimenting with hallucinogens at Harvard in the early 1960s. Walter Pahnke, a graduate student in theology, was also exploring inner space by means of drugs. His interest, however, was the relationship between drug-induced hallucinations and mystical experience. Here's an account of his experiment:

> Walter Pahnke was interested in the literature and experience of religious ecstasy. He trained housewives, presumably for their lack of bias, to identify passages in literature that qualified as transcendental or ecstatic accounts. Then he fed a group of divinity students controlled doses of psilocybin on Good Friday, 1962. The theology students soon after described their experiences while under the influence, and the housewives rated those confessions, mixed in among other narratives of religious ecstasy as well as other nonecstatic accounts, without knowing where they came from. The results were remarkable. The brigade of housewife readers identified a large proportion of the students' narratives as bona fide mystical encounters, and Pahnke concluded that drugs could simulate the transcendent ecstasy that lay at the source of so much religious tradition. Pahnke's work became known as the Good Friday Experiment and the reports by students as the Miracle of Marsh Chapel, named after the site on Harvard's campus where Pahnke collected his results. The age of scientific study of hallucinogens and their role in religious ecstasy had begun. But Pahnke's research raised a storm of criticism. If experience of God could be induced by a chemical, then what did that say about all the regalia and ritual of institutional religion?[38]

and meditation can lead to neurophysiological habituation.[39] One effect of this habituation is to shut down the body's proprioceptors which provide information about the body's location and orientation. This may produce the feeling that consciousness is no longer attached to the body. In other words, it may lead to an out-of-body experience.[40] Reports of such experiences are not uncommon among mystics. St. Theresa relates that "often my body would become so light that it lost all weight."[41] Christian mystic Heinrich Suzo also tells of a feeling of floating during his mystical experiences.[42]

Does all this mean that we must concur with Russell's judgment that these experiences are nothing more than self-induced fantasies? Not at all. The fact that mystical experiences have physical causes and are states of nonnormal consciousness doesn't prove that the experiences offer distorted views of reality, for normal consciousness may not provide the best perspective from which to view reality. As the

OBEs and Mystical Experience

Susan Blackmore, one of the world's leading authorities on out-of-body experiences (OBEs), claims that the same sorts of psychological mechanisms that generate these experiences can also generate mystical experiences. She writes in her book *Beyond the Body*:

We are selves. And selves, as we know from psychology, are constructed entities — or models. . . . We all build vast mental models of "me, here, now" based on our senses. It is this which provides the core of our consciousness from moment to moment. . . . The model of reality is sustained by the complex processing of the brain and changes as that processing changes. It is normally totally dependent on the input to our senses: on what we can see and hear and feel and the body image with which we integrate it all. That is "me, now." But what happens when there is not enough input, or confusing input, or when we are drugged or near death? The normal model of reality begins to break down, of course. . . . This, I think, provides the answer about OBEs. A sensible system, losing touch with external reality, uncertain as to what is "out there" and what is imagination, has to make a decision. Only one model of the world can actually represent "out there" and seem real. So which is it? I propose that when this breakdown occurs the most sensible thing the system can do is to ask itself (as it were) "Who am I? Where am I? What is going on?" and so reconstruct, on the basis of memory and imagination, what it thinks should be happening. And what are memory models like? We know from much work in psychology that many representations in memory are in bird's eye view. . . . Most OBErs are convinced by their illusion; they are sure that they are seeing the "real world." In this sense OBErs are like dreamers. But just as you can become lucid in a dream, and realize that it is all illusory, so you can in an OBE. You can realize the constructed nature of all these images — indeed of the basis of consciousness itself. In this way you can see into the essential emptiness of it all and the connectedness of everything which can be experienced. It is simultaneously total aloneness and complete oneness. This is a key insight into the mystical experience.[43]

philosopher and psychologist William James tells us, "for aught we know to the contrary, 103 or 104 degrees Fahrenheit might be a much more favorable temperature for truths to germinate and sprout in, than the more ordinary blood-heat of 97 or 98 degrees."[44] James's point is that since body chemistry plays a role in the production of all of our beliefs, we can't reject a belief simply because it can be shown to have an organic cause. If we did, "none of our thoughts and feelings, not even our scientific doctrines, not even our disbeliefs, could retain any value as revelations of the truth, for every one of them without exception flows from the state of their possessor's body at the time."[45] The fact that an experience is produced by a certain physiological state, then, can't, by itself, show that the experience is erroneous.

In fact, some influential thinkers have argued that the experiences produced by abnormal physical conditions are just as real as ordinary ones. They merely reveal an aspect of reality that is normally hidden to us. In this view, the brain and nervous system function as a reducing valve that blocks out those aspects of reality that have no survival value. Through spiritual exercises, drugs, or hypnosis, we can temporarily open up that reducing valve and let more of what's out there in, so to speak. Aldous Huxley, author of *Brave New World*, was convinced that this was what happened when he took mescaline. He claimed that the drug did not create the visions; it merely opened the door to certain ordinarily unseen dimensions of reality.

James was sympathetic to the view that there are modes of awareness normally hidden from view. He writes:

> our normal waking consciousness, rational consciousness as we call it, is but one special type of consciousness, whilst all about it, parted from it by the filmiest of screens, there lie potential forms of consciousness entirely different. . . . No account of the universe in its totality can be final which leaves these other forms of consciousness quite disregarded. . . . At any rate, they forbid a premature closing of our accounts with reality.[46]

But even though James was open to the possibility that mystical experience provides insights into the nature of reality, he was well aware that merely having such an experience did not guarantee its truth. "To come from [a mystical experience] is no infallible credential. What comes must be sifted and tested, and run the gauntlet of confrontation with the total context of experience, just like what comes from the outer world of sense."[47] In other words, mystical experiences aren't self-authenticating. Although they may seem more real, more true than any other experiences we've had, they may not be, for as we have seen:

Just because you believe that something is true doesn't mean that it is.

As philosopher Tobias Chapman puts it: "the psychological feeling of certainty does not guarantee truth and can, in fact, attach itself to the

Huxley on the Function of the Mind

In *The Doors of Perception,* Aldous Huxley reflects on his experiences with mescaline. The title of his book is taken from a line by the poet William Blake: "If the doors of perception were cleansed, every thing would appear to man as it is, infinite." The rock group, The Doors, allegedly took their name from the title of Huxley's book. Here's Huxley's theory of how minds are affected by drugs:

> Reflecting on my experience, I find myself agreeing with the eminent Cambridge philosopher, Dr. C. D. Broad, "that we should do well to consider much more seriously than we have hitherto been inclined to do the type of theory which Bergson put forward in connection with memory and sense perception. The suggestion is that the function of the brain and nervous system and sense organs is in the main eliminative and not productive. Each person is at each moment capable of remembering all that has ever happened to him and of perceiving everything that is happening everywhere in the universe. The function of the brain and nervous system is to protect us from being overwhelmed and confused by this mass of largely useless and irrelevant knowledge, by shutting out most of what we should otherwise perceive or remember at any moment, and leaving only that very small and special selection which is likely to be practically useful." According to such a theory, each one of us is potentially Mind at Large. But in so far as we are animals, our business is at all costs to survive. To make biological survival possible, Mind at Large has to be funnelled through the reducing valve of the brain and nervous system. What comes out at the other end is a measly trickle of the kind of consciousness which will help us to stay alive on the surface of this particular planet. . . . Most people, most of the time, know only what comes through the reducing valve and is consecrated as genuinely real by the local language. Certain persons, however, seem to be born with a kind of by-pass that circumvents the reducing valve. In others temporary by-passes may be acquired either spontaneously, or as the result of deliberate "spiritual exercises," or through hypnosis, or by means of drugs.[48]

most preposterous beliefs."[49] To determine the truth or falsity of a claim based on mystical experience, then, we must subject it to the same sort of scrutiny we would a claim based on ordinary experience.

A mystical experience can transform your life. It can infuse it with meaning, significance, and value. Where once you only saw pointless posturing, you may now see profound purpose. St. John of the Cross writes of the salutary effects of mystical experiences:

> They enrich it marvelously. A single one of them may be sufficient to abolish at a stroke certain imperfections of which the soul during its

James on Mysticism and Nitrous Oxide

In *The Varieties of Religious Experience,* James provides the following account of his experience with nitrous oxide (laughing gas):

> Nitrous oxide and ether, especially nitrous oxide, when sufficiently diluted with air, stimulate the mystical consciousness in an extraordinary degree. Depth beyond depth of truth seems revealed to the inhaler. This truth fades out, however, or escapes, at the moment of coming to; and if any words remain over in which it seemed to clothe itself, they prove to be the veriest nonsense. Nevertheless, the sense of a profound meaning having been there persists; and I know more than one person who is persuaded that in the nitrous oxide trance we have a genuine metaphysical revelation. . . . Looking back on my own experiences, they all converge towards a kind of insight to which I cannot help ascribing some metaphysical significance. The keynote of it is invariably a reconciliation. It is as if the opposites of the world, whose contradictoriness and conflict make all our difficulties and troubles, were melted into unity. Not only do they, as contrasted species, belong to one and the same genus, but one of the species, the nobler and better one, is itself the genus, and so soaks up and absorbs its opposite into itself.[50]

> whole life had vainly tried to rid itself, and to leave it adorned with virtues and loaded with supernatural gifts. A single one of the intoxicating consolations may reward it for all the labors undergone in its life— even were they numberless.[51]

Some take the profound effect mystical experiences have on people as evidence for the reality of what's experienced. But as Bertrand Russell replied to Father Copleston when he made such a claim,

> The fact that a belief has a good moral effect upon a man is no evidence whatsoever in favor of its truth. . . . Obviously the character of a young man may be — and often is — immensely affected for good by reading about some great man in history, and it may happen that the great man is a myth and doesn't exist, but the boy is just as much affected for good as if he did.[52]

Similarly, dreams may profoundly affect one's life for the better. (Scrooge comes to mind here.) Since changes in character can be brought about by false beliefs as well as true, such changes provide no evidence for the truth of their incipient beliefs.

While being mystical doesn't guarantee the truth of an experience, it doesn't guarantee the falsity of it either. It's entirely possible that mystical experiences do reveal aspects of reality that are normally

Russell's Mystical Experience

Although Bertrand Russell denies that the transforming powers of mystical experience are a sign of their validity, he nonetheless was himself transformed by a mystical experience. The following is an excerpt from his autobiography:

When we came home, we found Mrs. W undergoing an unusually severe bout of pain. She seemed cut off from everyone and everything by walls of agony, and the sense of the solitude of each human soul suddenly overwhelmed me. Ever since my marriage, my emotional life had been calm and superficial. I had forgotten all the deeper issues, and had been content with flippant cleverness. Suddenly the ground seemed to give way beneath me, and I found myself in quite another region. Within five minutes I went thru some such reflections as the following: the loneliness of the human soul is unendurable; nothing can penetrate it except the highest intensity of the sort of love that religious teachers have preached; whatever does not spring from this motive is harmful, or at best useless; it follows that war is wrong, that a public school education is abominable, that the use of force is to be deprecated, and that in human relations one should penetrate to the core of loneliness in each person and speak to that. . . . At the end of those five minutes I had become a completely different person. For a time, a sort of mystic illumination possessed me. I felt that I knew the inmost thoughts of everybody that I met in the street, and though this was, no doubt, a delusion, I did in actual fact find myself in far closer touch than previously with all my friends, and many of my acquaintances. Having been an Imperialist, I became during those five minutes . . . a Pacifist. Having for years cared only for exactness and analysis, I found myself filled with semi-mystical feelings about beauty, and with an intense interest in children and with a desire almost as profound as that of the Buddha to find some philosophy which should make human life endurable. A strange excitement possessed me, containing intense pain but also some element of triumph through the fact that I could dominate pain, and make it, as I thought, a gateway to wisdom. The mystic insight which I then imagined myself to possess has largely faded, and the habit of analysis has reasserted itself. But something of what I thought I saw in that moment has remained always with me, causing my attitude during the first war, my interest in my children, my indifference to minor misfortunes and a certain emotional tone in all my human relations.[53]

hidden to us. But the only way we can tell is by putting them to the test. If they are revelatory of reality, we should be able to corroborate them. The Dalai Lama, spiritual leader of Tibetan Buddhism, recognizes the importance of corroboration. At a conference on neuroscience held at Newport Beach, California, he remarked, "If there's good, strong evidence from science that such and such is the case and this is contrary to Buddhism, then we will change."[54] Truth, as the Dalai Lama realizes, should be able to withstand the closest scrutiny, for only that which can withstand such scrutiny deserves to be called true.

SUGGESTED READINGS:

Capra, Fritjof. *The Tao of Physics*. New York: Bantam, 1975.

James, William. *The Varieties of Religious Experience*. New York: Signet, 1958.

Katz, Steven T., ed. *Mysticism and Philosophical Analysis*. New York: Oxford University Press, 1978.

Neher, Andrew. *The Psychology of Transcendence*. Englewood Cliffs, N.J.: Prentice-Hall, 1980.

Stace, W. T. *Mysticism and Philosophy*. Philadelphia: Lippincott, 1960.

NOTES

1. Fritjof Capra, *The Tao of Physics* (New York: Bantam Books, 1975), p. 16.
2. Bertrand Russell, *Mysticism*. Quoted in Walter Kaufmann, *Critique of Philosophy and Religion* (Garden City, N.Y.: Doubleday, 1961), p. 315.
3. Capra, *Tao of Physics*, p. 294.
4. Lawrence LeShan, *The Medium, the Mystic, and the Physicist* (New York: Viking Press, 1974), p. 77.
5. A number of writers have made similar claims. See, for example, Michael Talbot, *Mysticism and the New Physics* (New York, Bantam Books, 1981); Amaury de Riencourt, *The Eye of Shiva* (New York: William Morrow, 1981; and Gary Zukav, *The Dancing Wu Li Masters* (New York: William Morrow, 1979).
6. Cited in Paul Kurtz, *The Transcendental Temptation* (Buffalo: Prometheus Books, 1991), p. 96.
7. Cited in Evelyn Underhill, *Mysticism* (New York: World/Meridian, 1972), p. 292.
8. Shankara, *Crest-Jewel of Discrimination* (Hollywood: Vedanta Press, 1975), p. 106.
9. Ibid., p. 72.
10. Ibid.
11. Ibid., p. 111.
12. Ibid., p. 110.
13. Ibid., p. 73.
14. Cited in Walpola Rahula, *What the Buddha Taught* (New York: Grove Press, 1974), pp. 25–26.
15. Ibid., p. 26.

16. Ibid., p. 51.

17. Capra, *Tao of Physics*, pp. 117–18.

18. See, for example, P .C. W. Davies and J. Brown, *Superstrings: A Theory of Everything?* (Cambridge: Cambridge University Press, 1989).

19. John Hick, *Death and Eternal Life* (San Francisco: Harper and Row, 1976), p. 324.

20. Enos E. Witmer, "Interpretation of Quantum Mechanics and the Future of Physics," *American Journal of Physics*, 35 (1967): 47.

21. Marilyn Ferguson, *The Aquarian Conspiracy* (Los Angeles: J. P. Tarcher, 1980), pp. 177–86.

22. William James, *The Varieties of Religious Experience* (New York: Signet, 1958), p. 292; Walter Stace, *Mysticism and Philosophy* (Philadelphia: J. B. Lippincott, 1960), p. 109ff.

23. Walter T. Stace, *Time and Eternity* (Princeton: Princeton University Press, 1952), p. 33.

24. William Alston, "Ineffability," *The Philosophical Review*, 65 (1956): 506–22.

25. Ludwig Wittgenstein, *Tractatus Logico-Philosophicus*, proposition 7.

26. Steven T. Katz, "Language, Epistemology, and Mysticism," in *Mysticism and Philosophical Analysis*, ed. Steven T. Katz (New York: Oxford University Press, 1978), pp. 39–40.

27. Ibid., p. 33.

28. Ibid., pp. 34–35.

29. Capra, *Tao of Physics*, p. 16.

30. Satprem, *Sri Aurobindo, or the Adventure of Consciousness* (New York: Harper and Row, 1968), p. 32.

31. Ibid.

32. Cited in Satprem, *Sri Aurobindo*, p. 37.

33. Robert Nozick, *Philosophical Explanations* (Cambridge: Harvard University Press, 1981), p. 158.

34. John Zubek, ed., *Sensory Deprivation* (New York: Appleton, 1969).

35. Charles Brownfield, *Isolation* (New York: Random House, 1965), pp. 13–31.

36. Joshua Slocum, *Sailing Alone Around the World* (New York: Sheridan House, 1954), pp. 39–42.

37. A. Mandell, "Toward a Psychobiology of Transcendence: God in the Brain," in *Psychobiology of Consciousness*, ed. J. Davidson and R. Davidson (New York: Plenum Press, 1980), pp. 379–464.

38. "A Short History of Consciousness," *Omni*, October 1993, p. 64.

39. B. K. Anand, G. S. Chhina, and Baldev Singh, "Some Aspects of Electroencephalographic Studies in Yogis," *Electroencephalography and Clinical Neurophysiology*, 13 (1961): 452–56.

40. Celia Green, *Out of the Body Experiences* (New York: Random House/Ballantine, 1973), p. 44.

41. Cited in James H. Leuba, *The Psychology of Religious Mysticism* (London: Routledge and Kegan Paul, 1929), pp. 250–58.
42. Cited in Ben-Ami Sharfstein, *Mystical Experience* (Indianapolis: Bobbs-Merrill, 1973), p. 135.
43. Susan Blackmore, *Beyond the Body* (Chicago: Academy Chicago Publishers, 1992), pp. 279–81.
44. James, *Religious Experience*, p. 30.
45. Ibid.
46. Ibid, p. 298.
47. Ibid., p. 326.
48. Aldous Huxley, *The Doors of Perception* (New York: Harper and Row, 1954), pp. 22–24.
49. Tobias Chapman, *In Defense of Mystical Ideas* (Lewiston, Maine: Edwin Mellen Press, 1989), p. 10.
50. James, *Religious Experience*, p. 298.
51. Quoted in James, *Religious Experience*, p. 317.
52. Bertrand Russell, "A Debate on the Existence of God," in *Bertrand Russell on God and Religion*, ed. Al Seckel (Buffalo: Prometheus Books, 1986), p. 136.
53. Bertrand Russell, *The Autobiography of Bertrand Russell*, vol. 1 (London: Unwin Hyman, 1946), p. 146.
54. Cited in Pamela Weintraub in "Masters of the Universe," *Omni*, March 1990, p. 89.

SEVEN

How to Assess a "Miracle Cure"

YOUR MIND CAN cure cancer.

Therapeutic touch can heal the body.

Acupuncture can alleviate chronic pain.

Homeopathic remedies are effective against influenza and asthma.

Psychic surgery can remove diseased tissue from your body without an incision.

Vitamin E supplements can dissolve breast lumps.

Firewalking can cure impotence.

Herbs can fight AIDS.

Which of these claims is true? Every one of them has actually been advocated, and sometimes strongly promoted. Most of them are considered extraordinary, even bizarre, by many people. But as you know by now, their weirdness alone doesn't mean that they're false. Maybe your mind really can shrink malignant tumors. Maybe it can't. A crucial question is, if you think that any of these claims is true or false, how do you know? If you believe or disbelieve any one of these claims, what are your reasons?

This question is fundamental. It's a question concerning epistemology. The fact is, many arguments over the effectiveness of offbeat treatments (sometimes called *alternative* or *unconventional medicine*) are essentially about epistemology — about the basis or grounds for believing that a certain therapy works or doesn't work. It's also the case that many people either never bother to rationally assess their reasons for belief in a treatment or give reasons that are simply inadequate, offering little or no support for their belief).

People can have numerous emotional motivations for believing a claim about the efficacy of a treatment. They may be compelled by fear of an illness or of the side effects of a particular treatment, by the emotional appeal of sales pitches or promises of relief, by the pleasing or reassuring demeanor of a certain practitioner, or by mistrust of physicians. Such feelings may deserve our understanding, but it should be clear that they provide no grounds for belief that a given treatment is effective or ineffective. They're *not* adequate reasons for supposing the truth of any claim that a treatment is effective.

> We are constantly misled by the ease with which our minds fall into the ruts of one or two experiences.
> —SIR WILLIAM OSLER

There are, however, other reasons that people offer in support of claims about the effectiveness of treatments. Here are some of the most common and persuasive:

1. I tried it, and it worked.
2. Someone else tried it, and it worked.
3. Dr. X says it works.
4. Dr. X's observations of several patients show that it works.
5. An ancient practice or folklore shows that it works.
6. A scientific study shows that it works.

In statements 1 and 2, personal experience is supposed to be a good enough reason. In 3 and 4, a doctor's authority or observations are offered as proof. In 5, it's the experience of past generations or social groups. In 6, it's the objective investigations of science. Each one of these reasons is probably assumed by millions of people to be perfectly adequate as proof or strong evidence of a treatment's power to help or cure.

But *are* they adequate? Can they help us decide if the claim that a treatment works — whether offbeat or not — is really true? Let's see by examining each of these rationales in turn.

PERSONAL EXPERIENCE

You have a headache. You drink a cup of herbal tea. In an hour your headache is gone. What could be more natural than to credit the tea for your pain relief? Isn't such a personal experience (what is often called *anecdotal evidence*) the best and most direct way to learn whether a treatment works?

Many people say yes. In fact, a large proportion of the claims made for unconventional therapies are based solely on personal experience. Testimonials by those who believe that they've been cured are common and often highly persuasive. These stories frequently go like this: "I had multiple sclerosis, and the doctors said that there was nothing they could do for me. I figured I had nothing to lose, so I tried daily megadoses of vitamin E. After one month, all my symptoms disappeared; the disease was gone, and the doctors were mystified. Vitamin E works."

The late Norman Cousins, former editor of *Saturday Review*, was one of many prominent people who put much weight on anecdotal evidence. He wrote books about his personal experience with overcoming disease. He even suggested that two instances of anecdotal evidence amount to a scientific replication of results. In *The Healing Heart* he says, "My heart attack gave me the opportunity to find out whether the same approach and technique that had worked so well before might work again. I had a chance to graduate from the anecdotal to the reproducible. The essence of the scientific method is reproducibility."[1]

Stories like Cousins's are always intriguing. But as you may have guessed from the discussion of personal experience in Chapter 3, anecdotal evidence is not always what it seems. Despite its strong appeal and despite the number of people who swear by it, *there are good reasons why personal experience generally cannot tell you if a treatment really works.* There are, in fact, good reasons to be guided by this principle:

> Personal experience alone
> generally cannot establish the
> effectiveness of a treatment beyond
> a reasonable doubt.

There are three reasons why this principle is true: many illnesses simply improve on their own; people sometimes improve even when given a treatment known to be ineffective; and other factors may cause the improvement in a person's condition.

The Variable Nature of Illness

Human physiology is immensely complicated. Drawing conclusions about what causes what inside the body is not as easy as figuring out what causes a car engine to misfire or a billiard ball to drop into the side pocket. One of the complexities that frequently confounds efforts to discover whether a treatment works is the self-limiting nature of illness. The fact is, most human ailments improve on their own — whether a treatment is administered or not. Diseases often simply disappear without any help from anybody. Plus, the symptoms of illnesses, even serious or terminal ones, can vary dramatically from day to day, with periods of both decline and improvement. Some chronic diseases like rheumatoid arthritis and multiple sclerosis (MS) can have spontaneous remissions, with symptoms vanishing for long periods of time — MS symptoms can disappear for years.

Even the course of cancer is variable. One cancer patient may live a few months; another patient with the same kind of cancer may live years. It's possible to calculate average survival times for certain cancers, but it's often extremely difficult to predict what will happen to a particular patient who gets a certain treatment or no treatment. This is one reason why doctors who predict how long a specific patient has to live are often wrong. When a patient does outlive a doctor's prediction, people sometimes credit whatever unconventional therapy the patient was taking at the time. Spontaneous remissions of cancer, even particularly lethal types, have also been documented. They're rare, and their frequency varies according to tumor type. But because they do happen, they undermine attempts to legitimately claim that a single instance of a cure was due to any particular treatment.

Often a treatment is administered when the patient's condition is deteriorating. Due to the natural variation in illness, such bad times are frequently followed by inevitable high points of improvement, so the treatment may get credit that it doesn't deserve.

So was it the herbal tea that cured your headache? Or did the headache go away on its own? Was it the vitamin E that cured the MS, or was it a spontaneous remission? Perhaps it was the treatments that did the trick. Perhaps it wasn't. The point is, because of the known variability of disease, a conclusion that the treatment worked is unfounded when based on personal experience alone.

The Placebo Effect

A peculiar fact about people is that sometimes even if they're given a treatment that's inactive or bogus, they'll respond with an improvement in the way they feel. As mentioned earlier, this response, called

Firewalking to Well-Being

For a fee, you can have an amazing personal experience and learn to do an extraordinary feat — you can walk barefoot across a red-hot bed of burning charcoal and not get burned! Yes, seminars are teaching the art of firewalking. They're promoting the idea that the practice requires esoteric skills and that mastering them can increase self-confidence, cure impotence and chronic depression, heal failing eyesight, help people stop smoking, and enhance powers of communication and persuasion. Anthony Robbins has been a major advocate of firewalking, leading many seminars and asserting that successful firewalking requires psychic or mental energy that protects the walker from burns. Science and health writer Kurt Butler, however, disputes Robbins's claims, pointing out — as several experts have — that firewalking is actually a matter of simple physics, not psychics:

> In response to [Robbins's] skullduggery, some friends and I held a firewalk and invited the public to join us for free. We received front-page newspaper coverage as well as coverage on local television news. In that event and others since, our coals have been at least as hot as Robbins's and our fire at least as long. We have been thanked for our demonstrations by grateful relatives for helping to dissuade loved ones from continuing to waste money on firewalking seminars and experiences. One mother said her daughter had already spent $35,000 following her firewalking guru to seminars and firewalks around the country. . . .
>
> In our events we have no seminar, positive thinking, or praying to invoke special powers or awaken dormant parts of our brain. In fact, following two minutes of safety instructions, our participants chant "hot coals" as they stride across the glowing bed. In over one hundred individual crossings, only one person was ever burned badly enough to raise a blister. Other groups of skeptics, most notably members of the Southern California Skeptics, have done similar demonstrations of firewalking. (Nevertheless, we all strongly urge against anyone trying to do it without advice and preferably direct supervision from an experienced person. Several safety and legal precautions are absolutely essential.)
>
> Firewalking is a physical feat, not a mental one. It is possible because charcoal, especially when coated with ashes, does not transfer heat rapidly to other objects. Its heat-transmission characteristics are similar to those of air. You can stick your hand into a very hot oven without burning yourself, but if you touch metal in the oven, you can be badly burned. The metal is no hotter than the air, but it transfers its heat much more quickly. . . .
>
> Glowing hot charcoals, of course, are not the same as hot air. The firewalkers walk (usually rapidly) on the charcoals — they don't stand around. If they did so they would be burned. Each foot is in contact with the heat for only about a second before being lifted. Moreover, the entire walk generally lasts less than seven seconds. Any longer exposure and the risk of burns is much greater.
>
> Walking on hot coals without sustaining injury is not a miraculous feat.[2]

the *placebo effect,* is not all in the mind—it can involve both psychological and physiological changes. What exactly is behind this effect isn't clear, but many experts say it depends on the power of suggestion.

In many illnesses about one-third or more of patients will get better when given a placebo. (Placebos can also cause negative side effects, just as drugs can.) People taking placebos have experienced relief of headaches, hay fever, tension, arthritis, nausea, colds, high blood pressure, premenstrual tension, mood changes, cancer, and other conditions. Many times the relief is only temporary. Placebo effects can be induced by sugar pills, worthless injections and devices, a practitioner's reassuring manner, and incantations—even by the act of walking into the doctor's office.[3]

Some people are more likely than others to get relief from placebos; in most cases, people don't respond to placebos at all. But it's difficult to tell who will respond and who won't. Having trust in the practitioner or believing in a therapy raises the chances that a placebo effect will happen. Even those who don't believe in a treatment, however, may have a placebo response.

The placebo effect can be especially impressive in the relief of pain. Psychologists Leonard Zusne and Warren H. Jones explain:

> It is well-known that expectations have a profound effect on the degree of distress that an individual will experience when in pain. Objectively measured, the anticipation of pain can be quite literally worse than the pain itself. . . . The placebo, a physiologically inert substance, can be as effective as a drug if there is expectation that it will work. The placebo effect has an obvious bearing on the relief of pain in faith healing. Clinical studies show that severe postoperative pain can be reduced in some individuals by giving them a placebo instead of a pain-killing drug, such as morphine. Some 35% of the cases studied experienced relief. On the other hand, only 75% of patients report relief from morphine.[4]

In the 1950s, some doctors thought they had discovered a cure for angina pectoris, a painful condition caused by an insufficient blood supply to the heart. Surgeons tried to improve the blood flow to the heart by tying off, or ligating, an artery inside the chest. The surgery was done on scores of patients, and most experienced dramatic improvement in their condition. But then some researchers decided to conduct a controlled study of the surgical procedure in angina patients. In their study, about half of the patients had their arteries tied off, and the others received a placebo — phony surgery in which they got an incision in their chests but no ligating of arteries. The results were eye-opening. Most patients in *both* groups experienced dramatic improvement in subjective symptoms (with one patient in the placebo

The power of suggestion to alter body function is well established by research with hypnosis. Blisters have been induced and warts made to disappear through suggestion.

—William T. Jarvis

group showing proof of improvement on electrocardiograms). None of the improvements, though, lasted longer than a few months.[5] Thus, the surgical procedure was shown to be no more effective than a placebo and was soon abandoned.

This study added angina pectoris to the long list of ailments susceptible to the placebo effect. More than that, it illustrates how the placebo effect confounds our attempts to use personal experience to conclude that a treatment really works. Maybe the treatment in question doesn't work at all, and we're simply witnessing a transitory placebo effect. If no controlled study had been done, how many people (including surgeons) would have concluded that the angina surgery was truly effective — that is, had a greater influence than a placebo? How many other angina surgeries would have been performed needlessly?

The risk of being misled by the placebo effect is why scientists include a placebo group in medical studies. The changes shown in the treatment group are compared to any changes in the placebo group. To be considered effective, the treatment under study must do better than sugar pills or sham therapies. Placebos may have a place in the modern practice of medicine. But they can also make worthless remedies look potent.

Overlooked Causes

You've had an upset stomach for two days. A friend rubs a crystal amulet across your belly, and in a few hours your stomach settles. Did the crystal heal you?

Maybe. But there are other possible causes of your relief, besides the placebo effect and natural fluctuations in your illness. Was there a change in your diet in the last day that finally eased your digestion? Was your cure caused by exercise, lack of exercise, change in bowel habits, altered daily routine, or standing on your head in yoga class? Was it the medication you took — or stopped taking? Was it the tremendous relief you got when you heard that your car was not going to be repossessed? Unfortunately, in personal experience it's extremely difficult to rule out such possible causes for any given improvement (or deterioration) in your condition. People, however, frequently ignore other possibilities and adopt the explanation that suits them. This habit is a reliable formula for reaching false conclusions.

The formula, nevertheless, is widespread. It's sometimes used, for example, by people who've undergone cancer treatment. They may have received both conventional and unconventional treatment, but they choose to credit only the unconventional.[6]

A Shark's Tale

Here's an entry in the annals of really-weird-but-briefly-famous-remedies. It was featured on none other than CBS-TV's "60 Minutes." Question: Would the "60 Minutes" segment as described below have impressed you? Would you have concluded that the remedy probably does in fact cure cancer? After you finish reading this chapter, consider these questions again.

Shark cartilage has been called to public attention by a "60 Minutes" program focused on the theories of biochemist William I. Lane, Ph.D., author of *Sharks Don't Get Cancer.* Narrator Mike Wallace began by calling attention to the book and stating that Lane says that sharks don't get cancer. The program focused on a Cuban study of twenty-nine "terminal" cancer patients who were given shark-cartilage preparations. Although the program contained many disclaimers, it was clearly promotional.

Wallace visited the site of the experiment, filmed several of the patients doing exercise, and said that most of the patients felt better several weeks after the treatment had begun. (The fact that "feeling better" does not indicate whether a cancer treatment is effective was not mentioned.) Two American cancer specialists then said that the results were intriguing. One, who was aligned with the health-food industry, said that three of the patients appeared to have improved. The other, who appeared to be solidly scientific, noted that evaluation was difficult because many of the x-ray films were of poor quality, but he thought that a few tumors had gotten smaller. (The reasons why this might not be significant were not mentioned.) After noting that shark cartilage was sold in health-food stores, Wallace remarked on the inadvisability of "going to the nearest health-food store" and was seconded by the radiation therapist who said it would be foolish to do so unless all else had failed. . . .

Like all animals, sharks *do* get cancer. Lane's book actually says so, although it claims that the number is "insignificant." The preface notes that "while *ALMOST No Sharks Get Cancer* might have been a bit more accurate, it would have been a rotten title." The Smithsonian Institution's *Registry of Tumors in Lower Animals* indicates that sharks even get cancers of their cartilage (chondromas).[8]

"Life would certainly be simpler if medical treatments could be tested as easily as puddings," says psychologist Ray Hyman.

But healing is far more complicated than cooking. If a woman says she sleeps better after being advised to change her position, should we accept this as evidence that a pendulum can determine "polarity"? If two patients improve after undergoing intense emotional experiences with Miss F [who practices "regression therapy," believing that most illnesses and emotional problems result from problems in previous lives], does this argue for the reality of "previous existences"? If scar tissue or abnormal cervical cells disappear after a patient consults a psychic healer, does this prove that psychic forces did the job?[7]

It's this whirl of possible causes that scientists try to control in properly conducted research. By controlling these confounding factors, scientists hope to narrow down the possibilities to the true cause or causes of a condition. This task requires a systematic, objective approach—something that personal experience, by definition, isn't.

For the above three reasons (and a few others), our principle must always guide us when we try to assess anecdotal evidence: *personal experience alone generally cannot establish the effectiveness of a treatment beyond a reasonable doubt.*

These reasons are reminders of the importance of considering alternative explanations when trying to make sense of any phenomenon—a principle we'll discuss in more detail later. To fail to consider alternative explanations—including the self-limiting and variable nature of illness, the placebo effect, and the presence of hidden causes—is to risk committing the *fallacy of false cause.* This common mistake is a matter of believing that two events are causally connected when in fact no such connection has been shown to exist. People can fall prey to this fallacy by concluding that the crow of the rooster causes the sun to rise, or that carrying an umbrella deters the rain, or that a treatment cured their ills while a dozen other possibilities go unconsidered.

It's also important to realize that if one person's personal experience generally can't provide reliable evidence of a treatment's efficacy, neither can the personal experiences of many people. If one person can commit the fallacy of false cause, so can a hundred. If one piece of evidence is invalid or unreliable, many more pieces of invalid or unreliable evidence don't make the case any stronger. This means that the many testimonials offered by practitioners or users to promote a favorite therapy generally don't prove much of anything—except perhaps that some people have strong beliefs about certain treatments. (Some consumer advocates also point out that many testimonials are faked.) Epidemiologist Thomas M. Vogt assesses the worth of testimonials this way:

> Suffice to say that testimonials are not reliable. The world is large, and one can find a large number of people to whom the most bizarre events have occurred. They all have personal explanations. The vast majority are wrong. It once seemed logical that the earth was flat, that pus helped wounds heal, that bloodletting cured most ills, and that pellagra was caused by a germ. In Ethiopia it is still widely believed that gonorrhea is

caused by urinating in the moonlight. There are lots of anecdotes to support each of these notions.[9]

The National Research Council expressed similar reservations about personal testimony in a report assessing popular techniques for enhancing human performance (including methods for reducing stress, altering mental states, and improving motor skills and learning):

> People are typically weak at identifying the range of [possible causes of positive changes in their lives], however simply they may be described, and at distinguishing the different ways in which the causal forces might operate. How can people know how they would have matured over time in the absence of an intervention (technique) that is being assessed? How can people disentangle effects due to a pleasant experience, a dynamic leader, or a sense of doing something important from effects due to the critical components of the treatment per se? Much research has shown that individuals are poor intuitive scientists and that they recreate a set of known cognitive biases. These include belief perseverance, selective memory, errors in attribution, and overconfidence. These biases influence experts and nonexperts alike, usually without one's awareness of them.[10]

It's not surprising, then, that numerous claims of the effectiveness of treatments have been shown to be false by controlled scientific testing though these same claims have been affirmed by many testimonials. Some examples: Vitamin C prevents the common cold; Laetrile (the trade name for a synthetic relative of the chemical amygdalin, found in apricot pits and other plants) fights cancer; the Feingold diet can prevent or treat attention deficit disorder (hyperactivity) in children.[11]

THE DOCTOR'S EVIDENCE

A physician says that megadoses of vitamin C can prolong the life of cancer patients. Another doctor avers that hair analysis (laboratory testing of a sample of human hair) can reveal a person's nutritional status. Still another doctor maintains that cellular therapy (the injection of animal cells into humans) can prevent aging. Must we conclude that these assertions are true because they come from doctors? Aren't doctors legitimate authorities, and shouldn't we rely on their say-so?

These are important questions because people often do accept a health claim solely because of a doctor's pronouncements and such pronouncements are sometimes false. The three claims just mentioned, for example, have actually been defended by some doctors even though they are false or unproven.

Quackery—the promotion and sale of useless remedies promising relief from chronic and critical health conditions— exceeds $10 billion a year.
—Claude Pepper

Weasels Are on the Loose!

Weaseling is a writing trick used in many fields, including advertising, politics, and health journalism. It's the use of certain words (called *weasel words*) to weaken a claim so that the author can say something without actually saying it and be shielded from criticism. Weaseling is often misleading yet allows the author to plead innocent to any charge of dishonesty. Perhaps the all-time prize-winning example of weaseling is the junk mail advertising come-on, "You may have already won a MILLION DOLLARS!!" Technically, the statement is true since it's physically possible that you *have* won a million dollars. But since the odds of your winning are often something like 1 in 50,000,000, the implication that you're close to being a millionaire is misleading—and, of course, is meant to be. The advertiser, however, can claim that nothing untruthful was uttered; the weasel word *may* gets him off the hook.

Some other examples:

• Let's say that in a study of laboratory rats, doses of garlic were found to inhibit the AIDS virus. Then you read this headline referring to the study: "Garlic may fight AIDS! " The head-line writer can claim that he said nothing untruthful since he merely pointed out that garlic *may* be effective against AIDS in humans. But since a rat study is extremely weak evidence for garlic's effects on the AIDS virus in humans (and most treatments found effective in animals rarely pan out in humans), the headline is misleading. Yet the writer can weasel out of any charge of dishonesty.

• Say 99.9 percent of nutritional scientists believe that taking doses of vitamin C does not prevent the common cold, and the remaining 0.1 percent believe that taking vitamin C does prevent colds. Then you read this statement in a magazine: "Good news: Some nutritional scientists believe that taking vitamin C can prevent colds." Technically, the claim is true. But it is very misleading because it doesn't tell you the whole story. The weasel word *some* allows the writer to weasel out of any blame.

• You come across an ad like this: "Formula 100B-Plus is packed with B vitamins and reportedly 'fires up' the metabolic systems that may contribute directly to bursts of energy. It may contain the combination of factors that

As noted previously, appeals to authority can indeed give us good reasons for accepting a claim. But the authority must be *qualified* to speak on the question at issue. To be qualified, an authority must have demonstrated expertise about the question at issue. It's this expertise that makes someone an authority. It's not the degree behind her name, or the school she attended, or her reputation among her peers—although all of these may be good indicators of whether she possesses the requisite expertise.

is possibly the most powerful 'ignition' for every functioning system. Experts theorize that 100B is the very best medicine to ensure daily stamina." This ad seems to promise extraordinary benefits from the product. But because of the weasel words *reportedly, may, possibly,* and *theorize,* it actually promises nothing.

In health journalism, *may* seems to be the favorite weasel word. The reason is probably that *may* can cover a multitude of meanings (or sins). *May,* which indicates a degree of probability, can be used to mean everything from "very probable but not certain" to "virtually no chance whatsoever." Too often, scientists use *may* to convey a certain level of probability regarding research results, then some journalists use the same word to imply a very different level of probability in the results.

In 1992 a *Time* magazine article on vitamins was criticized for one-sided reporting and weaseling. The National Council Against Health Fraud said, "The April 6 issue of *Time* read like [a] health food magazine as it shouted the headlines: 'New research shows they [vitamins] may help fight cancer, heart disease and the ravages of aging.' (ed. note: 'may' is a weasel word that automatically states 'may not'). . . . The article's false premise is that scientific positions which question the benefits of self-prescribed supplementation with glamour nutrients (i.e., those popularized by enthusiasts) are now outmoded. Scientists were selectively quoted. . . . Many who spoke favorably of supplements are, or have been, supported by the supplement industry."[12] *Probe* magazine also critiqued the *Time* article. It said that "in one *Time* table [the weasel word *may*] appears an incredible 15 times. But the powerful thrust of the piece, and the media message, is that the 'mays' are but quibbles."[13]

All words used to weasel, of course, can also have legitimate uses. They can be employed to add crucial qualifications to statements in order to increase precision or improve accuracy. How can you tell when weaseling is going on and when it isn't? You have to evaluate the subject, the writer, and the context. Generally, you should suspect weaseling when the words are used to imply more than what's justified or to shield the writer from criticism or blame in case his or her statements are challenged.

Medical doctors are, of course, authorities, assuming they have shown themselves to be effective healers. They're authorities in the diagnosis of disease and in applying therapeutic techniques and technology to their patients. They have the requisite know-how to treat human illness.

But are they authorities on which remedies work and don't work? Yes — *if they have the requisite expertise to answer the questions at issue.* And where does this expertise come from? As we'll soon see, generally it must be derived from objective, scientific investigation. In other words, doctors learn what works — that is, what is substantially effective in numerous patients — from science. Then they can use all their skill to apply the proven treatments. Some physicians, of course, may be scientists as well, conducting medical research, but this is a different role involving distinct skills.

Contrary to what many people believe, a doctor's work with patients generally can't give us the evidence required to assess the effectiveness of a therapy. For several reasons, doctors can't usually deduce that a treatment is valid by simply seeing patients and administering the treatment to them. The doctor is an authority on the efficacy of treatments if she knows the pertinent findings of medical science. In general, if she doesn't know this, she's no authority on efficacy, though she may know many other things about treatments (the best way to administer them, for example).

This distinction is important because occasionally a doctor will claim that treatment is effective based solely on his experience with his patients. Many people may assume that his experience alone is a good reason for accepting the claim. Generally it's not.

You might ask why a doctor could not give a treatment to several patients with the same illness, monitor what happens to them, keep records of their reactions, and then draw valid conclusions about the treatment's effectiveness. There are reasons why such actions would not be enough.

Accounts of a doctor's observations of individual patients are called *case reports* (also case series, case histories, and descriptive studies). They can be extremely valuable to other doctors and to medical scientists. "They are . . . invaluable documentaries that, once filed, may lead to exciting discoveries," says epidemiologist Stephen H. Gehlbach. Gehlbach goes on to note:

> Accounts of an unusual episode of poisoning or an atypical rash developing after administration of a new medication are examples of descriptive studies at their simplest. These reports alert clinicians about possible drug side effects, unusual complications of illnesses, or surprising presentations of disease.[14]

But, as Gehlbach points it, such accounts "do not provide detailed explanations for the cause of disease or offer the kind of evidence we need to evaluate the efficacy of a new treatment."[15]

Perhaps you've already guessed some of the reasons for this limitation of case reports. The variable nature of disease, the placebo effect, and overlooked causes can confound the doctor's attempt to draw firm conclusions about treatment efficacy, just as these factors confound attempts to pinpoint causes of symptom relief in our own personal experience. Though doctors monitor patients and keep records, case studies are compiled without the strict controls found in scientific studies, so confounding factors usually can't be ruled out. The doctor administered a treatment; the patient got better. But would the patient have gotten better anyway? Was it a placebo effect? Was some other factor involved? While the patient was being treated by the doctor, did the patient change his diet, his daily routine, his sleep patterns, his physical activities, his stress level? Was he taking some other treatment (maybe a self-treatment) while under the doctor's care? Case reports usually can't help us answer all these questions.

Case reports are also vulnerable to several serious biases that controlled research is better able to deal with. One is called *social desirability bias*. It refers to patients' tendency to strongly wish to respond to treatment in what they perceive as a correct way. People will sometimes report improvement in their condition after treatment simply because they think that's the proper response or because they want to please the doctor.

Another bias can come from doctors themselves. Called *investigator bias*, it refers to the well documented fact that investigators or clinicians sometimes see an effect in a patient because they want or expect to see it. (Recall the case of Professor Blondlot in Chapter 3.)

> One's investment in the results or anticipation of how subjects are likely to respond can easily become a self-fulfilling prophecy. This is not to impugn the integrity of investigators. Objectivity is difficult to master. It is difficult for surgeons not to find benefits from their favorite operative procedures to alleviate hemorrhoids or for social workers looking for evidence of child abuse and neglect not to uncover child maltreatment in a group known to be at high risk.[16]

Scientists use several techniques in medical research to try to minimize the effects of such biases. In case studies, bias is harder to control, and it often has sway.

For all the above reasons, we reach an inevitable conclusion about the doctor's evidence:

> Case studies alone generally cannot establish the effectiveness of a treatment beyond a reasonable doubt.

This principle and the preceding one (about personal experience) are especially handy tools in thinking about proposed treatments because

Doctors Reveal Amazing Healing Powers of Water
—TABLOID

often the only evidence offered in their favor is case studies or personal experience. Taken together, these principles create a new principle:

> When claims of a treatment's effectiveness are based solely on case studies or personal experience, you generally cannot know that the treatment is effective.

To think otherwise would be to accept claims arbitrarily, without good reasons — an open invitation to error.

These principles should cast considerable doubt on the "proof" offered in statements like "The home remedies presented here are more than just folklore — all come from the actual experience of doctors." Or "Millions of jars of the exciting Super-W Wrinkle-Removing Cream, which was developed by a pharmacist, have been purchased by women who are reporting wonderful results." Or "Dr. Miracle has documented remarkable results in over 100 patients who used his special formula."

Here are a few popular claims that have sometimes been supported with case studies or personal experience but that, to date, have essentially no firmer evidence in their favor:

- "Relaxation and mental imagery techniques can fight malignant tumors and extend the lives of cancer patients." Probably the most noted proponents of this claim have been O. Carl Simonton and Stephanie Simonton-Atchley, who wrote a best-selling book on the subject.[17]

- "It's possible to use just your hands to transfer energy to a sick person and thus promote healing." This technique, known as therapeutic touch, is used by many believers. Scientific studies have failed to provide any firm support for the claim.[18]

- "Pressing on certain areas of the hands or feet can eliminate the cause of disease in other parts of the body." This technique is called *reflexology* or *zone therapy*. Proponents insist that each part of the body is represented on zones of the hands or feet. They claim that it's possible to diagnose diseases by examining these areas and that pressing or massaging these zones affects the corresponding body part.[19]

- "Psychic surgeons can remove diseased tissue from the body without leaving a scar or wound on the skin." The ability to do such

There's gold in them thar' hills! And the rush is on. Pandering publishers, manufacturers, drugstores, "health food" stores, pharmaceutical firms, and bookstores all profit from the misinformation and mythology.
— KURT BUTLER

Cosmic Vitamins!

From a consumer health newsletter comes this report on the promotion of an unusual health product. Would you buy it?

> In-case-you-missed-it department. According to an ad in *Horoscope* magazine, "your astrological sign can predetermine health and well-being!" Fortunately, *Astrological Vitamins* "specifically formulated" to be "compatible with your own individual astrological sign" are now available so you can "protect your-self from your own health weaknesses!" The ad explains that "many astrologers believe Aries may have poor eyesight and vitamin A helps maintain normal vision" and that "Taurus is prone to throat problems and vitamin C may help increase resistance to colds." The cost is $22.95 for a 30-day supply (or $39.90 for a 2-month supply) plus a free crystal pendant for "luck, health, and long life."[21]

"psychic surgery" has been claimed by several practitioners, notably in Brazil and the Philippines. The personal experience of watching such a practitioner in action can be very impressive. Typically, a woman with a malignant stomach tumor will lie on her back. She'll remain wide awake as the psychic surgeon begins to knead the flesh on her stomach. Then the surgeon's fingers will seem to plunge into the woman's stomach as blood oozes from the area. The surgeon pulls out some bloody material, which he says is the tumor. The blood is wiped from the stomach, revealing no wound. The woman feels no pain and is relieved to see that her tumor is gone at last. Such performances, however, have been investigated and shown to be tricks, mere sleight-of-hand, in which the tissue (from animals) and blood (either a dye or also from animals) are palmed by the "surgeon" and brought into view only when their being seen will produce the desired effect.[20]

• "A macrobiotic diet is effective against cancer." Macrobiotics is a lifestyle and diet derived from Far Eastern ideas and promoted by many adherents in the United States. The diet is semivegetarian and low in fat. In recent years there have been many published accounts of people who say they have recovered from cancer because they ate a macrobiotic diet.[22] There have also been several case reports. Attempts have been made to compare the outcomes of these cases to those of patients with comparable cases of cancer who did not follow a macrobiotic diet. But this approach to evaluating a cancer treatment generally doesn't work:

Testing Iridology

There have been few scientific studies on the central claim of iridology — that diseases can be accurately detected by examination of the iris. (There's no shortage, however, of testimonials supporting the claim.) In the studies that have been done, though, iridology has failed. Science writer C. Eugene Emery Jr. investigated iridology and even arranged for a test of the diagnostic ability of three iridologists in Rhode Island (which they failed). Here he sums up the views of a prominent iridologist and the results of two scientific assessments of iridological diagnosis:

> Bernard Jensen, D.C., the leading American iridologist, claims to have worked with over 350,000 patients during almost 50 years of active practice. He states that "Nature has provided us with a miniature television screen showing the most remote portions of the body by way of nerve reflex responses." He also claims that iridology reveals "tissue strengths and weaknesses" as well as "nutritional and chemical needs." His booklet, *Iridology Simplified*, relates more than 30 diseases and conditions (including arthritis,

> biliousness, gallstones, obesity and tuberculosis) to "mineral deficiencies.". . .

> Jensen and two other practitioners were tested in a study published in the September 28, 1979 *Journal of the American Medical Association*. In this study, the iridologists were shown iris photographs of 143 patients, some with severe kidney disease and some with no evidence of kidney problems. The assessment of kidney problems was based on the levels of creatinine in the blood. When asked to identify the people with problems, all three iridologists failed the test.

> Five Dutch iridologists failed a similar test . . . when they tried to detect gallbladder disease by looking at slides of the iris of 39 patients with gallstones (proven by surgery the day after the slides were made) and 39 patients without gallstones (proven by ultrasound examination). The iridologists were correct only half the time (the result expected by chance), and did not agree among themselves about which patients had gallstones and which did not [*British Medical Journal* 297:1578 – 1581, Dec. 17, 1988].[25]

Except in rare circumstances, because of the heterogeneity of cancer patients' clinical courses, it is virtually impossible to predict what would have happened to a particular patient if he or she had had no treatment or a different treatment. Groups of patients who have chosen to take a particular treatment cannot be compared retrospectively with other groups of patients, even those with similar disease, to determine the effects of the treatment. The factors that set apart patients who take unconventional treatments from other cancer patients may be related to prognosis (these may be both physical and psychological factors), and the means do not exist currently to confidently "adjust" for these factors in analyses. Examples of retrospective evaluations that have turned out to be wrong are well documented.[23]

This chapter is mostly about claims of treatment efficacy, but the above cautions about basing such beliefs on personal experience and case studies also apply to claims about disease diagnosis. Here, too, we can find popular claims based solely on these less reliable grounds. For example, some people claim that it's impossible to diagnose states of health and disease anywhere in the body by examining only the iris (the colored part of the eyes). This is the basic claim of iridology (pronounced "eye-ridology"). In scientific tests, however, practitioners of iridology (called iridologists) have never been able to diagnose bodily states accurately.[24]

THE APPEAL TO TRADITION

Our understanding of the limitations of personal experience and case studies can now help us put ancient practice and folklore in perspective. The appeal to ancient practice says, "We know this treatment works because the repeated experience of generations shows that it does." An appeal to folklore says, "We know this treatment works because the experience of social or cultural groups shows that it does." But the fact is, the confounding factors and biases inherent in personal experience don't necessarily disappear just because personal experience has been repeated for 1,000 years or is shared by whole tribes.

We should remember that some of the ancient practices allegedly tested and found useful by generations of healers include things like bloodletting, leeching, and purging. Many herbs have reputations in folklore as potent remedies, yet are actually ineffective for the recommended uses or are highly toxic.[26]

The point is not that remedies backed by ancient practice or folklore don't work. Some do. Indeed, many modern treatments are actually based on such treatments. The point is that the mere fact that a treatment is supported by such revered experiences does not mean it works. Maybe it does; maybe it doesn't. Scientific testing can often reveal the answer, and ancient practice or folklore can sometimes provide leads.

THE REASONS OF SCIENCE

Now we come to a different set of reasons for accepting the claim that a treatment is efficacious—those based on science. The arguments often sound like this: "Scientific studies show that treatment X works." Or "Scientific research indicates that treatment X alleviates symptoms

The "Modus Operandi" of Quackery

Quackery is considered the promotion of false or unproven remedies for profit. Many consumer advocates say that health fraud and quackery are so pervasive in the United States that government agencies can't adequately handle the problem. So they urge consumers to learn how to recognize quackery and protect themselves from it. They also say that the practitioners and promoters of quackery often have the following characteristic behavior patterns:

1. They promise quick, dramatic, simple, painless, or drugless treatment or cures.

2. They use anecdotes, case histories, or testimonials to support claims. Prominent people such as actors, writers, baseball players, and even physicians may be used in testimonials. . . .

3. They use disclaimers couched in pseudomedical or pseudoscientific jargon. Instead of promising to treat or cure a specific illness or condition, they offer to "detoxify" the body, "strengthen the immune system," "balance body chemistry," or bring the body into "harmony with nature."

4. They may display credentials or use titles that might be confused with those of the scientific or medical community. Use of the terms professor, doctor, or nutritionist may be spurious. Their credentials may be from an unaccredited school or an organization that promotes non-scientific methods.

5. The results they claim have not been verified by others or published in a reputable scientific journal.

6. They claim that a single product or service can cure a wide range of unrelated illnesses.

7. They claim to have a secret cure or one that is recognized in other parts of the world but not yet known or accepted in the United States.

8. They claim to be persecuted by organized medicine and that their treatment is being suppressed because it is controversial or because the medical establishment does not want competition.

9. They state that medical doctors should not be trusted because surgery, x-rays, and drugs cause more harm than good. They say most doctors are "butchers" and "poisoners."

10. They claim that most disease is due to a faulty diet and can be treated by nutritional methods.

11. They use scare tactics to encourage use of the product or service advocated. They say lack of adequate intake of vitamins and minerals results in poor nutrition that may cause troublesome conditions. They state that food additives and preservatives may poison people.

12. They claim that most Americans are poorly nourished and need "nutrition insurance."

13. They advise vitamins and "health foods" for everyone.

14. They use hair analysis to determine nutritional needs.

15. They claim that natural vitamins are better than synthetic ones."[27]

of condition Y." These arguments derive their strength from this fact, which we express as a critical principle:

> Scientific evidence gained through controlled experiments — unlike personal experience and case studies — generally can establish the effectiveness of a treatment beyond a reasonable doubt.

Unfortunately, this principle alone won't get you very far. In books and magazines, in newspapers, on radio and television, and in private conversation, you're peppered with appeals to scientific evidence. In the world of health and medicine, the findings of science are cited by both orthodox and unorthodox practitioners to support both valuable and worthless treatments. Many assessments of the evidence are reliable and informative; others are biased and misleading. The stakes are high because the conclusions you draw from all this could dramatically affect your health. A magazine article might report that a scientific study of fifteen people shows that vitamin C cures cancer. An author might say that a study of thousands of people indicates that all adults should include walnuts in their diets. Someone on a talk show may conclude that you should never drink cola again because large doses of it caused tumors in labora-tory rats. What are you to make of such pronouncements? If you're not a scientist, how are you to evaluate these appeals to scientific evidence?

First, understand that it's indeed possible for nonscientists to make some reasonable judgments about medical evidence. Most of the time, of course, you must rely heavily on reliable authorities (as previously defined) for guidance. But even without such guidance you can often draw reasonable and useful conclusions about medical research *if you understand some of the peculiar characteristics and limitations of this kind of evidence.*

So let's begin with the essentials of this understanding and see how these considerations can help you assess the science behind claims of a treatment's efficacy.

Medical Research

The basic unit of scientific research in medicine is the study (in some cases called the *experiment*). Its purpose is to critically evaluate scientific hypotheses such as "Antibiotic X inhibits bacteria Y under certain conditions" or "Daily doses of vitamin B₆ can alleviate premenstrual syndrome in women." In a study, evidence is gathered through careful observation and experimentation. From beginning to end, the study is intended to be done under conditions that maximize objectivity, accuracy of measurement, and control over extraneous variables. The results of a well-done study can support (provide evidence for) the hypothesis or fail to support it. Sometimes studies are done on cells in a test tube, sometimes on laboratory animals, and sometimes on humans.

Scientific hypotheses are empirical statements — those whose truth can be confirmed by observation of the world. So scientific studies concern themselves with matters of empirical fact, not of value. Thus the results (the empirical findings) of medical studies can tell you what the facts are — not what to do about them. They can show that taking high doses of vitamin C over extended periods of time does not prevent occurrence of the common cold. They can't tell you what you should do about this information. The question of whether you should stop taking vitamin C, continue taking it, reduce your dose, start taking it, or make any other choice cannot be answered by medical studies on vitamin C. Certainly studies can give you information that may help you make a more informed decision, but they can't supply the values. Scientific studies aren't in that line of work.

When scientists complete a study, they try to get it published in a scientific journal. The best journals subject studies to peer review before publication — that is, experts examine the study to see whether it should be accepted for publication, changed to correct flaws, or rejected. If the study gets into print, other scientists can criticize it, use it, or try to repeat the study for themselves (a process called *replication*, a critical step in science). In this way, medical science can progress. Usually, when you read about a medical study in magazines or newspapers, it's been published in a journal, though not necessarily a peer-reviewed one. Often, though, the study is unpublished.

Behind this tidy picture of medical science, however, are some untidy facts you should know:

Single Studies. It may seem reasonable to assume that one medical study can usually offer conclusive evidence because it's conducted by scientists who try to be objective and conscientious and because, after all, it's *science*. But this assumption is false.

Conducting medical research is exacting work, and many things can go wrong — and often do. Several scientific reviews of medical studies have concluded that a large proportion of published studies are seriously flawed. (In the words of one review, "The mere fact that research reports are published, even in the most prestigious journals, is no guarantee of their quality."[28] An expert on the medical literature cautions, "the odds are good that the authors [of published clinical research] have arrived at invalid conclusions."[29]) Confounding variables and bias may creep in and skew results. The sample studied may be too small or not representative. The statistical analysis of data may be faulty. In rare cases, the data may even turn out to be faked or massaged. There may be many other detected or undetected inadequacies, and often these are serious enough to cripple a study and cast substantial doubt on its conclusions.

To minimize this potential for error, inadequacy, or fraud, medical scientists seek replication. Several studies yielding essentially the same results can render a hypothesis more probable than would a long study. "Two studies seldom have identical sources of error or bias," says Vogt. "With three or four studies, the chance is even less that the same flaws are shared."[30] All of this means that evidence for or against a certain treatment generally accumulates slowly. Despite the impression often left by the media, medical breakthroughs arising out of a single study are extremely rare.

For these reasons and a few more discussed below, we can say the following:

> Single medical studies generally cannot establish the effectiveness of a treatment beyond a reasonable doubt.

Unless you're a scientist or have some skill in the evaluation of the medical literature, eliminating doubt will have to rest on the reports of reliable authorities. In such a case, it's not reasonable for you to accept the claim of a treatment's efficacy based on one study unless most qualified experts are willing to do so.

This principle holds regardless of what spin the media, advertisers, and other nonscientists try to put on the meaning of a medical study. It also holds even when a scientist enthusiastically endorses the validity of his or her own studies. Scientists are human, too; as such, they sometimes allow their commitment to their own work to bias their perception and their judgment. We need to understand this — and guard against it.

Conflicting Results.   Somewhere you may have read these health claims prompted by scientific studies: taking vitamin E relieves angina pain, and taking vitamin E does not relieve angina pain. Or how about this pair: vitamin E eases fibrocystic breast disease (breast lumps), and vitamin E is not effective against fibrocystic breast disease. What's going on here?

As is often the case, the underlying conflict in these pairs is between the results of preliminary or flawed research and that of less preliminary, better-designed research. (The second claim in each pair is the better-supported claim.) Errors, of course, can cause conflicting results among studies. But also, the results of preliminary studies (in test tubes, on laboratory animals, or with only a few human subjects) often contradict those of more rigorous studies of many human subjects. This conflict is expected, just as we would expect discrepancies between the information revealed by a quick glance and a long, close look. Other problems arise when the media report preliminary study results as though they were well established. Then when different sets of hyped results conflict, there's confusion, and scientists look as though they can't make up their minds.

When the results of studies conflict, scientists try to sort things out. They criticize the existing studies; they do bigger and better studies. The process can continue for years until the issue is resolved.

Previously we discussed what to do when experts disagree. A corollary to that tenet will help you when faced with unresolved conflict among studies:

> When the results of relevant
> studies conflict, you cannot know
> that the treatment in question is
> effective.

This principle must guide nonscientists because they usually don't have the expertise to resolve conflict among studies or to take sides among disagreeing scientists. They can't simply choose the study results that support the claim they like best, nor can they assume that a conflict shows that a treatment being tested is effective for some people but not for others. It generally would be extremely difficult for nonscientists to judge whether they had good reasons (which would have to be both valid and technical) to decide a conflict and accept a disputed claim. In this case, the reasonable course is to suspend judgment until scientists resolve the conflict.

It may be possible, however, for nonscientists with some skill in assessing the medical evidence to acquire good reasons. A qualified expert, for example, could present them with reasons that they understood and judged to be valid and compelling.

Studies Conflicting with Fact.   Let's say that a new, well-designed study suggests, to everyone's surprise, that lifelong cigarette smoking *prevents* lung cancer in humans. Should we conclude that it's time to buy a carton of Camels and light up? Should we write our legislators and insist that the Surgeon General's warnings against cigarette smoking be expunged from every pack?

No—and not just because the revolutionary research is just a single study. The main reason is that the new finding that smoking prevents lung cancer would be contrary to a mountain of credible research repeated and verified countless times over many years. It is possible that this mountain of research is wrong and the new study right, but it would be unreasonable to assume so. To accept the new study would be to ignore the weight of evidence and thus to believe something arbitrarily. It would be more reasonable to believe that the new study is probably seriously flawed. The point is this:

> New study results that conflict
> with well-established findings
> cannot establish the effectiveness
> of a treatment beyond a reasonable
> doubt.

If, however, more and more research supports the revolutionary finding and the preponderance of evidence shifts conclusively in its favor, scientists must rethink the issue and probably discard the old view.

Limitations of Studies.   All medical studies are not created equal. Medical studies can vary in more than just quality. There are several different types, and they differ dramatically in their strength to support hypotheses about the efficacy of treatments or cause and effect. Scientists, and anyone else who tries to make sense of medical research, must understand these differences and give more weight to studies with the greater strength. They must also allow for the inherent limitations of different types of studies. On the next pages, we'll discuss the major types of medical studies, listed roughly from weakest to strongest in terms of their conclusiveness.

Is It Right to Promote Unproven Treatments?

In this chapter (and in this book) the focus has been on determining answers to questions about *what's true*. But in the world of health and medicine, such concerns are often intertwined with values—that is, *what's right*. One such value question that frequently arises is whether it's ethical to recommend or promote an unproven treatment—one that has little or no scientific evidence supporting its efficacy. The question often looms over remedies called "alternative" or "unconventional."

The issue is important because companies, advertisers, special interest groups, magazines, newspapers, TV talk shows, health practitioners, and others often do promote remedies and health practices that are unproven. This practice—for better or worse—can have enormous consequences for all of us.

Most medical scientists and health officials oppose the practice, sometimes warning that there isn't yet enough evidence to recommend a certain treatment to the public. Promoters of unproven treatments strongly disagree and sometimes ridicule officials for being "overly cautious" or "too conservative." Their most plausible arguments usually involve an appeal to the relative costs and benefits of a treatment. "What's the harm?" they may ask. "If the treatment itself is harmless, why shouldn't suffering people be given a chance to try it? There may be no strong evidence that it works, but if it does, the benefits to many people would be substantial. The costs to people—in terms of potential physical harm—are low. So on balance, it's best to urge people to try it; the possible benefits outweigh the possible costs." Promoters may believe that this argument is especially strong if the treatment has some pre-liminary evidence in its favor or if the monetary outlay for the treatment is low.

But is this really a good argument? Many on both sides in the debate would probably agree that weighing costs and benefits is a valid way to judge the issue. (This approach is based on the fundamental ethical insight that we ought to do what's likely to benefit people and avoid doing what's likely to harm them.) So the question reduces to whether promoting unproven treatments is likely to result in a net benefit to people. Does the promoter's argument show that his promoting leads to such benefit? Actually, his argument fails. It fails because it's too simplistic, neglecting to take into account important factors in the cost-benefit equation.

One such factor is *probability*. Few people would judge a treatment solely on the magnitude of its proposed benefit or harm. Most would want to take into account the probability that the proposed effects would happen. Someone may claim that rubbing a stone on your belly will cure cancer. The alleged benefit is enormous—but the likelihood of receiving this benefit is almost nil. If someone wanted to sell you such a "cancer-curing" stone for ten dollars, would you buy it? Probably not. The proposed benefit is great but not likely to happen. The cost, though, is a sure thing: if you want the stone, you'll have to pay the price. So on balance, the likely cost, though small, outweighs the unlikely benefits, though great.

But what's the probability that any unproven remedy will be effective? The evidence relating to the remedy can't tell us; by definition, it's too weak to help us figure probabilities. We can, however, make a reasonable assumption. Scientists know that the chances of new hypotheses being correct are very low simply because it's far easier to be wrong than to be right. For the same reason, the likelihood of new health claims turning out to be true is also low. Historically, most health hypotheses, when adequately tested, have been found to be false. In drug testing, for example, scientists may begin with thousands of substances proposed as medicines, some with preliminary evidence in their favor. In the end, after assessing them all, only a meager handful are proven effective in humans. Some promoters misjudge the cost-benefit of recommending a treatment because they either overestimate the probability of its effectiveness or don't consider the factor at all. They seem to assume that the odds of any proposed remedy being effective are close to fifty-fifty, especially if there's some preliminary evidence in its favor. This assumption is false.

When we plug realistic probabilities into our moral equation, the wisdom of promoting unproven treatments becomes suspect. Even if an unproven treatment has considerable possible benefits, is harmless, and costs little, it may be no bargain. In general, given the realistic probabilities, the most likely prospect is that the treatment will be ineffective. So, in fact, the odds are excellent that people who buy the treatment will waste their time and money. The likely cost outweighs the unlikely benefits. Promoting the treatment is not likely to result in a net benefit for people, but net harm. The possible benefit of a ten-dollar "cancer-fighting" rock may be great, but the low probability of its working makes buying it a bad deal. Promoting it would be unethical.

Clearly, the higher the cost of an unproven treatment, the less likely that promoting it will result in a net benefit. But there's more to the cost of an unproven treatment than many promoters realize. The monetary cost can vary tremendously and may not be low at all. (Many unconventional treatments cost hundreds or even thousands of dollars.) Other costs include the direct physical harm that a treatment can cause (nearly all treatments — drugs, surgery, herbs, vitamins, and others — cause some side effects). There's also an indirect cost: A few people (maybe many people) may take the promoter seriously and stop, postpone, or refuse a proven therapy to try the unproven one — a gamble that sometimes has tragic consequences. Then there's the very real emotional pain that false hope can often bring. In these ways, even a harmless therapy can cause harm. All these costs must be factored into the cost-benefit equation. Usually, they just make the promoter's argument weaker.

Now, it's possible that a person could apply the cost-benefit approach in her own life and rightly conclude that she *should* try an unproven remedy. She could calculate that any possible benefit, though very unlikely, is well worth the cost because no other treatment is possible or because she considers the cost inconsequential. Promoters, however, aren't privy to such personal information about those who try unproven remedies. Promoters can only weigh the probable impact of their actions on other people. If they do so honestly, they'll have to conclude that, generally, promoting unproven treatments does more harm than good.

Types of Studies

In Vitro Experiments.   Test-tube studies (*in vitro* means "within a glass") are the most fundamental kind of study — though they may or may not actually be done in test tubes. They can involve tissues and cells from both animals and people, but they're not carried out on *living* animals or people

This kind of research can offer weak supporting evidence for a hypothesis or important clues about how something in the human body might work. But one test-tube study or a hundred test-tube studies can't provide strong evidence for the effectiveness of a treatment in a living human. The reason is the enormous difficulty of extrapolating from the laboratory to a living organism. What transpires in a Petri dish may never happen in a living body. In the dish, a drug may dramatically affect nerve cells. But in the body, multitudes of different processes and substances might block, dilute, reroute, or inhibit that drug. Generally, the chances of test-tube results being duplicated in humans is low.

These points generate a principle:

> Test-tube studies alone generally cannot establish the effectiveness of a treatment beyond a reasonable doubt.

Nevertheless, you may occasionally encounter media coverage that assumes the opposite. Reports may focus on substances that have interesting effects in test tubes (inhibiting the AIDS virus, for example) and then imply (subtly or not so subtly) that the same effects will happen in humans. Those who publish such reports are either unaware of or willfully ignoring the limitations of test-tube studies.

Animal Studies.   Animal experiments can give scientists important leads in understanding human disease. They can give us clues about the possible value of drugs or the hazards of chemicals. They can offer support for a medical hypothesis — usually weak support, though once in a while the findings can be startling. But by themselves, animal studies can't show that a therapy works in humans, nor can they show that a substance is safe for humans. These facts are mostly due to the genetic and physiological differences between *Homo sapiens* and animals. Science and medical writer Victor Cohn sums up the differences this way:

Animals are often much like people in their reactions, and often very different. The challenge to scientists is to pick the right animal model for the subject — the human disease or risk or physiological change — being studied. Armadillos are reasonable models for the study of leprosy, cats for deafness, chimpanzees for AIDS, mice for cancer and epilepsy, rats for diabetes and aging, and dogs for many conditions, but no animal is a completely satisfactory model for any human disease.

Cortisone gives cleft palate to mice but not men. A dose of morphine that can kill a human merely anesthetizes a dog. Arsenic doesn't induce cancer in animals but does in man. A late colleague of mine would toss many an animal research story aside with the comment "Mice are not men."[33]

Also, extrapolating from animals to humans in studies of chronic diseases is especially risky. Such illnesses generally take a long time to develop in people. The lifespan of lab animals is usually much shorter than humans'.

It should be no surprise, then, that most treatments proven effective in animals usually don't pan out in humans. So our guiding principle must be the following:

> Animal studies alone generally
> cannot establish the effectiveness
> of a treatment beyond a reasonable
> doubt.

Still, many people do accept claims of effectiveness based solely on animal research. Thomas Vogt offers an interesting example:

from my files I found a[n] article from a daily San Francisco Bay area newspaper which was headlined: Heart Attacks from Lack of 'C'? The assistant professor quoted in the story had done studies on rabbits. He was quoted as saying, "I keep playing devil's advocate, asking all the questions my critics will ask. But all the pieces of the puzzle fit. It has to be right."

Next to that item was a news clipping from . . . the *National Enquirer*. The headline read: People Who Take Vitamin C Increase Their Chances of a Heart Attack. The "top medical researcher" quoted in this story had worked with rats and concluded that his experimental animals which "were essentially middle-aged, comparable to people in their forties and fifties," had higher cholesterol levels when fed vitamin C than did those fed similar diets without vitamin C. From this he inferred that the vitamins increased the risk of heart attack in humans. The problem with both of these stories is not that the studies were improperly performed, but rather that a single animal study had given rise to banner headlines and national publicity falsely inferring cause to their lack or excess of vitamin C.[32]

Observational Studies. Studies based on observing human subjects are also called *nonintervention* or *epidemiological studies*. They include several kinds of human studies whose names you often see in the titles of medical articles — case-control, cohort, cross-sectional, prospective. Their common feature is that they don't involve *intervening* in the subjects' lives to test something. They don't involve administering treatments. (This distinguishes them from intervention studies, usually called *clinical trials*, in which scientists do intervene in subjects' lives.)

Their purpose is to examine the natural course of health and disease. Sometimes this task is as straightforward as describing the incidence of or mortality rates for some disease. Usually, though, it involves the search for revealing *associations* between disease or health and other key factors. Scientists gather data about subjects, their health, and factors that may influence their health. Then they sort and analyze the data, making comparisons. One kind of observational study, for example, may uncover an association between the rate of cigarette smoking over ten years in women and women's ten-year mortality rate due to lung cancer. Another kind might find that people who have high-sodium diets are more likely to have hypertension. Still another might discover that the more fruits and vegetables people eat, the lower their risk of cancer.

The famous Framingham Heart Study is a cohort study that for years has monitored the health habits and physiological status of over 5,000 people in Framingham, Massachusetts. What it found, among other things, was that people with high serum cholesterol and high blood pressure were more likely to develop heart disease than those who didn't have these symptoms. These findings don't in themselves show that high cholesterol and high blood pressure *cause* heart disease — only that people with these symptoms are more likely to get the disease. In other words, those people are at greater risk.

The important thing to remember here is that observational studies alone — no matter how many thousands of subjects they iclude — *cannot* prove cause-and-effect relationships. They can onlyshow associations and thus hint at possible causal connections. It's even difficult for one observational study alone to demonstrate that a causal connection is likely. These studies can show that factor X is consistently linked to condition Y. But they can't demonstrate that X causes Y, or that Y causes X, or that there's any causal connection at all. Only controlled intervention studies can demonstrate such things.

Many observational studies with similar results, however, can build a strong case for cause and effect. It was many such studies involving thousands of people over several decades that showed that it was almost certain that cigarette smoking causes cancer. The findings of the Framingham Heart Study, along with a lot of other corroborating observational studies, became the basis for recommendations for reducing high blood pressure.

Scientists are keenly aware of how easy it is to uncover associations and how hard it is to determine whether these links are actually cause-and-effect relationships. If you select a group of people and compile data about their health, lifestyle, and environment, you could uncover hundreds of associations. You may find direct associations between shirt size and blood pressure, or body weight and ownership of Ford pickup trucks, or incidence of diabetes and choice of deodorant soap. But few of these links would be causal. It's possible to demonstrate that the incidence of AIDS has risen as VCR sales have risen. Do VCRs cause AIDS? The physical height of children increases as their lifetime total of hours spent watching television increases. Does television watching promote physical growth?

It may be tempting, when you read that daily intake of vitamin A is associated with a lower incidence of arthritis pain to conclude that vitamin A must cause arthritis pain to go away. But the conclusion would be unwarranted. It could be that people who take vitamin A also do several other things that are the real cause of less pain. Maybe people who take more vitamin A are also more likely to take their pain medication or get proper exercise. Or vitamin A could just be an indicator that other vitamins or nonvitamin factors are present in the body, and *they* are the real pain-relievers.

Pizza Cuts Heart Attack Risk
—Tabloid

In a cohort study of 31,208 Seventh-Day Adventists, scientists found that subjects who frequently ate nuts were less likely to die of coronary heart disease than those who ate nuts less often.[33] Does this mean that nuts can protect us from fatal heart attacks? Should we now make a big effort to work more nuts into our diets, as some people have suggested? This study may have been well conducted, and its data may be of very high quality. But it's an observational study, with all the limitations inherent in such research. Thus, this research is a long way from demonstrating that frequent consumption of nuts can prevent death from heart disease. Even to say "Frequent nut consumption had a protective effect" would be an overstatement. Generally, to show that a causal connection probably exists, *several* observational studies are required.

This gives us another principle:

Observational studies alone generally cannot establish the effectiveness of a treatment beyond a reasonable doubt.

Homeopathy: Does It Work?

Homeopathy is based on the idea that extremely tiny doses of substances that cause disease symptoms in a healthy person can cure people suffering from similar symptoms. Samuel Hahnemann (1755–1843), a German physician, was the first to apply this notion systematically. He also added what he called the "law of infinitesimals," the proposition that — contrary to the findings of science — the smaller the dose, the more powerful the medicine. So he treated people with drastically diluted substances — so diluted that, in many homoeopathic medicines, not even one molecule of the substance remains. Hahnemann admitted this but believed that the substances somehow left behind an imperceptible "spirit-like" essence that effected cures. This essence was supposed to revitalize the "vital force" in the body.

Today, the theory and practice of Hahnemann's homeopathy are still intact. There are hundreds of homeopathic practitioners in the United States (and hundreds more in other countries) and thousands of people who try homeopathic treatments.

But do homeopathic remedies really work? Medical experts say no and offer this alternative hypothesis: Homeopathic remedies act as placebos.

There are several factors that make the homeopathy hypothesis less likely than the placebo one. First, homeopathy postulates both an undetectable essence and an unknown mysterious force. Other things being equal, the more unproven assumptions a hypothesis rests on, the less likely it is to be true. These assumptions alone are serious problems for the homeopathy hypothesis. Homeopathy also conflicts with a massive amount of scientific experience regarding the action of substances in the human body. There isn't a single verified instance in pharmacology of any substance having a stronger effect the more diluted it becomes. Further, the existing scientific evidence in favor of homeopathy (reviewed below) is extremely weak. All of this shows that homeopathy is a much weaker hypothesis than the placebo hypothesis. In fact, in light of these concerns, the probability of homeopathic remedies being effective seems extremely low. New research that gives strong support to homeopathy, of course, could change this verdict.

Here's a recent summation of existing scientific evidence:

Since many homeopathic remedies contain no detectable amount of active ingredient, it is impossible to test whether they contain

Clinical Trials. Of all the different types of medical studies, clinical studies offer the strongest and clearest support for any claim that a treatment is effective because they can establish cause and effect beyond a reasonable doubt. This is true because clinical trials allow scientists to control extraneous variables and test one factor at a time. Properly conducted clinical trials have become the gold standard of

what their label says. They have been presumed safe, but unlike most potent drugs, they have not been proven effective against disease by double-blind testing.

Probably the best review of homeopathic research is the two-part article by A. M. Scofield, Ph.D., a British biochemistry professor. Published in 1984 in the *British Homeopathic Journal*, the article concludes: "Despite a great deal of experimental and clinical work there is only a little scientific evidence to suggest that homeopathy is effective. This is because of bad design, execution, reporting or failure to repeat promising experimental work and not necessarily because of the inefficacy of the system which has yet to be properly tested on a large enough scale. . . . It is hardly surprising in view of the quality of much of the experimental work as well as its philosophical framework, that this system is not accepted by the medical and scientific community at large."

In 1986, the British journal *Lancet* published a report that fifty-six hay fever patients who were given a homeopathic preparation of mixed grass pollens had fewer symptoms than a comparable group of fifty-two patients who received a placebo. In 1989, *Lancet* reported another study in which a homeopathic remedy showed modest benefit for flu-like symptoms. Future studies should include an independent laboratory analysis to ensure that the homeopathic products have not been adulterated with therapeutic amounts of drugs known to be effective.

In 1990, an article in *Review of Epidemiology* analyzed forty randomized trials that had compared homeopathic treatment with standard treatment, a placebo, or no treatment. The authors concluded that all but three of the trials had major flaws in their design and that only one of those three had reported a positive result. The authors concluded that there is no evidence that homeopathic treatment has any more value than a placebo.

Proponents trumpet the few "positive" studies as proof that "homeopathy works." Even if their results can be consistently reproduced (which seems unlikely), the most that the study of a single remedy for a single disease could prove is that the remedy is effective against *that* disease. It would not validate homeopathy's basic theories."[35]

medical evidence, having proven themselves again and again. As Cohn observes:

> Randomized clinical trials proved that new drugs could cut the heart attack death rate, that treating hypertension could prevent strokes, and that polio, measles, and hepatitis vaccines worked. No doctor, observing a limited number of patients, could have shown these things.[34]

In clinical trials designed to test treatment efficacy, an experimental group of subjects receives the treatment in question. A control group that's as similar to the experimental group as possible doesn't get the treatment. (Use of a control group makes the study a controlled trial.) Scientists then compare pertinent differences between the two groups to verify whether the treatment has any effect. The control group is essential. Without it, there's generally no way to tell whether the treatment really worked. With no control group, it's usually not possible to know whether the subjects' condition would have changed even without treatment, or that some factor besides the treatment (like the subjects' lifestyle) was responsible for any positive results, or that the placebo effect was at work, or that some change in the subjects' behavior after getting the treatment was what made the difference. By comparing results in the experimental group to those in the control group, researchers can determine whether the experimental treatment was more effective than would be expected due to these other factors alone.

To minimize confounding factors, subjects in the control group often receive a placebo. (Such a study is then referred to as a *placebo-controlled trial.*) Placebos are given as if they're effective therapy because, as mentioned previously, many people experience signs of improvement even when they're given a worthless treatment (the placebo effect). Scientists compare the results in the experimental group with that in the placebo control group. If the experimental treatment is truly effective — and not merely a placebo itself — it should perform much better than the placebo.

Frequently, especially in drug testing, the control group gets not a placebo but an already proven treatment. The purpose of the study is to determine if the new treatment works better than the established, or standard, one.

Another extremely important element in clinical trials is *blinding* — a practice used to ensure that subjects, and if possible researchers, don't know which subjects are getting the experimental treatment or the placebo. This practice is followed to avoid having knowledge of the experiment taint the results. If subjects know which therapy is the placebo and which the true treatment, some of them may feel better when they get the treatment, whether it's truly effective or not. Or if they know they've received a placebo, they may change their health habits to compensate. Or they may even try to obtain the true therapy on their own. Similar problems can affect the scientists conducting the study. If researchers know who received which treatment, they may unconsciously bias the test data. Well-designed clinical trials are *double-blind*, which means that neither the subjects nor the scientists know who's getting which treatment.

Now, many common missteps in both study design and execution can be fatal to a clinical trial, severely weakening the study or rendering its data useless. Most of these flaws can be detected only by qualified experts. But there are at least three study limitations that can often be apparent to nonscientists and that can seriously undermine a study's support for any claim as to a treatment's efficacy: the lack of a control group; faulty comparisons; and small sample sizes.

1. *Lack of a control group.* Without a control group, a clinical trial can generally prove very little, if anything. Clinical trials without a control group (called *uncontrolled*) are about as useful as evidence as are testimonials and case studies. If one uncontrolled trial proves little or nothing, having several that report the same results doesn't make the case any stronger.

2. *Faulty comparisons.* The experimental group and the control group should be as alike as possible in all important respects. When they are not alike, confounding factors can skew the study results. Let's say that a clinical trial is conducted to test the effectiveness of a new drug to prevent heart disease in men. One group of men takes the drug; a control group gets a placebo. After three years, the researchers discover that only a few of the men in the drug group developed heart disease, but many more men in the control group did. These results make the drug look pretty good. But what if you learn that the men in the drug group were, on average, ten years younger than the men in the control group? This fact would make the results very dubious because the incidence of heart disease is known to increase with age. Or what if a third of the control-group men smoke, and none of the men in the other group do? This fact would cast serious doubt on the results because smoking is a known cause of heart disease.

In clinical trials, it's frequently critical that groups be comparable in health status, occupation, race, age, income, nationality, and relevant behaviors like exercise and smoking. But these variables are often ignored, which seriously weakens study findings and claims based on them.

To protect against the problem of noncomparable groups, scientists use a technique called *randomization*. Subjects are *randomly* assigned to either the experimental or control group, with each subject having an equal chance to be assigned to each group. This helps to ensure that if there are any important differences in the subjects, the differences will be evenly distributed among both groups. This helps neutralize the kind of biases mentioned above, especially those the scientist isn't aware of. Lack of randomization in a clinical trial is usually a notable deficiency; sometimes it's a pivotal defect.

3. *Small numbers.* Some clinical studies may have fewer than thirty subjects. These are generally considered pilot studies, offering a quick and relatively inexpensive way to test a treatment's possibilities. They're designed to see if anything is out there, to determine if larger clinical trials should be done. But generally they cannot give much support to a claim that a treatment is effective. With so few subjects, the chance that some confounding variable will skew results is great. Also large is the chance of a small study suggesting that a treatment works when in fact it doesn't. (There's also the insidious problem of publication bias, a form of which is the tendency to publish studies that show positive results and not to publish studies yielding negative results. Publication bias is more likely when small studies are involved.) In addition, because small studies usually last for brief periods, they can't help us draw conclusions about long term conditions.

These three limitations of clinical trials can be decisive in our assessment of claims that a treatment works if those claims are supported by such studies. The operative principle is:

> Clinical trials with any of these limitations generally cannot establish the effectiveness of a treatment beyond a reasonable doubt.

It may be reasonable to believe that a specific case is an exception to this rule — but only if you have good reasons. As in most situations, these good reasons must come from qualified experts.

SUGGESTED READINGS

Barrett, Stephen, and William Jarvis, eds. *The Health Robbers.* Buffalo: Prometheus Books, 1993.

Gehlbach, Stephen. *Interpreting the Medical Literature.* New York: Macmillan, 1988.

Office of Technology Assessment. *Unconventional Cancer Treatments.* Washington, D.C.: U.S. Government Printing Office, 1990.

Stalker, Douglas, and Clark Glymour, eds. *Examining Holistic Medicine.* Buffalo: Prometheus Books, 1989.

Vogt, Thomas M. *Making Health Decisions.* Chicago: Nelson-Hall, 1983.

NOTES

1. Norman Cousins, *The Healing Heart* (New York: W. W. Norton, 1983), pp. 48–49.
2. Kurt Butler, *A Consumer's Guide to "Alternative Medicine"* (Buffalo: Prometheus Books, 1992), pp. 182–84.
3. Howard Brody, *Placebos and the Philosophy of Medicine* (Chicago: University of Chicago Press, 1980), pp. 8–24. See also Harold J. Cornacchia and Stephen Barrett, *Consumer Health: A Guide to Intelligent Decisions* (St. Louis: Mosby-Year Book, 1993), pp. 58–59.
4. Leonard Zusne and Warren H. Jones, *Anomalistic Psychology* (Hillsdale, N.J.: Lawrence Erlbaum Associates, 1982), p. 54.
5. L. A. Cobb, G. I. Thomas, D. H. Dillard, K. A. Merendino, and R. A. Bruce, "An Evaluation of Internal-Mammary-Artery Ligation by a Double-blind Technique," *New England Journal of Medicine*, 260 (1959): 1115–18.
6. American Cancer Society, *Dubious Cancer Treatment* (Baltimore: Port City Press, 1991), pp. 24, 75–76.
7. Ray Hyman, "Occult Health Practices," In *The Health Robbers*, ed. Stephen Barrett and William Jarvis (Buffalo: Prometheus Books, 1993), 29.
8. "Shark Cartilage in the News," *Nutrition Forum*, May/June 1993, p. 23.
9. Thomas M. Vogt, *Making Health Decisions* (Chicago: Nelson-Hall, 1983), p. 44.
10. Daniel Druckerman and John Swets, eds. *Enhancing Human Performance: Issues, Theories, and Techniques* (Washington, D.C.: National Academy Press, 1988), p. 35.
11. See Charles W. Marshall, "Can Megadoses of Vitamin C Help Against Colds?" *Nutrition Forum*, September/October 1992, pp. 33–36; Office of Technology Assessment, Congress of the United States, *Unconventional Cancer Treatments* (Washington, D.C.: U.S. Government Printing Office, 1990), pp. 102–7; and E. H. Wender and M. A. Lipton," The National Advisory Committee on Hyperkinesis and Food Additives—Final report to The Nutrition Foundation" (Washington, D.C.: The Nutrition Foundation, 1980).
12. *NCAHF Newsletter*, May/June, 1992.
13. *Probe*, May 1, 1992.
14. Stephen H. Gehlbach, *Interpreting the Medical Literature* (New York: Macmillan, 1988, p. 14.
15. Ibid., p. 14. The exceptions to this rule are rare, occurring only when cause-and-effect relationships are clear-cut and dramatic. One example is the effect of insulin on diabetic hyperglycemia; another is the impact of penicillin on pneumococcal pneumonia. These effects were accepted by scientists without demands for rigorously controlled studies.

16. Ibid., p. 90.

17. S. Matthews-Simonton, O. C. Simonton, and J. L. Creighton, *Getting Well Again* (New York: Bantam, 1978): American Cancer Society, *Dubious Cancer Treatment*, pp. 73–78; Office of Technology Assessment, *Unconventional Cancer Treatments*, pp. 35–36.

18. Philip E. Clark and Mary Jo Clark, "Therapeutic Touch: Is There a Scientific Basis for the Practice?" *Nursing Research*, 33 (January/February 1984); Susan M. Williams, "Holistic Nursing" in *Examining Holistic Medicine* (Buffalo: Prometheus Books, 1989), pp. 55–56.

19. Butler, *Consumer's Guide*, pp. 103–4.

20. W. A. Nolen, *Healing: A Doctor in Search of a Miracle* (New York: Random House, 1974); James Randi, *Flim-Flam* (Buffalo: Prometheus Books, 1982).

21. *Nutrition Forum*, September/October 1991, p. 39.

22. Michio Kushi and the East West Foundation, *The Macrobiotic Approach to Cancer. Toward Preventing and Controlling Cancer with Diet and Lifestyle* (Wayne, N.J.: Avery Publishing Group, 1982); A. J. Sattilaro and T. J. Monte, *Recalled by Life* (New York: Avon, 1982).

23. Office of Technology Assessment, *Unconventional Cancer Treatment*, p. 22.

24. Russell S. Worrall, "Iridology: Diagnosis or Delusion?" *Skeptical Inquirer*, 7 (1983): 23–35; P. Knipschild, "Looking for Gall Bladder Disease in the Patient's Iris," *British Medical Journal*, 297 (1988): 1578–81.

25. C. Eugene Emery Jr., *Nutrition Forum*, January/February 1989, p. 5.

26. Varro E. Tyler, *The Honest Herbal* (Binghamton, N.Y.: Haworth Press, 1993).

27. Harold J. Cornacchia and Stephen Barrett, *Consumer Health*, pp. 60–61.

28. P. G. Goldschmidt and T. Colton, "The Quality of Medical Literature: An Analysis of Validation Assessments," in *Medical Uses of Statistics*, ed. J. C. Bailar and F. Mosteller (Waltham, Mass.: New England Journal of Medicine Books, 1986), pp. 370–91.

29. John M. Yancey, "Ten Rules for Reading Clinical Research Reports," *The American Journal of Surgery*, 159 (June 1990): 533–39.

30. Thomas M. Vogt, *Making Health Decisions*, p. 84.

31. Victor Cohn, *News & Numbers* (Ames: Iowa State University Press, 1989), p. 72.

32. Thomas M. Vogt, *Making Health Decisions*, pp. 86–87.

33. "A Possible Protective Effect of Nut Consumption on Risk of Coronary Heart Disease," *Archives of Internal Medicine*, 152 (July 1992): 1416–24.

34. Victor Cohn, *News & Numbers*, p. 39.

35. Stephen Barrett, "Homeopathy: Is It Medicine?" in *The Health Robbers*, ed. Stephen Barrett and William Jarvis (Buffalo: Prometheus Books, 1993), pp. 198–99.

EIGHT
Science and Its Pretenders

THE SCIENTIFIC METHOD is the most powerful tool we have for acquiring knowledge. By its means we've discovered the structure of the atom and the composition of the stars, the causes of disease and cures for infection, the blueprint for life and the mechanisms of growth. Many people don't think of science as a search for the truth. Instead, they think of it as a means for creating commodities. When they think of science, they think of such things as televisions, VCRs, and CDs. Although scientific knowledge is used in the manufacture of these items, the production of such goods is not the goal of science. Science seeks to understand the general principles that govern the universe — not to produce gadgets.

Scientists are peeping Toms at the keyhole of eternity.
— ARTHUR KOESTLER

Gadget production is the province of technology, which applies scientific knowledge to practical problems. Unfortunately, technology has given science a bad name in some quarters. For although technology is responsible for such wonders as telephones, refrigerators, and microwaves, it is also responsible for such horrors as atomic bombs, chemical weapons, and industrial pollution. Some believe that even greater horrors are lurking in the wings. For example, recombinant DNA technology, which has given us the power to create new life forms, could destroy us if we use it to create organisms that alter the ecological balance of the planet. Computer technology, which has given us the power to create intelligent machines, also could destroy us if the machines we develop are smarter than we are. To save the human race from such ignoble ends, some believe that the scientific research behind these technologies should be stopped. Some knowledge, they claim, is simply not worth having.

While the potential for disaster that these technologies pose is significant, so is their potential for good. Recombinant DNA technology might be used to cure disease, solve the world's food shortage, and even clean up environmental pollution. Computer technology can help us improve our problem-solving abilities, communication systems, and manufacturing processes. Weighing risks and benefits is never easy. Whichever way the balance tilts, however, it's important to realize that knowledge itself is not the problem; the debate is over how that knowledge is applied.

The line between science and technology is often difficult to draw because the same persons may engage in both pursuits. Scientists, in conducting their investigations, may fabricate special apparatus, while technologists, in designing their mechanisms, may perform systematic experiments that lead to scientific discoveries. In general, however, we may say that science produces knowledge while technology produces goods. Scientists are primarily interested in knowing how something works while technologists are primarily interested in making something that works. The best indication for scientists that they know how something works is that they can successfully predict what it will do. Thus science seeks to understand the world by identifying general principles that are both explanatory and predictive.[1]

Critics (some of whom are scientists) disagree. They say that far from being an impartial search for the truth, science is an imperialistic ideology that champions a particular world view, namely, a mechanistic, materialistic, and atomistic one. Science, they claim, is committed to the view that the world is a great machine, composed of minuscule particles of matter that interact with each other like tiny

The dangers that face the world can, every one of them, be traced back to science. The salvations that may save the world will, every one of them, be traced back to science.

—ISAAC ASIMOV

Rifkin's Designer Genes

Jeremy Rifkin, author, lecturer, and president of the Foundation on Economic Trends, is one of those who believes that the risks associated with certain types of scientific research are so great that the research should be discontinued. He claims that research into the structure of DNA, for example, not only de-sacralizes nature, but threatens to destroy us all. Here's an excerpt from his *Declaration of a Heretic*:

> What a civilization discovers depends upon the conceptual framework it chooses to live by. In the West we chose to live by a world view that has led to the nuclear bomb and the engineering of the genetic blueprints of life. If this reality is less than comforting, it is even more disturbing to witness non-Western cultures rush to embrace both our scientific world view and the two powerful technologies that have been erected from it.

> Still, there is also reason to hope that this emergent reality can be challenged and surmounted. But to have any possibility of succeeding, we must first be willing to cast aside the technological determinism that has so gripped the consciousness of the culture. There is nothing inevitable about the split atom or the engineered gene. The fact is, there is a future that lies beyond both of these technologies: a future wholly free of the consciousness that nurtured and sustains these powerful realities.

> If this seems startling, it is understandable. The powers that be inform us that it is impossible to ever rid the idea of the bomb or genetic engineering from the thinking of the human race. They tell us that these discoveries can never be recalled, but, at best, only contained. They are wrong. The bomb and genetic engineering are not a fact of life like the coming and going of the seasons. They are inventions fashioned by human hands and conceived by the human mind. As such, they can be removed from both our culture and our consciousness.[2]

Would this be a desirable state of affairs? Would we be better off if we had decided not to try to unlock the secrets of the atom or the cell?

billiard balls. Such a world is inimical to human flourishing because it treats us like machines. It denies the importance of our thoughts, feelings, and desires, stripping us of our dignity and humanity.[3] The devastating effects of this approach to reality, they claim, can be witnessed by anyone who turns on the nightly news.[4]

What we need, they suggest, is a different world view, one that is more organic, holistic, and process-oriented. The world should be viewed not as a giant machine composed of isolated entities, but as a giant organism composed of interdependent processes. Only by adopting this sort of world view can we regain the social, psychological, and ecological balance necessary for continued survival on this planet.[5]

While it may be true that, at any one time, a particular world view is dominant in the scientific community, it would be a mistake to identify science with any particular world view. For science is a method of discerning the truth, not a particular body of truths. It is a way of solving problems, not a particular solution to them. Just as you cannot identify science with its applications, so you cannot identify it with its results. The world views held by scientists have changed radically over the years; as we've seen, the world view of quantum mechanics is far from the mechanistic world view of the seventeenth century.

Those who believe that we should adopt a more organic and holistic world view do so on the grounds that it offers a more accurate description of reality than does a mechanistic and atomistic one. That may well be the case, but the only way to find out is to determine whether there is any evidence to that effect, and the best way to make such a determination is to use the scientific method, for the scientific method provides the best means of assessing the accuracy of a theory.

SCIENCE AND DOGMA

It's tempting to say that what distinguishes science from all other modes of inquiry is that it takes nothing for granted. But this is not strictly true. For there is at least one proposition that must be accepted before any scientific investigation can take place — that the world is *publicly understandable*. This means at least three things: (1) the world has a determinate structure; (2) we can know that structure; and (3) this knowledge is available to everyone. Let's examine each of these claims in turn.

It is not what the man of science believes that distinguishes him, but how and why he believes it.

—BERTRAND RUSSELL

If the world had no determinate structure — if it were formless and nondescript — it couldn't be understood scientifically because it couldn't be explained or predicted. Only where there is an identifiable pattern can there be explanation or prediction. If the world lacked a discernible pattern, it would be beyond our ken.

But a determinate structure is not enough for scientific understanding; we also need a means of apprehending it. As we've seen, humans possess at least four faculties that put us in touch with the world: perception, introspection, memory, and reason. There may be others, but at present, these are the only ones that have proven themselves to be reliable. They're not 100 percent reliable, but the beauty of the scientific method is that it can determine when they're not. The scientific method is self-correcting, and as a result it is our most reliable guide to the truth.[6]

What makes scientific understanding public is that the information upon which it is based is, in principle, available to everyone. Anyone willing to make the appropriate observations can see for themselves whether any particular claim is true. No one has to take anybody's word for anything. Everything is out in the open, and it is open season on everything. To be accepted as true, a scientific claim must be able to withstand the closest scrutiny, for only if it does can we be reasonably sure that it's not mistaken.

SCIENTIFIC METHODOLOGY

The scientific method is often said to consist of the following four steps:

1. Observe
2. Induce general hypotheses or possible explanations for what we have observed
3. Deduce specific things that must also be true if our hypothesis is true
4. Test the hypothesis by checking out the deduced implications.[7]

But this conception of the scientific method provides a misleading picture of scientific inquiry—for scientific investigation can occur only after a hypothesis has been formulated, and induction is not the only way of formulating a hypothesis.

A moment's reflection reveals that data collection in the absence of a hypothesis has little or no scientific value. Suppose, for example, that one day you decide to become a scientist, and having read a standard account of the scientific method, you set out to collect some data. Where should you begin? Should you start by cataloguing all the items in your room, measuring them, weighing them, noting their color and composition, and so on? Should you then take these items apart and catalogue their parts in a similar manner? Should you note the relationship of these objects to one another, to the fixtures in the room, to objects outside? Clearly there's enough data in your room to keep you busy for the rest of your life.

From a scientific point of view, however, collecting this data wouldn't be very useful because it wouldn't help us evaluate any scientific hypotheses. The goal of scientific inquiry is to identify principles that are both explanatory and predictive. Without a hypothesis to guide our investigations, there is no guarantee that the information gathered would help us accomplish that goal.

How odd it is that anyone should not see that all observation must be for or against some view if it is to be of any service!
—CHARLES DARWIN

Philosopher Karl Popper graphically demonstrated the importance of hypotheses for observation:

> Twenty-five years ago I tried to bring home the same point to a group of physics students in Vienna by beginning a lecture with the following instructions: "Take pencil and paper; carefully observe, and write down what you have observed!" They asked, of course, what I wanted them to observe. Clearly the instruction, "Observe!" is absurd. (It is not even idiomatic, unless the object of the transitive verb can be taken as understood.) Observation is always selective. It needs a chosen object, a definite task, an interest, a point of view, a problem.[8]

Scientific inquiry begins with a problem — why did something occur? How are two or more things related? What is something made of? An observation, of course, is needed to recognize that a problem exists, but any such observation will have been guided by an earlier hypothesis.[9] Hypotheses are needed for scientific observation because they tell us what to look for — they help us distinguish relevant from irrelevant information.

Scientific hypotheses indicate what will happen if certain conditions are realized. By producing these conditions in the laboratory or observing them in the field, we can assess the credibility of the hypotheses proposed. If the predicted results occur, we have reason to believe that the hypothesis in question is true. If not, we have reason to believe that it's false.

In scientific work, those who refuse to go beyond fact rarely get as far as fact.
—THOMAS HUXLEY

Although hypotheses are designed to account for data, they rarely can be derived from data. Contrary to what the traditional account of the scientific method would have us believe, inductive thinking is rarely used to generate hypotheses. It can be used to formulate certain elementary hypotheses such as this one: Every fish ever caught in this lake has been a bass; therefore every fish that ever will be caught in this lake will be a bass. But it can't be used to generate the more sophisticated hypotheses scientists commonly use because scientific hypotheses often postulate entities that aren't mentioned in the data. The atomic theory of matter, for example, postulates the existence of atoms. All of the data upon which the atomic theory rests, however, can be described without mentioning atoms. Since scientific hypotheses often introduce concepts not found in their data, there can be no mechanical procedure for constructing them.[10]

Hypotheses are created, not discovered, and the process of their creation is just as open-ended as the process of artistic creation. There is no formula for generating hypotheses. That's not to say that the process of theory construction is irrational, but it *is* to say that the process is not mechanical. In searching for the best explanation, scientists are guided by certain criteria, such as testability, fruitfulness, scope, simplicity, and conservatism. Fulfilling any one of these criteria, however, is neither a necessary nor a sufficient condition for being a good hypothesis. Science therefore is just as much a product of the imagination as it is of reason.

Even the most beautifully crafted hypotheses, however, can turn out to be false. That's why scientists insist on checking all hypotheses against reality. Let's examine how this might be done in a particular case.

Science is our century's art.
—Horace Freeland Judson

Suppose you hypothesize that a new drug is an effective painkiller. To test this hypothesis, you might prescribe the drug to a number of patients. If a majority of those who took the drug report that they feel less pain, you may think that you have a good reason for believing that it works. But actually you don't, for as we've seen, the positive results you obtained may be due to the placebo effect. Since over one third of those who ingest a substance and believe that it is a painkiller will experience pain reduction even if the substance has no painkilling properties, you need to devise a test that will take the placebo effect into account.

One way of doing this is to divide the subjects into two groups, giving one group a placebo and the other the drug. In this case, if a majority of those taking the drug report less pain while only a third of those taking the placebo do, you have somewhat better grounds for believing that the drug is an effective painkiller. But you still don't *know* that it is, for the test you performed doesn't establish its effectiveness beyond a reasonable doubt. The reason for this is that those conducting the experiment may have unwittingly influenced the results. As we saw in Chapter 7, experimenters can affect the outcome of a test by conveying their expectations to their subjects in extremely subtle ways. It's possible that the experimenters unconsciously revealed to the subjects which pills were placebos and which weren't. It's also possible that the experimenters interpreted the subject's reports in accordance with their own expectations. Until the doubts raised by these possibilities are eliminated, the drug's actual effectiveness remains unknown.

These doubts can be removed by setting up a double-blind experiment in which neither the subjects taking the pills nor the experimenters themselves know which subjects received the drug. Experimenter effects are thus reduced to a minimum. But even the successful completion of such a test would not establish the drug's effectiveness beyond a reasonable doubt, for there could be other factors at work that you haven't taken into account. Not until others have replicated your results can you legitimately claim to know that the drug is effective. For only then can you be reasonably sure that none of the things that could go wrong with an experiment did go wrong.

It should be clear from this example why the scientific method is such an effective means of acquiring knowledge. Knowledge, you will recall, requires the absence of reasonable doubt. By formulating their hypotheses precisely and controlling their observations carefully, scientists attempt to eliminate as many sources of doubt as possible. They can't remove them all, but often they can remove enough of them to give us knowledge.

Not all sciences can perform controlled experiments, however, for not all natural phenomena can be controlled. Much as we might like to, there's little we can do about earthquakes, volcanoes, and sinkholes, let alone comets, meteors, and asteroids. So geological and astronomical hypotheses can't usually be tested in the laboratory. They can be tested in the field, however. By looking for the conditions specified in their hypotheses, geologists and astronomers can determine whether the events predicted actually occur.

Since many legitimate sciences don't perform controlled experiments, the scientific method can't be identified with the experimental method. In fact, the scientific method can't be identified with *any* particular procedure because there are many different ways to assess the credibility of a hypothesis. In general, *any procedure that serves to systematically eliminate reasonable grounds for doubt can be considered scientific.*

You don't have to be a scientist to use the scientific method. In fact, many of us use it every day; as Thomas H. Huxley realized, "Science is simply common sense at its best — that is, rigidly accurate in observation, and merciless to fallacy in logic." When getting the right answer is important, we do everything we can to ensure that both our evidence and our explanations are as complete and accurate as possible. In so doing, we are using the scientific method.

CONFIRMING AND CONFUTING HYPOTHESES

The results of scientific inquiry are never final and conclusive but are always provisional and open. No scientific hypothesis can be conclusively confirmed because the possibility of someday finding evidence to the contrary can't be ruled out. Scientific hypotheses always go beyond the information given. They not only explain what has been discovered; they also predict what will be discovered. Since there's no

Science is intelligence in action with no holds barred.
— P. W. BRIDGMAN

Science is organized common sense where many a beautiful theory was killed by an ugly fact.
— THOMAS H. HUXLEY

The Duhem Hypothesis

Pierre Duhem, a French philosopher of science, was perhaps the first to realize that hypotheses cannot be tested in isolation. Harvard philosopher Willard Van Orman Quine puts Duhem's insight this way: "Hypotheses meet the tribunal of experience as a corporate body." Here's how Duhem put it:

> People generally think that each one of the hypotheses employed in Physics can be taken in isolation, checked by experiment, then when many varied tests have established its validity, given a definitive place in the system of Physics. In reality, this is not the case. Physics is not a machine which lets itself be taken apart; we cannot try each piece in isolation, and in order to adjust it, wait until its solidity has been carefully checked; physical science is a system that must be taken as a whole; it is an organism in which one part cannot be made to function without the parts that are most remote from it being called into play, some more so than others, but all to some degree. If something goes wrong, if some discomfort is felt in the functioning of the organism, the physicist will have to ferret out through its effect on the entire system which organ needs to be remedied or modified without the possibility of isolating this organ and examining it apart. The watchmaker to whom you give a watch that has stopped separates all the wheel-works and examines them one by one until he finds the part that is defective or broken; the doctor to whom a patient appears cannot dissect him in order to establish his diagnosis; he has to guess the seat and cause of the ailment solely by inspecting disorders affecting the whole body. Now, the physicist concerned with remedying a limping theory resembles the doctor and not the watchmaker.[11]

guarantee that these predictions will come true, we can never be absolutely sure that a scientific hypothesis is true.

Just as we can never conclusively confirm a scientific hypothesis, we can never conclusively confute one either. There is a widespread belief that negative results prove a hypothesis false. This would be true if predictions followed from individual hypotheses alone, but they don't. Predictions can be derived from a hypothesis only in conjunction with a background theory. This background theory provides information about the objects under study as well as the apparatus used to study them. If a prediction turns out to be false, we can always save the hypothesis by modifying the background theory. As philosopher Philip Kitcher notes:

> Individual scientific claims do not, and cannot, confront the evidence one by one. Rather . . . "Hypotheses are tested in bundles." . . . We can

only test relatively large bundles of claims. What this means is that when our experiments go awry we are not logically compelled to select any particular claim as the culprit. We can always save a cherished hypothesis from refutation by rejecting (however implausibly) one of the other members of the bundle.[12]

To see this, let's examine Christopher Columbus's claim that the Earth is round.

Both Christopher Columbus and Nicholas Copernicus rejected the flat Earth hypothesis on the grounds that its predictions were contrary to experience. They argued that if the Earth were flat, all parts of a ship should disappear from view at the same rate as it sails out to sea. But that's not what is observed. To someone on shore, the lower part of a ship disappears before the upper part. As a result, they concluded that the Earth must not be flat. Furthermore, they argued, if the Earth were round, the lower part of a ship would disappear before the upper part. Since this is what is observed, the latter hypothesis is the more credible one.

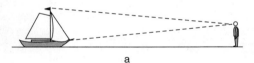

a

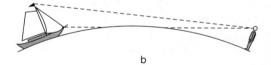

b

In a world where light travels in straight lines, Figure a shows what we should see if the Earth is flat while Figure b shows what we should see if the Earth is round.

But if the Earth were flat, all parts of a ship would fade from view at the same rate only if light travels in straight lines. If it traveled in curved lines, concave upwards, the lower part of a ship could well disappear from view before the upper part. As a ship sailed farther out to sea, the light from the lower part would curve into the ocean before the light from the upper part did, thus making the lower part invisible before the upper part.[13] So we can maintain the view that the Earth is flat as long as we're willing to change our view of the nature of light. In general, any hypothesis can be maintained in the face of seemingly adverse evidence if we're willing to make enough alterations in our background beliefs. Consequently, no hypothesis can be conclusively confuted.

a   b

In a world where light travels in curved lines, Figure a shows what we should see if a ship is close by and Figure b shows what we should see if the ship is farther away.

This does not mean, however, that every hypothesis is as good as every other. Although no amount of evidence logically compels us to reject a hypothesis, maintaining a hypothesis in the face of adverse evidence can be manifestly unreasonable. So even if we cannot conclusively say that a hypothesis is false, we can often conclusively say that it's unreasonable.

The flat Earth hypothesis, for example, is manifestly unreasonable — and yet it has defenders to this day. Although the voyages of Columbus and other seafaring explorers nearly killed the theory in the fifteenth century, it was resurrected in England in 1849 by an itinerant lecturer who called himself *Parallax* (his real name was Samuel Birley Rowbotham). The world, he argued, is a flat disc with the North Pole at its center and a 150-foot wall of ice — the South Pole — encircling its perimeter. According to Parallax, those who sail around the world simply travel in a big circle. What makes the lower part of a ship disappear before the upper part is atmospheric refraction and what he called the *zetetic law of perspective*.[14]

Exactly what the zetetic law of perspective is, is unclear. But its use by Rowbotham is instructive, for it illustrates a popular method for shielding hypotheses from adverse evidence: constructing ad-hoc hypotheses. A hypothesis threatened by recalcitrant data can often be saved by postulating entities or properties that account for the data. Such a move is legitimate if there's an independent means of verifying their existence. If there is no such means, the hypothesis is ad hoc.

Ad hoc literally means "after the fact." But it's not simply that a hypothesis is proposed after certain facts are established that makes it ad hoc (if that were the case, *all* hypotheses would be ad hoc). What makes a hypothesis ad hoc is that it can't be verified independently of the data it's supposed to explain.

For example, by 1844, it was known that the planet Uranus didn't follow the orbit predicted by Newton's theories of gravity and planetary motion. The observed orbit differed from the predicted

In days of old, When Knights were bold, And science not invented, The Earth was flat, And that was that, With no man discontented.
— ENGLISH VERSE

The Hollow Earth

Flat and round do not exhaust the possible conceptions of the Earth. How about hollow? The hollow Earth theory was first proposed by the astronomer Edmund Halley, the discoverer of Halley's comet, to account for various irregularities in compass readings noted by sailors. It has since become the property of cranks. Ted Schultz discusses its evolution:

> In 1818, U.S. Infantry Captain John Cleves Symmes, a hero of the War of 1812, announced his revolutionary theory that the earth is a hollow shell containing four additional concentric spheres, all accessible via polar openings thousands of miles across. Symmes proposed to lead an expedition to the "warm and rich land, stocked with thrifty vegetables and animals" that lay beyond the frozen North, inside the earth. In 1828, at the urging of Symmes' follower Jeremiah Reynolds, Congress actually approved the plan. The Secretaries of the Navy and Treasury prepared three ships for the adventure, but the newly elected President Andrew Jackson put an end to the project.
>
> If Symmes's ideas failed to inspire serious scientific investigation, they did inspire works of fiction, including Edgar Allan Poe's *Narrative of Arthur Gordon Pym* and *Manuscript Found in a Bottle*. Meanwhile, in 1869 a man named Cyrus Teed had a revelation. The earth was hollow all right but we live on the *inside*. Teed, who formed a religion around his theory, traveled around the country gathering followers and in 1894 he founded the Koreshan colony in Estero, Florida. Teed died in 1908, but the Koreshan colony exists to this day. A variation of Teed's idea, known as *Hohlweltehre*, or Hollow Earth Doctrine, was widely held in Nazi Germany.

> In 1906, William Reed's contribution to hollow-earth theory, *The Phantom of the Poles*, appeared. Reed dispensed with Symmes' idea of concentric spheres, describing instead a single hollow globe with polar openings and an undiscovered world of continents and seas within. He explained that the aurora borealis is nothing more than the reflection of forest fires and volcanoes in the earth's interior.
>
> In 1913, Marshal Gardner published *A Journey to the Earth's Interior*, or *Have the Poles Really Been Discovered*, followed in 1920 by an enlarged edition. While Reed had proposed that the inner earth is illuminated by sunlight penetrating through the polar openings, Gardner believed that it contains its own miniature sun, the light from which causes the auroras. He theorized that Eskimos are descended from inner-earth races, and that the mammoths found frozen in arctic ice originate there. . . .
>
> In 1964 Raymond Bernard's modestly titled *The Hollow Earth: The Greatest Geological Discovery in History* appeared. Borrowing heavily from the works of Reed and Gardner, Bernard expanded the theory to include flying saucers.[15]

According to Bernard, the people who live in the center of the earth are the survivors of a nuclear war between the inhabitants of Atlantis and Mu (a former island continent in the Pacific). Their relocation to the center of the Earth was necessary to escape the effects of the radiation produced by the war. The UFOs we observe are really Atlantean spaceships sent from the center of the Earth to keep tabs on us surface-dwellers.

orbit by two minutes of arc, a discrepancy much greater than that of any other known planet. In 1845, the astronomer Urbain Jean Joseph Leverrier hypothesized that the gravitational force of an unknown planet affected Uranus's motion. Using Newton's theories of gravity and motion, he calculated the planet's position. On the basis of those calculations, he requested that astronomer Johann Gottfried Galle in Berlin search a particular region of the sky for it. In less than an hour after Galle began his search, he noticed something that was not on his charts. When he checked again the next night, it had moved a considerable distance. He had discovered the planet that we now call Neptune!

If the aberrant orbit of Uranus had not been accounted for, Newton's theory would have been in jeopardy. So Leverrier's postulation of another planet can be seen as an attempt to save Newton's theory from negative evidence. But his hypothesis was not ad hoc, for it could be independently verified. If he had claimed, however, that some unknown and undetectable (occult) force was responsible for Uranus's erratic behavior, that would have been an ad-hoc hypothesis. For, by definition, there would be no way to confirm the existence of such a force.

When a scientific theory starts relying on ad-hoc hypotheses to be saved from adverse data, it becomes unreasonable to maintain belief in that theory. The phlogiston theory of heat provides a case in point.

The real purpose of scientific method is to make sure Nature hasn't misled you into thinking you know something you don't actually know.
—ROBERT M. PIRSIG

The scientific study of heat began in earnest shortly after Galileo's invention of the thermometer (or *thermoscope,* as he called it) in 1593. Over the years it was discovered that different substances absorb heat at different rates, that different substances change state (solid, liquid, gas) at different temperatures, and that different substances expand at different rates when heated. To explain these phenomena, German chemist Georg Ernst Stahl proposed in the late seventeenth century that all combustible substances and metals contain an invisible substance that came to be known as *phlogiston.*

Phlogiston was considered to be an elastic fluid composed of particles that repel one another. (This explained why things expand when heated.) These particles were thought to be attracted to particles of other substances with different strengths. (This explained why some things heat faster than others.) When particles of phlogiston come into contact with particles of another substance, they supposedly combined with it to form a new state of matter. (This explained why ice turns into water when heated.) Phlogiston also seemed to explain such things as why a substance turns to ash when burned (it loses phlogiston); why a metallic oxide turns back into a metal when heated with charcoal (it gains phlogiston); and why pounding on a substance can make it expand (it releases stored phlogiston). Because the phlogiston theory seemed to explain so much, it became the dominant theory of heat in the eighteenth century.

It always had its detractors, however, for phlogiston was a very mysterious substance. Not only was it colorless and odorless, it was weightless as well. Even though phlogiston was supposed to flow into substances that were heated, careful experiments had found that increases in temperature did not produce increases in weight. Phlogiston was also thought to flow out of substances that were burned. What ultimately led to the theory's demise, however, was the discovery that some substances actually gain weight when burned. Antoine Lavoisier found that when tin was burned, for example, the resulting metallic oxide weighed more than the original tin. If phlogiston were lost during burning, he argued, this wouldn't be the case.

Defenders of the phlogiston theory tried to account for this phenomenon by hypothesizing that the phlogiston in tin possessed negative weight, so that when it was lost, the tin gained weight. But this hypothesis was soon seen for what it really was — a desperate attempt to save the theory from the facts. Unlike Leverrier's postulation of the existence of the planet that was named Neptune, there was no way to independently confirm or confute the negative weight hypothesis. It was ad hoc in the truest sense of the term.

The moral of this story is that for a hypothesis to increase our knowledge, there must be some way to test it, for if there isn't, we have no way of telling whether or not the hypothesis is true.

CRITERIA OF ADEQUACY

The aim of science is not to open the door to everlasting wisdom, but to set a limit on everlasting error.

— BERTOLT BRECHT

To explain something is to offer a hypothesis that helps us understand it. For example, we can explain why a penny left outside turns green by offering the hypothesis that the penny is made out of copper and that when copper oxidizes, it turns green. But for any set of facts, it's possible to devise an infinite number of hypotheses to account for them. Suppose that someone wanted to know what makes fluorescent lights work. One hypothesis is that inside each tube is a little gremlin who creates light (sparks) by striking his pickax against the side of the tube. In addition to the one gremlin hypothesis, there is the two gremlin hypothesis, the three gremlin hypothesis, and so on. Because there is always more than one hypothesis to account for any set of facts and because no set of facts can conclusively confirm or confute any hypothesis, we must appeal to something besides just the facts in order to decide which hypothesis is the most reasonable. What we appeal to are *criteria of adequacy*. These criteria help us determine how well a hypothesis accomplishes the goal of increasing our knowledge. They are testability, fruitfulness, scope, simplicity, and conservatism.

Testability

Since science is a search for knowledge, it's interested only in those hypotheses that can be tested — if a hypothesis can't be tested, there is no way to determine whether it's true or false. Hypotheses, however, can't be tested in isolation, for, as we've seen, hypotheses have observable consequences only in the context of a background theory. So to be testable, a hypothesis, in conjunction with a background theory, must predict something more than the background theory alone.[16] If a hypothesis doesn't go beyond the background theory, it doesn't expand our knowledge, and hence is scientifically uninteresting.

The practical effect of a belief is the real test of its soundness.
—JAMES A. FROUDE

Take the gremlin hypothesis, for example. To qualify as scientific, there must be some test we can perform — other than turning on the lights — to detect the presence of gremlins. Whether there is such a test will depend on what the hypothesis tells us about the gremlins. If it tells us that they are visible to the naked eye, it can be tested by simply breaking open a fluorescent light and looking for them. If it tells us that they are invisible but sensitive to heat and capable of emitting sounds, it can be tested by putting a fluorescent light in boiling water and listening for tiny screams. But if it tells us that they are incorporeal or so shy that any attempt to detect them makes them disappear, it can't be tested and hence is not scientific.

Scientific hypotheses can be distinguished from nonscientific ones, then, by the following principle:

> A hypothesis is scientific only if it is testable, that is, only if it predicts something other than what it was introduced to explain.

The gremlin hypothesis predicts that if we turn on a fluorescent light, it will emit light. But this doesn't mean that the gremlin hypothesis is testable because the fact that fluorescent lights emit light is what the gremlin hypothesis was introduced to explain. That fact is part of its background theory. To be testable, a hypothesis must make a prediction that goes beyond its background theory. A prediction tells us that if certain conditions are realized, then certain results will be observed. If a prediction can be derived from a hypothesis and its background theory that cannot be derived from its background theory alone, then the hypothesis is testable.

Falsification and Psychoanalysis

Many writers have concurred with one of Popper's assertions, which is that psychoanalysis is not a legitimate scientific theory because it can't be falsified. No observation or experimental test can show the theory to be false because psychoanalysts can always invent a just-so story to account for any possible behavior. Popper explains his dissatisfaction with psychoanalysis as follows:

> The Freudian analysts emphasized that their theories were constantly verified by their "clinical observations." As for Adler, I was much impressed by a personal experience. Once, in 1919, I reported to him a case which to me did not seem particularly Adlerian, but which he found no difficulty in analyzing in terms of his theory of inferiority feelings, although he had not even seen the child. . . . But this means very little, I reflected, since every conceivable case could be interpreted in the light of Adler's theory, or equally of Freud's. I may illustrate this by two very different examples of human behavior: that of a man who pushes a child into the water with the intention of drowning it; and that of a man who sacrifices his life in an attempt to save the child. Each of these two cases can be explained with equal ease in Freudian and in Adlerian terms. According to Freud the first man suffered from repression (say, of some component of his Oedipus complex), while the second man had achieved sublimation. According to Adler the first man suffered from feelings of inferiority (producing perhaps the need to prove to himself that he dared to commit some crime), and so did the second man (whose need was to prove to himself that he dared to rescue the child). I could not think of any human behavior which could not be interpreted in terms of either theory. It was precisely this fact— that they always fitted, that they were always confirmed—which in the eyes of their admirers constituted the strongest argument in favour of these theories. It began to dawn on me that this apparent strength was in fact their weakness.[17]

Karl Popper realized long ago that untestable hypotheses cannot legitimately be called scientific. What distinguishes genuine scientific hypotheses from pseudoscientific ones, he claims, is that the former are *falsifiable*. Although his insight is a good one, it has two shortcomings: First, the term is unfortunate, for no hypothesis is, strictly speaking, falsifiable because it's always possible to maintain a hypothesis in the face of unfavorable evidence by making suitable alterations in the background theory.[18]

In making theories, always keep a window open so that you can throw one out if necessary.
—BELA SCHICK

The second weakness in Popper's theory is that it doesn't explain why we hold on to some hypotheses in the face of adverse evidence. When new hypotheses are first proposed, there is often a good deal of evidence against them. As philosopher of science Imre Lakatos notes, "When Newton published his *Principia*, it was common knowledge that it could not properly explain even the motion of the moon; in fact, lunar motion refuted Newton. . . . All hypotheses, in this sense, are born refuted and die refuted."[19] Nonetheless, we give credence to some and not others. Popper's theory is hard-pressed to explain why this is so. Recognizing that other criteria play a role in evaluating hypotheses makes sense of this situation.

Fruitfulness

One thing that makes some hypotheses attractive even in the face of adverse evidence is that they open new lines of research. That is, they predict hitherto unknown phenomena. Such hypotheses possess the virtue of *fruitfulness*. For example, Einstein's theory of relativity predicts that light rays traveling near massive objects will appear to be bent because the space around them is curved. At the time Einstein proposed his theory, common wisdom was that since light has no mass, light rays travel in Euclidean straight lines. To test Einstein's theory, physicist Sir Arthur Eddington mounted an expedition to Africa in 1919 to observe a total eclipse of the sun. If light rays are bent by massive objects, he reasoned, then the position of stars whose light passes near the sun should appear to be shifted from their true position. The shift should be detectable by comparing a photograph taken during the eclipse with one taken at night of the same portion of the sky. When Eddington compared the two photographs, he found that stars near the sun during the eclipse did appear to have moved more than those farther away, and that the amount of their apparent movement was what Einstein's theory predicted. (Einstein's theory predicted a deflection of 1.75 seconds of arc. Eddington observed a deflection of 1.64 seconds of arc, well within the possible error of measurement.)[20] Thus Einstein's theory had successfully predicted a phenomenon that no one had previously thought existed. In so doing, it expanded the frontiers of our knowledge.

Since hypotheses make predictions only in the context of a larger body of background information, Lakatos prefers to talk of *research programs* rather than hypotheses. According to Lakatos, what distinguishes good (progressive) research programs from bad (degenerating) ones is their fruitfulness.

All the research programs I admire have one characteristic in common. They all predict novel facts, facts which had been either undreamt of, or have indeed been contradicted by previous or rival programs. . . . What really count are dramatic, unexpected, stunning predictions; a few of them are enough to tilt the balance; where theory lags behind the facts, we are dealing with miserable degenerating research programs.[21]

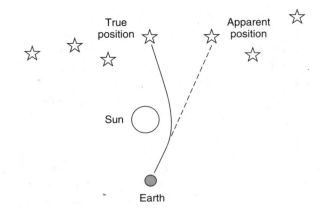

The effect of light bending near the sun.

True position

Apparent position

Sun

Earth

The classic case of a degenerating research program, he tells us, is Marxism:

> Has, for instance, Marxism ever predicted a stunning novel fact successfully? Never! It has some famous unsuccessful predictions. It predicted the absolute impoverishment of the working class. It predicted that the first socialist revolutions would take place in the industrially most developed society. It predicted that socialist societies would be free of revolutions. It predicted that there will be no conflict of interests between socialist countries. Thus the early predictions of Marxism were bold and stunning but they failed. Marxists explained all their failures: they explained the rising living standards of the working class by devising a theory of imperialism; they even explained why the first socialist revolution occurred in industrially backward Russia. They "explained" Berlin 1953, Budapest 1956, Prague 1968. They "explained" the Russian-Chinese conflict. But their auxiliary hypotheses were all cooked up after the event to protect Marxian theory from the facts. The Newtonian program led to novel facts; the Marxian lagged behind the facts and has been running fast to catch up with them.[22]

Marxism is a degenerating research program not only because it failed to predict any novel facts, but also because it is riddled with ad-hoc hypotheses. The lesson is clear:

> Other things being equal, the best hypothesis is the one that is the most fruitful, that is, makes the most novel predictions.

If two hypotheses do equally well with regard to all the other criteria of adequacy, the one with greater fruitfulness is better.

Having greater fruitfulness by itself does not necessarily make a hypothesis superior to its rivals, however, because it might not do as well as they do with respect to other criteria of adequacy. Velikovsky's theory of Venus's genesis demonstrates this point.

In 1950 Immanuel Velikovsky published *Worlds in Collision*, in which he argued that many of the ancient myths depicting worldwide catastrophes can be explained on the assumption that around 1500 B.C. Jupiter expelled a glowing ball of hot gases toward the Earth. This great ball of fire, which looked to observers on Earth like a gigantic comet, was later to become the planet Venus. As the Earth passed through its tail, Velikovsky claims, showers of meteorites fell to the Earth, exploding balls of naphtha filled the sky, and oil rained from the heavens. The gravitational pull of the comet became so great that it caused the Earth to tilt on its axis and slow its rate of rotation. Cities were laid waste by earthquakes, rivers reversed their course, and a gigantic hurricane ravaged the planet. Before Venus finally settled into its current orbit, it pulled Mars off course and sent that planet hurtling toward the Earth, thus igniting a whole new wave of catastrophes.[23]

Since Velikovsky thought that Venus was recently expelled from Jupiter, he predicted that it would still be hot. This prediction flew in the face of current scientific thinking, which held that Venus was cold and lifeless. The Pioneer space probe revealed, however, that Velikovsky was right: Venus is hot. At the time it was offered, then, Velikovsky's theory could claim fruitfulness among its virtues because it predicted a novel fact. Many of its other claims, however, appear to be physically impossible. Carl Sagan, for example, has calculated that the energy necessary to eject a mass the size of Venus from Jupiter is 10^{41} ergs, "which is equivalent to all the energy radiated by the Sun to space in an entire year, and one hundred million times more powerful than the largest solar flare ever observed."[24] Velikovsky does not say how Jupiter was able to generate such energy. Nor does he explain how the Earth was able to resume its normal rate of rotation after it slowed down. Other claims conflict with well-established laws in biology, chemistry, and astrophysics.[25] These laws may be mistaken, but unless Velikovsky can identify the correct laws and show that they explain astronomical events better than the currently accepted laws do, there is no reason to believe that those currently accepted laws are mistaken.

Scope

The *scope* of a hypothesis — or the amount of phenomena explained and predicted by it — is also an important measure of its adequacy; the more a hypothesis explains and predicts, the more it unifies and systematizes our knowledge and the less likely it is to be false because

He who proves things by experience increases his knowledge; he who believes blindly increases his errors.
— CHINESE PROVERB

Nazi Cosmology

Velikovsky wasn't the first to try to explain ancient myths in terms of celestial events. In 1696, British clergyman and mathematician William Whiston published his *New Theory of the Earth* in which he argued that the "chaos" from which the world developed was the tail of a large comet. The great flood of Noah, he claimed, began on Friday, November 28, 2349 B.C. when God sent another comet that passed near the earth and caused it to rain for forty days and forty nights. In 1882, Minnesota Irishman Ignatious Donnelly published *Ragnarok*, in which he argued that many of the events described in the Old Testament were the result of a comet passing close to the earth and dumping thousands of tons of dust on it. The view that became the official cosmology of the Nazis, however, claims that our world sprang from a colossal conflagration of fire and ice. In 1913, Hans Hörbiger, a Viennese mining engineer, published *Glazial-Kosmogonie* in which he argued that solar systems are formed by gigantic blocks of ice colliding with stars:

> Ignoring Kepler's laws of motion, which state that orbiting bodies travel in ellipses,

Hörbiger argued that these blocks of ice follow a spiral path, so that they eventually collide with the star, causing an enormous explosion. The star ejects a molten mass of rotating matter which forms a new solar system.

Hörbiger's belief that planets follow a spiral path led him to suggest that there were originally four moons orbiting the Earth, of which our present Moon is the only remaining one. The last collision of a moon with the Earth, some 13,000 years ago, he claimed, caused the disappearance of Atlantis — the continent that the Nazis believed was the original home of the Aryan race.

Himmler was particularly impressed with Hörbiger's theories, and a treatise on the cosmic ice theory was published as one of a series of handbooks for the SA (the paramilitary wing of the Nazi Party). And Hitler himself declared that he would build an observatory in his home town of Linz, dedicated to the three great cosmologists: Copernicus, Kepler — and Hans Hörbiger.[26]

the more evidence it has in its favor. For example, one reason that Einstein's theory of relativity came to be preferred over Newton's theories of gravity and motion is that it had greater scope. It could explain and predict everything that Newton's theories could, as well as some things that they couldn't. For instance, Einstein's theory could explain a variation in Mercury's orbit, among other phenomena.

It had been known since the middle of the nineteenth century that the planet Mercury's perihelion (the point at which it is closest to the sun) does not remain constant — that point rotates slowly, or *precesses*, around the sun at the rate of about 574 seconds of arc per century. Using Newton's laws of motion and gravity, it was possible to account for about 531 seconds of arc of this motion. Leverrier tried to account for the missing 43 seconds of arc in the same way he had accounted for the discrepancies in the orbit of Uranus—by postulating the existence of another planet between Mercury and the sun. He named this planet *Vulcan* (*Star Trek* fans take note), but repeated observations failed to find it. Einstein's theory of relativity, however, can account for the precession of Mercury's perihelion without postulating the existence of another planet. According to relativity theory, space is curved around massive objects. Since Mercury is so close to the sun, the space it travels through is more warped (again *Star Trek* fans take note) than is the space that the rest of the planets travel through. Using relativity theory, it is possible to calculate the extent to which space is thus bent. It turns out to be just enough to account for the missing 43 seconds of arc in the precession of Mercury's perihelion.[27]

The fact that Einstein's theory had greater scope than Newton's was a powerful argument in its favor. As the physicist P. Langevin proclaimed at the Paris Academy of Sciences:

> This theory is the *only one* that permits one actually to represent all the known experimental facts and that possesses moreover the remarkable power of prediction confirmed in so astonishing a manner by the deviation of light rays and the displacement of spectral lines in the gravitational field of the sun.[28]

For Langevin, Einstein's theory is superior to Newton's because it has greater explanatory and predictive power. The principle he's relying on is this one:

> Other things being equal, the best hypothesis is the one that has the greatest scope, that is, that explains and predicts the most diverse phenomena.

Simplicity

Interestingly enough, even though considerations of fruitfulness and scope loomed large in the minds of many of those who accepted Einstein's theory, *simplicity* was what Einstein saw as its main virtue. He wrote: "I do not by any means find the chief significance of the general theory of relativity in the fact that it has predicted a few minute observable facts, but rather in the simplicity of its foundation and

Seek simplicity and distrust it.
—ALFRED NORTH WHITEHEAD

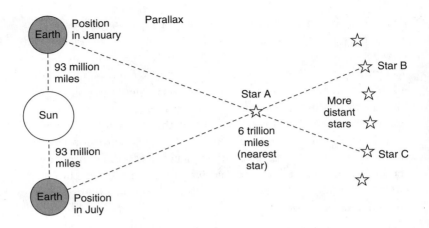

Parallax: As the Earth travels around the sun, the stars that appear to be behind the nearest star change.

in its logical consistency."[29] For Einstein, simplicity is a theoretical virtue *par excellence*.

Simplicity is notoriously difficult to define.[30] For our purposes, however, we may say that the simpler of two hypotheses is the one that makes the fewest assumptions.[31] Simplicity is valued for the same reason that scope is — the simpler a theory is, the more it unifies and systematizes our knowledge and the less likely it is to be false because the fewer ways there are for it to go wrong.

Since the time of Thales (arguably the West's first scientist), simplicity has been an important criterion of theory selection. To take but one example: Copernicus's heliocentric theory, which claimed that the Earth revolved around the sun, could explain no more than Ptolemy's geocentric theory, which claimed that the sun revolved around the Earth. In terms of scope and fruitfulness, then, Copernicus's theory had no advantage over Ptolemy's. In fact, Copernicus's theory had the disadvantage of being inconsistent with observed data. If Copernicus's theory were true, opponents charged, then stars nearer the Earth should seem to change their position relative to more distant stars as the Earth moved around the sun. But no such apparent change in position (known as *parallax*) was observed. This predictive failure did not move Copernicus and his followers to abandon the theory, however, for they believed that stars were too far away to exhibit parallax. It turns out that they were right: the nearest star is six trillion miles away. It wasn't until 1838, almost 300 years after Copernicus's death, that stellar parallax was finally observed. (The parallax was observed when more powerful telescopes were finally available to observe stars more precisely.) Copernicus's theory, however, had

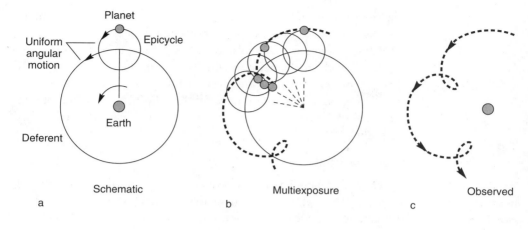

long since become the accepted explanation of the structure of the solar system.

Scientists accepted Copernicus's theory in the face of such seemingly adverse evidence because it was simpler than Ptolemy's. One of the most difficult features of planetary motion to account for is the fact that certain planets, at certain times, seem to reverse their direction of travel. Ptolemy accounted for this retrograde motion by assuming that planets orbit their orbits, so to speak. He assumed that they travel in a circle (known as an *epicycle*) around a point that is itself traveling in a circle around the earth (known as a *deferent*).

Copernicus showed that many of these epicycles were unnecessary hypotheses adduced to maintain the view that planets travel in circles around the Earth. Because Copernicus's theory could explain planetary motion without using as many epicycles, it was simpler than Ptolemy's. The criterion at work here is this:

> Other things being equal, the best hypothesis is the simplest one, that is, the one that makes the fewest assumptions.

As we've seen, hypotheses often explain phenomena by assuming that certain entities exist. The simplicity criterion tells us that, other things being equal, the fewer such assumptions a theory makes, the better it is. When searching for an explanation, then, it's wise to cleave to the principle known as *Occam's razor* (in honor of the medieval philosopher, William of Occam, who formulated it): Do not multiply entities beyond necessity. In other words, assume no more than is required to explain the phenomenon in question.

One of the most famous applications of this principle was made by the French mathematician and astronomer Pierre Laplace. After Laplace presented the first edition of his theory of the universe to Napoleon, Napoleon is said to have asked, "Where does God fit into your theory?" Laplace matter-of-factly replied: "I have no need of that hypothesis."[32]

Conservatism

Since consistency is a necessary condition of knowledge, we should be wary of accepting a hypothesis that conflicts with our background information. As we've seen, not only does accepting such a hypothesis undermine our claim to know, it also requires rejecting the beliefs it conflicts with. If those beliefs are well established, the chances of the new hypothesis being true are not good. In general, then, the more *conservative* a hypothesis is (that is, the fewer well-established beliefs it conflicts with), the more plausible it is.[33] The criterion of conservatism can be stated as follows:

> Other things being equal, the best hypothesis is the one that is the most conservative, that is, the one that fits best with established beliefs.

Things aren't always equal, however. It may be perfectly reasonable to accept a hypothesis that is not conservative provided that it possesses other criteria of adequacy. Unfortunately, there's no foolproof method for determining when conservatism should take a backseat to other criteria.

Indeed, there is no fixed formula for applying *any* of the criteria of adequacy. We can't quantify how well a hypothesis does with respect to any of them, nor can we definitively rank the criteria in order of importance. At times we may rate conservatism more highly than scope, especially if the hypothesis in question is lacking in fruitfulness. At other times we may rate simplicity higher than conservatism, especially if the hypothesis has at least as much scope as our existing hypothesis. Choosing between theories is not the purely logical process it is often made out to be. Like judicial decision making, it relies on factors of human judgment that resist formalization.

The least questioned assumptions are often the most questionable.
—PAUL BROCA

This does not mean that the process of theory selection is subjective. There are many distinctions we can't quantify that nevertheless are perfectly objective. We can't say, for example, exactly when day turns into night or when a person with a full head of hair turns bald. Nevertheless, the distinctions between night and day or baldness and hirsuteness are as objective as they come. There are certainly borderline cases that reasonable people can disagree about, but there are also clearcut cases where disagreement would be irrational. It would simply be wrong to believe that a person with a full head of (living) hair is bald. If you persisted in such a belief, you would be irrational. Similarly, it would simply be wrong to believe that the phlogiston theory is a good scientific theory. In general, if you believe a theory that clearly fails to meet the criteria of adequacy, you are irrational.

CREATIONISM, EVOLUTION, AND CRITERIA OF ADEQUACY

Criteria of adequacy are what we appeal to when trying to decide which hypothesis best explains a phenomenon. The best hypothesis is the one that meets the criteria of adequacy better than any of its competitors. To make a rational choice among hypotheses, then, it's important to know what these criteria are and how to apply them. Thomas Kuhn agrees. "It is vitally important," he tells us, "that scientists be taught to value these characteristics and that they be provided with examples that illustrate them in practice."[34]

In recent years, a number of people (as well as a number of state legislatures) have claimed that the theory of creationism is just as good as the theory of evolution and thus should be given equal time in the classroom. Our discussion of the criteria of adequacy has given us the means to evaluate this claim. If creationism is just as good a theory as evolution, then it should fulfill the criteria of adequacy just as well as evolution does. Let's see if this is the case.

The theory of evolution, although not invented by Darwin, received its most impressive formulation at his hand. In 1859, he published *The Origin of Species*, in which he argued that the theory of evolution by natural selection provided the best explanation of a number of different phenomena:

> It can hardly be supposed that a false theory would explain, in so satisfactory a manner as does the theory of natural selection, the several large classes of facts above specified. It has recently been objected that this is an unsafe method of arguing; but it is a method used in judging of the

common events of life, and has often been used by the greatest natural philosophers.[35]

Darwin found that organisms living in isolated habitats (such as islands) have forms related to but distinct from organisms living in neighboring habitats, that there are anatomical resemblances between closely related species, that the embryos of distantly related species resemble one another more than the adults of those species, and that fossils show a distinct progression from the simplest forms to the most complex.[36] The best explanation of these facts, Darwin argued, was that organisms adapt to their environment through a process of natural selection. The hypothesis that all creatures were created by God in one fell swoop, he argued, offers no explanation for these facts.

Darwin realized that many more creatures are born than live long enough to reproduce, that these creatures possess different physical characteristics, and that the characteristics they possess are often inherited from their parents. He reasoned that when an inherited characteristic (like an opposable thumb) increased a creature's chances of living long enough to reproduce itself, that characteristic would be passed to the next generation. As this process continued, the characteristic adapted to survival would become prevalent throughout the species. This was the process that Darwin called *natural selection*, which was the driving force behind evolution. Darwin was not aware of the mechanism by which these characteristics were transmitted. The discovery of that mechanism—the science of genetics—has further bolstered Darwin's theory, for it has been found that the number of chromosomes and their internal organization is similar among closely related species.[37]

Creation science or scientific creationism holds that the universe, energy, and life were created from nothing relatively recently (around 6,000 to 10,000 years ago); that living things could not have developed from a single organism through mutation and natural selection; that there is very little variation among members of the same species; that humans did not develop from the apes; and that the Earth's geology can be explained by the occurrence of various catastrophes, including a worldwide flood.[38] This account of the creation of the universe and its inhabitants is derived primarily from the Bible's Book of Genesis.[39]

Those who espouse this view believe the theory of evolution to be a pernicious doctrine with disastrous social consequences. Henry Morris, Director of the Institute for Creation Research, and Martin Clark, for example, assert:

> Evolution is thus not only anti-Biblical and anti-Christian, but it is utterly unscientific and impossible as well. But it has served effectively

as the pseudo-scientific basis of atheism, agnosticism, socialism, fascism, and numerous other false and dangerous philosophies over the past century.[40]

Teaching creationism, they believe, will help counter these consequences by putting God back in the classroom. Promoting religion in the public schools, however, is a violation of the establishment clause of the First Amendment, which reads: "Congress shall make no law respecting an establishment of religion." Consequently, the courts have consistently found laws requiring the teaching of creationism to be unconstitutional. Supreme Court Justice William Brennan explains:

> Because the primary purpose of the Creationism Act is to advance a particular religious belief, the act endorses religion in violation of the First Amendment. . . . The act violates the establishment clause of the First Amendment because it seeks to employ the symbolic and financial support of government to achieve a religious purpose.[41]

Our concern, however, is not with the constitutionality of the teaching of creationism, but with its adequacy as a scientific theory. We want to know whether creationism really is as good a theory as evolution.

Ironically, even though creationists have taken to calling their theory scientific in an attempt to garner public support, they openly admit that it's nothing of the sort. They don't see this as a problem, however—because they don't believe that evolution is a scientific theory either! Duane Gish, Director of the Institute for Creation Research, explains: "There were no human witnesses to the origin of the Universe, the origin of life or the origin of a single living thing. These were unique, unrepeatable events of the past that cannot be observed in nature or recapitulated in the laboratory. Thus, neither creation nor evolution qualifies as a scientific theory, and each is equally religious."[42] Gish here is appealing to the principle of testability discussed earlier. His claim is that since neither creationism nor evolution is testable, neither can be considered a scientific theory.

But is it true that neither is testable? A hypothesis is testable if it predicts something other than what it was introduced to explain. Evolution clearly meets this criterion, for, as we've seen, it explains why the number and internal organization of chromosomes are so similar among closely related species. But that's not all. It can also explain numerous other facts discovered by immunology, biochemistry, and molecular biology.[43] So evolution is testable. If the facts about the transmission of hereditary information had turned out differently, evolution might well have been abandoned.

Creationism is also testable because it makes a number of claims that can be checked by observation. It claims, for example, that the

Religion, which should most distinguish us from the beasts, and ought most particularly to elevate us, as rational creatures, above brutes, is that wherein men often appear most irrational, and more senseless than beasts themselves.
—JOHN LOCKE

universe is 6,000 to 10,000 years old, that all species were created at the same time, and that the geographical features of the Earth can be explained as the result of tidal waves created by the great flood of Noah. All these claims can be tested. All these claims conflict with well-established scientific findings.[44] So not only is creationism testable, it has been tested—and found wanting.

Gish writes as if the lack of human witnesses makes the two theories untestable and therefore religious. But if that lack rendered a theory religious, a lot of what passes for science would have to be reclassified as religion, for many phenomena studied by scientists can't be witnessed by humans. Nobody, for example, ever has seen or ever will see the interior of the sun. But that doesn't mean that any theory about what goes on inside the sun is theological. Theories about the internal structure of stars can be tested by observing their behavior. Similarly, theories about the creation of the universe or living things can be tested by observing the behavior of objects in the universe or creatures on the Earth.

One piece of evidence that Darwin cited in favor of the theory of evolution is that there is a progression among fossils from the simplest, in the oldest strata, to the most complex, in the most recent layers. Creationists claim that this evidence is no evidence at all because—they say—the age of rock strata is determined by the complexity of the fossils it contains. In other words, creationists claim that evolutionists argue in a circle—they date rock strata by the fossils they contain and then date fossils by the rock strata in which they're found.[45]

Creationists don't deny that the simplest fossils are often found at the lowest point in fossil beds. They account for this fact by assuming that after the great flood of Noah, the simplest forms of life (marine life) would be the first to be deposited on the sea floor. All creatures—dinosaurs as well as humans—came into existence at the same time. They were all washed away in a great flood, and the fossils that remain are found in their present order not because of their relative age but because of their relative buoyancy.

Creationists who make this argument must then explain how the creatures alive today survived the flood. Most follow the Bible and claim that they were saved by Noah and his ark. The ark, of course, presents a problem. To save all living creatures, according to one calculation, it had to carry at least 25,000 species of birds, 15,000 species of mammals, 6,000 species of reptiles, 2,500 species of amphibians, and more than 1 million species of insects.[46] Moreover, since creationists believe that men and dinosaurs walked the earth at the same time, the ark must have contained two of each species of dinosaur;

that is, it included two Supersauruses (which were 100 feet long and weighed up to 55 tons each) and two Apatosauruses (up to 70 feet long and 20 tons) — not to mention two hungry 7-ton Tyrannosauruses. How Noah, his wife, and three sons, and their wives could possibly have built an ark big enough to hold all these creatures — let alone feed and water them and clean out their stalls — is something that creationists are curiously silent about.

The fact is, however, that no geological or anthropological evidence indicates that a worldwide flood occurred during the last 10,000 years.[47] Furthermore, the claim that the evolutionist's argument from the fossil record is circular is simply mistaken, for there are many ways to date fossils independent of the rock strata they're found in.

One such method is carbon dating. Carbon-14, a radioactive isotope of carbon, is created in the upper atmosphere when nitrogen is bombarded by cosmic rays. Like all radioactive isotopes, it decays at a constant rate. Since the Earth is constantly being bombarded by cosmic rays, however, the ratio of carbon-14 to ordinary carbon (carbon-12) in the upper atmosphere remains constant. Living creatures take up both kinds of carbon in the ratio found in the upper atmosphere. When a creature dies, it takes in no new carbon, however, so the ratio of carbon-14 to carbon-12 in its remains will diminish as the carbon-14 decays. By determining the ratio of carbon-14 to carbon-12 in a fossil, then, it's possible to calculate its age. Using this method, many fossils have been found to be much older than 10,000 years — many, in fact, are millions of years old.

The age of the universe can also be calculated, independently of both fossils and rock strata. By determining how far apart the galaxies are and how rapidly they are moving away from each other, it's possible to determine when the outward expansion of the universe began. Present estimates put the age of the universe at something like 15 to 20 billion years, a far cry from the 6,000 to 10,000 years claimed by creationists.

These facts are hard to ignore. If the creationists believe that they aren't really facts, the burden of proof is on them to show why not. Do scientists have an inadequate understanding of how carbon-14 is created? Are they mistaken about its rate of decay? Have they misjudged the distance between the galaxies or their rate of motion? Unless the creationists can show that current dating methods are in error, there's no reason to take their theory seriously.

This disagreement about the age of the universe and living things points out one of the major failings of creationism: it does not cohere with well-established beliefs. In other words, it fails to meet the criteria of conservatism. As Isaac Asimov has pointed out, creationism

Did Adam and Eve Have Navels?

If the universe is only 10,000 years old, why does it seem so much older? Why, for example, do we find fossils that seem to be millions of years old? One possible response is to say that God put them there to test our faith. This view is not favored by modern day creationists, however, for it puts God in a bad light. As one creationist remarks: "This would be the creation, not of an appearance of age, but of an appearance of evil, and would be contrary to Gods [sic] nature."[48] The creationists do not want to make God out to be a deceiver.

Nineteenth-century British naturalist Philip Gosse, however, argued that if God created the world, he had to create it with vestiges of a past, so why not assume that God created it with vestiges of a great past? Martin Gardner elucidates his argument:

Gosse admitted geology had established beyond any doubt that the earth had a long geological history in which plants and animals flourished before the time of Adam. He was also convinced that the earth was created about 4,000 B.C., in six days, exactly as described in *Genesis*. How did he reconcile these apparently contradictory opinions? Very simply. Just as Adam was created with a navel, the relic of a birth which never occurred, so the entire earth was created with all the fossil relics of a past which had no existence except in the mind of God! . . .

"It may be objected," writes Gosse, "that to assume the world to have been created with fossil skeletons in its crust—skeletons of animals that never really existed—is to charge the Creator with forming objects

cannot be adopted "without discarding all of modern biology, biochemistry, geology, astronomy—in short, without discarding all of science."[50] That's a pretty high price to pay for adopting a theory. If the creationists can't make up for this lack of conservatism by demonstrating that their theory has greater fruitfulness, scope, or simplicity than evolution, it can't be considered as good a theory as evolution.

Creationism is not a fruitful theory because it hasn't predicted any novel facts. It has made some novel predictions—such as that the universe is from 6,000 to 10,000 years old, that all creatures were created at the same time, that there was a worldwide flood, and so on—but none of them has been born out by the evidence. Evolution, on the other hand, has predicted that the chromosomes and proteins of related species should be similar, that mutations should occur, that organisms should adapt to changing environments, and so on, all of which have been verified. In terms of fruitfulness, then, evolution is superior to creationism.

Nothing in biology makes sense except in the light of evolution.

— THEODOSIUS DOBZHANSKY

whose sole purpose was to deceive us. The reply is obvious. Were the concentric timber-rings of a created tree formed merely to deceive? Were the growth lines of a created shell intended to deceive? Was the navel of the created Man intended to deceive him into the persuasion that he had a parent?"

This question of whether Adam had a navel is by no means a forgotten one. A few years ago North Carolina's Congressman Carl T. Durham and his House Military Affairs subcommittee objected to a cartoon of Adam and Eve in Public Affairs Pamphlet no. 85 (*The Races of Mankind* by Ruth Benedict and Gene Weltfish). The cartoon disclosed a pair of navels. The subcommittee thought this had something to do with communism. [Apparently they associated navels with evolution and evolution with communism.] Their fears were somewhat allayed when it was pointed out that Michelangelo had painted a navel on Adam in his Sistine Chapel Murals.

So thorough is Gosse in covering every aspect of this question that he even discusses the finding of coprolites, fossil excrement. Up until now, he writes, this "has been considered a more than ordinarily triumphant proof of real preexistence." Yet, he points out, it offers no more difficulty than the fact that waste matter would certainly exist in the intestines of the newly-formed Adam. Blood must have flowed through his arteries, and blood presupposes chyle and chyme, which in turn presupposes an indigestible residuum in the intestines. "It may seem at first sight ridiculous," he confesses, ". . . but truth is truth."[49]

Evoluton is also superior to creationism in terms of simplicity. Simplicity, remember, is a measure of the number of assumptions a theory makes. Evolution assumes a lot less than creationism. For one thing, it doesn't assume the existence of God. For another, it doesn't assume the existence of unknown forces. That creationism makes both of these assumptions was made clear by Gish:

> We do not know how the Creator created, what processes He used, *for He used processes which are not now operating anywhere in the natural universe.* This is why we refer to creation as Special Creation. We cannot discover by scientific investigation anything about the creative processes used by the Creator.[51]

Creationism, then, assumes the existence of a supernatural being with supernatural powers. Since evolution makes neither of these assumptions, it is the simpler theory.

The major advantage of evolution over creationism, however, is its scope or explanatory power. Evolution has served to systematize and unify discoveries from a number of different fields. "In fact," claims Isaac Asimov, "the strongest of all indications as to the fact of evolution and the truth of the theory of natural selection is that all the independent findings of scientists in every branch of science, when they have anything to do with biological evolution at all, *always* strengthen the case and *never* weaken it."[52] Evolution fits well with what we know about the universe. It not only explains the facts uncovered by Darwin, but many others as well. Creationism, on the other hand, does not fit well with what we know about the universe and can't even explain Darwin's data. Furthermore, it raises more questions than it answers. How did the creator create? What caused the worldwide flood? How did creatures survive it? Why does the world seem so much older than it is? A theory that raises more questions than it answers doesn't increase our understanding; it decreases our understanding.

It stands to the everlasting credit of science that by acting on the human mind it has overcome man's insecurity before himself and before nature.

—Albert Einstein

Moreover, appealing to the incomprehensible can never increase our comprehension. Suppose you're an engineer charged with explaining why a bridge collapsed and someone remarks, "I know why it collapsed. It collapsed because an incomprehensible being zapped it with an incomprehensible force." Because you are interested in exploring all possibilities, you inquire, "Can you tell me any more about this being or this force?" "No," he replies. "Do you have any tangible evidence that this occurred?" you ask. "No," he admits. At this point you would do well to thank him for his help and show him to the door.

Is this a theory you should take seriously? Would you be remiss if you left it out of your final report? Of course not. Such a theory explains nothing. Yet it's just such a theory that the creationists are pushing. The creator and his means of creation, they claim, are beyond human comprehension. But if they are, appealing to them can't increase our understanding. As a result, creationism explains nothing; its scope is nil.

Creationism can be considered as good a theory as evolution only if it meets the criteria of adequacy as well as evolution does, but it doesn't. With respect to each criterion of adequacy — testability, conservatism, fruitfulness, simplicity, and scope — creationism actually does much worse than evolution. Consequently, the creationists' claim that creationism is as good a theory as evolution is totally unfounded.

Before we leave the topic of creationism, a few remarks on the creationists' rhetorical strategy would be in order. Creationists often attack evolution by citing a specific fact that they believe evolution can't account for. But notice how hypocritical this strategy is. On the one hand, they claim that evolution is untestable (and therefore un-scientific) while on the other, they claim that it fails certain tests. They can't have it both ways. If evolution is untestable, no data can count against it. If data counts against it, it can't be untestable.

Creationists also assume that any data that counts against evolution counts in favor of creationism.[53] But to argue in this way is to commit the fallacy of *false dilemma;* it presents two alternatives as mutually exclusive when, in fact, they aren't. Gish sets up the dilemma this way: "Either the Universe arose through naturalistic, mechanistic evolutionary processes, or it was created supernaturally."[54] This is a false dilemma for a number of reasons. In the first place, there is no need to assume that the universe was created even if evolution is not supported. The universe, as many non-Western peoples believe, may be eternal, that is, without beginning or end. Those who believe that the universe was created by God usually believe that God is eternal. If God can be eternal, why not the universe?[55] Secondly, evolution is not the only natural account of creation, and Genesis is not the only supernatural account. Theories of creation are as varied as the cultures that conceived them. Some believe that the universe developed naturally from the void (the Vikings) while others believe that it's the supernatural work of the devil (the Gnostics). Thus, even if the creationists could totally discredit evolution, they would not thereby prove their own position, for there are many other alternatives. Only by demonstrating that creationism meets the criteria of adequacy at least as well as its rivals can creationists hope to show that their theory is a viable one.

PARAPSYCHOLOGY

Creationists do not use the scientific method to test their hypotheses, but parapsychologists do. For this reason, among others, the Parapsychological Association was granted affiliate status with the American Association for the Advancement of Science in 1969.

Parapsychology is the study of extrasensory perception (ESP) and psychokinesis. Extrasensory perception, as the name suggests, is perception that is not mediated by an organism's recognized sensory organs. There are three main types of ESP: telepathy, or perception of another's thoughts without the use of the senses; clairvoyance, perception of distant objects without the use of the senses; and precognition, perception of future events without the use of the senses. Psychokinesis is the ability to affect physical objects without the use of the body, that is, by simply thinking about them. These phenomena are often grouped together under the heading *psi phenomena.*

Probability and Belief

Why do so many of us believe that we have experienced ESP? Because we are not good at estimating the probabilities of unlikely coincidences, says parapsychologist Susan Blackmore. As a result, we consider certain events to be much more unlikely than they really are. Blackmore explains:

> Tom Troscianko and I, at the University of Bristol, hypothesized that if the origin of belief in ESP lies in misjudgments of probability, then we would expect believers (usually referred to as "sheep") to be less accurate in their probability judgments than goats (disbelievers). This we tested by giving schoolchildren, university students, medical workers and others, a set of computerized tests.
>
> In general the goats did better at these tasks, as we predicted, and as is consistent with the idea (but does not prove) that the sheeps' errors are responsible for their belief in ESP. Interestingly, the university students did no better than the schoolchildren which implies that these judgments are not improved by education. Another well-known error lies in "subjective random generation." Put simply, most people have no idea of how random numbers behave. When they are asked to generate a string of random numbers many people avoid repeating the same digit twice—it is as though they think that this would not be random.
>
> At the University of Zurich in Switzerland, Peter Brugger and his colleagues have been exploring the relationship between this error and belief in the paranormal. In keeping with our hypothesis they found that sheep avoided pairs more than goats did—in both real ESP experiments and in tests of random string generation. They suggest that most, if not all, of the major findings in parapsychology can be attributed to errors in random number generation or response bias."[56]

Many of us have had experiences that seem to fall into one of these categories. We may have thought of a friend moments before she phoned us, or sensed that a loved one was in danger only to find out that he or she actually was, or dreamt about winning a jackpot and then won it. Such experiences appear to be common. One study of over 1,400 American adults found that 67 percent had "experienced ESP."[57] But as we've seen, we can't always take our experiences at face value. What seems to be inexplicable often turns out to have a rather mundane explanation. Before we accept the reality of psi phenomena, then, we should be sure that the phenomena in question can't be explained in terms of well-understood processes.

Some think that the world would be a much more interesting place if psi were a reality. On a personal level, for example, telepathy could improve our communication skills, precognition help us prepare for the future, and psychokinesis help us achieve our goals. On the national and international level, however, the consequences could be even more remarkable. Imagine being able to read your enemies' minds, examine their secret documents without breaking into their headquarters, and disarm their weapons by thought alone. J. B. Rhine, one of the first to study psi in the laboratory, had this to say about the prospect of harnessing psi energy:

> The consequences for world affairs would be literally colossal. War plans and crafty designs of any kind, anywhere in the world, could be watched and revealed. With such revelation it seems unlikely that war could ever occur again. There would be no advantage of surprise. Every secret weapon and scheming strategy would be subject to exposure. The nations could relax their suspicious fear of each other's secret machinations.
>
> Crime on any scale could hardly exist with its cloak of invisibility thus removed. Graft, exploitation, and suppression could not continue if the dark plots of wicked men were to be laid bare.[58]

But would a fully developed psi capability really be such a boon? What if there were people who could read your thoughts, see what you're doing every minute of the day, and control your body with their minds? Wouldn't that make possible a form of social control more horrific than that portrayed in either George Orwell's *1984* or Aldous Huxley's *Brave New World?* Martin Gardner thinks so. He sees psi powers as "tools with a far wider scope for repression and terror than the mere tapping of a phone, opening of a letter, or electronic eavesdropping."[59]

Strange thoughts beget strange deeds.
—PERCY BYSSHE SHELLEY

The military potential of psi has not escaped the watchful eye of the Pentagon. Columnist Jack Anderson reported in 1981 that the Pentagon's top secret "psychic task force" had spent over $6 million in 1980 alone trying to develop psi weapons. Our military leaders knew that the Soviets had been conducting serious psychic research since the 1930s and that Stalin had hoped to develop psychic weapons to counter America's nuclear threat. Apparently the Pentagon's top brass was anxious to close what they perceived as an ESP gap.

In the 1970s, books such as Sheila Ostrander and Lynn Schroeder's *Psychic Discoveries Behind the Iron Curtain* created the impression that the Soviets were well on the way to harnessing psychic energy. There were stories of Russian women who could separate the white of an egg from its yolk after it had been dropped into an aquarium (an impressive feat because it couldn't have been done with hidden magnets or strings) and psychokinetically stop the heartbeat of frogs. If such energies could be focused and amplified, no American would be safe.

But it wasn't the military implications that got J. B. Rhine interested in psi phenomena. It was the philosophical implications. Like

The Army and ESP

In 1984, the National Research Council was asked by the Army Research Institute to investigate the possibility of using paranormal phenomena to enhance human performance. The Army was particularly interested in its potential military applications.

In their view, ESP, if real and controllable, could be used for intelligence gathering and, because it includes "precognition," ESP could also be used to anticipate the actions of an enemy. It is believed that PK, (psychokinesis), if realizable, might be used to jam enemy computers, prematurely trigger nuclear weapons, and incapacitate weapons and vehicles. More specific applications envisioned involve behavior modification; inducing sickness, disorientation, or even death in a distant enemy; communicating with submarines; planting thoughts in individuals without their knowledge; hypnotizing individuals at a distance; psychotronic weapons of various kinds; psychic shields to protect sensitive information or military installations; and the like. One suggested application is a conception of the "First Earth Battalion," made up of "warrior monks," who will have mastered almost all the techniques under consideration by the committee, including the use of ESP, leaving their bodies at will, levitating, psychic healing, and walking through walls.[60]

Many paranormal phenomena were studied, including remote viewing, psychokinesis, telepathy, and plant perception. The committee drew the following conclusions:

Overall, the experimental designs are of insufficient quality to arbitrate between claims made for and against the existence of the phenomena. While the best research is of higher quality than many critics assume, the bulk of the work does not meet the standards necessary to contribute to the knowledge base of science. Definitive conclusions must depend on evidence derived from stronger research designs."[61]

the creationists, Rhine believed that a widespread acceptance of materialism would have disastrous social consequences.

The most far-reaching and revolting consequence lies in what would happen to volitional or mental freedom. Under a mechanistic determinism the cherished voluntarism of the individual would be nothing but idle fancy. Without the exercise of some freedom from physical law, the concepts of character responsibility, moral judgment, and democracy would not survive critical analysis. The concept of a spiritual order, either in the individual or beyond him, would have no logical place whatever. In fact, little of the entire value system under which human society has developed would survive the establishment of a thoroughgoing philosophy of physicalism.[62]

Symbols in a deck
of Zener cards.

If psi was real, he thought, the materialist world view would have to
be abandoned and one more in tune with traditional values could take
its place.

J. B. Rhine began his research into psi phenomena in 1930 at
Duke University. Using a deck of cards designed by his colleague Carl
Zener, Rhine tried to determine whether it was possible for a subject
to correctly identify the symbols on the cards without coming into
sensory contact with them. There are twenty-five cards in a Zener
deck: five cards each of five different symbols — a cross, a star, a circle, wavy lines, and a square. One run consists of an attempt to identify the symbol on each card in the deck. By pure chance, in any one
run, a respondent should be able to correctly identify the symbols on
five of the cards.

In Rhine's earliest and most successful experiments, the subject
and the experimenter sat at opposite ends of a table in the middle of
which was a thin partition that prevented the subject from seeing the
cards. To test for telepathy, the experimenter would look at the cards
one by one, and the subject would try to identify the symbol the experimenter was looking at. To test for clairvoyance, the experimenter,
without looking at the symbols on the cards, would pick them up one
by one, and the subject would try to identify the symbol that was on
the card the experimenter held. Alternatively, the deck would be shuffled and placed face down on the table and the subject would try to
identify the symbol on each card starting from the top and reading
down through the deck. To test for precognition, the subject would
write down ahead of time the order the cards would be in after having been shuffled. (A successful outcome of this test, however, does
not necessarily prove the existence of precognition, for the subject
could have used psychokinesis to influence the shuffle.)

In 1934 Rhine published his results in a book entitled *Extrasensory
Perception*. (Rhine coined the term.) Out of nearly 100,000 attempts,
Rhine's subjects averaged 7.1 correct identifications per run. Since

Psychic Trains

An Associated Press story from 1989 shows the tragic consequences of overestimating one's psychic powers:

E. Frenkel, one of the Soviet Union's growing number of psychic healers and mentalists, claimed he used his powers to stop bicycles, automobiles and streetcars.

He thought he was ready for something bigger, so he stepped in front of a freight train. It didn't work.

The engineer of the train that ran Frenkel over said the psychic stepped onto the tracks with his arms raised, his head lowered and his body tensed.

The daily *Sovietskaya Rossiya* yesterday said investigators looking into Frenkel's decision to jump in front of a train near the southern city of Astrakhan found the answer in the briefcase he left by the side of the track.

"First I stopped a bicycle, cars, and a streetcar," Frenkel wrote in notes that the investigators found. "Now I'm going to stop a train."

Frenkel apparently felt he had found the secret of psychic-biological power and that his effort to halt a train would be the ultimate test of his powers, according to the notes. "Only in extraordinary conditions of a direct threat to my organism will all my reserves be called into action," he wrote.[63]

only five correct identifications per run would be expected by chance, the odds against Rhine's results being due to chance are well over a googol to one. (A googol is a one followed by a hundred zeros.) On the basis of his research, Rhine concluded that there must be some form of nonphysical energy at work:

> Might not the same logic that has produced the concepts of the various energies involved in physical theory profitably be followed to the point of suggesting that psi energy be hypothesized? . . . It is no great jump from the broad concept of energy as it now prevails in physical theory over to the notion of a special state of energy that is not interceptible by any of the sense organs. . . . It may be tentatively proposed, then, that back of the phenomena of psi must exist an energy that interoperates with and interconverts to those other energetic states already familiar to physics.[64]

But is this really the best explanation of the evidence? To determine whether it is, we'll have to explore some alternative hypotheses and see whether any of them meet the criteria of adequacy better than Rhine's.

The criteria of simplicity and conservatism tell us that, when we are attempting to explain something,

> ## We should accept an extraordinary hypothesis only if no ordinary one will do.

Rhine's early research, however, does not require an extraordinary hypothesis. It can be fully explained in terms of quite ordinary forms of information transfer. Psychologists Leonard Zusne and Warren Jones explain:

> Chance was clearly not producing Rhine's results. It was opportunities to establish the identity of the cards by sensory means. These were so numerous and so readily available that much of Rhine's work during the 1930s may be safely ignored. Testing often occurred in a face-to-face situation, with minimal screening between the agent and the percipient or none at all. When an agent sits across the table from the percipient, the latter can see the backs of the cards. At one time, the ESP cards had been printed with such a heavy pressure that the symbols became embossed in the card material and could be read from the back. In 1938, it was discovered that the symbols could also be seen through the cards, which, of course, allows room for fingertip reading of the backs of the cards and, if they are marked, of their sides.
>
> The instructions that accompany the ESP cards, which were made available to the public in 1937, indicate that an 18 x 24 inch piece of plywood would be sufficient for screening purposes. It is decidedly not. A small screen still allows the percipient to see the faces of the cards if the agent wears glasses, and even if the agent does not, because the card faces are also reflected from the agent's corneas. Changes in facial expression give away clues that are not concealed by small screens. Larger screens still allow the percipient to hear the agent's voice. If the agent also serves as the recorder, which was routine in Rhine's experiments, voice inflections are as useful a source of information as are facial expressions. Furthermore, the sound of the pen or pencil wielded by the agent as he or she records the calls can be also utilized by a person who is skilled at it or learns the skill when tested over a sufficiently large number of trials. Involuntary whispering on the part of the recording agent cannot be excluded as an additional source of information. When the distance between the percipient and the cards was increased, scores dropped.[65]

Given all the opportunities for sensory leakage, there is no reason to believe that anything extrasensory was going on. The best explanation of Rhine's results, then, is that the subject, either consciously or unconsciously, sensed the identity of the cards by ordinary means.

The reason this explanation is the best is that it's the simplest and most conservative one that accounts for the data.

There is something else to notice about Rhine's hypothesis. He tells us that there is some sort of nonphysical energy involved, but he doesn't tell us enough about this energy to allow for any independent confirmation of it. As a result, his hypothesis is ad hoc. It's no better than the hypothesis that gremlins cause fluorescent light bulbs to light up. In fact, it's no better than the hypothesis that gremlins (rather than energy) cause ESP by carrying messages back and forth between the experimenter and the percipient. Until we learn enough about Rhine's energy to make an independent determination of its existence, there is no good reason to believe that it exists.

If Rhine's energy really existed, others should be able to detect it in the same sorts of situations that Rhine did. But this is not the case. Very few of those who have repeated Rhine's experiments have gotten his results. Psychologist J. Crumbaugh's experiences are typical:

> At the time [1938] of performing the experiments involved I fully expected that they would yield easily all the final answers. I did not imagine that after 28 years I would still be in as much doubt as when I had begun. I repeated a number of the then current Duke techniques, but the results of 3,024 runs of the ESP cards — as much work as Rhine reported in his first book — were all negative. In 1940 I utilized further methods with high school students, again with negative results.[66]

Psychologist John Beloff was also unable to find any positive evidence for psi:

> I recently completed a seven-year programme of parapsychological research with the help of one full time research assistant. No one would have been more delighted to obtain positive results than we, but for all the success we achieved, ESP might just as well not have existed. . . . I have not found on comparing notes with other parapsychologists . . . that my experience is in any way out of the ordinary.[67]

Because there are so many ways that an experiment can go wrong, we can't be sure that an effect is real (rather than an artifact of the experimental setup) unless it can be repeated by others. But in the field of parapsychology, there are no repeatable experiments. Even the same researchers, using the same subjects, can't achieve similar results every time. Consequently, there is good reason to doubt that psi is real.

That's not to say that psi is unreal, however. No amount of evidence (or lack of it) could prove that, because it's impossible to prove a universal negative. What the lack of repeatable experiments shows is that no one is justified in believing that psi exists because the evidence available doesn't establish that claim beyond a reasonable doubt.

The greatest wonder of all is the regularity of nature.

— GEORGE DANA BOARDMAN

Perhaps parapsychologists haven't been able to devise a repeatable experiment because they haven't identified the relevant variables yet. Scientists, whenever possible, perform controlled experiments to ensure that the relevant variables remain the same each time an experiment is performed. If they didn't, the experiment would be worthless. So one explanation of the parapsychologist's lack of repeatable experiments is that the factors necessary for proper psi functioning have not been identified.

Parapsychologists have their own explanations for the inability of others to replicate their experiments, however. One of the most common is the *sheep-goat effect*, studied extensively by Gertrude Schmeidler.[68] According to this hypothesis, the results of psi experiments are influenced by the attitudes of the experimenter. If the experimenter doubts the existence of psi (a goat), the experiment won't succeed; if the experimenter believes in the existence of psi (a sheep), the experiment will succeed. But what of experimenters like J. Crumbaugh and John Beloff who claim that they began their research as sheep? Don't they show that the sheep-goat effect is mistaken? Not according to this argument, which holds that while they may have consciously believed in psi, they must have unconsciously doubted it. D. Scott Rogo, for example, claims that Susan Blackmore's failure to find any evidence for the existence of psi in her sixteen years of research is due to her unconscious bias against it.[69]

The ad-hoc character of this hypothesis should be obvious. There's no way to test it because no possible data could count against it. Every apparent counterexample can be explained away by appeal to the unconscious. Moreover, accepting it would make the whole field of parapsychology untestable. No unsuccessful experiments could count against the existence of psi because they could simply be the result of experimenter bias. This sort of reasoning convinces many that parapsychology is a pseudoscience.

But parapsychologists need not reason this way, and many don't. According to Ray Hyman, over 3,000 parapsychological experiments have been performed, many by competent investigators.[70] Some do appear to be successful. But none are consistently repeatable, and many of the most impressive experiments have turned out to be fraudulent.

For example, in London between 1941 and 1943, parapsychologist Samuel Soal tested a subject named Basil Shackleton by using cards that had brightly painted pictures of animals on them instead of the usual Zener symbols. Soal's theory was that subjects might do better if they had more interesting material to work with. Although Shackleton only scored at chance levels with the target cards, his guesses correlated remarkably well with the card immediately following the target card. It was estimated that the odds of that happening by chance were greater than 10^{35} to 1.

Many considered Soal's research to be the best evidence available for psi. Whately Carrington, for example, said:

> If I had to choose one single investigation on which to pin my whole faith in the reality of paranormal phenomena, or with which to convince a hardened skeptic (if this be not a contradiction in terms), I should unhesitatingly choose this series of experiments, which is the most cast-iron piece of work I know, as well as having yielded the most remarkable results.[71]

We now know, however, that Soal fudged his data. An assistant in many of the Shackleton experiments, Gretl Albert, told one of Soal's colleagues that she had seen him altering the records. Later computer analysis of the records has shown that Soal either altered them or didn't get his random numbers in the way he said he did.[72]

Another prominent case of experimenter fraud involves Walter J. Levy Jr., the man Rhine picked to succeed him as head of his parapsychology laboratory. Levy was caught unplugging an automatic scoring machine in an attempt to have it record an abnormally high number of hits.

Certainly not all parapsychologists (nor all parapsychological subjects) are frauds. But because parapsychology has had more than its fair share of them, we should not accept the results of a psi experiment unless we can establish beyond a reasonable doubt that they're not due to fraud. One way to guard against fraud is to enlist the aid of a professional magician. Project Alpha, described in the box, underscores the importance of this precaution.

The evidence currently available does not establish the existence of psi beyond a reasonable doubt because the experiments upon which it is based are not repeatable. It has been claimed, however, that even though no particular experiment is repeatable, all the successful experiments taken together establish the existence of psi beyond a reasonable doubt. John Beloff, for example, has written:

> It is not my contention that any of the aforegoing experiments were perfect . . . or beyond criticism. . . . Moreover, unless a much higher level of repeatability becomes possible, the skeptical option, that the results can be attributed to carelessness or to conscious or unconscious cheating on the part of one or more of the experimenters, remains open and valid. Nevertheless, it is my personal opinion that these . . . investigations represent an overwhelming case for accepting the reality of psi phenomena.[73]

Everyone's entitled to their opinion, of course, but the important question from our point of view is whether Beloff's opinion is justified.

Project Alpha

An experiment provides evidence for ESP only if the results cannot be accounted for in terms of ordinary sensory perception (OSP). Unfortunately, scientists are not particularly adept at determining when a result could be due to OSP because they are not trained in the art of deception. Professional magicians, however, are. As a result, parapsychologists would do well to make use of their expertise. Project Alpha, conceived by James (the Amazing) Randi, provides a dramatic demonstration of the need for magicians in the psi lab.

In Project Alpha, two young magicians, Steve Shaw and Michael Edwards, with Randi's advice, went to the McDonnell Laboratory for Psychical Research at Washington University in St. Louis, Missouri. The McDonnell laboratory was probably the best-funded psychical laboratory in the world; it had been created with a $500,000 grant from James McDonnell, chairman of the board of the McDonnell-Douglas Aircraft Corporation.

Shaw and Edwards easily convinced the research staff at the McDonnell Laboratory that they had genuine psychic powers. They were tested by the laboratory for a period of three years. They rarely failed to achieve "psychic" feats. Metal was bent "paranormally," minds were read, the contents of sealed envelopes were mysteriously divined, fuses sealed in protective containers burned out, and mysterious pictures appeared "psychically" on film inside cameras. . . . Randi reports in detail on the simple ways in which these deceptions were carried out.

Before Shaw and Edwards began to be tested at the McDonnell Laboratory, Randi wrote to the director, Dr. Peter Phillips, a physics professor at Washington University. Randi outlined the type of controls that the lab should use to guard against sleight of hand and other such trickery. He also offered to come to the lab, at his own expense and without public acknowledgment, to assist in the preparation of "trick-proof" experiments. Randi's offer was rejected and his advice ignored. The controls that were placed on Shaw and Edwards were totally inadequate to prevent their use of trickery. Even when videotapes of their feats showed fairly clearly, to anyone watching them carefully, how the trick had been done, the enthusiastic laboratory staff failed to catch on."[74]

Can individually unconvincing studies be collectively convincing? No. What a study lacks in quality cannot be made up in quantity. The evidence generated by questionable studies remains questionable, no matter how many of them there are.

There is a great deal of anecdotal evidence for psi phenomena. Many individuals have had experiences that they believe are inexplicable in terms of known physical laws. But as we saw in Chapter 3, many strange experiences can be accounted for in terms of well-known perceptual processes, such as hypnogogic and hypnopompic imagery, pareidolia, cryptomnesia, selective attention, subjective validation, the Forer effect, the autokinetic effect, and so on. Because, outside of the laboratory, we can't establish beyond a reasonable doubt that these factors are *not* at work, we can't accept anecdotal evidence at face value.

One further body of evidence must be included in any examination of psi — that obtained by gambling casinos. As Terence Hines observes, "One can consider every spin of the roulette wheel, every throw of the dice, every draw of the card in gambling casinos the world over as a single trial in a worldwide ongoing study in parapsychology."[75] If psi were a reality, casino winnings should vary from what's predicted by the laws of chance. But they don't. The billions of trials conducted each year by casinos all over the world provide no evidence for the existence of psi. It has been claimed that the reason for this is that psi cannot be used for personal gain. Such ad-hoc hypotheses, however, should not keep us from giving this evidence its due.

There are non-ad-hoc hypotheses that can explain the casino data, however. One is that it is just too noisy in casinos for psi to operate. Recent experiments using sensory deprivation techniques seem to lend credibility to this hypothesis.

Recognizing that if psi exists, it must be an extremely weak force, parapsychologist Charles Honorton has tried to detect its presence by reducing normal sensory input to a minimum. Subjects in his experiments are put in a *ganzfeld* designed to block out sensory information. The ganzfeld is produced by putting ping pong balls over the subjects' eyes and headphones over their ears. A bright red light is shown through the ping pong balls and white noise played through the headphones. After being in this condition for about fifteen minutes, the subjects begin to hallucinate. What they see is similar to the hypnogogic images sometimes seen right before falling asleep. Once the subjects have reached this state, the senders — usually relatives or friends — try to transmit to the subjects the contents of a minute-long video. The clip is chosen randomly by a computer out of forty sets of four clips each. Thus even the experimenter has no way of knowing what clip is being played at any particular time. Once the senders have viewed the clip, the subjects are asked to describe the images they are seeing. Honorton's hypothesis is that if psi exists, the images seen by the subjects should match the images transmitted by the senders more often than would be expected by pure chance. At the end of each session, the subjects are shown all four clips in the set and asked to identify which one most closely resembles the images they were seeing.

By chance alone, the subjects should be able to identify the correct clip 25 percent of the time. Honorton's 240 subjects did so 34 percent of the time. The odds against this happening by chance are over a million to one.

This is not the first ganzfield experiment to have been conducted. It was designed specifically to meet the objections of Ray Hyman, one of the most outspoken critics of such studies. Honorton realized that the best experiment would be the least objectionable, and that the best way to eliminate objections is to please your harshest critic. He apparently succeeded. "There are a lot of minor things I could quibble with," says Hyman, "but Honorton met most of the objections I had."[76] Until the results are replicated, however, Hyman points out that they do not provide credible evidence for the existence of psi. Attempts to replicate Honorton's experiment, however, are underway. If they are successful, we may have to start rethinking our world view.

SUGGESTED READINGS

Goldstein, Martin, and Inge Goldstein. *How We Know: An Exploration of the Scientific Process.* New York: Plenum Press, 1980.

Gardner, Martin. *Science: Good, Bad, and Bogus.* Buffalo: Prometheus Books, 1981.

Grim, Patrick, ed. *Philosophy of Science and the Occult.* Albany: State University of New York Press, 1982.

Hansel, C. E. M. *ESP and Parapsychology: A Critical Re-evaluation.* Buffalo: Prometheus Books, 1980.

Hempel, Carl. *Philosophy of Natural Science.* Englewood Cliffs, N.J.: Prentice-Hall, 1966.

Kitcher, Philip. *Abusing Science: The Case Against Creationism.* Cambridge, Mass.: MIT Press, 1982.

Klemke, E. D., Robert Hollinger, and A. David Kline, eds. *Introductory Readings in the Philosophy of Science.* Buffalo: Prometheus Books, 1980.

Quine, W. V., and J. S. Ullian. *The Web of Belief.* New York: Random House, 1970.

NOTES

1. Carl Hempel, "Valuation and Objectivity in Science," in *Physics, Philosophy and Psychoanalysis: Essays in Honor of Adolf Grünbaum,* ed. R. S. Cohen and L. Laudan (Boston: Reidel, 1983), pp. 91ff.

2. Jeremy Rifkin, *Declaration of a Heretic* (Boston: Routledge and Kegan Paul, 1985), pp. 79–80.

3. See, for example, B. F. Skinner, *Beyond Freedom and Dignity* (New York: Bantam Books, 1972).

4. Bruce Holbrook, *The Stone Monkey* (New York: William Morrow, 1981), pp. 50–52.

5. Fritjof Capra, *The Turning Point* (New York: Bantam Books, 1983).

6. Charles Sanders Peirce, *Collected Papers*, vol. 5, ed. Charles Hartshorne, Paul Weiss, and Arthur Burks (Cambridge: Harvard University Press, 1931–58), para. 575–83.

7. Kenneth L. Feder, *Frauds, Myths, and Mysteries* (Mountain View, Calif.: Mayfield, 1990), p. 20.

8. Karl Popper, *Conjectures and Refutations: The Growth of Scientific Knowledge* (New York: Basic Books, 1965), p. 46.

9. Ibid., p. 47.

10. Carl Hempel, *Philosophy of Natural Science* (Englewood Cliffs, N.J.: Prentice-Hall, 1966), pp. 14ff.

11. Pierre Duhem, *Aim and Structure of Physical Theory* (Princeton: Princeton University Press, 1953), Chapter 6, reprinted in *Readings in the Philosophy of Science*, ed. Herbert Feigl and May Brodbeck (New York: Appleton-Century-Crofts, 1953), pp. 240–41.

12. Philip Kitcher, "Believing Where We Cannot Prove," *Abusing Science* (Cambridge: MIT Press, 1982), p. 44.

13. Irving Copi, *Introduction to Logic*, 6th ed. (New York: Macmillan, 1982), pp. 488–94.

14. Robert Schadewald, "Some Like It Flat," in *The Fringes of Reason: A Whole Earth Catalog*, ed. Ted Schultz (New York: Harmony Books, 1989), p. 86.

15. Ted Schultz, "Jumping Geography," in *Fringes of Reason*, Schultz, p. 89.

16. Hempel, *Philosophy of Natural Science*, p. 31.

17. Popper, *Conjectures and Refutations*, p. 35.

18. Popper is not unaware of this method of saving theories from negative evidence. He calls it a *conventionalist twist* or a *conventionalist stratagem*. See Popper, *Conjectures and Refutations*, p. 37.

19. Imre Lakatos, "The Methodology of Scientific Research," *Philosophical Papers*, vol. 1 (New York: Cambridge University Press, 1977), pp. 6–7.

20. Nathan Spielberg and Byron D. Anderson, *Seven Ideas That Shook the Universe* (New York: John Wiley, 1987), pp. 178ff.

21. Ibid.

22. Ibid.

23. Immanuel Velikovsky, *Worlds in Collision* (New York: Dell, 1969).

24. Carl Sagan, *Broca's Brain* (New York: Ballantine, 1979), p. 115.

25. Ibid., pp. 113ff.

26. Frank Smyth, "Nazi Occult," in *The Occult Connection*, ed. Peter Brookesmith (London: Macdonald & Co., 1988), p. 60.

27. Spielberg and Anderson, *Seven Ideas*, pp. 180–81.

28. P. Langevin, *C. R. Acad. Sci.* 173 (1921): 831.

29. Albert Einstein, *Forum Philosophicum,* 1, no. 173 (1930): 183.

30. Hempel, *Philosophy of Natural Science,* pp. 40ff.

31. There is no formula for counting assumptions, but nevertheless their number can be arrived at through various qualitative considerations. See, for example, Paul Thagard, "The Best Explanation: Criteria for Theory Choice," *The Journal of Philosophy,* 75, no. 2 (February 1978): 86ff.

32. Capra, *The Tao of Physics,* p. 46.

33. W. V. Quine and J. S. Ullian, *The Web of Belief* (New York: Random House, 1970), pp. 43–44.

34. Thomas Kuhn, "Reflections on My Critics," in *Criticism and the Growth of Knowledge,* ed. Imre Lakatos and Alan Musgrave (Cambridge: Cambridge University Press, 1970), p. 261.

35. Charles Darwin, *The Origin of Species* (New York: Collier, 1962), p. 176.

36. I. Michael Lerner, *Heredity, Evolution, and Society* (San Francisco: W. H. Freeman, 1968), pp. 35–39.

37. Ibid., pp. 39–42.

38. Section 4a of Act 590 of the Acts of Arkansas of 1981, "Balanced Treatment for Creation-Science and Evolution-Science Act."

39. Judge William Overton, *McLean v. Arkansas Board of Education,* cited in Jeffrey G. Murphy, *Evolution, Morality and the Meaning of Life* (Totowa, N.J.: Rowman and Littlefield, 1982), p. 146.

40. Henry Morris and Martin Clark, *The Bible Has the Answer,* cited in Overton, *McLean v. Arkansas Board of Education,* in Murphy, *Evolution, Morality,* p. 123.

41. Cited in Garvin McCain and Erwin Segal, *The Game of Science* (Pacific Grove, Calif.: Brooks/Cole, 1988), p. 19–20.

42. Duane Gish, "The Genesis War," *Science Digest,* October 1981, p. 82.

43. Lerner, *Heredity, Evolution, and Society,* p. 39ff.

44. Larry Laudan, "Science at the Bar: Causes for Concern," in Murphy, *Evolution, Morality,* p. 150.

45. Martin Gardner, *The New Age: Notes of a Fringe Watcher* (Buffalo: Prometheus Books, 1991), pp. 93–98.

46. Feder, *Frauds, Myths, and Mysteries,* p. 174.

47. Ibid., pp. 176–79.

48. Henry M. Morris, ed., *Scientific Creationism* (San Diego: Creation-Life Publishers, 1974), p. 210.

49. Martin Gardner, *Fads and Fallacies in the Name of Science* (New York: Dover, 1957), pp. 125–26.

50. Isaac Asimov and Duane Gish, "The Genesis War," *Science Digest,* October 1981.

51. Cited in Murphy, *Evolution, Morality,* p. 136.

52. Asimov and Gish, "Genesis War," p. 87.

53. Ibid., p. 82.

54. Ibid.

55. Even though the big bang happened only 15 billion years ago, it could have been the result of a prior "big crunch" (gravitational collapse) or our universe may have "budded off" (grown out of) a previously existing universe.

56. Susan Blackmore, "The Lure of the Paranormal," *New Scientist* 22 (1990): 62–65.

57. A. Greeley, "Mysticism Goes Mainstream," *American Health*, January/February 1987, pp. 47–49.

58. J. B. Rhine, *The Reach of the Mind* (1947), Chapter 11.

59. Martin Gardner, *The Whys of a Philosophical Scrivener* (New York: Quill, 1973), p. 58.

60. Daniel Druckman and John Swets, eds., *Enhancing Human Performance: Issues, Theories, and Techniques* (Washington, D.C.: National Academy Press, 1988), p. 171.

61. Ibid., p. 206.

62. J. B. Rhine, "The Science of Nonphysical Nature," in *Philosophy and Parapsychology*, ed. Jan Ludwig (Buffalo: Prometheus Books, 1978), p. 126.

63. *The Morning Call*, October 2, 1989, p. A7.

64. J. B. Rhine, "Science of Nonphysical Nature," pp. 124–25.

65. Leonard Zusne and Warren Jones, *Anomalistic Psychology* (Hillsdale, N.J.: Lawrence Erlbaum Associates, 1982), pp. 374–75.

66. J. Crumbaugh, "A Scientific Critique of Parapsychology," *International Journal of Neuropsychiatry*, 5 (1966): 521–29.

67. John Beloff, *Psychological Sciences* (London: Crosby Lockwood Staples, 1973), p. 312.

68. G. R. Schmeidler, "Separating the Sheep from the Goats," *Journal of the American Society for Psychical Research*, 39, no. 1 (1945): 47–50.

69. D. Scott Rogo, "Making of Psi Failure," *Fate*, April 1986, 76–80.

70. Ray Hyman, "A Critical Historical Overview of Parapsychology," in *A Skeptic's Handbook of Parapsychology*, ed. Paul Kurtz (Buffalo: Prometheus Books, 1985), pp. 3–96.

71. Quoted in Ibid., p. 50.

72. C. Scott and P. Haskell, "'Normal' Explanations of the Soal-Goldney Experiments in Extrasensory Perception," *Nature*, 245 (1973): 52–54.

73. John Beloff, "Seven Evidential Experiments," *Zetetic Scholar*, 6 (1980): 91–94.

74. Terence Hines, *Pseudoscience and the Paranormal* (Buffalo: Prometheus Books, 1988), pp. 93–94.

75. Hines, *Pseudoscience and the Paranormal*, p. 85.

76. John McCrone, "Roll Up for the Telepathy Test," *New Scientist*, May 15, 1993, pp. 29–33.

NINE
Case Studies in the Extraordinary

L ET'S TAKE STOCK.

In the preceding chapters, we've explored several essential principles that can empower our thinking about weird phenomena. We've seen, among other things, that even in the realms of weirdness, it's not true that anything is possible: Some things are logically impossible; some things are physically impossible; some things are technically impossible. On the other hand, some things that people believe are impossible may be possible after all. But we've also seen that just because something is logically or physically possible doesn't mean that it's real.

We've examined why personal experience doesn't always provide reliable evidence for believing something. We've seen that, in themselves, strong feelings of subjective

The pure and simple truth is rarely pure and never simple.
—OSCAR WILDE

certainty regarding a personal experience don't increase the reliability of that experience one bit. Only if we have no good reasons to doubt a personal experience can we accept it as a reliable guide to what's real — and there are often many grounds for doubt. As the basis for a claim — whether about UFOs, ghosts, witches, or the curative power of vitamin C — personal experience is frequently shakier than we realize.

We've seen why we can't escape the fact that there is indeed such a thing as objective truth. There is a way the world is. The idea that truth is relative to individuals, to societies, or to conceptual schemes is unreasonable. Similarly, the fashionable notions that people create their own reality or create reality by consensus have little to recommend them.

We've investigated what it means to say that we know something. We can know many things — including weird things — if we have good reasons to believe them and no good reasons to doubt them. We have good reasons to doubt a proposition when it conflicts with other propositions we have good reasons to believe, when it conflicts with well-established background information, or when it conflicts with expert opinion regarding the evidence. If we have good reason to doubt a proposition, we can't know it. The best we can do is proportion our belief to the evidence. If we don't know something, a leap of faith can never help us know it. We can't make something true just by believing it to be true. To accept a proposition on faith is to believe it without justification. Likewise, mystical experience doesn't provide us with a privileged way of knowing. Claims of knowledge based on mystical experience must pass the same rational tests as any other kind of experience.

The path of sound credence is through the thick forest of skepticism.
—George Jean Nathan

We've explored why — even though the scientific method can never prove or disprove anything conclusively — science is our most reliable means of establishing an empirical proposition beyond a reasonable doubt. It offers us a model for assessing new hypotheses, or claims, about all manner of extraordinary events and entities — a model that can serve scientists and nonscientists alike. If we want to know whether a hypothesis is true, we'll need to use this model in one form or another. The model requires that we judge a new hypothesis in light of alternative, competing hypotheses and apply to each of these alternatives the best yardsticks we have — the criteria of adequacy — to see which hypothesis measures up. Under pressure from the criteria of adequacy, some hypotheses may collapse from the lack of sturdy evidence or sound reasons to support them. Other hypotheses may not tumble completely but will be shown to be built on weak and rickety foundations. One, though, may emerge as the best hypothesis of them all, strong and tall because it rests on a firm base of good reasons.

In this chapter, we bring all these analytical tools together. We try to show how to coherently apply all our preceding principles to actual weird claims. This chapter, then, is the applications section of this volume, which is, as we've mentioned before, essentially a book of *applied epistemology.*

First, we'll sketch out a procedure that can help you evaluate, step-by-step, any extraordinary claim that you come across. It's a formula for inquiry that reminds you of the principles already discussed, suggests when and how they come into play, and guides you toward your own reasoned conclusions about the truth of a claim. The formula isn't carved in stone — it's simply one way to show how to apply the principles that we all must apply if we're to make sense of any unusual (or not so unusual) claim.

The rest of the chapter demonstrates how we authors have already put this formula to work to assess several popular, extraordinary claims and arrive at supportable conclusions. We try to show by example how to, well, think about weird things. The conclusions we reach are neither unique (many scientists and philosophers have reached similar conclusions) nor infallible. We do think, however, that they're based on the best of reasons — which is all anyone can ask of any conclusion worthy of acceptance. You are, of course, free to reject our conclusions. If you do, we hope that you do so for good reasons — and that by now you understand the difference between good and bad reasons and why the difference is crucial.

THE SEARCH FORMULA

Our formula for inquiry consists of four steps, which we represent by the acronym SEARCH. The letters stand for the key words in the four steps:

1. *S*tate the claim.
2. Examine the *E*vidence for the claim.
3. Consider *A*lternative hypotheses.
4. *R*ate, according to the *C*riteria of adequacy, each *H*ypothesis.

Judge a man by his questions rather than his answers.

—VOLTAIRE

The acronym is arbitrary and artificial, but it may help you remember the formula's vital components. Go through these steps any time you're faced with an extraordinary claim.

Note that throughout this chapter we use the words *hypothesis* and *claim* interchangeably. We do so because any weird claim, like any claim about events and entities, can be viewed as a hypothesis — as an explanation of a particular phenomenon. Thinking of weird claims as hypotheses is important because effectively evaluating weird claims involves essentially the same hypothesis-assessing procedure used in science.

Step 1: State the Claim

Before you can carefully examine a claim, you have to understand what it is. It's vital to state the claim in terms that are as *clear* and as *specific* as possible. "Ghosts are real" is not a good candidate for examination because it's vague and nonspecific. A better claim is "The disembodied spirits of dead persons exist and are visible to the human eye." Likewise, "Astrology is true" is not much to go on. It's better to say, "Astrologers can correctly identify someone's personality traits by using sun signs." Even these revised claims aren't as unambiguous and definitive as they should be. (Terms in the claims, for example, could be better defined. What is meant by "spirit"? What does it mean to "correctly identify someone's personality traits"?) But many of the extraordinary claims you run into are of this caliber. The point is that before examining any claim, you must achieve maximum clarity and specificity of what the claim is.

Step 2: Examine the Evidence for the Claim

Ask yourself what reasons there are for accepting the claim. That is, what empirical evidence or logical arguments are there in the claim's favor? Answering this question entails taking inventory of both the quantity and quality of the reasons for believing that the claim is true. An honest and thorough appraisal of reasons must include:

1. *Determining the exact nature and limitations of the empirical evidence.* This means assessing not only what the evidence is but whether there are any reasonable doubts regarding it. You have to try to find out if it's subject to any of the deficiencies we've previously discussed — the distortions of human perception, memory, and judgment; the errors and biases of scientific research; the difficulties inherent in ambiguous data. Sometimes even a preliminary survey of the facts may force you to admit that there really isn't anything mysterious that needs explaining. Or perhaps investigating a little mystery will lead to a bigger mystery. At any rate, attempting an objective assessment of the evidence takes courage. Many true believers have never taken this elementary step.

2. *Discovering if any of these reasons deserve to be disqualified.* As we've seen, people frequently offer considerations in support of a claim that

should be discounted. These include wishful thinking, faith, unfounded intuition, and subjective certainty. The problem is that these factors aren't reasons at all. In themselves, they can't provide any support for a claim.

3. *Deciding whether the hypothesis in question actually explains the evidence.* If it doesn't — if important factors are left out of account — the hypothesis is not a good one. In other words, a good hypothesis must be relevant to the evidence it's intended to explain. If it isn't, there's no reason to consider it any further.

Step 3: Consider Alternative Hypotheses

It's never enough to consider *only* the hypothesis in question and its reasons for acceptance. If you ever hope to discover the truth, you must also weigh *alternative* hypotheses and their reasons.

Take this hypothesis, for example: Rudolph the Red-Nosed Reindeer — Santa's funny, flying, furry headlight — is real and lives at the North Pole. As evidence for this hypothesis we could submit these facts: Millions of people (mostly children) believe Rudolph to be real; his likeness shows up everywhere during the Christmas holidays; given the multitude of reindeer in the world and their long history, it's likely that at some time a reindeer with flying capabilities would either evolve or be born with the necessary mutations; some people say that they have seen Rudolph with their own eyes. We could go on and on and build a fairly convincing case for the hypothesis — soon you may even come to believe that we were on to something.

The hypothesis sounds great by itself, but when considered alongside an alternative hypothesis — that Rudolph is a creature of the imagination created in a Christmas song — it looks ludicrous. The song hypothesis is supported by evidence that's overwhelming; it doesn't conflict with well-established theory in biology (as the real-Rudolph hypothesis does); and, unlike its competitor, it requires no postulations about new entities.

This third step involves creativity and maintaining an open mind. It requires asking whether there are other ways to account for the phenomenon at hand and, if there are, what reasons there are in favor of these alternative hypotheses. This step involves applying step two to all competing explanations.

It's also important to remember that, when people are confronted with some extraordinary phenomenon, they often immediately offer a hypothesis involving the paranormal or supernatural and then can't imagine a natural hypothesis to account for the facts. As a result, they

No man really becomes a fool until he stops asking questions.
— CHARLES STEINMETZ

assume that the paranormal or supernatural hypothesis must be right. But this assumption is unwarranted. Just because you can't think of a natural explanation doesn't mean there isn't one. It may be (as has often been the case throughout history) that you're simply unaware of the correct natural explanation. As pointed out in Chapter 2, the most reasonable response to a mystifying fact is to keep looking for a natural explanation.

We all have a built-in bias that urges us to latch onto a favorite hypothesis and ignore or resist all alternatives. We may believe that we needn't look at other explanations since we know that our favorite one is correct. This tendency may make us happy (at least for a while), but it's also a good recipe for delusion. We must work to counteract this bias. Having an open mind means being willing to consider any possibility and changing your view in light of good reasons.

Step 4: Rate, According to the Criteria of Adequacy, Each Hypothesis

Now it's time to weigh competing hypotheses and see which are found wanting and which are worthy of belief. Simply cataloguing the evidence for each hypothesis isn't enough. We need to consider other factors that can put that evidence in perspective and help us weigh hypotheses when there's no evidence at all, which is often the case with weird things. As discussed in Chapter 8, these potent factors are the criteria of adequacy. By applying them to each hypothesis, we can often eliminate some hypotheses right away, give more weight to some than others, and decide between hypotheses that may at first seem equally strong.

All is mystery; but he is a slave who will not struggle to penetrate the dark veil.

—Benjamin Disraeli

1. *Testability.* Ask: Can the hypothesis be tested? Is there any possible way to determine whether the hypothesis is true or false? Many hypotheses regarding extraordinary phenomena aren't testable. This doesn't mean they're false. It means they're worthless. They are merely assertions that we'll never be able to know. What if we claim that there is an invisible, undetectable gremlin in your head that sometimes causes you to have headaches. As an explanation for your headaches, this hypothesis is interesting but trivial. Since by definition there's no way to determine if this gremlin really exists, the hypothesis is amazingly uninformative. You can assign no weight to such a claim.

2. *Fruitfulness.* Ask: Does the hypothesis yield observable, surprising predictions that explain new phenomena? Any hypothesis that does so gets extra points. Other things being equal, hypotheses that make accurate, unexpected predictions are more likely to be true than hy-

potheses that don't. (Of course, if they yield no predictions, this in itself doesn't show that they're false.) Most hypotheses regarding weird things don't make observable predictions.

3. *Scope.* Ask: How many different phenomena can the hypothesis explain? Other things being equal, the more it explains, the less likely it is to be mistaken. In Chapter 3 we discussed the well-confirmed hypothesis that human perception is constructive. As we pointed out, the hypothesis explains a broad range of phenomena, including perceptual size constancy, misperception of stimuli, hallucinations, pareidolia, certain UFO sightings, and more. A hypothesis that explains only one of these phenomena (for example, the hypothesis that UFO sightings are caused by actual alien spacecraft) would be much less impressive—unless it had other things in its favor like compelling evidence.

4. *Simplicity.* Ask: Is this hypothesis the simplest explanation for the phenomenon? Generally, the simplest hypothesis that explains the phenomenon is the best, the one least likely to be false. *Simplest* means makes the fewest assumptions. In the realm of weird things, this is often a matter of postulating the existence of the fewest entities. Let's say you get into your car one morning, put the key in the ignition, and try to start the engine but find that it won't start. One hypothesis for this phenomenon is that the car battery is dead. Another is that a poltergeist (a mischievous spirit) has somehow caused your car not to start. The battery hypothesis is the simplest (in addition to being testable, able to yield predictions, and capable of explaining several phenomena) because it doesn't require postulating the existence of any mysterious entities. The poltergeist hypothesis, though, does postulate the existence of an entity (as well as assuming that the entity has certain capabilities and tendencies). Thus the criterion of simplicity shows us that the battery hypothesis has the greater chance of being right.

5. *Conservatism.* Ask: Is the hypothesis consistent with our well-founded beliefs? That is, is it consistent with the empirical evidence—with results from trustworthy observations and scientific tests, with natural laws, or with well-established theory? Trying to answer this question takes you beyond merely cataloguing evidence for hypotheses to actually assigning weight to hypotheses *in light of all the available evidence.* Other things being equal, the hypothesis most consistent with the entire corpus of our knowledge is the best bet, the one most likely to be true.

It follows that a hypothesis that flies in the face of extremely well-established evidence must be assigned a very low probability. Say, for example, that someone claims that yesterday thousands of cats and dogs rained down from the sky in Texas. This strange happening is logically possible, of course, but it conflicts with an enormous amount of human experience regarding objects that fall from the sky. Maybe one fine day cats and dogs will indeed tumble from the clouds and surprise us all. But based on a massive amount of experience, we must assign a very low probability to such a possibility.

What if someone claims to have built a perpetual motion machine, a device that, to work, must successfully circumvent one of the laws of thermodynamics. (A perpetual motion machine is supposed to function without ever stopping and without needing to draw on an external source of power — it supplies its own energy; this violates the law of conservation of mass-energy, which says that mass-energy can't be created or destroyed.) The laws of thermodynamics are supported by a massive amount of empirical evidence gathered throughout centuries. There have also been numerous failed attempts to build a perpetual motion machine. In light of such evidence, we're forced to conclude that it's very unlikely that anyone could avoid the laws of thermodynamics. Unless someone is able to produce good evidence showing that it can be done, we must say that the above claim is highly improbable.

Likewise, if someone puts forth a hypothesis that conflicts with a highly confirmed theory, the hypothesis must be regarded as improbable until good evidence shows that the hypothesis is right and the theory wrong. Paranormal claims then are, by definition, improbable. They conflict with what we know, with mountains of evidence. Only good evidence to the contrary can change this verdict.

DOWSING

Dowsing — as it's called in England, New England, New York, and Pennsylvania — is the practice of detecting underground water by using a Y-shaped stick (known as a *divining rod* or *dowsing rod*), a pendulum, or another device. (It's also called *water witching* or *divining*.) It's a folk tradition that's hundreds of years old, derived from sixteenth-century Europe. Dowsers claim to be able to detect the presence of underground water by walking over a given terrain and holding the two branches of the dowsing rod (one in each hand) with its point facing skyward away from the body. When the point of the rod dips toward the ground, that's supposed to indicate that water is beneath the dowser. Some dowsers claim not only to tell where water is, but at what depth and how much.

It seems to the dowser (and sometimes to observers) that the rod moves on its own, as though under the influence of some hidden force. The rod's gyrations are often so violent that the bark comes off in the dowser's hands.

Dowsers offer a variety of explanations for why the rod moves. Some say vaguely that dowsers get their power from Moses, who is said to have hit a rock with a stick and water gushed forth. Some claim that a magnetic or electrical attraction between dowser and rod is at work. Some say that the dowser detects water through psychic ability, and this information is revealed through unconscious muscle reactions transmitted to the divining rod. Some assert that mysterious and unknown forces or radiations act on the dowser or rod.

Obviously there's no shortage of hypotheses regarding water witching. For simplicity's sake, we'll select two hypotheses that reflect actual claims made by dowsers and apply the SEARCH formula to them. The first concerns the dowser's avowed ability to find water; the second concerns the cause of the divining rod's movements.

Hypothesis 1: *Through the use of a dowsing rod, certain persons can detect underground (or hidden) water better than through chance guessing and without the use of clues in the environment.* This, in plain language, is the standard claim of water witching, though there are many variations on the theme.

What evidence do dowsers offer to support this hypothesis? First, there are personal testimonials, eyewitness accounts, and case histories, featured prominently in prodowsing books like the classic *The Divining Hand.*[1] To many people, such anecdotal evidence seems very persuasive. But it's subject to many of the same deficiencies found in any other kind of personal experience — unconscious filling in or altering of reports to conform to what's expected or desired, reporting only dowsing successes while ignoring failures, conscious or unconscious omission of crucial facts from accounts, the machinations of constructive perception, and more. Even many water witching proponents have viewed such evidence as unreliable.[2]

Second, there are field tests — observations of dowsers in action, made for the specific purpose of testing the dowser's ability. Because they're tests, they usually have fewer deficiencies than anecdotal evidence. But like anecdotal evidence, they suffer from a critical flaw. They lack an objective standard by which to judge a dowser's performance. One standard is how successful a nondowser would be at finding water at the same location by chance alone. (Underground water is generally prevalent. In many places, if wells were dug at several randomly chosen spots, it's likely that water would be found at some of

This dowser uses a nylon rod to check the ground for oil deposits. A valid test of such a dowser must assess, among other things, whether he can find oil better than a nondowser using ordinary environmental clues.

them. The hypothesis in question states that the dowser must perform *better* than would be expected by chance.) Another standard is how successful a nondowser would be at finding water under the same conditions using environmental clues. (We know that groundwater experts can find underground water by simply observing surface clues like vegetation, soil color, and surface water. The hypothesis states that dowsers can find water without using these clues.) Any test that can't rule out the possibility that a dowser found water by chance guessing or by using surface clues can't be considered good evidence for the power of dowsing.

We can state the leading alternative to the above hypothesis like this: *The dowser's success in detecting underground or hidden water is due to chance or to the conscious or unconscious use of clues from the environment.* Evidence supporting this hypothesis has come from many controlled experiments using objective standards to assess dowsers' performance. In these tests, dowsers have not been able to find water any better than would be predicted by chance. Typically, the dowsers agree to all testing procedures, and are completely confident of their own abilities, but then couldn't do any better than would be expected from lucky guesses — and sometimes they performed far worse than groundwater experts did.[3]

A dowser holds a hazel twig in the conventional manner. Because groundwater is prevalent, it can often be found by chance alone.

Now, let's apply the criteria of adequacy to these competing hypotheses. We can see at once that they're both testable. We can also see that the dowsing hypothesis earns no points for fruitfulness because, to date, it hasn't predicted any hitherto unknown phenomena. The dowsing hypothesis also doesn't measure up to the alternative hypothesis in scope. The latter hypothesis offers chance as an explanation, which—unlike the dowsing hypothesis—can explain a vast number of other phenomena. As far as simplicity goes, the two explanations are equal; neither postulates any new entities or makes other assumptions.

So far, the dowsing hypothesis seems less credible than its competitor. The last criterion, conservatism, is the one that's most telling in this instance. On this score, the dowsing hypothesis is clearly inferior. It's simply not consistent with the empirical evidence. On the other hand, the alternative hypothesis is well supported by the best evidence. What's more, the dowsing hypothesis conflicts with much human experience regarding the discovery of unseen things. There's just no good evidence that anyone has ever found water through the power of dowsing.

Based on all of the above, we have to say that the dowsing hypothesis is probably false and the alternative most likely to be correct.

But why does the divining rod move? Let's select from the many possibilities a hypothesis concerning the rod's movements. Hypothesis 2: *An unknown form of radiation emanating from underground water pulls on the divining rod, causing it to move.*

Alas, there's no evidence for this hypothesis—or for any other hypothesis positing unknown or paranormal forces in dowsing. The leading rival hypothesis, however, has considerable supporting evidence. It says: *The movement of the divining rod in the dowser's hands is caused by suggestion and unconscious muscular activity in the dowser.*

Research has demonstrated the reality of ideomotor action—the phenomenon of a person's ideas creating in the body tiny muscular reactions that the person isn't consciously aware of. Just thinking about a certain physical action (like an arm moving or a fist closing) causes minute reactions in the muscles that would be used in such actions. Even the mere suggestion of physical action—whether the suggestion comes from oneself or others and even if it is unconscious—is enough to trigger these muscle reactions. Additional suggestions magnify the muscle movements; the movements are also enhanced if the muscles are already under a lot of tension, as they are in dowsers. (In dowsing, such muscle action can easily affect the rod noticeably because the slightest movement in wrists or hands can set the rod dipping.) Research has shown, for example, that a person holding a pendulum (a small weight on a string) can be given a suggestion that the pendulum will move in a certain way. Despite the person trying to hold his or her arm and hand perfectly still, the pendulum will indeed move in the way suggested due to unconscious muscle activity. That the person is not aware of this effect is expected. The heightened muscle tension masks neural feedback from the muscles so that their movements can seem autonomous.

All the physiological and psychological factors involved in the dowsing experience seem to be an excellent recipe for dramatic movements in the divining rod. As psychologists Leonard Zusne and Warren Jones point out:

> In an interested and attentive onlooker, the performance of a dowser creates the same muscular tensions, albeit on a smaller scale. An invitation to try the rod for oneself and the assurance that it will work constitute additional suggestion, and the muscular tension pattern is repeated in an enhanced manner as the novice begins dowsing. Concentration on the task and expectation serve to recruit the excitation and minute contractions of separate muscle fibers until a larger muscular contraction occurs and the rod . . . dips at the exact spot where it had previously dipped for the diviner. The beginner is convinced that it was some external force that moved the rod.[4]

Pendulum Power

Some dowsers use a pendulum instead of a divining rod. A pendulum can be simply an object suspended from a string. Psychologist Terence Hines explains the surprising "power" of such a device.

> The pendulum is usually held at arm's length and is said to swing back and forth, under its own power and with no attempt to induce swinging on the part of the dowser. It swings when the dowser is over water or whatever other substance is being searched for. The pendulum can also be used, it is said, to divine the sex of an unborn child: hold the pendulum over the mother's belly and it will swing one way for a boy, the other for a girl. The pendulum has also been used to determine the guilt or innocence of an accused person and to reveal all sorts of hidden knowledge.
>
> The pendulum seems to be swinging back and forth under its own power and the one holding it claims, quite honestly, to be making no conscious attempts to influence its movement. In reality, as for the dowsing rod, small arm movements, which are not registered in the brain, are responsible for the pendulum's movement. This can be demonstrated quite neatly by having the string that suspends the pendulum draped over some stationary object. Movement stops, even though the person is still holding the string and the pendulum is still free to swing, if there really were psychic forces causing its movement. In an interesting experiment, [researchers] further demonstrated the nature of the pendulum's movement. In one case, subjects could see the pendulum they were holding, in another they couldn't. Movement was greater when they could see it. Movement was even greater, by a factor of ten, when subjects were asked to imagine that the pendulum was moving, as opposed to when they were asked to imagine that it was not. Finally, if they observed some other type of oscillating motion, this also increased the amount of pendulum movement. None of these effects would be expected if the pendulum's movement were caused by some psychic force.[5]

Unless we are told more about the unknown force, the hypothesis that it exists is neither testable nor fruitful. The ideomotor hypothesis, however, is testable, has greater scope, and is simpler than the unknown force hypothesis. The ideomotor hypothesis postulates no new entities; the unknown force hypothesis does. So even if there were no empirical evidence for either hypothesis, these facts would lead us to reject the radiation hypothesis.

But there *is* evidence. As we've seen, the ideomotor hypothesis is most consistent with that evidence. Further, the existence of the unknown form of radiation conflicts with a vast amount of human experience. Conservatism alone shows the radiation hypothesis to be

It is always easier to believe than to deny. Our minds are naturally affirmative.
—JOHN BURROUGHS

improbable. It also reveals its rival as superior. In fact, thus far, the ideomotor hypothesis seems to be the most likely.

UFO ABDUCTIONS

In recent years, books, magazines, movies, and television talk shows have circulated an amazing hypothesis: Alien beings are abducting ordinary people, manipulating them in strange ways (performing experiments on them, having sex with them, or otherwise terrifying them), and then releasing their victims and vanishing. In the best-selling book *Communion,* author Whitley Strieber suggested that he was abducted by aliens with large heads and strange eyes and that they forced him to endure horrific treatment, including having a needle inserted into his head and an instrument put into his anus.[6] Later the book was made into a movie with the same name. The book *Intruders* by Budd Hopkins presents dramatic case histories of people who claim to have endured UFO abductions.[7] Hopkins suggests that aliens have abducted hundreds of people and used them in disturbing genetic experiments, then released them.

He that will not reason is a bigot; he that cannot reason is a fool; and he that dares not reason is a slave.

—WILLIAM DRUMMOND

In many cases, before any abduction story surfaces, the victims first experience a vivid dream or nightmare (sometimes in childhood) involving eerie, other-worldly creatures. Or they experience "missing time," the realization that they don't remember what happened to them during a certain period. Or they see an odd light in the night sky that they identify as a UFO. Later, when the victims are hypnotized to try to learn more about these strange occurrences, an abduction experience is fully revealed. While under hypnosis, the abductees report in stunning detail what they believe they saw or felt during abduction, what the aliens looked like, and, in some cases, what the aliens said. The technique called *regressive hypnosis* has been the favored method for uncovering details of an abduction and for authenticating it. Some people, however, have recounted a UFO-abduction experience or produced details about it without undergoing hypnosis.

Now let's apply the SEARCH formula to the abduction hypothesis and to some of the leading alternatives and see what happens.

Hypothesis 1: *Alien beings have abducted several people, interacted with them in various ways, and then released them.* Proponents of this hypothesis point to several pieces of evidence. First and foremost, there's the striking testimony elicited during hypnosis, which is thought to be a kind of truth serum, a way to retrieve accurate details about a person's experience of past events. There's also testimony that arises without the aid of hypnosis. There's the fact that the alleged abductees' stories

Alien Astronauts from Yesteryear

The UFO abduction is but one variation on the theme of alien visitors. In 1968 Swiss author Erich von Däniken offered his own ideas on the subject in his book *Chariots of the Gods?* His basic assertion was that aliens visited earth in the distant past, dramatically influenced the development of humanity, and left convincing archaeological proof of their visit. Here archaeologist Kenneth L. Feder examines one of von Däniken's main hypotheses:

> The first implicit claim concerns the existence of prehistoric drawings or sculptures of aliens from outer space and early writings about their visits. It is an intriguing thought. Hundreds, thousands, even tens of thousands of years ago, flying saucers or spaceships landed on our planet in a burst of fire and smoke. Out came space-suited aliens, perhaps to take soil samples or study plant life (just like E.T. in the [Stephen] Spielberg movie). Upon completion of their mission, they got back into their spaceships and took off for home.
>
> Secreted in the bushes, behind the rocks, an ancient human sat transfixed, having watched the entire scene unbeknownst to our alien friends. This Cro-Magnon, Neolithic, or Medieval man rushed home to tell others of the marvelous sight of the fiery "chariots" of the "gods" (thus, the title for von Däniken's book) that had come down from heaven. He would tell of how the Gods or angels (or devils) had silver skins (spacesuits) and bubbleheads (space helmets). Artistic renderings would be made on cave walls and pots. Descriptions would be passed down from generation to generation, especially if the space Gods came back again and again, reinforcing the entire idea of Gods from the heavens. Descriptions would be written of the wondrous spectacle of the Gods coming to earth. Our ancestors would wait for their return, as perhaps we wait to this very day.
>
> Fascinating? Undoubtedly! Wonderful, if true? Absolutely! Backed up by inductive and deductive scientific reasoning, evidence, and proof? Unfortunately, no.
>
> This first von Däniken scenario can be called the *Inkblot Hypothesis*. . . . [In psychological "inkblot" testing (using Rorschach tests)] the picture seen in an inkblot is entirely dependent upon the mind of the viewer. The images themselves are not necessarily anything in particular. They are whatever you make them out to be, whatever you want them to be.
>
> Von Däniken's approach is analogous to an inkblot test. Although he is describing actual images, these images belong to a different culture. Without an understanding of the religious, artistic, or historic contexts to the drawings or images within the culture that produced them, von Däniken's descriptions of the images tell us more about what is going on in his mind than about what was in the minds of the ancient artists.
>
> For example, an image identified by von Däniken as an astronaut with a radio antenna might be more easily explained as a shaman or priest with an antler headdress. Von Däniken sees spacemen because he wants to, not because they really are there.

(continued)

Here is another example. High up on a plain in the Andes Mountains, prehistoric people called the *Nazca* constructed a spectacular complex of shapes on the highland desert. Most are long lines, etched into the desert surface, crisscrossing each other at all angles. The most interesting, however, are actual drawings, rendered on an enormous scale (some are hundreds of feet across), of animals such as fish, monkeys, and snakes.

The figures and lines were made by clearing away the darker surface rocks, exposing the lighter desert soil beneath. They are remarkable achievements because of their great size, but certainly not beyond the capabilities of prehistoric people. Remember, these drawings were not carved into solid rock with extraterrestrial lasers; they were not paved over with some mysterious substance from another world. They were, in essence, "swept" into existence. Science writer Joe Nickell, an investigator of extreme claims . . . has duplicated the technique of making Nazca-like designs with a small crew, some rope, and a few pieces of wood. Amazing, perhaps. Unbelievable, no.

And what does von Däniken have to say about the Nazca markings? Almost yielding to rationality, he admits that "they could have been laid out on their gigantic scale by working from a model and using a system of coordinates," which is precisely how Nickell accomplished it. Not to disappoint us, however, von Däniken prefers the notion that "they could also have been built according to instructions from an aircraft." Relying on the "inkblot approach," he says, "Seen from the air, the clear-cut impression that the 37-mile-long plain of Nazca made on me was that of an airfield."

Please remember Occam's Razor here. On the one hand, for the hypothesis that the ancient people of South America built the lines themselves, we need only assume that they were clever. The archaeological record of the area certainly lends support to this. On the other hand, for von Däniken's preferred hypothesis, we have to assume the existence of extraterrestrial, intelligent life (unproven), assume that they visited the earth in the distant past (unproven and not very likely), assume that they needed to build rather strange airfields (pretty hard to swallow), and then, for added amusement, instruct local Indians to construct enormous representations of birds, spiders, monkeys, fish, and snakes. Those assumptions are bizarre, and the choice under Occam's Razor is abundantly clear.

We can go on and deduce some implications for our preferred hypothesis: we should find evidence of small-scale models, we should find the art style of the desert drawings repeated in other artifacts found in the area, and we might expect the Nazca markings to be part of a general tradition in western South America of large-scale drawings. When we test these predictions, we determine that we do find such supporting evidence.[8]

seem to be so similar, that many abductees report the experience of missing time, and that a few of them (including Whitley Strieber) have passed lie detector tests. There's also physical evidence, like mysterious scars on abductees' bodies and areas of dead grass on the ground suggesting a UFO landing.

As for hypnosis, it's not the revealer of truth that many believe it to be. Research has shown that even deeply hypnotized people can willfully lie and that a person can fake hypnosis and fool even very experienced hypnotists. More to the point, research also shows that when hypnotized subjects are asked to recall a past event, they will fantasize freely, creating memories of things that never happened. Martin T. Orne, one of the world's leading experts on the use of hypnosis to obtain information about past events, sums up the situation like this:

> The hypnotic suggestion to relive a past event, particularly when accompanied by questions about specific details, puts pressure on the subject to provide information. . . . This situation may jog the subject's memory and produce some increased recall, but it will also cause him to fill in details that are plausible but consist of memories or fantasies from other times. It is extremely difficult to know which aspects of hypnotically aided recall are historically accurate and which aspects have been

This earth-drawing, or geoglyph, of a monkey was constructed on a plain in the Andes Mountains by a prehistoric people called Nazca. Such large-scale drawings can be produced with simple tools and require no extra-terrestrial help.

confabulated [made up and confused with real events]. . . . There is no way, however, by which anyone — even a psychologist or psychiatrist with extensive training in the field of hypnosis — can for any particular piece of information determine whether it is actual memory versus a confabulation unless there is independent verification.[9]

Orne and other experts have also emphasized how extremely suggestible hypnotic subjects are and how easy it is for a hypnotist to unintentionally induce pseudomemories in the subject:

> If a witness is hypnotized and has factual information casually gleaned from newspapers or inadvertent comments made during prior interrogation or in discussion with others who might have knowledge about the facts, many of these bits of knowledge will become incorporated and form the basis of any pseudo-memories that develop. . . . If the hypnotist has beliefs about what actually occurred, it is exceedingly difficult for him to prevent himself from inadvertently guiding the subject's recall so that [the subject] will eventually "remember" what he, the hypnotist, believes actually happened.[10]

Orne describes a simple experiment he has repeatedly conducted which shows the limits of hypnotism. First he verifies that a subject went to bed at a certain time at night and slept straight through until morning. Then he hypnotizes the subject and asks her to relive that night. Orne asks the subject if she heard two loud noises during the night (noises that didn't, in fact, happen). Typically, the subject says that she was awakened by the noises and then describes how she arose from bed to investigate. If Orne asks her to look at the clock, the subject identifies a specific time — at which point the subject was actually asleep and in bed. After hypnosis, the subject remembers the nonevent as though it actually happened. A pseudomemory was thus created by a leading question that may seem perfectly neutral.

A study has even been conducted to see if people who had never seen a UFO nor were well informed about UFOs could, under hypnosis, tell "realistic" stories about being abducted by aliens. The conclusion was that they can. The imaginary abductees easily and eagerly invented many specific details of abductions. The researchers found "no substantive differences" between these descriptions and those people who have claimed to be abducted.[11]

Research also suggests that hypnosis not only induces pseudomemories, but also increases the likelihood that they'll become firmly established. As psychologist Terence Hines says:

> What hypnosis does do — and this is especially relevant to the UFO cases — is to greatly increase hypnotized subjects' confidence that their hypnotically induced memories are true. This increase in confidence occurs for both correct and incorrect memories. Thus, hypnosis can create

false memories, but the individual will be especially convinced that those memories are true. People repeating such false memories will seem credible because they really believe their false memories are true. Their belief, of course, does not indicate whether the memory is actually true or false.[12]

Proponents of the abduction hypothesis, however, point out that a few people have told of being abducted by a UFO before they were hypnotized. This testimony is relevant to the issue — but it's also subject to all the questions of reliability that we must ask of any human testimony. Given what we know about the witnesses and the circumstances of their experience (to be discussed shortly), we must rate this testimonial evidence as weak.

The similarity of abductee stories also gives little support to hypothesis 1. Critics point out that there's little wonder that the stories have so much in common since UFO abduction has become a universally familiar theme, thanks to books, movies, and television. Psychologist Robert A. Baker says:

> Any one of us, if asked to pretend that we had been kidnapped by aliens from outer space or another dimension, would make up a story that would vary little, either in details or in the supposed motives of the abductors, from the stories told by any and all of the kidnap victims reported by [Budd] Hopkins. Our imaginative tales would be remarkably similar in plot, dialogue, description, and characterization to the close encounters of the third kind and conversations with little gray aliens described in *Communion* or *Intruders*. The means of transportation would be saucer-shaped, the aliens would be small, humanoid, two-eyed, and gray or white or green, and the purpose of their visits would be to: 1) save our planet; 2) find a better home for themselves; 3) end nuclear war and the threat we pose to the peaceful life in the rest of the galaxy; 4) bring us knowledge and enlightenment; and 5) increase the aliens' knowledge and understanding of other forms of life.[13]

The similarities in many abduction stories can also be created by a hypnotist who has unwittingly cued the same pseudomemories in all his subjects. This is most likely to happen when the hypnotist lacks proper training in hypnotism and has strong beliefs about what actually happened to the subject — a state of affairs that may be the norm.

On closer inspection, the phenomenon of missing time seems to provide little support for the abduction hypothesis either. One reason is that the phenomenon is actually a common, ordinary experience — especially when people are anxious or under stress:

> Typically, motorists will report after a long drive that at some point in the journey they woke up to realize they had no awareness of a preceding

period of time. With some justification, people will describe this as a "gap in time," a "lost half-hour," or a "piece out of my life."[14]

In addition, many cases of missing time in abduction stories have been investigated and found to have fairly prosaic explanations.[15]

Passing a lie detector test doesn't lend credence to an abduction story either. Polygraph tests are still used in criminal investigations, employment screenings, and elsewhere. Nevertheless, recent research has established that polygraph testing is an extremely unreliable guide to someone's truthfulness.[16]

The physical evidence is equivocal. Scars or cuts on abductees could have been caused by aliens — or they could have happened accidentally without the subject's knowing how, just as we all occasionally discover scratches or cuts on our bodies without remembering how they got there. They could have also been intentionally self-inflicted. There's no corroborating evidence to show that they are, in fact, alien-inflicted. The story is much the same with dead-grass areas. There's no direct evidence linking them to UFO landings. Some of them, however, have been shown to be the work of a type of fungus that dehydrates the grass (sometimes in a circular pattern called a Fairy Ring) and makes it appear burnt. Let us consider some alternative explanations.

Hypothesis 2: *People who report being abducted by aliens are suffering from serious mental illness.* In other words, nobody has been abducted; people who make abduction claims are just plain crazy. Actually, it wouldn't be surprising to find that a few of these people were psychotic. But the idea that a large proportion of them are crazy isn't supported by the evidence.

Not every alleged abductee has undergone psychological testing, but a few have. The Fund for UFO Research asked Elizabeth Slater, a professional psychologist, to study nine people who claimed to have been abducted by aliens. During the study, Slater wasn't aware of the subjects' abduction claims. After extensive testing of these nine, she concluded that none of them were psychotic or crazy.[17] Other research has come up with similar findings.

Of course, psychologists and psychiatrists know that a person needn't be insane to exhibit extremely strange behavior or to have very weird experiences. It is also worth noting that Slater commented that the subjects, though sane, couldn't be considered completely normal. She said that they "did not represent an ordinary cross-section of the population," that several of them could be characterized as "odd or eccentric," and that under stressful conditions six of the nine showed a "potential for more or less transient psychotic experiences involving a loss of reality testing along with confused and disordered thinking that can be bizarre."[18]

Hypothesis 3: *People who report being abducted by aliens are perpetrating a hoax.* A few tales of UFO abduction are suspicious or have been found to be hoaxes. Philip Klass, for example, has shown that the Travis Walton abduction story (eventually made into the movie *Fire in the Sky*) was a probable hoax.[19] But there's no evidence that the majority of abduction tales are put-ons. Most observers agree that those who make abduction claims are apparently sincere.

Hypothesis 4: *Reports of alien abductions are fantasies arising from people with "fantasy-prone personalities," and these fantasies may be further elaborated and strengthened through hypnosis.* Scientists have discovered that some people, though they appear normal and well-adjusted, frequently have very realistic wide-awake hallucinations and fantasies and often have experiences that resemble those induced by hypnosis. The researchers who uncovered this phenomenon describe it this way:

> [This research] has shown that there exists a small group of individuals (possibly 4% of the population) who fantasize a large part of the time, who typically "see," "hear," "smell," and "touch" and fully experience what they fantasize; and who can be labeled fantasy-prone personalities. Their extensive and deep involvement in fantasy seems to be their basic characteristic and their other major talents — their ability to hallucinate voluntarily, their superb hypnotic performances, their vivid memories of their life experiences, and their talents as psychics or sensitives — seem to derive from or grow out of their profound fantasy life.[20]

When these people are deep in fantasy, they have a decreased awareness of time and place, just as many abductees say they do (the experience of missing time). Also, not only are they easily hypnotized, but they show hypnotic behavior all the time, even when not hypnotized:

> When we give them "hypnotic suggestions" such as suggestions for visual and auditory hallucinations, negative hallucinations, age regression, limb rigidity, anesthesia, and sensory hallucinations, we are asking them to do for us the kind of thing they can do independently of us in their daily lives.[21]

Interestingly enough, some research suggests that people who claim to have been abducted by aliens are in fact fantasy-prone personalities. In one study, a biographical analysis was done on 154 people who said they had been abducted or had several contacts with aliens. It was found that 132 of these subjects seemed normal and healthy but had many fantasy-prone personality characteristics.[22] Baker has suggested that Whitley Strieber, author of *Communion*, fits the fantasy-prone personality mold:

Men become civilized, not in proportion to their willingness to believe, but in proportion to their readiness to doubt.

—H. L. MENCKEN

Anyone familiar with the fantasy-prone personality who reads Strieber's *Communion* will suffer an immediate shock of recognition! Strieber is a classic example of the fantasy-prone type: easily hypnotized, amnesiac, from a very religious background, with vivid memories of his early years and a very active fantasy life—a writer of occult and highly imaginative novels featuring unusually strong sensory experiences, particularly smells and sounds and vivid dreams.

Strieber's wife was questioned under hypnosis by Hopkins. With regard to some of Strieber's visions, she says, "Whitley saw a lot of things that I didn't see at that time." "Did you look for [a bright crystal in the sky]?" "Oh, no. Because I knew it wasn't real." "How did you know it wasn't real? Whitley's a fairly down-to-earth guy—" "No, he isn't. . . ." "It didn't surprise you hearing Whitley, that he sees things like that?" "No."[23]

There's also evidence that sleep-related hallucinations (called, you may remember, hypnogogic and hypnopompic) happen more frequently to fantasy-prone people. And there's reason to believe that these phenomena play a role in UFO abduction stories. We know that many UFO abductions allegedly happen after the victim has gone to bed and involve the feeling of being paralyzed or seeming to float outside of the body. Such hallucinations seem absolutely real and thus are referred to as waking dreams. They're not an indication of mental illness; they happen to normal, sane, and rational people. Baker explains their telltale signs:

> There are a number of characteristic clues that tell you whether a perception is or is not a hypnogogic or hypnopompic hallucination. First, it always occurs before or after falling asleep; second, one is paralyzed or has difficulty in moving, or on the other hand, one may float out of one's body and have an out-of-body experience; third, the hallucination is unusually bizarre, i.e., one sees ghosts, aliens, monsters, etc.; fourth, after the hallucination is over, the hallucinator typically goes back to sleep; and, fifth, the hallucinator is unalterably convinced of the reality of the entire experience.[24]

Strieber himself, says Baker, had such an hallucination:

> Strieber's *Communion* contains a classic, textbook description of a hypno-pompic hallucination, complete with the wakening from a sound sleep, the strong sense of reality and of being awake, the paralysis (due to the fact that the body's neural circuits keep our muscles relaxed to help preserve our sleep), and the encounter with strange beings. Following the encounter, instead of jumping out of bed and going in search of the strangers, Strieber, typically, goes back to sleep. He even reports that the burglar alarm had not gone off—proof again that the intruders were mental rather than physical. On another occasion Strieber reports awakening and believing that the roof of his house is on fire and that aliens

are threatening his family. Yet his only response to this is to go peacefully back to sleep — again, clear evidence of a hypnopompic dream.

Strieber, of course, is convinced of the reality of these experiences. This, too, is expected. If he were not convinced of their reality, the experience would not be hypnopompic nor hallucinatory.[25]

Finally, it's clear that if a fantasy-prone person experiences a fantasy about being abducted by aliens and then is hypnotized by a hypnotist who asks leading questions and believes in UFO abductions, the fantasy is likely to be confirmed or elaborated, to be very convincing to others, and to be believed as absolutely true by the abductee.

Hypothesis 5: *Reports of alien abductions arise from dreams and are then elaborated or strengthened through hypnosis.* We know that the adventures of many people claiming to be abductees actually began with a compelling dream. First they said that they dreamed that they had had contact with a UFO or were abducted, then — while under hypnosis — they told in detail of an actual alien abduction. This was the case, for example, with many abductees featured in Hopkins's *Intruders.* As Hines says:

> It is thus easy to understand how, for example, a frightening dream about being abducted by a UFO can come to seem real to an individual who is repeatedly hypnotized to recall further details of the experience and is explicitly told by the hypnotist that the experience is real. If the individual already has difficulty telling reality from fantasy, the process of becoming convinced that the dream or fantasy was real will occur more rapidly. It is no rare event for someone to have a dream that, at least briefly, may seem to have really happened. In fact, almost everyone has had dreams that, upon awakening, were so vivid that it was not possible, for a while at least, to decide whether they really happened or not.[26]

Now let's apply the criteria of adequacy to these alternative hypotheses. All are testable, so we must rely on the other four criteria to help us choose among the possibilities. Using these four, let's first see if we can eliminate some of the hypotheses.

Hypotheses 2 through 5 can probably be given similar weight in terms of fruitfulness, scope, and simplicity, but hypotheses 2 and 3 are clearly inferior to the other two in conservatism. They conflict with existing evidence; hypotheses 4 and 5, on the other hand, are consistent with a great deal of evidence.

Now the contest is between hypotheses 1, 4, and 5. We can now see that hypothesis 1 comes out the loser to the other three on every count. Hypothesis 1 has yielded no novel predictions. Hypotheses 4 and 5 have greater scope, for they offer explanations that can be applied to several phenomena, not just claims of alien abductions. In

What happened to me was terrifying. It seemed completely real.

— WHITLEY STRIEBER

terms of simplicity, hypothesis 1 must be given less credence than the other hypotheses because it postulates new entities — aliens.

In light of the criterion of conservatism, we see that the evidence in favor of hypothesis 1 is extremely weak; the evidence for the other two alternatives is much stronger. In addition, hypothesis 1 conflicts with a great deal of human experience regarding visitors from outer space; so far, we have no good evidence that anyone has ever detected any aliens. Moreover, the probability of the Earth being visited by aliens from outer space must be considered very low (but not zero) in light of what we know about the size of the universe, the estimated likelihood of extraterrestrial life, and the physical requirements of space travel.

For all the above reasons, the abduction hypothesis must be considered improbable. Hypotheses 4 and 5 appear much more likely. But we have no grounds for choosing one of these to the exclusion of the other. In fact, they may each be a correct explanation for a portion of alien abduction claims. Also, though they appear to be good hypotheses, they may not be the only good ones. Our list of alternative hypotheses isn't intended to be exhaustive. Further research could narrow the field. In the meantime, our analysis has yielded a conclusion supported by good reasons: The abduction hypothesis is untenable, and there are indeed reasonable alternatives.

CHANNELING

Channeling is generally thought to be the receiving of messages from a disembodied entity via a person (the channel or channeler). The entity is supposed to be external to the person's consciousness. In recent years, many people have claimed to be channels for a bewildering glut of entities including Moses, Jesus, Einstein, Merlin of Camelot, the archangel Michael, a Hopi Indian named Barking Tree, a group of dolphins, a 2,000-year-old man named Mafu, and someone called Ramtha who was born on Atlantis and conquered the world 35,000 years ago. People who have claimed to be channels include Jane Roberts (channel of *The Seth Material,* discussed in Chapter 4), spoon-bending psychic Uri Geller, nineteenth-century occult superstar Helene Petrovna Blavatsky (1831–1891), Kevin Ryerson (featured in Shirley MacLaine's best-seller *Out on a Limb*), and a host of others both famous and obscure. (Edgar Cayce, 1877–1945, "the sleeping prophet" who produced many trance teachings, is sometimes regarded as a channeler. But according to him, the psychic information he produced came from his own subconscious.)

J Z Knight, one of the most prominent of recent channelers, here purportedly channels Ramtha, a 35,000-year-old entity from Atlantis.

When receiving communications from an entity, a channel will typically appear to go into a trance and then take on mannerisms and speech that seem foreign to the channel but presumably are characteristic of the entity. (Some channels convey an entity's words not through speech, but through writing, using pen or pencil to record the communication while in a trance. This is sometimes called *automatic writing*. A few channels use a Ouija board.) The resulting messages are usually believed to be profound, insightful, prophetic — and definitely not originating with the channel.

The term *channeling* is new, but the phenomenon goes back a long way, as psychologist James Alcock points out:

> It is sometimes claimed that all shamans and prophets, including the Oracle of Delphi, Moses, and even Jesus Christ, were channelers, but a less heady view places the origin of channeling with the renowned mystic Emanuel Swedenborg (1688–1772), who was the first Western medium in that he conversed with the souls of departed men and women rather than just with spirits. . . . The next major milestone in the history of channeling occurred in 1848, when Mr. and Mrs. John Fox of Hydesville, New York, heard a number of mysterious rappings in their home, rappings that seemed always to occur in the presence of two of their children, Kate (1841–1892) and Margaret (1838–1893). By

Common sense is very uncommon.
— HORACE GREELEY

assigning a different number of raps to each letter of the alphabet, the rappings were deciphered as being messages from the world beyond. The Fox sisters subsequently enjoyed a worldwide reputation as mediums, starting an interest in mediumship that was to endure well into the twentieth century. Although they confessed in later years that they had created the rappings themselves by using their toes, ankles, and knees, even today there are some who disbelieve their confessions.[27]

The channeling hypothesis has several competitors. Let's examine four of the main ones and see how all five fare under the SEARCH formula.

Hypothesis 1: *Persons known as channels or channelers receive messages from disembodied entities that are external to the persons' consciousness.* Perhaps the most striking evidence for this claim is the impressive performances of channels in apparent trance. A channel's gestures, facial expressions, and speech may suddenly and dramatically change. An alien personality seems to arise in place of the channel's usual one. The channel may speak with a strange accent and in a compelling style. To many, witnessing such a scene is eerie and convincing.

The content of the communications is said to be further evidence. The messages are deemed to be so wise and profound that they couldn't possibly be generated by the channel. The channel, it is often thought, has neither the education nor the intellect to create such material.

Most channeled entities claim that they lived on earth a very long time ago or never had a physical existence. So there's very little information about past lives that can be checked out with records and historical accounts. Some entities, though, have ventured predictions about the future.

For several reasons, we must rate all this evidence as extremely weak. The channel's performance is indeed impressive. But this in itself doesn't show that the entity is real and arises from outside the channel's consciousness. There are many other ways to account for the channeling performance, as we'll see.

As for the content of the messages, critics who have examined it report that it's not extraordinary at all. According to psychologist Graham Reed:

> The best data available for the study of the intellectual activities of channelers are the spoken messages they produce, as represented by recordings, transcripts, and a profusion of published works. Much has been made of the sagacity and profound insights communicated by such messages. These alleged qualities have been regarded as clear proof of the messages' supernatural origins because, it is argued, the channelers themselves have neither the erudition nor the intellectual power to produce

such material without help. But in actual fact, if the messages are examined objectively, ignoring their assumed origins, they prove to be simplistic, repetitive, and extremely vague. They quite lack the clarity, the tightness of argument, and the succinctness of expression that characterize productive thinking. On the contrary, they seem to consist solely of strings of loosely associated gobbets of naive ideas and verbal formulae. They are well within the intellectual capacity of channelers of even moderate education. What they do require is high and facile verbal fluency, together with a loosening of cognitive controls.[28]

Alcock's analysis is similar:

What do these eternal entities have to tell us now that they can so readily communicate with this world? Their basic message, which reflects well-established themes found in occult literature, is that we are spiritual and immortal beings in a universe that is essentially spiritual. We move through a series of embodied and disembodied lives until we eventually unite with God, and indeed, within each of us is some form of projection of God. By learning to contact that part of God within us, we can harness a force that will allow us to surmount our problems and find happiness and success. We create our own realities; and so if we want to be happy, we simply need to create a happy reality. There is no need for us to follow a guru, for we are as gods, each one of us.

This message is presented in different ways by different channelers. Often it is hard to discern it from the noisy claptrap in which it is packaged. Indeed, modern channelers are responsible for some of the most outrageous rubbish imaginable, often delivered in almost childishly silly accents and peppered with repetitive cliches. Consider, for example, some of Ramtha's pseudoarchaic prose: "I be that which is termed indeed, servant unto God Almighty, that which is called the Principal Cause, the Light Force, the Element, that which is termed the Spirit, that which is conclusive all of Itself, that which is termed the All in All, that which is called life indeed." Ramtha might be well-advised to contact Moses or Joshua for some advice on style.[29]

In addition, several entities have been found to speak in ways that are linguistically implausible. Linguist Sarah Grey Thomason provides several examples, including this one:

I analyzed the tape-recorded speech of one entity who is claimed to have a specific location in time and space: Matthew, whose channel is Marjorie Turcott. On the tape a man named Don Hayes introduces Marjorie and Matthew, and he gives useful background information about two of Matthew's past lives. Matthew lived his main past-life as a poor, blind fiddle-player in Scotland in the early sixteenth century. He told Hayes and/or Marjorie that he was born in Aberdeen but moved as a small child to "a seaport town" called the Firth of Forth. Right away he has a problem: The Firth of Forth is a body of water, not a town. Hayes goes on to give, in Matthew's dialect and words, an account of how Matthew was killed at the age of 15. In this account, Matthew uses at least two words that no one else was using during his lifetime. One of them is *rapscallion*, which is first recorded almost 200 years later in a 1699 text. The other is *bully boy*, which existed in Matthew's day only in the meaning "good friend, fine fellow" (as it is used by Shakespeare in 1599); the meaning Matthew gives the word, "a tyrannical coward," doesn't appear until 1699. Besides these words, some of Matthew's grammatical constructions are unknown, then and now, in the variety of Scots English spoken in Matthew's native region.[30]

Thomason also examined the speech of Julie Winter of New York who channels Mika, "an energy entity":

> When Mika appears, he speaks in a high, unnatural tone, often a monotone: his vowel sounds are drawn-out and distorted, but not consistently distorted in the same way, as they would be if his non-American-sounding speech were genuine. His voice quality. . . . is unlike any type of voice characteristic of any natural human language.
>
> When I checked specific phonetic traits in which Mika's speech differs from ordinary American English (including his channeler's dialect)—for instance, his *r*'s, which were often trilled, and several vowel sounds—I found a lack of the systematicity that is characteristic of all of the world's languages and dialects. Many words were pronounced sometimes with an un-English sound and sometimes with an English sound. Other words were always pronounced one way or the other, but instead of patterned substitutions Mika had random and inconsistent replacement of particular American English sounds with sounds that do not occur in American English. Moreover, the American-style pronunciations were especially frequent when Mika became excited (judging by his tempo, pitch, and loudness)—just the opposite of what one would expect if he were a nonnative speaker of American English who was still practicing the use of sounds foreign to him.
>
> All of this makes Mika highly implausible as a human linguistic animal. His unpatterned sound substitutions, strange voice quality, and tendency to sound more American under pressure are all easy to explain if the channeler is faking his speech, but they are hard to explain away under the supposition that he is a genuine "entity" independent of his channeler.[31]

The medium is the message.

—MARSHALL
MCLUHAN

In many cases, the channeled information isn't as foreign to the channel's own experience as some people believe. Jane Roberts, for example, was an author, poet, and avid reader who, according to her husband, already understood—before Seth—many of the concepts that Seth would later deal with. She studied, among other things, Eastern religions, shamanism, and voodooism. Ted Schultz points to other similar instances:

Edgar Cayce's trance readings on matters of health, for instance, owe a lot to a homeopathic physician named Wesley Ketchum, with whom he associated in his early years, while his readings on occult philosophy stem from his association with Arthur Lammers and other Theosophists who were attracted to him. In turn, many of the pronouncements of the popular modern-day trance channel Kevin Ryerson can be traced to Cayce's teachings, which he is known to have studied at the Association for Research and Enlightenment in Virginia Beach, Virginia.

Helen Schucman, the psychologist who channeled the immensely popular *Course in Miracles,* is personally bewildered by its supposed source: Jesus Christ. But Esalen co-founder Michael Murphy points out: "She was raised on that kind of literature. Her father owned a meta-physical bookshop." And transpersonal psychologist Ken Wilber says: "There's much more of Helen in the *Course* than I first thought. She was brought up mystically inclined. At four she used to stand out on the bal-cony and say that God would give her a sign of miracles to let her know that he was there. Many ideas from the *Course* came from the new thought or metaphysical schools she had been influenced by. . . . I found also that if you look at Helen's own poetry, you're initially very hard pressed to find any difference between that and the *Course.*"[32]

It's also clear that channeled messages often contradict one an-other. The entities of different channels have presented us with elab-orate descriptions of the cosmos and humanity's place in it, but these descriptions differ so much that they simply can't be reconciled with one another. Finally, as Schultz says, if channeled information is taken at face value,

We would have to wonder why so many channeled predictions didn't come true, like the coming of the saucer people predicted for 1952 by the entity Sananda, the rising of Atlantis predicted by Edgar Cayce for the late 1960s, or the landing of a fleet of UFOs "some years, or sooner" after 1972, predicted by Uri Geller's entity Hoova. Obviously channeled information is not always true. And this leads to the inevitable question: How do you tell what is true and what is not?[33]

The famous Ramtha (channeled by a woman named J Z Knight) pre-dicted, in 1985, that in three years a great holocaust would come and cities would be wiped out by disease. He also predicted that at the end of 1985, the United States would be engulfed in a major war, and a discovery in Turkey would reveal a great pyramid with a shaft reach-ing to the center of the earth.

Hypothesis 2: *Channels are mentally ill, suffering from psychotic dis-orders.* It's true that while channeling, channels do exhibit behaviors that could technically be classified as psychotic. Their reports are by definition classifiable as systemized delusions — they tell about

Don't live on a fault line. It's a zipper.
— THE ENTITY RAMTHA

How to Channel Martians

Today's channels specialize in channeling entities that have characteristics similar to those found in modern science fiction. Latter-day entities are said to be from other dimensions, from exotic civilizations, and from outer space. Most nineteenth-century spiritualists, however, channeled "spirit guides" who were more likely to be American Indians, Tibetans, and "Hindoos." One spiritualist, though, was way before her time.

In his 1901 classic, *From India to the Planet Mars* (New York: Harper), psychologist Theodore Flournoy describes his two-year case study of "Hélène Smith" (real name: Catherine-Elise Müller), a particularly dramatic French Swiss medium whose exceptional ability to enter a trance state produced, besides Martians, visitations from earthly personages like Cagliostro, Marie Antoinette, and "Simandini" (a 15th-century Indian princess).

Mademoiselle Smith's rich visions of Mars included "carriages without horses or wheels, emitting sparks as they glided by; houses with fountains on the roof; a cradle having for curtains an angel made of iron with outstretched wings." Lakes were blue-pink, the ground peach-colored, the sky greenish-yellow. Martians, who looked just like humans, wore large robes, flat hats, and sandals. A Martian named Asante used a hand-held flying machine that looked like a carriage-lantern. Through automatic painting, Mlle. Smith produced full-colored representations of Martian houses, plants, and animals. Most interesting of all, she spoke and wrote in the Martian language on many occasions.

Flournoy painstakingly recorded and studied the trance languages of Mlle. Smith. Through careful analysis, he demonstrated that, though her "Martian" language sounded and looked quite alien, it was an exact analogue of both written and spoken French, Mlle. Smith's native tongue. Each Martian letter had its equivalent in French, and the syntax was also identical. Apparently, Mlle. Smith's unconscious mind had invented and remembered what was essentially a written and spoken code.[34]

experiences that can be regarded as essentially auditory or tactile hallucinations; they manifest the "formal thought disorders" characteristic of schizophrenics; and they have a "blurring of ego boundaries," a problem in their sense of self and individuality.[35] Despite these symptoms, as Reed (a psychologist) points out, it's not likely that channels are psychotic:

> Debate about whether some or all channelers are psychotic is misplaced. In view of the symptoms . . . how can the matter be in question? Simply because channelers are able to turn the "symptoms" on or off at will. True psychotic symptoms are not under conscious control. If they are delib-

Turn-of-the-century medium Hélène Smith claimed to channel Martians and produced rich descriptions of Martian life as well as these paintings of Martian architecture and landscape.

erately manifested, this would be taken, in the psychiatric clinic, to constitute malingering.[36]

Hypothesis 3: *Channels are fakes, consciously pretending to receive messages from disembodied entities.* It's likely that at least some channels are indeed frauds. The inducements, both financial and psychological, to be a channeling fraud can be enormous. People have paid up to $1,500 apiece for a seminar with J Z Knight, for instance. But none of this shows that most latter-day channels are faking. Currently there isn't enough empirical evidence to help us determine how many people are phony channels. There is evidence, however, that most of the great mediums of the nineteenth century were frauds.[37]

Hypothesis 4: *Channels display features of the psychological phenomenon known as dissociation.* The idea that our consciousness is a unified whole, functioning as a single unit, is an illusion, say psychologists. Research has revealed that our consciousness is frequently divided, with separate parts of our mind functioning virtually independently of each other. It's as though, at times, there's more than one person operating inside us. Psychologists Zusne and Jones elaborate on this principle:

> Our attention is not always directed at one thing only. In arguments or debates, we not only attend to what our opponent is saying, but also to our own thought process that is preparing a rebuttal to be delivered as soon as the opponent stops speaking. The professional piano player may continue executing a complex piece while engaging in a lively conversation at the same time. Whether our attention jumps back and forth quickly between two objects or whether two mental processes may be occurring simultaneously are questions that are being currently investigated.
>
> The situation becomes baffling when we realize that, sometimes, we may not be at all aware of any of the activity that is going on in one of the channels of attention. It is a common experience to begin to day-dream while continuing to read a book. One may realize later that one has read a paragraph or page without remembering any of the material. It is as if one's mind worked along two different channels at the same time with amnesia following. The forgotten material may be retrieved, however, using such techniques as hypnosis. This example of an every-day case of divided consciousness has all of the characteristics of the most spectacular instances of this phenomenon. There is no dividing line.[38]

When we fail to recognize these parts of ourselves as belonging to us, when we view them as separate, then they're said to be *dissociated* from the rest of our consciousness. Sometimes this dissociation can be very pronounced, even in people who are not at all psychotic. Under the right circumstances, a dissociated subdivision of a person's consciousness may seem to that person like another voice, a separate consciousness, a different entity. (Cases of multiple personality differ in degree from other forms of dissociation; they're examples of the inability to integrate dissociated subpersonalities.) Several psychologists say that dissociation is what's behind possession states, speaking in tongues (glossolalia), water witching, and channeling.

Researchers have repeatedly induced impressive examples of dissociation through hypnosis:

> Very recent experimental work that dramatically demonstrates divided consciousness has been done by E. R. Hilgard. Hilgard, in a classroom

demonstration, hypnotized a subject, instructing him that he would cease to hear. Loud noises near the subject produced no response. When a student in the classroom suggested that a portion of the subject's consciousness could be registering something because there was nothing wrong with the subject's hearing, Hilgard agreed, and presented this idea to the subject in a quiet voice, asking to lift a finger if indeed part of him could still hear anything. The subject's finger rose. He immediately asked to be awakened in order to find out what was happening because he had felt his finger rise (the subject was blind). Hilgard awakened him but in the awake state, all the subject could remember was what had happened just before he was hypnotized, and that while he was "deaf," he had amused himself by doing problems in his head until he felt his finger rise. In experiments on hypnotic pain control, Hilgard has obtained similar evidence for the existence of what he calls the "hidden observer." For instance, a girl was hypnotized and the suggestion was given that she would feel no pain when her left hand was immersed in ice-cold water. A further suggestion was given that her right hand would not be subject to hypnosis and would write down the degree of pain actually experienced in terms of a number between 0 and 10. Although the girl's verbal report indicated no pain (0), her right hand kept recording increasing levels of pain — 5, 6, 7, 8.[39]

The trance state is itself an instance of dissociation, and once in such a state people can easily encounter the autonomous parts of consciousness that may appear to be entities from "out there." (People can readily self-induce a trance, as many channels do. Trance states can be attained through self-hypnosis, as well as hypnosis, sensory overstimulation, hyperventilation, and drugs.)

The unity of consciousness is illusory.

—Ernest R. Hilgard

Speaking of that predecessor of the modern channel, the medium, Zusne and Jones say that:

> The "true" medium is one who dissociates readily. Proneness to dissociation, repeated practice, and the expectant and supportive atmosphere of the seance room combine to make the medium's performance what it is: a smooth and reliable passage into the trance state and the impressive welling up of autonomous portions of her divided consciousness that are taken as the manifestations of the spirits of the dead.[40]

Hypothesis 5: *Channeling is an instance of cryptomnesia.* As discussed in Chapter 3, cryptomnesia is the remembering of something without recalling the memory's source so that it seems like an original thought or the result of extraordinary phenomena. Baker thinks that cryptomnesia may, in rare cases, explain channeling:

> Relaxation and suggestion can easily trigger the release of hundreds of buried memories that are connected in complex associative chains, and that, once revived, appear to come from "out of the blue," since the

original stimulus and storage has long been forgotten. Once these subconscious or unconscious sources have been tapped and the creative wellsprings have released the flood of fantasy material that is organized and made semilogical by the conscious cognitive processes, even the individual undergoing the experience is astounded. To onlookers and bystanders the channel does appear to speak with the tongues of angels and bring messages from the gods.[41]

Again, there's no empirical evidence to suggest how much of a role cryptomnesia plays in channeling, although some critics (like Baker) believe the role to be minimal.

So what can we make of these hypotheses? First, all are testable, and so must be distinguished by using the other four criteria. Hypotheses 2 through 5 seem to be relative equals in fruitfulness, scope, and simplicity, but hypothesis 2 appears inferior to the others in conservatism. Existing evidence suggests that mental illness is not a good explanation for channeling. So we can eliminate 2 from the running.

When we weigh the remaining four hypotheses, we see that the channeling hypothesis is the clear loser. It has predicted no new facts, it explains little besides the channeling phenomena, and it's less simple than the other three. These hypotheses, on the other hand, can explain many different types of behavior and can do so without postulating any new entities.

Moreover, the channeling hypothesis is much less conservative than hypotheses 3 through 5. The channeling hypothesis is supported by extremely weak evidence. Plus, it conflicts with a massive amount of human experience — we just don't have any good evidence of a single instance of communication from a disembodied entity. The evidence regarding hypotheses 3 through 5, however, shows that they're each a reasonable possibility. Each one may be the correct explanation for a portion of channeling cases. But to date, there doesn't seem to be enough evidence to clearly establish one of them as better than the others.

We have excellent reasons, then, to rate the channeling hypothesis as highly improbable. We also have good reasons to say that, among all the hypotheses we considered (and there may be other good ones we haven't examined), hypotheses 3 through 5 are the best explanations for the channeling phenomenon.

NEAR-DEATH EXPERIENCES

Benjamin Franklin once remarked in a letter to Jean-Baptist Leroy, "In this world, nothing is certain but death and taxes." A number of

[Spiritualists] are lacking not only in criticism but in the most elementary knowledge of psychology. At the bottom they do not want to be taught any better, but merely to go on believing.

—CARL GUSTAV JUNG

The Amityville Horror-Mongers

Psychological dissociation is not only an explanation for channeling, but for possession states as well. However, in the case of the most famous demon possession case of all — the Amityville Horror — other, more mundane explanations have been offered.

The Amityville story is about George and Kathy Lutz and their children, who lived in a "possessed" house in Amityville, New York, and were said to be the victims of some relentless, supernatural terror. Their tale was popularized in the book *The Amityville Horror* by Jay Anson, which was based on interviews with the Lutzes. Melvin Harris, famed investigator of unexplained mysteries, says that there's nothing horrific or supernatural about this story. He files this report:

> [The Amityville Horror is an] incredibly grim story, if true, but so like fiction that it prompts the question: Was there ever an authentic horror in the first place? Competent investigators unite in their answer — emphatically they say no!

Doctor Stephan Kaplan, director of the Parapsychology Institute of America, has written: "After several months of extensive research and interviews with those who were involved in the 'Amityville Horror' . . . we found no evidence to support any claim of a 'haunted house.' What we did find is a couple who had purchased a house that they economically could not afford. It is our professional opinion that the story of its haunting is mostly fiction" (*Theta*, no. 4, 1977).

Jerry Solfvin of the Psychical Research Foundation visited the house and wrote:

"The case wasn't interesting to us because the reports were confined to subjective responses from the Lutzes, and these were not at all impressive or even characteristic of these cases" (*Skeptical Inquirer*, Summer 1978).

But the most damning report of all originates with investigators Rick Moran and Peter Jordan. They went to Amityville and interviewed people mentioned in the book. The results were startling. To begin with, the police rejected the book's claim that they had investigated the house. In particular, Sergeant Cammorato denied that he'd ever entered the place while the Lutzes were in residence. Yet the book has Cammorato touring through the house and even inspecting a "secret room" in the basement — tales that turned out to be so much eyewash.

Then Father Mancuso (real name Pecorara), who's featured throughout the book, also flatly denied that he'd ever entered the Lutz home. So, that tale about his blessing the building and about the phantom voice that ordered him out is quite bogus. As well as that, the pastor of the Sacred Heart Rectory dismissed as "pure and utter nonsense" the Lutzes' yarn about "an unrelenting, disgusting odor that permeated the Rectory" — alleged "Scent of the Devil" that was supposed to have driven the priests out of their building.

In fact, little in the book stood up to close scrutiny. Local repairmen and locksmiths knew nothing of the paranormal damages they were supposed to have rectified.

(continued)

The Amityville Horror-Mongers (continued)

Not even the story that the Lutzes were driven out of the house by hauntings stood up. The real reasons for their exit were much more prosaic — a cash crisis and a near breakdown. . . .

[Attorney William Weber] admitted helping to sensationalize the Lutzes' story. In an Associated Press release of July 27, 1979, he said: "We created this horror story over many bottles of wine that George [Lutz] was drinking. We were really playing with each other. . . ."

The Lutzes themselves have provided ample proof of their unreliability. The proof is contained in the interviews they gave before the book came into being.

For a start, there's the account published in the *Long Island Press*, on January 17, 1976. In this article George Lutz sets out his experiences at 112 Ocean Avenue. But his story centers around things that were "sensed" and not seen. In fact, he contradicts earlier stories about "flying objects," "moving couches," and "wailing noises." . . .

Just over a year later, though, George Lutz came out with a new version of the events. . . . He related it to journalist Paul Hoffman and it appeared in the April 1977 issue of *Good Housekeeping*. [It] contradicts George's earlier account and is in conflict with the Anson book as well![42]

researchers, however, believe that Franklin was at best only half right. Taxes may indeed be inevitable, but death — understood as the annihilation of the self — may not even occur. Our physical bodies will no doubt die. But that, they say, doesn't mean that *we* will die, for there is evidence that we can survive the death of our physical bodies. The most impressive evidence for immortality, it is claimed, comes from near-death experiences.

The term *near-death experience* (NDE) was coined by Dr. Raymond Moody to describe a family of experiences he found common to those who had narrowly escaped death. His initial findings were based on in-depth interviews with some fifty people who had either clinically died (their heart and lungs had stopped functioning) and were later revived or who had faced death as a result of an accident, injury, or illness. What he discovered was that while no two people had exactly the same experience, their experiences shared a number of common elements. In 1975, he published the results of his research in his bestselling *Life After Life*. There he offered the following "ideal" or "complete" account of the near-death experience.

A man is dying and, as he reaches the point of greatest physical distress, he hears himself pronounced dead by his doctor. He begins to hear an uncomfortable noise, a loud ringing or buzzing, and at the same time feels himself moving very rapidly through a long dark tunnel. After this, he suddenly finds himself outside of his own physical body, but still in the immediate physical environment, and he sees his own body from a distance, as though he is a spectator. He watches the resuscitation attempt from this unusual vantage point and is in a state of emotional upheaval.

After a while, he collects himself and becomes more accustomed to his odd condition. He notices that he still has a "body," but one of a very different nature and with very different powers from the physical body he has left behind. Soon other things begin to happen. Others come to meet and to help him. He glimpses the spirits of relatives and friends who have already died, and a loving, warm spirit of a kind he has never encountered before — a being of light — appears before him. This being asks him a question, nonverbally, to make him evaluate his life and helps him along by showing him a panoramic, instantaneous playback of the major events of his life. At some point he finds himself approaching some sort of barrier or border, apparently representing the limit between earthly life and the next life. Yet, he finds that he must go back to the earth, that the time for his death has not yet come. At this point he resists, for by now he is taken up with his experiences in the afterlife and does not want to return. He is overwhelmed by intense feelings of joy, love, and peace. Despite his attitude, though, he somehow reunites with his physical body and lives.

Later he tries to tell others, but he has trouble doing so. In the first place, he can find no human words adequate to describe these unearthly episodes. He also finds that others scoff, so he stops telling other people. Still, the experience affects his life profoundly, especially his views about death and its relationship to life.[43]

Although none of the people Moody had interviewed for *Life After Life* had experienced all of the elements described above, he has since come across a number of people who have had the complete experience.[44]

When it first appeared, Moody's account of the near-death experience was met with a good deal of skepticism. Doctors who had resuscitated hundreds of patients said they had never encountered it. Others claimed that his sample was too small to be significant.[45] Nevertheless it sparked a great deal of interest among both professionals and laymen. A number of scientists and doctors began their own studies of the phenomena. To disseminate the results of this research, the Association for the Scientific Study of Near-Death Phenomena was founded in 1977.

More extensive and better controlled research has, for the most part, corroborated Moody's findings. The near-death experience as

Moody described it is fairly common among those who have survived a close brush with death. In fact, research suggests that if you come close to death or clinically die and are resuscitated, your chances of having such an experience are about fifty-fifty.

Dr. Fred Schoonmaker, chief of cardiovascular services at St. Luke's Hospital in Denver, had been studying near-death experiences for over a decade before Moody published *Life After Life.* He published the results of his research in 1979.[46] Out of the 2,300 cases he examined, most of whom had suffered cardiac arrest, 60 percent reported having a near-death experience of the sort described by Moody. Dr. Michael Sabom, a cardiologist in Atlanta, interviewed seventy-eight people who were known to have nearly died. He found that 42 percent of them had an experience like that Moody described.[47] A 1982 Gallup poll found that one in seven Americans had narrowly escaped death and that one in twenty had had a near-death experience.[48] One of the most detailed studies of the near-death experience was conducted by Dr. Kenneth Ring, a psychologist in Connecticut. Using hospital records and newspaper advertisements, he was able to identify 102 people who had been in a life-threatening situation. They were asked to provide a general description of their experience and then were questioned about the specific details. Almost 50 percent of the people in his sample had a near-death experience.[49]

Dr. Ring divided the near-death experience into five stages:

1. Peace and a sense of well-being.
2. Separation from the body.
3. Entering the darkness.
4. Seeing the light.
5. Entering the world of light.[50]

The earlier stages were reported more frequently than the latter. Sixty percent of his subjects reached the first stage, 37 percent reached the second, 23 percent reached the third, 16 percent reached the fourth, and 10 percent reached the fifth. What stage (if any) one reached was unaffected by one's age, sex, or religion. In fact, cross-cultural studies have found that the core elements of the experience are the same no matter what the person's background. Psychologists Karlis Osis and Erlendur Haraldsson, for example, examined the near-death experiences of Indian swamis and found that they did not differ essentially from those reported in the West.[51]

Given that near-death experiences are common and universal, what can we conclude about them? Do they provide evidence for the immortality of the soul? Moody thinks so. He believes that the best explanation of these experiences is that the soul or psyche leaves the body at death and travels to another world.[52] This is undoubtedly what most people would like to believe, so let's consider this hypothesis first.

Hypothesis 1: *During a near-death experience, the soul or psyche leaves the physical body and travels to another world.* Moody cites two reasons for taking near-death experiences at face value: first, those who have them can often accurately report what was going on around them while they were clinically dead; and second, their personalities are often transformed by the experience.[53] They no longer fear death, and their life becomes infused with a new sense of meaning, purpose, and value.

In Chapter 6 we saw that the fact that one is transformed by an experience doesn't imply its reality. As Russell pointed out, one's personality can be changed by reading a novel, but this doesn't mean that the characters in the novel are real. Nevertheless, the transforming power of the near-death experience is an important aspect of the experience, which must be accounted for by any adequate explanation.

Moody provides the following example of knowledge supposedly gained during the near-death experience:

> A forty-nine-year-old man had a heart attack so severe that after thirty-five minutes of vigorous resuscitation efforts, the doctor gave up and began filling out the death certificate. Then someone noticed a flicker of life, so the doctor continued his work with the paddles and breathing equipment and was able to restart the man's heart.
>
> The next day, when he was more coherent, the patient was able to describe in great detail what went on in the emergency room. This surprised the doctor. But what astonished him even more was the patient's vivid description of the emergency room nurse who hurried into the room to assist the doctor.
>
> He described her perfectly, right down to her wedge hairdo and her last name, Hawkes. He said that she rolled this cart down the hall with a machine that had what looked like two Ping-Pong paddles on it (an electroshocker that is basic resuscitation equipment).
>
> When the doctor asked him how he knew the nurse's name and what she had been doing during his heart attack, he said that he had left his body and—while walking down the hall to see his wife—passed right through nurse Hawkes. He read the name tag as he went through her, and remembered it so he could thank her later.
>
> I talked to the doctor at great length about this case. He was quite rattled by it. Being there, he said, was the only way the man could have recounted this with such complete accuracy.[54]

But the man's body was there. Is it really inconceivable that he got this information from his senses? Isn't it possible that he saw nurse Hawkes during a prior visit to the hospital or when he came in? Perhaps he passed her in the hall or saw her working behind a desk. And isn't it possible that the surgeons referred to her by name during the procedure? Perhaps one of the surgeons said something like, "Nurse Hawkes, please hand me the paddles." Even if this was said while he was lying clinically dead on the operating table, he could have heard it because the brain doesn't cease to function at the same time that the heart and lungs do. Hearing is the last sense to be lost.[55] Since the information the patient had could have been obtained by ordinary means, this case provides no compelling reason for believing that his soul left his body.

Moody admits that the evidence he has gathered in his twenty-two years of looking at near-death experience "isn't enough scientific proof to show conclusively that there is life after death."[56] Nevertheless he is convinced "that NDEers do get a glimpse of the beyond, a brief passage into a whole other reality."[57] Our concern is whether such a belief is justified.

Moody suggests that only conclusive proof is scientifically acceptable. But as we've seen, this is not the case, for nothing in science *can* be proved conclusively. The standard of justification in science is the same as that of common sense: a claim is justified if it is beyond a reasonable doubt, and it is beyond a reasonable doubt if it provides the best explanation of something. So our question is whether the evidence from near-death experiences establishes the belief in life after death beyond a reasonable doubt.

Moody is right that the most compelling evidence for his theory is the fact that NDEers accurately perceive reality while in the midst of their experience. He is right, too, that this evidence is not acceptable evidence of the existence of the soul — though he is wrong as to why that's the case. The problem is not that the evidence fails to prove conclusively that the soul leaves the body, but that it fails to prove the claim beyond a reasonable doubt. It fails to do so because the information may have been obtained through ordinary channels. To establish that it isn't, more controlled observation would be required.

One way to study near-death experiences under controlled conditions would be to artificially induce death (as was done in the movie *Flatliners*), have the subjects try to identify specific objects chosen through a double-blind procedure, and then revive them. Ethical considerations, however, prevent us from performing such experiments.

Fortunately, it's not necessary to kill people to check the veracity of out-of-body perception, for out-of-body experiences can be induced by other means. Meditation, stress, drugs, and exhaustion, for example, are known to produce out-of-body experiences. There are even people who claim to be able to produce them at will. Studies of these people by parapsychologists have produced equivocal results, however, leaving no solid evidence that accurate out-of-body perception occurs. After reviewing all of the major studies, Susan Blackmore, the world's leading expert on out-of-body experiences, concludes:

> All these experiments were aimed at finding out whether subjects could see a distant target during an OBE [out-of-body experience]. At best there are a very few properly controlled experiments (some critics would say, none) which have provided unequivocal evidence that a subject could detect anything by other than normal means. Although the experimental OBE may differ from the spontaneous kind, a simple conclusion is possible from the experimental studies. That is, OBE vision, if it occurs, is extremely poor.[58]

The experimental evidence, then, does not establish beyond a reasonable doubt that one can acquire knowledge of the physical world during an out-of-body experience.

The soul hypothesis, however, faces a number of other difficulties. For example, how are we to conceive of the soul? Apparently it has a location in space because people report that it can float around rooms and travel through walls. It also apparently has a shape because people describe it as a body with arms, legs, and so on. So it can't be totally nonphysical. What, then, is it made of? Moody is silent on this point. Since it has some physical properties, you would expect that it would be detectable. All attempts to detect it, however, have failed. Investigators have used ultraviolet and infrared devices, magnetometers, thermometers, and thermistors in the attempt to register the presence of the soul.[59] No attempts, however, have been successful.

If the soul can acquire knowledge about our world while it is out of the body, it must interact with that world. But if it interacts with the world, it must be observable. Psychologist William Rushton explains:

> We know that all information coming to us normally from the outside is caught by the sense organs and encoded by their nerves. And that a tiny damage to the retina (for instance) or its nerves to the brain produces such characteristic deficiencies in the visual sensation that the site of the damage may usually be correctly inferred. What is this OOB [out-of-body] eye that can encode the visual scene exactly as does the real eye, with its hundred million photoreceptors and its million signaling optic nerves? Can you imagine anything but a replica of the real eye that could manage to do this? But if this floating replica is to see, it must catch light, and hence cannot be transparent, and so must be visible to people in the vicinity.
>
> In fact floating eyes are not observed, nor would this be expected, for they only exist in fantasy.[60]

Since the soul is not observable, it's doubtful that it can acquire knowledge while out of the body. The problem is this. If the soul is physical, it should be detectable. The fact that we haven't detected it casts doubt on its physicality. If it's nonphysical, however, it's unclear how it could have a shape and a position in space or acquire knowledge of our world. Without more information about the nature of the soul and its commerce with the physical world, there is no good reason to take the nonphysical soul hypothesis seriously. For in the absence of such information, all it tells us is that something, we know not what, acquires information, we know not how, and goes someplace, we know not where. Needless to say, this is not very enlightening.

One of the most popular hypotheses regarding near-death experiences was championed by astronomer Carl Sagan in his book *Broca's Brain*.[61] First proposed by the psychologists Stanislov Grof and Joan Halifax, this hypothesis claims that near-death experiences are vivid recollections of the birth experience.[62] This explanation can apparently account for the universality of near-death experiences, for being born is an experience that all humans share. It can also apparently account for the experience of traveling through a tunnel (entering the darkness) and seeing the light, for that is what many imagine the birth experience to be like. As a result, it deserves a closer examination.

Hypothesis 2: *Near-death experiences are vivid recollections of the birth experience.* This hypothesis assumes that we can remember our birth and that what we remember is traveling down a long tunnel. Studies of infant cognition, however, indicate that their brains are not fully enough developed to remember specific details of their birth.[63] And even if they could, it's doubtful that they would remember the experience as traveling down a long tunnel for during birth their faces are pressed against the walls of the birth canal. Fetuses don't see anything until they've emerged from the uterus.

Moreover, if near-death experiences were based on birth memories, then those who were born by Cesarean section should not have tunnel experiences. Susan Blackmore tested this prediction by sending a questionnaire to 254 people, 36 of whom had been born by Cesarean section. She found that people born by Cesarean section were just as likely to have tunnel experiences as those who weren't. So the best test we have so far of the birth memory hypothesis has turned out negative.[64]

To fully explain the near-death experience, the birth memory hypothesis would have to tell us why only birth in particular is relived at death and not some other experience. One suggestion is that because our physiological condition at death is similar to that at birth, it trig-

Moody's Crystal Ball

Psychologist Raymond Moody, who popular- ized the notion of near-death experience, has recently taken to investigating another weird thing — *scrying*.

Scrying, which comes from the word *descry*, meaning "to reveal," involves staring in- tently into anything from a clear mountain lake to a polished mirror or crystal ball. "Cultures all over the world have made the discovery that people gazing into a clear depth will have remarkable visual experi- ences," says Moody. These "visions" may con- tain faces of people known and unknown, childhood memories, or even minidramas involving the characters in one's life.

While scrying has long been associated with the occult, Moody doesn't think there is anything paranormal about the practice. "The images reported by my patients seem indistinguishable from hypnogogic im- agery," he says, referring to the images that people commonly report as they drift off to sleep. The only thing even remotely un- canny about these images from the uncon- scious, adds Moody, is "that people report the imagery as arising from within the crys- tal ball, mirror, or whatever they are using."

Of the 100-plus people he has worked with, Moody says, more than half have reported seeing images in a crystal ball. For this reason Moody believes that scrying can be a useful psychotherapeutic technique. Scrying, he adds, may be more effective than the traditional Rorschach test, which involves interpreting a series of inkblots. "Because the person is gazing into a clear depth," he says, "you know that what the person sees is plainly coming from within."

Psychiatrists and psychologists are gen- erally unfamiliar with scrying. "I've never heard of it," says psychiatrist Stephen Barrett of Allentown, Pennsylvania, "and haven't the slightest idea if it's valid."[65]

gers memories of it, in much the same way that smells trigger memo- ries associated with them. But are the physiological conditions of birth and death really that similar? Can these conditions be produced under any other circumstances? If so, why aren't those situations re- called? Until these questions are answered, the birth memory expla- nation can't be considered a satisfactory one.

Hypothesis 3: *Near-death experiences are hallucinations caused by chemical reactions in the brain.* Because various drugs can produce experiences of exactly the same sort as those reported by near-death survivors, some investigators claim that near-death experiences are simply chemically induced hallucinations. Psychologist Ronald Siegel, for example, has found that all of the core elements of the near-death experience can be elicited by means of drugs.[66] Consequently, he hypothesizes that the stress of being near death causes the brain to manufacture chemicals that create the near-death experience.

Moody objects to this explanation on the grounds that people can have a near-death experience even though they have no detectable brain activity.[67] Dr. Schoonmaker, for example, reported fifty-five cases in which subjects had a flat EEG (electroencephalogram) and nevertheless had a near-death experience. Moody's objection is not decisive, however, because an EEG measures the activity of only the outermost portions of the brain. As Moody himself admits, "brain activity can be going on at such a deep level in the brain that surface electrodes don't pick it up."[68] So the fact that people with flat EEGs have reported near-death experiences doesn't rule out the hallucination hypothesis.

Furthermore, even if people with a flat EEG had absolutely no brain activity, the fact that near-death experiences were reported by people with flat EEGs wouldn't prove that those experiences could not result from brain activity. The near-death experience could have occurred either before or after the flat EEG. Since we can't pinpoint the exact time of a near-death experience, we can't be sure that it happened while the EEG was flat.

The biggest problem with the hallucination hypothesis is that it doesn't explain why the hallucinations at death are so similar. Drugs are capable of producing all sorts of hallucinations, and the hallucinations they produce are usually dependent on set and setting (expectations and environment). So why do people with such different backgrounds have such similar experiences? As Susan Blackmore asks, "Why a tunnel and not, say, a gate, doorway, or even the great River Styx? Why the light at the end of the tunnel? And why always above the body, not below it?"[69] Until we know what chemicals are involved and why they have the effects they do, the hallucination hypothesis doesn't tell us much.

Some people have suggested that chemical changes in the brain are responsible for near-death experiences and that those changes are the result of *cerebral anoxia,* or loss of oxygen in the brain.[70] When a patient clinically dies, the heart and lungs cease to function, and consequently the brain no longer receives oxygen. Those who make this argument point out that in the initial stages of oxygen deprivation, a person usually experiences a sense of well-being and power. If the condition persists, he or she often becomes deluded and may experience hallucinations. But the hallucinations associated with oxygen deprivation are not always the same as those associated with the near-death experience. And those who recover from cerebral anoxia usually recognize their hallucinations as hallucinations; those who've had a near-death experience often maintain that their experiences were real, even more real than those of waking life.[71] Finally, it should be noted that Dr. Schoonmaker, who often had the opportunity to measure the amount of oxygen in the blood at the time of cardiac arrest, reported a number of subjects who had a near-death experience even though their blood contained enough oxygen to maintain average brain functioning.[72] The cerebral anoxia hypothesis can't adequately account for a number of factors relating to the near-death experience.

Hypothesis 4: *The near-death experience is the result of the brain trying to construct a stable model of reality after the normal sources of input have been disrupted.* Susan Blackmore claims that in order to understand near-death experiences, we have to understand how our brains distinguish illusion from reality. Our brains, she tells us, are information-processing mechanisms that try to make sense out of the information they receive by constructing models of reality. The model we take to be real at any one time is the one that is the most stable, that is, the one that fits best with the available information. As she puts it:

> Our brains have no trouble distinguishing "reality" from "imagination." But this distinction is not given. It is one the brain has to make for itself by deciding which of its own models represents the world "out there." I suggest it does this by comparing all the models it has at any time and choosing the most stable one as "reality."[73]

When our normal sources of information are disrupted, as when we are under severe stress or near death, our models of reality will become unstable. In that case, the brain will try to construct a stable model by using the only information available to it, namely, memory. Remembered events, however, have a peculiar characteristic: they are always seen from a bird's-eye point of view. Try to remember the last time you walked down the beach or through the woods, for example. If you're like most of us, you'll see yourself from above. This aspect of our memories, she claims, helps explain out-of-body experiences. These experiences are simply the result of a memory model of reality taking over from a sensory model.[74]

One advantage of Blackmore's hypothesis is that it can account for the perceived reality of the out-of-body experience. Since reality is whatever our most stable model says it is, if a memory model becomes the most stable, then it will be taken to be real.

Extraordinary events can have a profound effect on us, especially if they are considered to be real. The events that occur during an NDE are, to say the least, extraordinary, and since they're part of an NDEer's most stable model of reality at the time, they seem real. It's no wonder, then, that people often come away from an NDE with a radically altered view of the world.

Other features of the near-death experience, Blackmore claims, can be accounted for by appeal to the physiology of the brain. We know, for example, that the brain produces opiumlike substances called *endorphins* in response to certain types of stress. The feeling of peace and well-being so often associated with near-death experiences, then, can be explained as the result of the brain's production of these natural painkillers.

We also know that brain activity is kept in check by the inhibitory action of certain nerve cells. If this action is reduced (as it can be during near-death experiences), then brain activity increases. If it increases in the visual cortex, tunnel experiences are produced due to the way our visual field is mapped onto our visual cortex.[75] So the experience of moving through a tunnel can be explained as the result of increasing noise in the visual cortex. Also, these chemical reactions, based as they are on fundamental human biochemistry, explain the universality of the images and sensations in NDEs.

Blackmore's hypothesis, then, does an admirable job of accounting for the major features of the near-death experience. Is it the best hypothesis? Let's review the bidding.

The soul hypothesis has not born any epistemological fruit, for it has not predicted any heretofore unknown phenomena, nor is it testable. It is also less simple and less conservative than any of the other hypotheses considered, for it postulates more entities than they do and the entities postulated are not recognized by our current best theories. The scope of this theory is also questionable, for as we saw in the case of creationism, you can't explain the unknown by appeal to the incomprehensible.

The birth memory hypothesis is inconsistent with what we know about the nature of the birth experience and has not lived up to its predictions. The hallucination hypothesis has trouble explaining the similarity of the hallucinations, the perceived reality of the out-of-body experience, and the transforming effects of the near-death experience. Blackmore's memory theory, on the other hand, can explain all of these aspects of the near-death experience and many others as well. Its scope, therefore, is greater than that of any of the other theories.

Another of its virtues is testability. It predicts that those who are better at imagining things from a bird's-eye view will have more out-of-body experiences than those who aren't. This prediction has been borne out by research conducted by both psychologist Harvey Irwin and Blackmore herself.[76] So her theory is fruitful as well.

It is also more simple and conservative than the soul hypothesis, and at least as simple and conservative as the other two, because its assumptions don't contradict any well-established findings. On balance, then, it would appear that Blackmore's theory provides the best explanation of the near-death experience.

These considerations should not be taken as the final word on the matters investigated here. We've simply tried to present our best thinking about them. You may disagree — but if you do, we trust that it's on the basis of good reasons.

Now that you know the difference between good and bad reasons, you have the basic intellectual tools necessary to evaluate all sorts of claims, weird and otherwise. We hope that you use these tools, for the quality of your life is determined by the quality of your decisions, and the quality of your decisions is determined by the quality of your reasoning.

SUGGESTED READINGS

Abell, George O., and Barry Singer, eds. *Science and the Paranormal.* New York: Charles Scribner's Sons, 1981.

Frazier, Kendrick, ed. *Paranormal Borderlands of Science.* Buffalo: Prometheus Books, 1981.

Gardner, Martin. *The New Age: Notes of a Fringe Watcher.* Buffalo: Prometheus Books, 1991.

Randi, James. *Flim Flam!* Buffalo: Prometheus Books, 1982.

Schultz, Ted, ed. *The Fringes of Reason.* New York: Harmony Books, 1989.

NOTES

1. Christopher Bird, *The Divining Hand* (New York: E. P. Dutton, 1979).
2. Evon Z. Vogt and Ray Hyman, *Water Witching U.S.A.* (Chicago: University of Chicago Press, 1979).
3. Ibid.
4. Leonard Zusne and Warren H. Jones, *Anomalistic Psychology* (Hillsdale, N.J.: Lawrence Erlbaum Associates, 1982), p. 252.
5. Terence Hines, *Pseudoscience and the Paranormal* (Buffalo: Prometheus Books, 1988), pp. 292–93.
6. Whitley Strieber, *Communion* (New York: William Morrow, 1987).
7. Budd Hopkins, *Intruders* (New York: Random House, 1987).
8. Kenneth L. Feder, *Frauds, Myths, and Mysteries* (Mountain View, Calif.: Mayfield, 1990), pp. 136–39.
9. Martin T. Orne, "The Use and Misuse of Hypnosis in Court," *International Journal of Clinical and Experimental Hypnosis,* October 1979, pp. 311–41.
10. Ibid.

11. A. H. Lawson and W. C. McCall, "What Can We Learn from the Hypnosis of Imaginary Attackers?" *MUFON UFO Symposium Proceedings* (Seguin, Tex.: Mutual UFO Network, 1977), pp. 107–35.

12. Hines, *Pseudoscience and the Paranormal*, p. 195.

13. Robert A. Baker, *They Call It Hypnosis* (Buffalo: Prometheus Books, 1990), p. 247.

14. Ibid., p. 252.

15. Philip J. Klass, *UFO Abductions: A Dangerous Game*, updated edition (Buffalo: Prometheus Books, 1989).

16. U.S. Office of Technology Assessment, *Scientific Validity of Polygraph Testing: A Research Review and Evaluation* (Washington. D.C.: Office of Technology Assessment, 1993, November) (OTA-TM-H-15); D. Lykken, *A Tremor in the Blood* (New York: McGraw-Hill, 1981).

17. Elizabeth Slater, "Conclusions on Nine Psychologies" in *Final Report on the Psychological Testing of UFO "Abductees,"* ed. R. Westrum (Mt. Rainier, Md.: Fund for UFO Research, 1985), pp. 17–31.

18. Ibid.

19. Klass, *UFO Abductions*, pp. 25–37.

20. S. C. Wilson and T. X. Barber, "The Fantasy-Prone Personality: Implications for Understanding Imagery, Hypnosis, and Parapsychological Phenomena," in *Imagery: Current Theory, Research and Application*, ed. A. A. Sheikh (New York: John Wiley, 1983).

21. Ibid.

22. K. Basterfield and R. Bartholomew, "Abductions: The Fantasy-Prone Personality Hypothesis," *International UFO Review*, 13(3), May-June 1988): 9–11.

23. Baker, *They Call It Hypnosis*, p. 247.

24. Ibid., p. 250.

25. Ibid., 251.

26. Hines, *Pseudoscience and the Paranormal*, p. 203.

27. James E. Alcock, "Channeling: Brief History and Contemporary Context," *The Skeptical Inquirer*, Summer 1989, p. 381.

28. Graham Reed, "The Psychology of Channeling," *The Skeptical Inquirer*, Summer 1989, p. 385.

29. James E. Alcock, "Channeling," p. 382.

30. Sarah Grey Thomason, "'Entities' in the Linguistic Minefield," in *The Skeptical Inquirer*, Summer 1989, p. 394.

31. Ibid., p. 393.

32. Ted Schultz, ed., *The Fringes of Reason: A Whole Earth Catalog* (New York: Harmony Books, 1989), p. 62.

33. Ibid., p. 64.

34. Ibid., p. 57.

35. Reed, "Psychology of Channeling," p. 388.
36. Ibid.
37. Paul Kurtz, "Spiritualists, Mediums, and Psychics: Some Evidence of Fraud," in *A Skeptics Handbook of Parapsychology* (Buffalo: Prometheus Books, 1985), pp. 177–223; Hines, *Pseudoscience and the Paranormal*, pp. 19–39.
38. Zusne and Jones, *Anomalistic Psychology*, p. 225.
39. Ibid., p. 227.
40. Ibid., p. 233.
41. Baker, *They Call It Hypnosis*, p. 261.
42. Melvin Harris, *Investigating the Unexplained* (Buffalo: Prometheus Books, 1986), pp. 11–14.
43. Raymond A. Moody Jr., *Life After Life* (New York: Bantam Books, 1975), pp. 21–23.
44. Raymond A. Moody Jr., *The Light Beyond* (New York: Bantam Books, 1988), p. 7.
45. Ibid., pp. 4–5.
46. Fred Schoonmaker, "Denver Cardiologist Discloses Findings After 18 Years of Near-Death Research," *Anabiosis,* 1 (1979): 1–2.
47. Michael Sabom, *Recollections of Death* (New York: Harper and Row, 1982).
48. Susan Blackmore, "Near-Death Experiences: In or Out of the Body?" *Skeptical Inquirer,* 16 (1991): 36.
49. Kenneth Ring, *Life at Death* (New York: Coward, McCann and Geoghegan, 1980). p. 32.
50. Ibid., p. 40.
51. Karlis Osis and Erlendur Haraldsson, "OBE's in Indian Swamis: Sathya Sai Baba and Dadaji," in *Research in Parapsychology 1976,* ed. J. D. Morris, W. G. Roll, and R. L. Morris (Metuchen, N.J.: Scarecrow Press, 1980), pp. 142–145.
52. Moody, *Light Beyond*, pp. 196–97.
53. Ibid., p. 197.
54. Ibid., pp. 170–71.
55. Blackmore, "Near-Death Experiences," p. 43.
56. Moody, *Light Beyond*, p. 197.
57. Ibid.
58. Susan J. Blackmore, *Beyond the Body* (Chicago: Academy Chicago Publishers, 1992), p. 199.
59. Ibid., pp. 200ff.
60. William Rushton, "Letter to the Editor," *Journal of the Society for Psychical Research,* 48 (1976): 412, cited in Blackmore, *Beyond the Body*, pp. 227–28.
61. Carl Sagan, *Broca's Brain* (New York: Ballantine Books, 1974), pp. 356ff.

62. S. Halifax and J. Halifax, *The Human Encounter with Death* (New York: E.P. Dutton, 1977).

63. C. B. Becker, "The Failure of Saganomics: Why Birth Models Cannot Explain Near-Death Phenomena," *Anabiosis*, 2 (1982): 102–9.

64. Susan Blackmore, "Birth and the OBE: An Unhelpful Analogy," *Journal of the American Society for Psychical Research*, 77, 229–38.

65. Patrick Huyghe, "Moody's Crystal Ball," *Omni*, June 1989, p. 90.

66. Ronald Siegel, "Life After Death," in *Science and the Paranormal*, ed. George O. Abell and Barry Singer (New York: Scribner's, 1981), pp. 159–84.

67. Moody, *Light Beyond*, pp. 180–82.

68. Ibid., p. 182.

69. Blackmore, "Near-Death Experiences: In or Out of the Body?" *Skeptical Inquirer*, 16 (1991): 34–35.

70. Hines, *Pseudoscience and the Paranormal*, p. 69.

71. Dina Ingber, "Visions of an Afterlife," *Science Digest*, January/February 1981, p. 142.

72. Ibid.

73. Susan Blackmore, "Near-Death Experiences," p. 41.

74. Ibid., p. 42.

75. Ibid., p. 40.

76. Ibid., p. 42.

APPENDIX
Informal Fallacies

WHEN WE GIVE reasons for accepting a claim, we are making an argument. The reasons we give are called the *premises* of the argument, and the claim that they allegedly support is called the *conclusion*. If the premises are acceptable, and if they adequately support the conclusion, then our argument is a good one. If not—if the premises are dubious, or if they do not justify the conclusion—then our argument is fallacious. A fallacious argument is a bogus one, for it fails to do what it purports to do, namely, provide a good reason for accepting a claim. Unfortunately, logically fallacious arguments can be psychologically compelling. Since most people have never learned the difference between a good argument and a fallacious one, they are often persuaded to believe things for no good reason. To avoid holding irrational beliefs, then, it is important to understand the many ways in which an argument can fail.

An argument is fallacious if it contains (1) unacceptable premises, (2) irrelevant premises, or (3) insufficient premises.[1] Premises are *unacceptable* if they are at least as dubious as the claim they are supposed to support. In a good argument, you see, the premises provide a firm basis for accepting the conclusion. If the premises are shaky, the argument is inconclusive. Premises are *irrelevant* if they have no bearing on the truth of the conclusion. In a good argument, the conclusion follows from the premises. If the premises are logically unrelated to the conclusion, they provide no reason to accept it. Premises are *insufficient* if they do not establish the conclusion beyond a reasonable doubt. In a good argument, the premises eliminate reasonable grounds for doubt. If they fail to do this, they don't justify the conclusion.

So when someone gives you an argument, you should ask yourself: Are the premises acceptable? Are they relevant? Are they sufficient? If the answer to any of these questions is no, then the argument is not logically compelling.

UNACCEPTABLE PREMISES

Begging the Question

An argument begs the question — or argues in a circle — when its conclusion is used as one of its premises. For example, some people claim that one should believe that God exists because the Bible says so. But when asked why we should believe the Bible, they answer that we should believe it because God wrote it. Such people are begging the question, for they are assuming what they are trying to prove, namely that God exists. Here's another example: "Jane has telepathy," says Susan. "How do you know?" asks Jill. "Because she can read my mind," replies Susan. Since telepathy is, by definition, the ability to read someone's mind, all Susan has told us is that she believes that Jane can read her mind because she believes that Jane can read her mind. Her reason merely reiterates her claim in different words. Consequently, her reason provides no additional justification for her claim.

False Dilemma

An argument proposes a false dilemma when it presumes that only two alternatives exist when in actuality there are more than two. For example, "Either science can explain how she was cured or it was a miracle. Science can't explain how she was cured. So it must be a miracle." These two alternatives do not exhaust all the possibilities. It's possible, for example, that she was cured by some natural cause that scientists don't yet understand. Because the argument doesn't take this possibility into account, it's fallacious. Again: "Either have your horoscope charted by an astrologer or continue to stumble through life without knowing where you're going. You certainly don't want to continue your wayward ways. So you should have your horoscope charted by an astrologer." If someone is concerned about the direction his or her life is taking, there are other things he or she can do about it than consult an astrologer. Since there are other options, the argument is fallacious.

IRRELEVANT PREMISES

Equivocation

Equivocation occurs when a word is used in two different senses in an argument. For example, consider this argument: "(i) Only man is rational. (ii) No woman is a man. (iii) Therefore no woman is rational." The word *man* is used in two different senses here: in the first premise it means human being while in the second it means male. As a result, the conclusion doesn't follow from the premises. Here's another example: "It's the duty of the press to publish news that's in the public interest. There is great public interest in UFOs. Therefore the press fails in its duty if it does not publish articles on UFOs." In the first premise, the phrase *the public interest* means the public welfare, but in the second, it means what the public is interested in. The switch in meaning invalidates the argument.

Composition

An argument may claim that what is true of the parts is also true of the whole; this is the fallacy of composition. For example, consider this argument: "Subatomic particles are lifeless. Therefore anything made out of them is lifeless." This argument is fallacious because a whole may be greater than the sum of its parts; that is, it may have properties not possessed by its parts. A property had by a whole but not by its parts is called an *emergent* property. Wetness, for example, is an emergent property. No individual water molecule is wet, but get enough of them together and wetness emerges.

Just as what's true of a part may not be true of the whole, what's true of a member of a group may not be true of the group itself. For example, "Belief in the supernatural makes Joe happy. Therefore, universal belief in the supernatural would make the nation happy." This doesn't follow because everybody's believing in the supernatural could have effects quite different from one person's believing in it. Not all arguments from part to whole are fallacious, for there are some properties that parts and wholes share. The fallacy lies in *assuming* that what's true of the parts is true of the whole.

Division

The fallacy of division is the converse of the fallacy of composition. It occurs when one assumes that what is true of a whole is also true of its parts. For example: "We are alive and we are made out of subatomic particles. So they must be alive too." To argue in this way is to ignore the very real difference between parts and wholes. Here's another example: "Society's interest in the occult is growing. Therefore Joe's interest in the occult is growing." Since groups can have properties that are not had by their members, such an argument is fallacious.

Appeal to the Person

When someone tries to rebut an argument by criticizing or denigrating its presenter rather than by dealing with the argument itself, that person is guilty of the fallacy of appeal to the person. This fallacy is referred to as *ad hominem*, or "to the man." For example: "This theory has been proposed by a believer in the occult. Why should we take it seriously?" Or: "You can't believe Dr. Jones's claim that there is no evidence for life after death. After all, he's an atheist." The flaw in these arguments is obvious: an argument stands or falls on its own merits; who proposes it is irrelevant to its soundness. Crazy people can come up with perfectly sound arguments, and sane people can talk nonsense.

Genetic Fallacy

To argue that a claim is true or false on the basis of its origin is to commit the genetic fallacy. For example: "Jones's idea is the result of a mystical experience, so it must be false (or true)." Or: "Jane got that message from a Ouija board, so it must be false (or true)." These arguments are fallacious because the origin of a claim is irrelevant to its truth or falsity. Some of our greatest advances have originated in unusual ways. For example, the chemist August Kekulé discovered the benzene ring while staring at a fire and seeing the image of a serpent biting its tail. The theory of evolution came to British naturalist Alfred Russell Wallace while in a delirium. Archimedes supposedly arrived at the principle of displacement while taking a bath, from which he leapt shouting "Eureka!" The truth or falsity of an idea is determined not by where it came from, but by the evidence supporting it.

Appeal to Authority

We often try to support our views by citing experts. This sort of appeal to authority is perfectly valid—provided that the person cited really is an expert in the field in question. If not, it is fallacious. Celebrity endorsements, for example, often involve fallacious appeals to authority because being famous doesn't necessarily give you any special expertise. The fact that Dionne Warwick is a great singer, for example, doesn't make her an expert on the efficacy of psychic hot lines. Similarly, the fact that Linus Pauling is a Nobel Prize winner doesn't make him an expert on the efficacy of vitamin C. Pauling claimed that taking massive doses of vitamin C would help prevent colds and increase the life expectancy of people suffering from cancer. That may be the case, but the fact that he said it doesn't justify our believing it. Only rigorous clinical studies confirming these claims can do that.

Appeal to the Masses

A remarkably common but fallacious form of reasoning is: "It must be true (or good) because everybody believes it (or does it)." Mothers understand that this is a fallacy; they often counter this argument by asking: "If everyone jumped off a cliff, would you do it, too?" Of course you wouldn't. What this shows is that just because a lot of people believe something or like something doesn't mean that it's true or good. A lot of people used to believe that the Earth was flat, but that certainly didn't make it so. Similarly, a lot of people used to believe that women should not have the right to vote. Popularity is not a reliable indication of either reality or value.

Appeal to Tradition

We appeal to tradition when we argue that something must be true (or good) because it is part of an established tradition. For example: "Astrology has been around for ages, so there must be something to it." Or "Mothers have always used chicken soup to fight colds, so it must be good for you." These arguments are fallacious because traditions can be wrong. This becomes obvious when you consider that slavery was once an established tradition. The fact that people have always done or believed something is no reason for believing that we should continue to do or believe something.

Appeal to Ignorance

The appeal to ignorance comes in two varieties: using an opponent's inability to disprove a conclusion as proof of the conclusion's correctness, and using an opponent's inability to prove a conclusion as proof of its incorrectness. In the first case, the claim is that since there is no proof that something is true, it must be false. For example: "There is no proof that the parapsychology experiments were fraudulent, so I'm sure they weren't." In the second case, the claim is that since there is no proof that something is false, it must be true. For example: "Bigfoot must exist because no one has been able to prove that he doesn't." The problem with these arguments is that they take a lack of evidence for one thing to be good evidence for another. A lack of evidence, however, proves nothing. In logic, as in life, you can't get something for nothing.

Appeal to Fear

To use the threat of harm to advance one's position is to commit the fallacy of the appeal to fear. It is also known as swinging the big stick. For example: "If you do not convict this criminal, one of you may be her next victim." This is fallacious because what a defendant might do in the future is irrelevant to determining whether she is responsible for a crime committed in the past. Or "You should believe in God because if you don't you'll go to hell." Such an argument is fallacious because it gives us no reason for believing that God exists. Threats extort; they do not help us arrive at the truth.

INSUFFICIENT PREMISES

Hasty Generalization

You are guilty of hasty generalization, or jumping to conclusions, when you draw a general conclusion about all things of a certain type on the basis of evidence concerning only a few things of that type. For example: "Every medium that's been investigated has turned out to be a fraud. You can't trust any of them." Or "I know one of those psychics. They're all a bunch of phonies." You can't make a valid generalization about an entire class of things from observing only one — or even a number of them. An inference from a sample of a group to the whole group is legitimate only if the sample is representative — that is, only if the sample is sufficiently large and every member of the group has an equal chance to be part of the sample.

Faulty Analogy

An argument from analogy claims that things which resemble one another in certain respects resemble one another in further respects. For example: "The Earth has air, water, and living organisms. Mars has air and water. Therefore Mars has living organisms." The success of such arguments depends upon the nature and extent of the similarities between the two objects. The greater their dissimilarities, the less convincing the argument will be. For example, consider this argument: "Astronauts wear helmets and fly in spaceships. The figure in this Mayan carving seems to be wearing a helmet and flying in a spaceship. Therefore it is a carving of an ancient astronaut." Although features of the carving may bear a resemblance to a helmet and spaceship, they may bear a greater resemblance to a ceremonial mask and fire. The problem is that any two things have some features in common. Consequently an argument from analogy can be successful only if the dissimilarities between the things being compared are insignificant.

False Cause

The fallacy of false cause consists of supposing that two events are causally connected when they are not. People often claim, for example, that because something occurred after something else it is caused by it. Latin scholars dubbed this the fallacy of *post hoc, ergo propter hoc,* which means "After this, therefore because of this." Such reasoning is fallacious because from the fact that two events are constantly conjoined, it doesn't follow that they are causally related. Night follows day, but that doesn't mean that day causes night. Suppose that ever since you wore crystals around your neck you haven't caught a cold. From this you can't conclude that the crystals caused you to stay healthy, because any number of other factors could be involved. Only if it has been established beyond a reasonable doubt that other factors were not involved—through a controlled study, for example—can you justifiably claim that there is a causal connection between the two events.

NOTE

1. Ludwig F. Schlecht, "Classifying Fallacies Logically," *Teaching Philosophy,* 14:1 (1991), pp. 53–64.

Credits

by Kenneth L. Feder. Copyright © 1990 by Mayfield Publishing Company. **Pages 259, 261** From *The Skeptical Inquirer,* Summer 1989. Reprinted by permission. **Pages 261, 262** From *The Skeptical Inquirer,* Summer 1989. Reprinted by permission. **Page 277** Reprinted by permission of OMNI, © 1989, OMNI Publications International, Inc.

ILLUSTRATIONS

Pages 1, 12, 33, 69, 150, 285 The Bettman Archive. **Page 41** Courtesy NASA Headquarters, Mountain View, CA. **Page 61** The Granger Collection, New York. By permission. **Page 187** UPI/Bettman. **Pages 196, 197** From *Introduction to Logic,* 6th ed., by Irving M. Copi. Reprinted with the permission of Macmillan College Publishing. Copyright © 1982 by Irving M. Copi. **Pages 204, 209** From *Seven Ideas That Shook the Universe,* by Nathan Spielberg and Bryon D. Anderson. Copyright © 1987, Wiley Science Editions. Reprinted by permission of John Wiley & Sons, Inc. **Page 208** From *An Introduction to Philosophical Analysis,* 3rd ed., by John Hospers, p. 171. Copyright © 1988. Reprinted by permission of Prentice-Hall, Englewood Cliffs, NJ. **Pages 244, 245** John Beckett. Courtesy of Adam Hart-Davis. **Page 251** Bate Littlehales, © National Geographic Society. **Page 259** From *I Am Ramtha.* Copyright © 1988 Beyond Words Publishing, Inc., Hillsboro, OR. **Page 265** From *The Fringes of Reason,* Harmony Books, 1989.

Index

objectivist vs. relativist

realist vs. idealist